High Leverage Practices for Intensive Interventions

High Leverage Practices for Intensive Interventions provides special education teachers with descriptions and practical instructions on how to use High Leverage Practices (HLPs) to improve student outcomes. Since many students with disabilities spend their school day in inclusive general education classrooms, these intensive interventions are often delivered in separate or tier 3 settings to meet the students' individualized needs. Each chapter focuses on a specific High Leverage Practice with explanations of its purpose and essential components, accompanied by examples for use with small groups of students or the individual student. This accessible and comprehensive guide is key for pre-service teachers in special education programs or those who provide intensive interventions with students.

James McLeskey is Professor in the School of Special Education, School Psychology, and Early Childhood Studies at the University of Florida, and project staff member for the CEEDAR Center.

Lawrence Maheady is Professor and Horace Mann Endowed Chair in the Exceptional Education Department at SUNY Buffalo State.

Bonnie Billingsley is Professor of Teaching and Learning at Virginia Tech. She teaches in both the teacher preparation and doctoral programs at Virginia Tech.

Mary T. Brownell is a Distinguished Professor of Special Education at the University of Florida and Director of the Collaboration for Effective Educator Development, Accountability and Reform (CEEDAR) Center.

Timothy J. Lewis is Curators' Distinguished Professor of Special Education, Director of the University of Missouri Center for School-wide Positive Behavior Support, and Co-director of the Center on Positive Behavioral Interventions and Supports (PBIS).

Sheila R. Alber-Morgan is Professor of Special Education at The Ohio State University and a Board Certified Behavior Analyst (BCBA-D). Her research focuses on using behavioral interventions to increase academic performance for individuals with disabilities.

High Leverage Practices for Intensive Interventions

Edited by James McLeskey,
Lawrence Maheady,
Bonnie Billingsley,
Mary T. Brownell,
Timothy J. Lewis, and
Sheila R. Alber-Morgan

A Co-publication with the Council for
Exceptional Children

Routledge
Taylor & Francis Group

NEW YORK AND LONDON

Designed cover image: © Getty Images

First published 2023
by Routledge
605 Third Avenue, New York, NY 10158

and by Routledge
4 Park Square, Milton Park, Abingdon, Oxon, OX14 4RN

Routledge is an imprint of the Taylor & Francis Group, an informa business

ISBN: 9781032233376 (hbk)
ISBN: 9781032231068 (pbk)
ISBN: 9781003276876 (ebk)

DOI: 10.4324/9781003276876

Typeset in Minion
by Newgen Publishing UK

Contents

Contributors

Terese C. Aceves, Loyola Marymount University
Sheila R. Alber-Morgan, Ohio State University
Abigail A. Allen, Clemson University
Tammy Barron, Western Carolina University
Bonnie Billingsley, Virginia Tech
Gino D. Binkert, George Mason University
Mary T. Brownell, University of Florida
Lindsay M. Griendling, University of Virginia
Jihyae Choe, George Mason University
Michelle M. Cumming, Florida International University
Dane Marco Di Cesare, Brock University
Kelly Durso, George Mason University
Julie Esparza Brown, Portland State University
Sara Estrapala, University of Missouri
Lauren L. Foxworth, The College of New Jersey
Grace L. Francis, George Mason University
Dawn W. Fraser, John Hopkins University
Marilyn Friend, UNC-Greensboro-Emeritus
Marcella M. Gallmeyer, Ohio State University
Patricia Gann, Florida International University
Kristall J. Graham Day, Ohio Dominican University
Andrew L. Hashey, SUNY Buffalo State College
William L. Heward, Ohio State University
Elizabeth A. Hicks, Michigan State University
Sara D. Hooks, Towson University
Tara L. Kaczorowski, Daemen University
Ryan O. Kellems, Brigham Young University
Michael J. Kennedy, University of Virginia
Moira Konrad, Ohio State University
Stephen D. Kroeger, University of Cincinnati
Rachel L. Kunemund, University of Virginia
Timothy J. Lewis, University of Missouri

Krishna Leyva, Alexandria (VA) Public Schools
Blair P. Lloyd, Vanderbilt University
Lawrence Maheady, SUNY Buffalo State
Troy V. Mariage, Michigan State University
James McLeskey, University of Florida
Barbara S. Mitchell, Kansas State University
Kevin Monnin, George Mason University
Sarah A. Nagro, George Mason University
Kristen Merrill O'Brien, George Mason University
Mary T. Peters, Ohio State University
Marney S. Pollack, Vanderbilt University
Ashley Rila, University of Iowa
Kristen R. Rolf, Utah State University
Terrance M. Scott, University of Louisville
LaRon A. Scott, University of Virginia
Timothy A. Slocum, Utah State University
Talida M. State, Montclair State University
Joshua P. Taylor, University of Maine
Alana Telesman, Ohio State University
Taneika Tukan, Alexandria (VA) Public Schools
Colleen K. Vesely, George Mason University
Jocelyn Washburn, University of Kansas
Margaret P. Weiss, George Mason University
Amanda Yurick, Cleveland State University
Imad Zaheer, St. John's University
Alyxandra Zavodney, Ohio State University

Acknowledgments

From the very beginning, a large number of scholars and practitioners have freely given of their time to support work related to the development and use of HLPs for special education teachers. This book is an extension of that collective work by professionals with expertise in a range of critical areas that are needed to support students with disabilities and others who struggle to learn and need intensive interventions. We want to express our appreciation to all of the chapter authors for this book, who pulled from their rich experiences to provide information to support teacher candidates and practicing teachers as they learned to use HLPs to provide students with intensive interventions. We especially appreciate that all contributors to this book worked without compensation, and all of the royalties from this book will be used to support the work of the Council for Exceptional Children. We'd also like to thank our editors at Routledge/Taylor & Francis, first Misha Kydd and later Nicole Salazar, as well as Olivia Powers at Routledge who provided support as we developed a plan, wrote this book, and moved to the final product. In addition, we appreciate the support from Suriya Rajasekar and her production team, and our copy editor Rob Wilkinson as they handled many details to move us toward the final production of this book. Finally, we would like to thank a large group of professionals who reviewed chapters and provided authors with valuable feedback regarding how the chapters might be improved. These reviewers are listed below.

Chapter Reviewers HLPs for Intensive Interventions

Reesha Adamson, Missouri State University
Stephenson Beck, North Dakota State University
Christina Billman, Ohio State University
Rick Brigham, George Mason University
Diane Bryant, University of Texas-Austin
Shannon Budin, SUNY Buffalo State College
Shweta Chandrashekhar, University of Wisconsin-Madison
Lindsey Chapman, University of Florida
Julie Clark, University of Wisconsin-Madison
Caitlin Criss, Georgia Southern University
Scott Dueker, Ball State University
Kate Fishley, Ohio Dominican
Jeremy Ford, Boise State University
Nick Gage, WestEd
Lenwood Gibson, City University of New York, Queens College
Shaina Haines, University of Vermont
Andrew Hashey, SUNY Buffalo State
Heather Hatton, University of Missouri
John Hosp, University of Massachusetts-Amherst
Elizabeth Hughes, Penn State University
Ya-yu Lo, University of North Carolina-Charlotte
Dana McCaleb, Virginia Tech
John McKenna, University of Massachusetts-Lowell)
Whitney Miller, Virginia Tech
Stephanie Morano, University of Virginia
Kelsey Morris, University of Missouri
April Mustian, Winthrop University
Robert O'Neil, University of Utah
Alba Ortiz, University of Texas-Austin
Robin Parks-Ennis, University of Alabama-Birmingham
Kathleen Puckett, Arizona State University
Dan Pyle, Weber State University

Nicole Pyle, Utah State University
Wendy Rodgers, Virginia Commonwealth University
Kim Rice, Arizona State University
Claudia Rinaldi, Lasell University
Chad Rose, University of Missouri
Zachary Rossetti, Boston University
Mary Sawyer, Fit Learning Atlanta
Kara Shawbitz, Ohio State University
Brandi Simonsen, University of Connecticut
Rosemary Tralli, Educational Consultant, Connecticut
Susan Wilczynski, Ball State University
Charlie Wood, University of North Carolina-Charlotte

Introduction

James McLeskey, Lawrence Maheady, Bonnie Billingsley, Mary T. Brownell, Timothy J. Lewis, and Sheila R. Alber-Morgan

"Special education teachers must be flexible problem solvers who not only have expertise in using highly effective practices, but also are proficient in monitoring the effectiveness of these practices with individual students and making decisions regarding changes in practice as needed. This routine analysis of practice and its effect on important student outcomes is foundational for effective special education teachers."

(McLeskey et al., 2017, p. 8)

By definition, students with disabilities are those who struggle with learning academic content or meeting social/behavioral expectations in schools. Special education teachers obviously have a central role in addressing the needs of these students. While "all beginning teachers are challenged to teach in ways that are responsive to students' needs, special education teachers face the challenge of teaching students with some of the most complex learning and behavioral difficulties" (McLeskey et al., 2017, p. 8). Extensive research has shown that substantially improving the learning of students with disabilities requires that special education teachers have a deep, comprehensive understanding of student learning to support the use of "highly responsive, explicit, systematic instructional and behavioral interventions" (p. 8).

The HLPs that are addressed in this book emerged from a national movement among teacher educators across disciplines (e.g., elementary education, science, mathematics, foreign language, and special education) to specify effective practices that would form the core curriculum for practice-based teacher preparation programs (Maheady et al., 2019; McDonald et al., 2013; Windschitl, 2019). After identifying core practices or HLPs, faculty in these programs would then design experiences that would be used to systematically prepare teacher education candidates to use these practices in classrooms (Brownell et al., 2019; McDonald et al., 2013). HLPs have been defined as "practices that are essential to effective teaching and fundamental to supporting student learning" (McLeskey et al., 2019, p. 332). Furthermore, the practices are (1) supported by research as improving student learning or behavior; (2) broadly applicable across content areas; and (3) frequently used in the classroom (McLeskey & Brownell, 2015).

In 2016, the Council for Exceptional Children approved a set of 22 high leverage practices (HLPs) for K-12 special education teachers that are intended to be foundational as these teachers provide

DOI: 10.4324/9781003276876-1

instruction that is highly responsive and effective in meeting the needs of students with disabilities who manifest complex learning and behavioral difficulties (McLeskey et al., 2017). These practices may be used as a core curriculum for teacher preparation, as well as for teacher induction and continuing professional development for practicing teachers (Billingsley et al., 2019; Maheady et al., 2019). Furthermore, the practices are intended to be used across settings and severity levels of disability. For example, in a previous book we focused on how these practices could be used in inclusive general education classrooms (i.e., tiers 1 and 2) (McLeskey et al., 2022). In this book, our goal is to focus on the use of the HLPs to address the needs of students with mild to moderate disabilities who have complex learning and behavioral needs which require the use of intensive interventions delivered in small groups or to individual students. It should be noted that another book has been published by Routledge that addresses the use of the HLPs to address complex learning and behavioral needs of students with extensive support needs or severe disabilities (Pennington et al., 2022).

Narrowing the Focus

This book is intended to be a practical resource for preservice and inservice special education teachers as they learn to use HLPs in their classrooms. These practices are clearly not all of the teaching skills that are needed for a special educator to be successful. However, the HLPs are intended to provide a level of proficient practice for all special education teachers, and serve as a foundation of skills for developing other aspects of practice as beginning teachers continue to learn and become highly accomplished professionals as their teaching careers progress.

We recognize that a single chapter cannot comprehensively address any of the HLPs and provide examples of the full range of how they might be used. We thus asked chapter authors to narrow their chapter's focus to ensure they could provide useful information and rich examples related to the use of these practices for providing intensive interventions. Given this focus, the described practices should be particularly useful for special education teachers, and also may be applicable for teachers who provide intensive instruction to students who are not identified with disabilities (e.g., reading specialists).

In the following sections we provide some background information regarding the development of the High Leverage Practices for Special Education teachers. Initially we address how these HLPs were identified. This is followed by a brief description of each of the 22 HLPs.

How Were the HLPs Identified?

In 2014, the Council for Exceptional Children identified 12 participants for a High Leverage Practices Writing Team, and charged this group with developing a set of HLPs for K-12 special education teachers. Members of this group were primarily teacher educators with extensive experience preparing special education teachers and working in schools. This group initially agreed on four key areas of practice that were important for all special education teachers: collaboration, assessment, social/emotional/behavioral practices, and instruction.

Based on the work of others who had developed HLPs in elementary education and other areas (Ball et al., 2009; Grossman et al., 2009; McDonald et al., 2013; Windschitl et al., 2012), the group then identified criteria (see Table 0.1) that would be used to identify the practices. These criteria included identifying practices that are frequently used in the classrooms and that had been shown to improve student learning or behavior. Additional criteria ensured that these practices were practical and useful for teacher education and professional development, and were limited in number and could be taught to novices at a reasonable level of proficiency in a preparation program. It should be noted that while a primary criterion was that the HLPs should focus on instructional practice (including behavioral practices), collaboration and assessment practices were also included that

Table 0.1 Criteria for Identifying High Leverage Practices

Applicable and Important to the Everyday Work of Teachers

- Focus directly on instructional practice

- Occur with high frequency in teaching

- Research-based and known to foster important kinds of student engagement and learning

- Broadly applicable and usable in any content area or approach to teaching

- So important that skillfully executing them is fundamental to effective Teaching

---

Applicable and Important to Teacher Education

- Limited in number (about 20) for a teacher education program

- Can be articulated and taught

- Novices can begin to master

- Can be practiced across university and field-based settings

- Grain size (i.e., how detailed should the practice be) is small enough to be clearly visible in practice, but large enough to preserve the integrity and complexity of teaching

- System (or group of HLP) considerations

  - embody a broader theory regarding the relationship between teaching and learning than would individual practices.

  - support more comprehensive student learning goals (the whole is more than the sum of its parts)

Source: Ball et al., 2009; Grossman et al., 2009; McDonald et al., 2013; Windschitl et al., 2012.

address major functions of the role of special education teachers. While there is strong research support for at least one of these practices (i.e., HLP 6—that addresses formative assessment or using assessment information to make instructional decisions), most of the practices in these areas were viewed as essential to the role of special education teachers, and in most cases had policy support for their inclusion.

Members of the HLP Writing Team used research on effective practices and the wisdom of practice as they began exploring possible core practices. This information was used to develop an initial draft of HLPs which was subsequently critically examined in focus group interviews over several months with teacher educators, teachers, and administrators. Based on this feedback as well as feedback from conference presentations, the core practices were revised by the HLP Writing Team and reduced in number from 26 to 22. Feedback was then sought for the revised list of practices using an on-line survey and a presentation at a professional conference for teacher educators. Using all of this feedback and further critical examination of the practices, the HLP Writing Team reduced the list to the final set of 22 high leverage practices. These practices were then subjected to review and feedback by the Representative Assembly (RA) of the Council for Exceptional Children (CEC), resulting in further changes. The final version of the HLPs were approved by the CEC Board in July 2016.

In the following section, we provide basic information describing the HLPs organized by major areas of practice or essential teaching functions used by special education teachers—Collaboration, Assessment, Social/Emotional/Behavioral Practices, and Instruction. Each of these sections includes a brief introduction to the section and a list of HLPs. The 22 HLPs are intended to provide a foundation for preparing effective special education teachers from initial preparation through induction and beyond. For more extensive descriptions of each HLP and research and/or policy support for each practice, see McLeskey and colleagues (2017).

What are the 22 HLPs for Special Education Teachers?

The HLPs are organized around the four major areas of practice for special education teachers: collaboration, assessment, social/emotional/behavioral practices, and instruction. The following sections provide brief introductions to each area of practice, followed by a list of HLPs related to the area of practice. It should be noted that the wording for HLPs 8 and 22 are the same, but HLP 8 applies to student behavior and feedback, while HLP 22 applies to feedback related to academic performance. It should also be noted that the introductions to these sections are taken from a book published by CEC (McLeskey et al., 2017, pp. 15–17).

Collaboration high leverage practices. Effective special education teachers collaborate with a wide range of professionals, families, and caregivers to assure that educational programs and related services are effectively designed and implemented to meet the needs of each student with a disability. Collaboration allows for varied expertise and perspectives about a student to be shared among those responsible for each student's learning and well-being. This collective expertise provides collaborators with a more comprehensive understanding of each student's needs, and this knowledge is used to more effectively plan and implement instruction and services that benefit the student.

Teachers use respectful and effective communication skills as they collaborate with others, considering the background, socioeconomic status, culture, and language of the families and the professionals with whom they work. They focus collaborative activities on designing each student's instructional program to meet clearly specified outcomes and collecting data and monitoring progress toward these outcomes. Effective and purposeful collaboration should enlist support from district and school leaders, who foster a collective commitment to collaboration, provide professional learning experiences to increase team members' collaborative skills, and create schedules that support different forms (e.g., IEP teams, co-teachers, teachers and families, teachers and paraprofessionals) of ongoing collaboration. The three high leverage practices related to collaboration are listed below.

1. Collaborate with professionals to increase student success.
2. Organize and facilitate effective meetings with professionals and families.
3. Collaborate with families to support student learning and secure needed services.

Assessment high leverage practices. Assessment plays a foundational role in special education. Students with disabilities are complex learners who have unique needs that exist alongside their strengths. Effective special education teachers have to fully understand those strengths and needs. Thus, these teachers are knowledgeable regarding assessment and are skilled in using and interpreting data. This includes formal, standardized assessments that are used in the identification of students for special education services, the development of their Individualized Education Programs (IEPs), and to inform their ongoing services. Formal assessments such as statewide exams also provide data regarding whether students with disabilities are achieving state content standards and how their academic progress compares to students without disabilities. Teachers are also knowledgeable regarding and skillful in using informal assessments, such as those used to evaluate students' academic, behavioral, and functional strengths and needs. These assessments are used to develop students' IEPs, design and evaluate instruction, and monitor student progress. As reflective practitioners, teachers are also continuously analyzing the impact and effectiveness of their own instruction. Finally, teachers are knowledgeable regarding how context, culture, language, and poverty might influence student performance, navigating conversations with families and other stakeholders, and choosing appropriate assessments given each student's profile. This is an especially important consideration, given the over-representation of culturally and linguistically diverse students and those from high poverty backgrounds in special education. The three high leverage practices related to assessment are listed below.

4. Use multiple sources of information to develop a comprehensive understanding of a student's strengths and needs.
5. Interpret and communicate assessment information with stakeholders to collaboratively design and implement educational programs.
6. Use student assessment data, analyze instructional practices, and make necessary adjustments that improve student outcomes.

Social/emotional/behavioral high leverage practices. Effective special education teachers establish a consistent, organized, and respectful learning environment to support student success. To do this, they employ several practices that are critical in promoting student social and emotional well-being. First, effective teachers focus on increasing appropriate behavior by adopting an instructional approach and explicitly teaching social skills and offering multiple opportunities to practice appropriate social behaviors across the school day followed by positive specific feedback. Second, they implement evidence-based practices to prevent social/emotional behavioral challenges and provide early intervention at the first sign of risk. Third, effective teachers provide increasingly comprehensive supports through a team-based problem-solving strategy, to match the intensity of student challenges guided by behavioral assessment. Finally, they implement all behavioral supports, even those in response to significant problem behavior, in a caring, respectful, and culturally relevant manner. Effective teachers recognize that academic and behavioral support strategies are more effective when delivered within the context of positive and caring teacher and student relationships. The four high leverage practices related to social/emotional/behavioral practices are listed below.

7. Establish a consistent, organized, and respectful learning environment.
8. Provide positive and constructive feedback to guide students' learning and behavior.
9. Teach social behaviors.
10. Conduct functional behavioral assessments to develop individual student behavior support plans.

Instruction high leverage practices. Teaching students with disabilities is a strategic, flexible, and recursive process as effective special education teachers use content knowledge, pedagogical knowledge (including evidence-based practice), and data on student learning to design, deliver, and evaluate the effectiveness of instruction. This process begins with well-designed instruction. Effective special education teachers are well-versed in general education curricula and other contextually relevant curricula. They use appropriate standards, learning progressions, and evidence-based practices in conjunction with specific IEP goals and benchmarks to prioritize long- and short-term learning goals and plan instruction. This instruction, when delivered with fidelity, is designed to maximize academic learning time, actively engage learners in meaningful activities, and emphasize proactive and positive approaches across tiers of instructional intensity.

Teachers use the best available evidence, professional judgment, and knowledge of individual student needs. They value diverse perspectives and incorporate students' background, culture, and language to make instructional decisions. Their decisions result in improved student outcomes across varied curriculum areas and in multiple educational settings. They use teacher-led, peer-assisted, student-regulated, and technology-assisted practices fluently, and know when and where to apply them. They continually analyze instruction and monitor student progress in ways that allow them to improve student learning and refine their professional practice. The 12 high leverage practices related to instruction are listed below.

11. Identify and prioritize long- and short-term learning goals.
12. Systematically design instruction toward a specific learning goal.
13. Adapt curriculum tasks and materials for specific learning goals.
14. Teach cognitive and metacognitive strategies to support learning and independence.
15. Provide scaffolded supports.
16. Use explicit instruction.
17. Use flexible grouping.
18. Use strategies to promote active student engagement.
19. Use assistive and instructional technologies.
20. Provide intensive instruction.
21. Teach students to maintain and generalize new learning across time and settings.
22. Provide positive and constructive feedback to guide students' learning and behavior. (Note that this HLP focuses on instruction, while HLP 8 focuses on behavior.)

Wrap Up

This chapter provides background information regarding what HLPs are and why they are important. A brief description was provided regarding how the HLPs were developed and organized around key teaching functions for special educators—collaboration, assessment, social/emotional/behavioral practices, and instruction. Finally, a brief introduction to the HLPs for K-12 special education teachers was provided.

More extensive information regarding each of the 22 HLPs is provided in the chapters that follow. Each chapter begins with a general introduction to the HLP. Given the complexity of the HLPs, chapter content could not address every component and application of the practice. This required chapter authors to carefully select critical applications of each practice that would be useful for teachers as they learn to use the practice. A narrowing the focus section is provided in each chapter to describe how and why this was done. This is followed by descriptions of the components or essential functions of the HLP and general information regarding how to use the practice. Then the majority of each chapter is used to provide rich examples of the application of the practice in real-life contexts. Each chapter concludes with a brief wrap up, tips for using the HLP, and a short list of key resources for learning to use the practice.

Tips

1. As you will readily recognize from briefly reviewing the 22 HLPs addressed in this book, it is prudent to be selective in determining which practices you will initially learn to use. This decision will obviously be influenced by your teaching role and the needs of your students. We recommend that you carefully review the HLPs to see which will be most useful to improve your practice and better meet your students' needs. No matter where you start, we encourage you to not hesitate, but to pick a couple of HLPs and dive into the practices!

2. We also encourage you to take advantage of teachers around you who have skill related to the HLPs. Our experience indicates that in most schools, there are teachers who have expertise related to many of the HLPs. If you know a teacher who is skilled in using one or more of the HLPs, seek them out, pick their brain for resources, observe their teaching. Furthermore, if possible, have them observe you, provide feedback and respond to application-related questions regarding the HLP.

3. We encourage you not only to learn from others about using HLPs, but also to share your expertise with others as you become skilled in using these practices. We have found these types of collaborations among teachers to be the most effective approach to ensuring that many

teachers become well versed in using effective practices. Furthermore, educators who share their practices with others are more likely to sustain the use of these practices over time. All the best as you explore the HLPs. We hope you'll find that these practices are useful in improving your practice and addressing the needs of students that are addressed using intensive interventions.

References

Ball, D. L., Sleep, L., Boerst, T., & Bass, H. (2009). Combining the development of practice and the practice of development in teacher education. *Elementary School Journal, 109*, 458–76.

Billingsley, B., Bettini, E., & Jones, N. (2019). Supporting special education teacher induction through high-leverage practices. *Remedial and Special Education, 40*(6), 365–79.

Brownell, M., Benedict, A., Leko, M., Payton, D., Pua, D., & Tudor-Richards, C. (2019). A continuum of pedagogies for preparing teachers to use HLPs. *Remedial and Special Education, 40*(6), 338–55.

Grossman, P., Hammerness, K., & McDonald, M. (2009). Redefining teaching: Re-imagining teacher education. *Teachers and teaching: Theory and practice. 15*(2), 273–90.

Maheady, L., Patti, A., Rafferty, L., & del Prado Hill, P. (2019). School-university partnerships: One institution's efforts to integrate and support teacher use of high-leverage practices. *Remedial and Special Education, 40*(6), 356–64.

McDonald, M., Kazemi, E., & Kavanaugh, S. (2013). Core practices of teacher education: A call for a common language and collective activity. *Journal of Teacher Education, 64*(5), 378–86.

McLeskey, J., Billingsley, B., Brownell, M., Maheady, L., & Lewis, T. (2019). What are high-leverage practices for special education teachers and why are they important? *Remedial and Special Education, 40*(6), 331–7.

McLeskey, J., Berringer, M., Billingsley, B., Brownell, M., Jackson, D., Kennedy, M., Lewis, T., Maheady, L., Rodriguez, J., Scheeler, M. C., Winn, J., & Ziegler, D. (2017). *High-leverage practices in special education.* CEC and CEEDAR Center.

McLeskey, J., & Brownell, M. (2015). *High leverage practices and teacher preparation in special education.* CEEDAR Center. Retrieved from http://ceedar.education.ufl.edu/reports/.

McLeskey, J., Maheady, L., Billingsley, B., Brownell, M., & Lewis, T. J. (Eds.) (2022). *High leverage practices for inclusive classrooms* (2nd Ed.). Routledge/Taylor & Francis.

Pennington, R., Jones Ault, M., Courtade, G., Jameson, J.M., & Ruppar, A. (2022). *High Leverage Practices and Students with Extensive Support Needs.* Routledge/Taylor & Francis.

Windschitl, M., Thompson, J., Braaten, M., & Stroupe, D. (2019). Sharing a vision: How communities of educators improve teaching. *Remedial and Special Education, 40*(6), 380–90.

Windschitl, M., Thompson, J., Braaten, M., & Stroupe, D. (2012). Proposing a core set of instructional practices and tools for teachers of science. *Science Education, 96*(5), 878–903.

Section I
Collaboration High Leverage Practices
Bonnie Billingsley and Jocelyn Washburn

The Individuals with Disabilities Education Act (IDEA) requires that professionals and families collaborate in areas such as assessment and eligibility, Individual Education Programs (IEPs), and the transition of students with disabilities to post-school settings. Collaboration is also needed to meet the needs of students as they are increasingly served in inclusive settings (Williamson et al., 2019) and to coordinate programs and services when they occur across multiple environments. Thus, special educators, general educators, specialists, paraprofessionals, and families need to work together in specific ways to assure each student's program is deliberately planned, implemented, and assessed to support positive learning outcomes. Thus, collaboration is a primary and crucial responsibility for professionals.

A key tenet across chapters in Section I is the importance of developing positive and trusting relationships that support productive interactions among all involved with each student. Effective collaborators understand the importance of effective communication, as they listen to others and share their expertise to support each student's learning. Professionals also need to learn about and develop relationships with and advocate for students and families who differ from their own backgrounds (e.g., ethnicity, race, language, family structure, beliefs) and consider families' contributions and preferred ways to communicate.

In this first section of the book, we address collaboration in three specific contexts. Chapter 1 focuses on how special and general educators work together to plan instruction, co-teach, assess student performance, and problem-solve. Chapter 2 provides overall guidance for structuring and leading meetings for students in need of intensive interventions. Chapter 3 describes the importance of respect, equity, and advocacy as professionals work with parents, caregivers, and families (e.g., Turnbull et al., 2021), with a focus on immigrant families. The authors also consider ways for professionals to reduce language and cultural misunderstandings that are often barriers to effective communication. Case studies are used across chapters to illustrate collaborative practices.

The first two chapters address collaboration within a Multi-Tiered System of Support (MTSS) framework. Intensifying instruction may include increasing the number of sessions, the length of sessions, and opportunities for feedback and practice as well as decreasing group size, distractions, and heterogeneity (Fuchs et al., 2017). As instruction becomes more intensive for students, effective collaboration may intensify accordingly. As examples, co-teachers need additional planning time to

DOI: 10.4324/9781003276876-2

incorporate intensive instruction into their lessons, and to use co-teaching approaches that allow for small group instruction. Professionals also need an environment that allows careful and deliberate collaborative work, without distractions.

In summary, planning and delivering intensive interventions for students with disabilities require more than special education teacher; rather, teams made up of professionals and family members collaborate to plan and implement comprehensive and responsive academic and behavioral programming to support student learning. Teachers should consider additional learning activities to continue to develop their skills as they use collaborative practices, and seek out support from leaders, colleagues, or cultural brokers if they need additional support.

References

Fuchs, L. S., Fuchs, D., & Malone, A. S. (2017). The taxonomy of intervention intensity. *Teaching Exceptional Children*, *50*(1), 35–43. https://doi.org/10.1177%2F0040059917703962

Turnbull, A., Turnbull, R., Francis, G. L., Burke, M., Kyzar, K., Haines, S. J., Gershwin, T., Shepherd, K.G., Holdren, N., & Singer, G. (2021) *Families and Professionals: Trusting Partnerships in General and Special Education* (8th edition). Pearson.

Williamson, P., Hoppey, D., McLeskey, J., Bergmann, E., & Moore, H. (2019). Trends in LRE placement rates over the past 25 years. *Journal of Special Education*, 53, 236–44. https://doi.org/ 10.1177/0022466919855052

1
Collaborate with Professionals to Increase Student Success[1]

Margaret P. Weiss
George Mason University
Jocelyn Washburn
University of Kansas, Center for Research on Learning
Marilyn Friend
University of North Carolina at Greensboro
Tammy Barron
Western Carolina University

Introduction

Collaboration is an important part of teachers' professional lives as they work together to improve student learning. Teachers within and sometimes across schools engage in varied types of instructional collaboration together, including using student data to discuss how to improve instruction in a specific content area or using lesson study to consider how to teach a particular math concept. During quality collaboration, teachers share their knowledge, use student data to plan and modify their instruction, and provide feedback to each other. Although collaboration requires time and preparation, it is worth the effort. Researchers have found that quality collaboration leads to both teacher improvement and higher student achievement (Ronfeldt et al., 2015), and is an important source of colleague support (De Jong et al., 2019).

In special education, collaboration has specific meanings as professionals and families work together so that each student with a disability has a program that is designed and coordinated to meet their unique needs. For example, varied combinations of individuals, including principals, teachers, related service personnel, paraprofessionals, and families may meet informally or formally to address the needs of a student with a disability. This chapter addresses how colleagues, specifically co-teachers, collaborate to increase student success. Colleagues often work together in different ways to address a student's needs. For example, they may meet one time to make decisions about selecting a specific assistive technology device for a student, meet periodically to use screening data to identify students requiring more intensive assistance, and meet daily as they plan, teach, and evaluate the use of an intervention to meet a student's needs. Collaboration may also involve co-teaching, which typically involves a special and general education teacher instructing in the same classroom.

DOI: 10.4324/9781003276876-3

Co-teaching is frequently used to provide students with disabilities access to inclusive classrooms and the general education curriculum, while providing specialized instructional strategies to facilitate their learning (Cook & Friend, 2010).

Collaborating with colleagues provides ongoing opportunities to create and support justice-oriented experiences for professionals, families, and students, so all experience a sense of belonging in schools. A vision for equitable and inclusionary practices and the willingness for professionals to collaborate toward this vision creates a purpose-driven motivator behind honing one's interpersonal skills and collaborative practices. When students with disabilities are in general education classrooms, educators provide them with access to what already exists (i.e., curriculum and setting), yet there are additional steps needed to truly include them in the classroom. Teachers who collaborate to include students with disabilities in the general education classroom can reauthor what it means to share decision-making power, lesson design, instructional responsibilities, and the assessment of student learning.

Narrowing the Focus

In this chapter, we describe critical collaborative practices between special and general education teachers to increase students' opportunities to learn. We then provide an example of how they collaborate to integrate intensive interventions (Tier 3) for students with disabilities in a general education classroom through co-teaching.

Chapter Overview

1. Identify collaborative formats, resources, and processes that support intensive interventions in the general curriculum classroom.
2. Describe interpersonal skills that support collaboration.
3. Describe how co-teaching models support intensive interventions.
4. Illustrate effective collaboration and co-teaching for Nathan, an elementary student identified with autism who receives intensive intervention.

Using the HLP: Collaborative Practices that Support Intensive Interventions

Collaboration involves *how* colleagues make decisions and work together (Friend, 2021). Cook and Friend (2010) identified six characteristics of collaboration: (1) it is voluntary; (2) involves parity (i.e., each member's contribution is equally valued); (3) includes at least one shared goal; with (4) shared responsibilities for key decisions; (5) pooled resources; and (6) joint accountability for outcomes. It is important that professionals have a mutual understanding of what constitutes collaboration, otherwise they may have different expectations, which can interfere with effective team functioning. In this section, we consider collaborative format and resources, collaborative processes, and the interpersonal skills needed to support intensive interventions for students with disabilities.

Intensive interventions are necessary to help students with persistent learning and behavioral needs who are not making adequate progress through small group interventions or toward their individualized education program goals (National Center for Intensive Intervention, 2022). Within a Multi-Tiered System of Support (MTSS), intensive intervention usually falls in Tier 3 where teachers use practices supported by evidence to address persistently low academic achievement and/or high-intensity or frequent behavior issues (National Center for Intensive Intervention, 2022). The skills being taught through these intensive interventions must be integrated and supported in the general education classroom so that the student can generalize the skills learned within the intervention to other settings. This requires intentional and ongoing collaboration between teachers and data collection across settings.

Collaboration Formats and Resources

The ways in which teachers collaborate to support students with disabilities may differ from teacher collaboration for other instructional purposes. Examples include:

- Departmental or grade levels teams may include a special educator, and collaboration will occur to discuss content, activities, assessments, and the accessibility of these for students with disabilities, or
- A special educator and general educator may collaborate around co-teaching a course where students with disabilities only receive special education services in this setting, or
- A special educator and general educator may collaborate through consultation, without direct collaboration during instruction.

Collaboration regarding intensive interventions may also include a combination of these examples, such as:

- One special educator delivers the intensive intervention and consults with another special educator who co-teaches with a general educator in 10th grade English, or
- The special educator may deliver the intensive intervention *and* co-teach with the general educator in a course where the student receiving the intervention participates, or
- In an intensive intervention setting, a special educator may collaborate with a paraeducator during instruction.

Given the variability of collaboration formats, the collaborative practices for intensive interventions need to be flexible. Collaboration will only work if all partners are able to participate, and it is more difficult to get multiple people to a same-time, face-to-face space than it is to use other means of collaboration. Using technology can facilitate collaboration when face-to-face options are not available. For example, storing lesson plans on shared drives allows multiple people to provide feedback or suggest revisions before implementation. Using standard forms in applications such as Microsoft Forms or Qualtrics may make data collection/observer reports much easier to collect and share. Meeting via Zoom would facilitate off hours or off-site collaboration.

For all types of collaboration, participants need access to relevant resources. In relation to collaborating to support intensive intervention, examples of shared resources include the intensive intervention plan, universal screening and progress monitoring data (e.g., reading scores), and information provided within the Individual Education Program (IEP), such as Present Level of Performance, goals, and accommodations. During co-teaching, both teachers need access to instructional materials (e.g., course textbooks and teacher's editions) and classroom data (e.g., gradebook). No matter the formats, structures, or resources used to facilitate collaboration between teachers, effective interpersonal and communication skills are critical for success.

Collaborative Processes

Additionally, it is important to think about approaching collaborative tasks in a systematic way. Using systematic and negotiated decision-making processes or protocols allows teams to accomplish tasks effectively without having to change procedures with each discussion. Teachers involved in an MTSS framework typically use protocols that support decision making, but there are many examples available. For teachers who co-teach, there are modified lesson plan templates that support the integration of specially designed instruction, and there are planning processes that facilitate collaborative instructional decision making. For example, teachers may use processes such as the SMARTER

Planning and Instructional Cycle (https://sim.ku.edu/smarter-planning) or the "What, How, and Who" questioning process. During intensive intervention planning teachers may use school or district planning tools based on MTSS (www.csun.edu/sites/default/files/10-Tips-for-Using-Co-Planning-Time-More-Efficiently.pdf).

In addition to the above, problem-solving processes also facilitate collaboration. For example, problem solving involves a series of steps that professionals can use to systematically consider varied alternatives. These include: (1) analyzing the need for a problem-solving process; (2) identifying the problem; (3) brainstorming possible solutions; (4) evaluating these solutions; (5) selecting a solution and planning for its implementation, implementing the solution; and (6) evaluating the effectiveness of the solutions, continuing, discontinuing, or revising as needed (see Friend & Barron, 2022).

Interpersonal Skills for Collaboration

Teachers also need to be aware of and use interpersonal skills that enhance collaboration, as they engage with others to work toward common goals. Table 1.1 provides examples of interpersonal skills that support collaboration, outlining considerations for listening, question-asking, non-verbal

Table 1.1 Interpersonal Skills that Support Collaboration

Interpersonal skill	Description
Listening actively	Effective listening is crucial to communication. First, the listener takes in the information being shared, perhaps mentally repeating it to maintain attention and remember what is said; then the listener conveys to the speaker that listening is occurring which communicates that full attention is given to the concerns and insights expressed.
Asking questions	Effective question-asking is an active process integral to constructive communication. The use of open-ended questions is particularly helpful to understanding others' perspectives as it invites an elaborated response versus questions that can be answered with a yes, no or a phrase. For example, "what types of behaviors are interfering in the classroom?" allows the respondent to draw from their experience with the student.
Paraphrasing	Relaying a summary of what the speaker just shared is paraphrasing. It is helpful to check that you heard another's perspective accurately, especially in challenging situations. It involves demonstrating understanding and ensuring communication accuracy.
Recognizing nonverbal communication	Signaling positive communication through open body language (e.g., arms open, appropriate eye contact, leaning forward) can be used to encourage engagement and supports the development of rapport. In addition, facial expressions may convey interest, boredom, or annoyance.
Acknowledging diverse perspectives*	Working with others who bring diverse backgrounds or educational experiences provides new perspectives and ideas as teachers collaborative to meet student needs. A key way to encourage diverse perspectives is to work to achieve parity, as members are more likely to participate when they feel their perspectives are welcomed and valued.

Source: Adapted from Friend & Barron (2022).

Note: * Chapters 2 and 3 address considerations for working with family members from diverse backgrounds.

communication, and addressing diverse perspectives. This is not intended to be a comprehensive list, rather we focus on specific behaviors that help demonstrate respect and foster trust. Collaborators may find that not all interactions will proceed smoothly during the early stages of their relationships as they are establishing norms. Even further, conflicts are a natural part of interactions. In some cases, a conflict might elevate into a problem to resolve. Clarifying goals, identifying areas of agreement, and using problem-solving approaches or protocols can help collaborators work through differences. Problem-solving approaches or protocols can also be used to facilitate group interactions, so all have opportunities to generate and evaluate possible solutions to a problem. Practicing effective interpersonal skills may lead to more productive and gratifying collaborative experiences.

Collaboration for Co-Teaching

Co-teaching most often occurs in a general education setting, includes two teachers instructing students in the same classroom, and is a means to provide access to the general curriculum and specially designed instruction for students with disabilities in an inclusive classroom. Co-teaching relies on effective communication skills and a commitment to collegial collaboration and is one example of how collaboration can support intensive intervention. Co-teaching involves collaborating through each cycle of instruction: planning, instructing, and assessing student learning.

When two professionals collaborate through co-planning, co-instructing, and co-assessing, they can support intensive intervention in an inclusive classroom. Students with intensive support needs require that the two teachers intentionally co-plan from the outset of lesson design, including ways to practice and provide feedback on the skills being learned in intensive intervention settings. Based on curricular goals and student learning needs, co-teachers then choose which co-teaching approaches (shown in Figure 1.1) are appropriate when co-instructing and co-assessing. These six approaches support teachers in making important decisions about their active roles and responsibilities when delivering instruction.

Supporting the Integration of Intensive Intervention in Co-Taught Classrooms

Intensive intervention and instruction (HLP 20) are designed to match the needs of each student or address a lack of expected progress. One way to intensify instruction is by increasing the number of explicit instruction (HLP 16) elements in the lesson. Within co-taught classrooms, students require varied degrees and dosage of explicit instruction to meet their learning goals. For example, student A requires frequent feedback and reinforcement to make progress on their learning goals, while student B requires intermittent feedback, but also scaffolded support through modeling of cognitive processes and physical behaviors to complete the same task. Teachers can provide a continuum of explicit instruction feasibly within a co-taught class by using co-teaching approaches. As shown in Figure 1.1, three of the co-teaching approaches use whole group instruction, and three of the co-teaching approaches use small group instruction.

During whole group instruction, two teachers are actively engaged in instructional delivery, thus they should have increased effectiveness and efficiency over that of one teacher. In addition, each teacher performs distinctive roles to support the integration of intensive intervention. During instructional delivery, students are provided with targeted assistance; data on student performance is collected; and strategic learning can be modeled. With these whole group approaches, the focus of supporting intensive intervention is directed at generalizing skills learned as part of an intervention to new settings, with new tasks and grade level material.

Alternatively, using approaches that incorporate small group instruction provides each teacher with opportunities to differentiate content and methodology as well as make instruction more explicit and systematic. Specifically, the special educator may apply higher levels of explicit instruction to smaller numbers of students, and the general education teacher may deliver lesser degrees of

Co-teaching Approach	Classroom Layout	Roles of Two Teachers	Feature of Intensive Intervention in Example	Example
One Teaching, One Assisting		While one teacher delivers instruction, the other teacher provides targeted support throughout the class.	Behavior, engagement, and motivation support	While one teacher instructs on social studies concepts, the other teacher circulates to provide intermittent reinforcement of on-task, appropriate behavior and identifies instructional cues for students for notetaking and tracking information.
One Teaching, One Observing		While one teacher delivers instruction, the other teacher gathers data.	Attention to transfer	While one teacher introduces the historic context for a class novel, the other teacher records key behaviors of two students who are working on transferring a new strategy for maintaining attention and focus during whole class instruction.
Teaming		Two teachers share instructional delivery and have distinctive roles.	Explicit Modeling of Cognitive and Physical Behaviors	While one teacher presents and explains a worked example in math, the other teacher provides the steps in writing at the front of the room.

Co-teaching Approach	Classroom Layout	Roles of Two Teachers	Feature of Intensive Intervention in Example	Example
Parallel Teaching		Each teacher instructs a half of the class at the same time.	Differentiate content, methodology, or instructional delivery to achieve the same learning goal	During a math lesson, both teachers use the concrete-representational-abstract (CRA) method. As planned based on student learning needs, one teacher provides extra practice using manipulatives before moving to representation and abstract. The other teacher moves through CRA quicker and spends more time with abstract practice.
Station Teaching		Each teacher instructs a small group, and commonly one group of students works independently. The groups rotate.	Increased opportunities for practice with descriptive, corrective feedback	One teacher provides explicit instruction on predicting word meanings based on affixes, while the other teacher leads instruction on writing sentences using the new vocabulary words. The smaller teacher-student ratio allows for increased feedback. At the independent station, students create word part memory tables.
Alternative Teaching		While one teacher instructs a larger portion of the class, the other teacher instructs a small group of students.	Pre-teach content	One teacher facilitates an enrichment exercise with most of the class, the other teacher instructs a small group to pre-teach vocabulary words for the science lesson to be introduced next.

Figure 1.1 Supporting the Integration of Intensive Intervention in a Co-Taught Class

explicit instruction to a larger number of students without disabilities. Likewise, when small group instruction is used, instruction can be intensified, and increased features of intensive intervention can be incorporated within the co-taught class.

In the case study that follows, co-teachers collaborate to include one student's intensive needs within their co-taught class.

Case Study: Supporting Nathan through Collaboration and Co-Teaching

Middletown Elementary is in a small rural town outside of an Indigenous Community in the Great Plains Region. Its population is 200 students across grades one through five. There are two local industries outside of farming in the area: a trucking company and a tool die company. Most of the families in the community have at least one member who works for one of the two companies or works on one of the industry farms. The community center sits at the border of the Community and the town and is the hub of both communities. It includes the local library which provides free, reliable internet access. It also includes a small, volunteer historical preservation society that preserves the customs and history of the tribe.

Nathan is a 10-year-old fifth grader at Middletown Elementary. He has been at this school since preschool, receiving speech-language therapy since he was three. He was born in the Indigenous community but lives just outside it with his maternal Aunt Ruth and Uncle Daryl who are very involved with his education. Nathan reached most of his developmental milestones a little later than average; however, Nathan did not develop as his peers in early language, often seemed aloof, and exhibited restricted, repetitive behaviors such as arm flapping when agitated. Upon recommendation by their pediatrician, Ruth and Daryl had Nathan evaluated by a psychologist and he was diagnosed with autism spectrum disorder (ASD) soon after he came to live with them. He generally thrives within his family: he has a positive demeanor, enjoys school, and completes his chores at home with little prompting. His aunt and uncle participate in all of Nathan's IEP meetings and monitor his academic progress and social development closely. Ruth and Daryl learned about autism through the internet and a local support group for parents. Nathan and his aunt and uncle participate in most of the tribal events and most of the families in the community know them. Nathan is particularly interested in the cultural traditions and dress of his heritage, spending hours at the community center on Saturdays. He spends much of his time creating drawings of Indigenous dress, activities, and birds. Nathan's teachers have posted his drawings in the classroom and school, and the art teacher encourages his artistic talents. Ruth and Daryl have invited the teachers to some of the tribal events, which has helped teachers to understand their community. These informal interchanges have supported a trusting relationship between Nathan's family and the school.

In kindergarten and first grade, Nathan received special education in a separate setting due to his difficulty with social interactions and agitation when in groups of children in classroom settings. He received applied behavior therapy services at school and at home through kindergarten and first grade which greatly reduced his repetitive rocking, arm flapping, and attempts to leave the classroom or recess area. His academic performance in reading and writing was on grade level so in second grade, Nathan's IEP team decided to begin integrating him into general education classes. His second-grade teacher, Mr. Grundy, worked closely with the paraprofessional who supported Nathan, and his inclusion in art, music, and social studies was successful. As Nathan participated with his peers, teachers noticed that he had a difficult time following oral directions and learning content delivered in whole group instruction. For example, Nathan would often just sit and listen to his social studies teacher while his peers took notes and then would watch what the other students did after directions were given before he would begin. He also needed many more practice opportunities to master new vocabulary and sight words than his peers. During fourth grade, Ms. Anderson, Nathan's special education teacher, learned that Nathan showed initiative in art class, and was rarely agitated during these weekly classes. She worked with Mr. Bures, the art teacher, to support Nathan's social skill development in fourth grade, giving him structured opportunities to share and describe his art in small group settings.

Nathan is now a fifth-grade student and is served much of the day in co-taught classrooms. Nathan's grades and progress monitoring data indicate that he is making progress in all classes. He has developed self-soothing strategies when agitated and does not attempt to leave the room. Nathan is successful in cuing his teachers when he feels overwhelmed, and his behavior plan allows him to take a break from the classroom in situations that cause anxiety by going to a "safe" room. Nathan's IEP goals are currently focused on improving his social interaction skills with other students, increasing his use of strategies to address his auditory processing needs, and developing content vocabulary. Ms. Anderson co-teaches reading, writing, social studies, and math with Nathan's fifth grade teacher, Ms. Lightfoot.

Part I: Co-Planning

Ms. Anderson and Ms. Lightfoot sit catty-corner from each other during their common planning period to discuss an upcoming math lesson. They both have their laptops with a shared lesson plan document open to record their instructional decisions and roles and responsibilities during the lesson. There are 18 students in their class. Five of these students are identified as students with disabilities, including students with specific learning disabilities, hearing loss, and autism. Ms. Lightfoot initiates the planning conversation, "Ok, so our next unit is on fractions and decimals. The learning objectives are for the students to (a) represent and identify equivalencies among fractions and decimals, with and without models; and (b) compare and order fractions, mixed numbers, and/or decimals in each set, from least to greatest and greatest to least." They need to collaborate on how best to help all students, with special attention on Nathan so he has opportunities to achieve these objectives.

Next, Ms. Anderson asks, "Would it make sense for us to focus on their conceptual understanding of fractions first? Then, we could move into comparing fractions to decimals as well as comparing and ordering them." However, Ms. Lightfoot explains she feels strongly that a fifth-grade math class needs to prepare students for work in middle school and beyond. In the past, she has begun class with a brief review of the previous day's lesson, taught relevant vocabulary, modeled solving a new problem, and then presented a similar problem that the students must work together in small groups to solve. Ms. Anderson listens attentively and contemplates how to integrate their viewpoints.

Ms. Anderson shares the *IEP-at-a-Glance* she made for each student on her caseload for easy reference while planning. This one-page document includes IEP goals, accommodations, and notes about required specially designed instruction. She points out that a few students have difficulty with recognizing and interpreting information (i.e., processing deficits). "Let's look at Nathan specifically," as she reviews aloud, "Nathan has a great deal of difficulty moving from concrete to abstract understanding. For example, he mastered all his math facts in addition, subtraction, and multiplication. However, when asked to apply a conceptual understanding of addition or multiplication to applied or word problems, he is not able to identify what the question is asking and is not able to identify the operation necessary to solve the problem." Ms. Lightfoot nods to show understanding, and says, "I see what you mean. Also, in the past, fractions have been challenging for most students." Together, they decide that the evidence-based practice of following the concrete-representational-abstract (CRA) approach during math instruction will be a good fit for the learning objectives and to meet students' learning needs. They can differentiate the amount of practice for each stage in the CRA approach. Specifically, some students, like Nathan, will need to spend more time practicing with manipulatives (e.g., fraction bars), whereas other students will be able to practice with a few examples and proceed to practicing with representational (e.g., tallies, pictures) and abstract (i.e., fractions written on paper) problems.

Ms. Anderson refers to the options for co-teaching approaches, "How about if we use *Parallel Teaching*? I could instruct students who we predict need more practice with concrete and representational practice; you could work with students who need less of these types of practices and move to practicing with additional abstract examples." She continues by pointing out that this small group co-teaching approach will allow them to interact with the students more than a whole group approach. Ms. Lightfoot adds, "That'll work great! To build on this idea, we could give each other a signal when our group is ready for the next part of the lesson. If some students in one of our groups are not ready yet, then we could switch to *Alternative Teaching*. For example, all students who are ready could work with partners for additional practice, and the students who need more practice could stay with us. This way, we could give them more feedback within this smaller group size." With these two co-teaching approaches, they will be able to vary the type and amount of practice as well as opportunities for feedback based on the students' needs, while still achieving the same learning goal.

Ms. Anderson smiles and leans forward. Next, she brings up Nathan's social skills. Nathan does not typically participate in class discussion, even when students ask him direct questions. Often, he will just copy the answers the other students have written down without interacting with the group or asking for help. Mrs. Anderson has data demonstrating that Nathan asks to go to his safe room more frequently in math than in any other class. Ms. Anderson says, "As they will be working in small groups, this will be a chance for Nathan to practice the social skills he's been learning during intensive intervention. I will be providing this instruction just prior to our math block, so I'll cue Nathan on our walk to class by encouraging him to use the sentence starters we wrote during intervention for asking questions and sharing his thoughts. We will have also just completed an exercise to compare numbers which will serve as a scaffold for comparing fractions. I'll remind Nathan to try the problems on his own first before checking with a peer or me." As a recap of their collaborative planning session, Table 1.2 shows an excerpt of their lesson plan.

Part II: Co-Instructing and Co-Assessing

"It's time for math. Let's get ready to go," says Ms. Anderson. The intensive instruction group packs up materials and lines up at the door. They had just finished a lesson with social stories on how to ask for help and participate in discussions with peers and Nathan participated throughout their time together. As the group walks through the hall, Ms. Anderson goes through her practice routine with Nathan. Having planned the lesson with Ms. Lightfoot, Ms. Anderson knows that Nathan will be working with other students in smaller groups on fractions and he will need to be engaged and interactive to get the necessary practice opportunities. Nathan appears calm and ready today. Ms. Anderson lets him know that he will be working in a group with Elan, his best friend.

When they enter the room, Ms. Anderson gives Ms. Lightfoot a nod indicating that Nathan and the group had a productive session, and everyone is calm and ready to learn. The students in the room are putting away their lesson materials and moving to their seats. Ms. Lightfoot addresses the class once everyone is seated, stating that they are going to shift to math where they will work on comparing fractions using their fraction bars. Ms. Anderson tells the class that, because they are going to be using the fraction bars, they are going to split into two groups: one with Ms. Anderson and one with Ms. Lightfoot. She says the names of the students who will be at a table with Ms. Lightfoot near the window and asks the students to move there. The rest of the students, including Nathan and Elan, are to move to the table by the door. During their planning session, Ms. Lightfoot and Ms. Anderson put all the necessary materials together and tucked them into shelves near their tables. Once everyone is settled, the teachers go to their groups and start the lesson. They sit at opposite ends of their group table so that they can see each other and communicate about how the lesson is going.

Table 1.2 Excerpt of a Co-Taught Lesson Plan

Unit 2: Fractions and Decimals
Learning Objectives:
- represent and identify equivalencies among fractions and decimals, with and without models
- compare and order fractions, mixed numbers, and/or decimals in a given set, from least to greatest and greatest to least

Co-Teaching Approach	Roles & Responsibilities	Primary Activity	Materials
One-Teaching/ One-Assisting	Ms. Lightfoot introduces the lesson goals and expectations for participation in group instruction. Ms. Anderson cues Nathan prior to lesson and circulates to ensure students are gathering their materials for small group instruction.	Warm-up	Practice sheet with one problem
Parallel Teaching	With her group of 10 students, Ms. Lightfoot gives a basic review of fractions with fraction bars. Then, she uses I Do, We Do, You Do with the CRA approach to compare and order fractions. With her group of 8 students, Ms. Anderson gives a basic review of fractions with fraction bars. Then, she uses I Do, We Do, You Do with the CRA approach to compare and order fractions.	Differentiated use of CRA approach with fractions	Fraction Bars Practice sheet with 15 problems Bookmark with sentence starters for Nathan
Alternative Teaching	Most students participate in partner practice with additional problems. Ms. Lightfoot and Ms. Anderson each work with an even smaller group of students or partners on these problems, depending on their progress during Parallel Teaching. Both teachers prompt students in their small group to think aloud with concrete or representational problems (as needed) and monitor student work to solve abstract problems.	Partner Practice with additional abstract examples Students think aloud for additional C-R practice and move to abstract examples	Practice sheet with 5 abstract problems Extra practice sheets for C-R and Fraction Bars

Both teachers begin with a basic review of using fraction bars. They ask students to create different fractions at the tables and have the students talk through their thinking. Nathan is following along and often checks the others around him before making his own fraction with the bars. But Ms. Anderson encourages him to ask his neighbor for assistance, if needed. The room gets a little noisy with students in both groups talking, but Nathan is not distracted. The teachers share eye contact and nod to indicate that things are going ok. Ms. Anderson begins her explicit instruction on comparing fractions by asking the students to create two fractions (with common denominators) and then asking them to compare numerators and denominators and determining which one is greater than or less than the other by stacking them next to each other. After multiple practice opportunities, most of the students in both groups are catching on and can draw the comparisons instead of using the bars!

Another nod from Ms. Anderson and Ms. Lightfoot says to the class, "Ok, friends! Ms. Anderson and I see that you are on your way to mastering comparing fractions with common denominators. I am going to assign you a partner and give you four practice comparisons to do on your own. Remind me what the procedures are for working with partners?"

After chorally responding with the procedures, Ms. Anderson identifies the pairs of students and directs them to work in a specific space. One pair from her group, Amanda and Teresa, are directed to work at the table with Ms. Lightfoot as Ms. Anderson could see from their time with her that they still needed some support and feedback before working independently. She directs Nathan and Elan to stay at the table with her. All students work through the same practice problems; however, Amanda, Teresa, Nathan, and Elan continue to work with the teachers using the bars and drawing the results on their worksheets. Ms. Lightfoot directs Amanda and Teresa to work on one practice problem on their own as she watches and listens.

Satisfied that they are headed in the right direction, Ms. Lightfoot gets up and moves through the room, examining the student responses and providing feedback. She observes Nathan put all his fraction bars in the middle of his worksheet and begin to rub both eyes with his fists and rock slightly. She knows that this means Nathan is frustrated and cannot move on. Ms. Lightfoot moves over to the table where Nathan is sitting and says, "Nathan, I need your help. Would you please come over to my table and help me put away my fraction bars? I've gotten them all mixed up while I was using them." Slowly, Nathan complies and follows Ms. Lightfoot to her table. There she speaks softly to him, gives him the fraction bar box, and asks him to first put away the thirds pieces. "Great, Nathan! You are right—those are the thirds fraction bars. Can you hand me all the half fraction bars? How many half fraction bars should we find, Nathan?" Nathan continues to help Ms. Lightfoot while Ms. Anderson finishes the problems with Elan.

Reflections About Collaborative Practices

During co-planning, special educator, Ms. Anderson, and general educator, Ms. Lightfoot used their interpersonal skills, identified clear goals for the lesson, drew upon student data to form groups, and selected evidence-based practices and co-teaching approaches to support intensive intervention. Throughout their co-planning, they listened carefully to each other and showed support for diverse perspectives by asking questions and reinforcing each other's ideas. During co-instructing, their communication remained strong by using nonverbal gestures, and their parity was evident in how they shared roles and responsibilities throughout the lesson. Finally, both Ms. Anderson and Ms. Lightfoot were informally assessing student mastery of the learning objectives as they observed them completing practice problems. When they noticed most students were ready, they moved them to working in pairs independently. When Ms. Lightfoot realized that Nathan was frustrated with the practice problems, she redirected him to complete tasks related to the objectives but that he was confident in completing. During their next planning session, Ms. Lightfoot and Ms. Anderson reflected on the students' learning, and identified additional ways in which to include more small group practice opportunities for students like Nathan who took longer to master the fractions concepts.

Wrap Up

Collaboration can make a difference in what teachers accomplish and what students achieve; however, it requires commitment to high standards for this work. Effective collaboration requires professionals who understand what collaboration means and have developed both knowledge about professional collaboration and the interpersonal behaviors that support positive relationships. In addition, to collaborate effectively, teachers need to share their expertise about the student, the content being taught, and the teaching practices that have the strongest evidence for promoting learning for students with disabilities. Finally, teachers need supportive contexts for collaboration, including the time, schedules, and resources needed for this important responsibility.

Tips

1. *Continue to learn about effective intensive interventions for students with disabilities.*
   Effectively participating in collaboration for intensive interventions requires an understanding of content taught, intensive interventions in the area of content taught, varied types of student data, how to analyze and chart student data, and decision-making processes. Teachers should consider their own professional knowledge and learning goals to engage in on-going professional learning through professional development programs, and use high-quality resources such as the IRIS modules https://iris.peabody.vanderbilt.edu/resources/
2. *Seek out support from principals or mentors as needed to support collaboration.*
   Teachers may find it difficult to collaborate if they do not have the schedules, time, resources, or space for this work. Professional development may also be necessary to support specific types of collaboration (e.g., co-teaching). Principals and mentors are often a source of support.
3. *Take time to learn about and practice communication skills.* Everyone can improve their communication skills and teachers can use everyday interactions as an opportunity to practice these skills. Also, use the interpersonal content earlier in this chapter to take a personal inventory of how you see your strengths for collaboration (e.g., preparation for collaboration) and specific behavior you desire to modify as you collaborate (e.g., tendency to interrupt in conversations). For example, before each meeting remind yourself to notice if you interrupt others and focus on reducing any interruptions over time. Teachers may also request feedback about their communication and collaborative skills from trusted colleagues. In addition, groups of teachers may want to reflect about their collaboration process on a periodic basis and identify goals for change. Given the centrality of collaboration to teachers' work, continue to learn about effective communication through books, articles, and web materials. For example, this resource provides detailed information about communication with others www.newconversations.net/

Note

1 The first two authors contributed equally to this manuscript.

Key Resources

Journal Articles and Books

Barron, T., Friend, M., Dieker, L., & Kohnke, S. (2021). Co-teaching in uncertain times: Using technology to improve student learning and manage today's complex educational landscape. *Journal of Special Education Technology*, 01626434211033579.

Chitiyo, J. (2017). Challenges to the use of co-teaching by teachers. *International Journal of Whole Schooling*, 13, 55–66.

Friend, M. (2019). *Co-teach!: Building and sustaining effective classroom partnerships in inclusive schools* (3rd ed.). Marilyn Friend, Inc.

Friend, M., Cook, L., Hurley-Chamberlain, D., & Shamberger, C. (2010). Co-teaching: An illustration of the complexity of collaboration in special education. *Journal of Educational and Psychological Consultation*, 20, 9–27. doi: 10.1080/10474410903535380

Murawski, W. W., & Hughes, C. E. (2021). Special educators in inclusive settings: Take steps for self-advocacy! *Teaching Exceptional Children*, 53(3), 184–93.

Rivers, D. (2012). *The seven challenges workbook: Communication skills for success at home and work.* www.newconversations.net/

Rodgers, W., & Weiss, M. P. (2019). Specially designed instruction in secondary co-taught mathematics courses. *Teaching Exceptional Children, 51,* 276–85. https://doi.org/10.1177/004005991 9826546

Stewart, E. M. (2019). Reducing ambiguity: Tools to define and communicate paraprofessional roles and responsibilities. *Intervention in School and Clinic, 55*(1), 52–7.

Weiss, M. P., & Rodgers, W. (2020) Instruction in co-taught secondary classrooms: Three elements, two teachers, one unique idea. *Psychology in the Schools, 57,* 959–72. https://doi.org/10.1002/pits.22376

Website Materials

Communication for Collaboration

https://connectmodules.dec-sped.org/connect-modules/learners/module-3/

TTACOnline.org

http://ttaconline.org/Resource/JWHaEa5BS77n8SA6lK7xng/Resource-hlp-highlight-tool---hlp-1-collaborate-with-professionals-to-increase-student-success-vdoe-ttac-at

http://ttaconline.org/Resource/JWHaEa5BS75SnS7BmwvFtw/Resource-co-teaching-a-workbook-for-achieving-the-perfect-union-loudoun-county-public-schools

https://ttaconline.org/Resource/JWHaEa5BS74rMLN0lAD9Jg/Resource-chalk-it-up-to-experience-tips-from-real-co-teachers-of-virginia-august-2020

Team teaching: How to improve one's game www.youtube.com/watch?v=3RcEuYG9UNc

References

De Jong, L., Meirink, J., & Admiraal, W. (2019). School-based teacher collaboration: Different learning opportunities across varied contexts. *Teaching and Teacher Education, 86,* 1–12. https://doi.org/10.1016/j.tate.2019.102925

Cook, L., & Friend, M. (2010). The state of the art of collaboration in special education. *Journal of Educational and Psychological Consultation, 20*(1), 1–8.

Friend, M. (2021). *Interactions: Collaboration skills for school professionals* (9th ed.). Pearson.

Friend, M. & Barron, T. (2022). *High leverage practices for inclusive practices* (2nd edition). In J. McLeskley, L. Maheady, B. Billingsley, M. T. Brownell, & T. J. Lewis, *High Leverage Practices for Inclusive Classrooms* (2nd edition). Routledge.

National Center for Intensive Intervention. (2022). *What is data-based individualization?* https://intensiveintervention.org/data-based-individualization

Ronfeldt, M., Farmer, S. O., McQueen, K., & Grissom, J. A. (2015). Teacher collaboration in instructional teams and student achievement. *American Educational Research Journal, 52*(3), 475–514.

2
Organize and Facilitate Effective Meetings with Professionals and Families

Jocelyn Washburn
University of Kansas
Center for Research on Learning

Bonnie Billingsley
Virginia Tech
School of Education

Introduction

Students with disabilities, by definition, require individualized, specially designed instruction to meet their unique needs. Addressing the needs of each student with a disability requires a high level of collaboration and coordination among professionals and family members. There are several different types of meetings, including Individual Educational Program (IEP) meetings, professional collaboration meetings, and others designed for specific purposes as the child's needs may change throughout the year. IEP meetings are held at least annually to outline the goals and services each student will receive and are typically developed by parents/caregivers, teachers, administrators, related services personnel, and transition specialists. Professional collaboration meetings are regularly scheduled meetings to plan, monitor, and adjust the student's plan to meet their IEP goals. Other types of meetings may include those that are initiated by professionals or parents to address some aspects of a student's program. Examples include manifest determination meetings and developing plans to strengthen home-school communication. This chapter focuses on collaboration during intensive intervention meetings with professionals and families to support students' achievement and well-being.

Special education teachers often have the responsibility for coordinating and leading varied types of meetings; however, school psychologists and principals sometimes fulfill this role. Leaders need to develop organizational skills to coordinate meeting logistics to accomplish key meeting goals, collaborative skills to work effectively with others from diverse backgrounds, and the skills to draw upon *every* participant's knowledge and expertise in decision making. Leaders will likely confront typical meeting barriers, such as lack of time, problematic schedules, and disagreements. However, with careful planning, meetings can be used to support coordinated and effective instructional programs for students with disabilities.

Leaders have an important responsibility to involve parents as partners in their child's education. More specifically, they should consider the needs of families and caregivers, and consider how to include parents and family members from minoritized groups and those with different backgrounds

DOI: 10.4324/9781003276876-4

and cultures. Key considerations include holding, "high expectations about parents and their participation, developing trust with families, respecting family culture, avoiding jargon, equalizing relationships, and recognizing family strengths and expertise" (Cheathem & Lim-Mullins, 2018, p. 42). When working with bilingual family members, leaders need to consider their language preferences, backgrounds, and perspectives; otherwise, they may inadvertently silence them, preventing meaningful dialogue (Cheatham et al., 2018). Taking time to value families and their contributions is important to building positive relationships and developing trust (Blue-Banning et al., 2004).

In summary, effective meetings provide opportunities for professionals and families to share their expertise and coordinate their efforts so that students with disabilities have the best possible opportunities to achieve and meet their individual goals. In this sense, meetings are ground zero for sharing goals, coordinating instructional plans, selecting evidence-based practices, and monitoring each student's progress over time. Leaders should work to promote positive relationships and productive interactions among all participants, with the priorities of enhancing "student learning, achievement, positive behavior, and attendance" as well as to reduce participants' stress and improve their self-efficacy (Francis et al., 2016, p. 281).

Narrowing the Focus

This chapter has two primary purposes. In the first part, we briefly review key guidelines that address features for planning and leading effective meetings. In the second part, we focus on the decision-making processes during regularly scheduled collaboration meetings, specifically intensive intervention meetings, consistent within a Multi-Tiered System of Supports (MTSS) framework. Intensive interventions are designed to increase student achievement and well-being in the foundational areas of literacy, mathematics, and social and behavioral skills. It is important to involve parents and caregivers in IEP meetings where the annual objectives are determined for each child. During intensive intervention meetings, parents are not likely to attend all of these meetings, as they happen on a regular basis, two or more times a month.

Chapter Overview

1. Provide guidelines for leading effective meetings.
2. Describe the decision-making steps used during intensive intervention meetings.
3. Illustrate intensive intervention meetings using a two-part case study.

Using the HLP: Guidelines for Leading Effective Meetings

Productive meetings require preparation before the meeting, effective facilitation during the meeting, and specific follow-up actions. Table 2.1 provides basic guidelines to consider when preparing for and leading varied types of meetings. The first three tasks in Table 2.1 are straightforward in most situations (i.e., identify meeting goals, determine participants, and schedule the meeting). It is easier to accomplish these tasks efficiently if you have certain tools available. For example, having a folder on your computer with scheduling tools such as Doodle, drafts of meeting invitations that can be edited, and a checklist of actions for meetings should help you complete these tasks efficiently. In some cases, meeting attendees may need to participate using virtual tools (e.g., Google Meet, Zoom). It is important to anticipate any challenges related to hosting a remote meeting and to support participants in their ability to actively engage in the meeting (see https://thedigitalwo rkplace.com/articles/virtual-meeting-best-practices-7-ways-to-improve-your-remote-meetings/ for details).

Table 2.1 Leading Effective Meetings

Meeting Checklist	Examples
A. Set the Stage for the Meeting	
1. Identify meeting goals/ purposes	• Develop IEP • Review progress monitoring data and create/modify instructional plan • Create home-school communication plan • Listen to and address parent and caregiver concerns
2. Determine participants	• Progress monitoring meeting: general education teacher, paraprofessional • IEP meetings: family members, administrators, general and special educator (possibly student)
3. Schedule meeting & invite participants	• Consider others' schedules • Share purpose, date, time, place, and meeting length • Determine if some or all attendees will participate virtually (e.g., Google Meet, Zoom)
4. Share how participants might prepare prior to meeting	• Consider priorities for student • Bring assessments: e.g., literacy progress monitoring results, work samples • Parents and caregivers consider child's needs and possible goals
B. Facilitate the Meeting	
1. Share expectations or ground rules	• Identify a set of behaviors or ground rules for regularly scheduled meetings and share virtual meeting etiquette, if applicable • Begin and end the meeting on time • Share the meeting goal • Set positive tone by sharing something positive • Use guided questions or a checklist for instructional decision-making
2. Model inclusiveness and parity	• Plan for accessibility needs (e.g., interpreters) • Encourage parity by facilitating discussion and encouraging all to participate • Model openness and listen carefully to participants • View disagreements as part of human interactions rather than something to be avoided • Use active listening to demonstrate understanding (restate using own words)
3. Keep the meeting on track	• Gently remind group of the meeting goals if it gets off track • Use a problem-solving approach when concerns are expressed • Encourage a forward view ("It seems the issue is…so how might we move forward") • Consider another meeting if there is not time to address concerns or if another person, such as the principal needs to be present
4. Summarize key points and next steps	• At the end of meeting, summarize meeting accomplishments • Identify needed follow-up activities, determine who is responsible for each and timelines for completion

Source: Summarized from Washburn & Billingsley (2022).

Facilitating meetings requires a commitment to collaboration and an understanding of how to achieve parity. Parity means creating equal opportunities for input among all meeting participants so each person attending feels comfortable sharing their expertise, suggesting ideas, and expressing concerns. Parents, caregivers, and professionals have unique backgrounds and experiences with the student that are relevant to planning their educational program. Family members and caregivers are more likely to share their knowledge if they feel welcomed, supported, and have trusting relationships with school staff (Francis et al., 2016). Additionally, if participants take time to listen to each other and understand each other's perspectives, differences in backgrounds or perspectives are not necessarily barriers to communication (Lake et al., 2019).

Meeting participants may disagree. If the meeting leader views disagreements as part of human interactions, they will be more likely to listen carefully, paraphrase others' needs, and consider varied goals, and solutions. Conflicts are less likely to arise (and take hold) when participants are open to others' ideas, are unguarded, and listen to others' perspectives (Lake et al., 2019). If meeting norms allow for and accept conflict, participants may be more comfortable both listening to divergent views and sharing their perspectives with others. Table 2.1 also includes possible strategies to consider if participants are no longer working toward the stated meeting goals or if conflicts arise (i.e., keep the meeting on track; Washburn & Billingsley, 2022).

In summary, successful meetings involve positive interactions and equal and meaningful participation among all attendees (Beck & DeSutter, 2021). Participants know what will be addressed ahead of time and how they can prepare for the meeting. In addition to facilitating student learning, positive interactions also provide school staff and parents with social supports, including opportunities to develop trusting relationships with each other, to problem solve and share expertise, and to support each other's efforts.

Leading Intensive Intervention Meetings

Students who need intensive interventions have complex learning challenges that are best solved when teams combine their expertise and use data to monitor growth. When teams collaborate using student progress monitoring data, they gain a comprehensive understanding of the student's progress over time and use this data to make systematic adaptations to the content or delivery of the intervention to best reach a student's learning needs. Table 2.2 provides an overview of intensive intervention meetings.

During intensive intervention meetings, participants use assessment data to identify students' learning goals, develop plans, and monitor their progress. To facilitate these meetings, leaders need knowledge about: (1) a variety of assessment measures such as screening, formative assessments, benchmark tests, and skill-based assessments and how to communicate results to stakeholders (see Chapters 5–7); (2) how to analyze and chart student data in varied areas of student performance (example shown in Figure 2.1), curricular demands and interventions to provide the basis for sound instructional decisions; and (3) decision-making processes (see examples in Table 2.2).

Collaborating with professionals through intensive intervention team meetings maximizes the effectiveness of a process known as data-based individualization (DBI; Lindström et al, 2019). DBI is a framework for providing and adapting intensive interventions. "At its core, DBI depends upon a validated intervention program implemented with fidelity. Teachers set an appropriate goal for a student and monitor progress weekly using carefully selected measures. Ideal progress monitoring tools are (a) linked to instruction; (b) sensitive to growth; and (c) easy to administer" (Lindström et al., p. 113). We illustrate the use of DBI in the forthcoming case studies.

Table 2.2 Overview of Steps in Intensive Intervention Meetings

Leaders:	Example:
1. Select a step-by-step process to guide instructional decision-making, such as guiding questions or a checklist.	Step 1. What are the key goals for the student? Step 2. What is the student's current level? Step 3. How will the student meet instructional goal(s)? Step 4. How will the student's progress be monitored and assessed (e.g., measurement, frequency)?
2. Prior to the meeting, request from participants specific data appropriate to the purpose of the meeting.	Pre-test or baseline assessments Benchmark assessment results Behavior/performance checklists Progress charts for interventions Other data (e.g., cumulative file, standardized assessments, discipline record, student work examples, observations)
3. Use data within the step-by-step process selected in 1 and 2 above as progress is reviewed in periodic meetings and determine appropriate next steps (e.g., continue current intervention because it is working or modify it because progress is insufficient).	See Figure 2.1 which shows Kasey's progress on decoding checks.

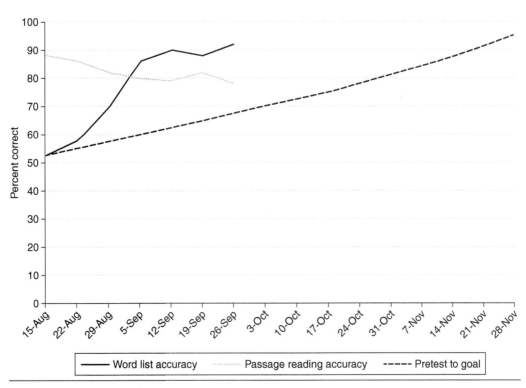

Figure 2.1 Kasey's Decoding IEP Goal Progress

Case Study Part 1: Leading an Initial Progress Monitoring Meeting

In this case study, Ms. Lopez, a special education teacher who instructs an intensive reading intervention class for ninth graders, leads a one-hour team meeting with two ninth-grade English Language Arts (ELA) teachers after their monthly ELA department meeting. This example shows their first regularly scheduled meeting and includes several interrelated purposes:

- to communicate about student progress in the intervention and their ELA coursework,
- to gather formative data to make instructional decisions within the intervention,
- to collaborate regarding instructional methods and resources for prompting generalization of skills learned during the intervention in the ELA class and activating generalization within the intervention.

Dilicia Thoma, an instructional support paraprofessional, attends as she supports one of the students in the classroom. Aletha Pack, the school's literacy coach, also attends because she facilitates professional learning, including intervention fidelity checks, for Ms. Lopez.

Preparing for an Effective Meeting

Ms. Lopez, the special education teacher, decides that the most time-efficient manner to collaborate with her ELA colleagues is to request a team meeting following the regularly scheduled, monthly ELA department meetings. To prepare for the team meeting, Ms. Lopez considers what is possible to accomplish in this first meeting. She determines the most time-sensitive goals and represents them on a meeting agenda shown in Table 2.3. She sends the meeting goals to the ELA teachers, along with the agenda and a request to bring needed assessments or work samples. In this request, she also solicits any additional agenda items they might want to add.

Table 2.3 Intensive Intervention Team Meeting Agenda

Intensive Intervention Team Meeting
August 23, 4:30–5:30 pm
Location: ELA Department Chair's Classroom

Prior to the meeting: Please consider your priorities for student learning goals in your ELA course and bring any initial pre-test results and other relevant assessments (e.g., student work samples) to share at the meeting. If you have additional agenda items to address, please let me know.

AGENDA

Welcome and Meeting Goals
- to communicate about student progress in the intervention and their ELA coursework
- to gather formative data to make instructional decisions within the intervention
- to promote transfer of reading skills to ELA assignments

Learn about Students' Reading Progress

Intervention Overview

Strategy Transfer and Generalization
   QR Code for Padlet Activity:

Be sure to mark your calendar for our next meeting: September 24
Same time, Same place!

Table 2.4 Two-Way Communication About Student Reading Progress

Please keep the top-half of this sheet in a locked cabinet.

Special Education Teacher: Ms. Lopez, rlopez@school.org, 555-1234

Student: K.L.   Case Manager: Jamal Williams

IEP Reading Goals:

By the end of the IEP period, when given a list of 40 multisyllabic words containing closed, open, consonant-vowel-e, and vowel team syllable types, the student will be able to decode 38/40 (95%) words correctly as measured by teacher records.

By the end of the IEP period, when given a grade-level nonfiction passage, Kasey will identify the main idea and provide at least two details related to the main idea with 90% accuracy in three out of four trials.

Current Reading Level: 680 Lexile

Please return to Ms. Lopez by Friday, September 2.

Student: K.L.

How did the student perform on any ELA pre-tests?

What observations have you made about the student's reading participation in your course?

Please provide at least one passage from your course for practice during intervention.

When considering the main purposes for the meeting, she decides handouts will help. First, she develops an intervention overview with a few specific strategies that students are learning currently along with suggested cues that teachers can use with her students to support strategy transfer to their ELA coursework. She also prepares an individualized communication sheet (Table 2.4) for each student they teach who is enrolled in the intervention. The top half of the handout communicates the student's progress in the intervention, current reading level, and IEP goals for reading. The bottom half of the sheet includes questions for the teachers to share with Ms. Lopez about the student's progress on reading tasks in their ELA course. Hoping that the team meeting will be interactive, she prepares a Padlet to gather ideas simultaneously about how students might use reading strategies with their ELA reading assignments.

Communication Tool

In addition to meeting goals and logistics, all meeting leaders, including Ms. Lopez, need to consider areas that might be particularly sensitive or where there may be disagreements. By doing this, they make plans for how issues should be presented, if there are parameters for discussing the issues, and if a decision cannot be achieved, what might be their next step. Thus, in preparation for this meeting, Ms. Lopez predicts that scaffolding support for reading grade-level text will be a common

Table 2.5 Collaborative Problem-Solving Protocol

PROBLEM-SOLVING WORKSHEET

Problem-Solving Team Members:	Role:
Rosa Lopez	Special Education Teacher
Josie Strothcamp	ELA Teacher
Bob Miller	ELA Teacher
Dilicia Thoma	Paraprofessional
Althea Pack	Literacy coach

Problem:
How will students who are reading around the 4th grade level read their literature book which is written at the 9th grade level?

Details:
the literature book five grade levels higher than the students' current reading levels
students read outside of class

Alternative Solutions:
Read aloud software
Audio version of literature book
Assign a different short story to read with lower readability
Provide a graphic organizer
Pre-teaching key vocabulary

Solution to Be Tried First:
providing scaffolds, such as graphic organizers and pre-teaching vocabulary

Implementation Steps	When	Who
Check with the students' case managers about their read aloud accommodations	Tomorrow	Ms. Lopez

How Will the Plan Be Monitored? Each team meeting, we will revisit this challenge and share additional solutions, including what's working and what's not working

What Are the Criteria for Success? Homework completion: students prepared by having read the assigned passage in the book; students prepared for class discussion

Date and Time of Next Meeting: September 24

Source: Adapted from Knackendoffel et al. (1992).

challenge, so she brings a collaborative problem-solving protocol (Knackendoffel et al., 1992) to support instructional decision-making (see Table 2.5).

Facilitating an Effective Initial Meeting

At the start of the meeting, Ms. Lopez thanks the ELA teachers for staying after the department meeting and reviews the meeting agenda, shares the three handouts, and clarifies the purpose for the meeting. She states, "I'm pleased we will be collaborating across our courses because we share several students. Today we will discuss individual student reading progress and ideas for strategies to encourage reading growth and independence (purpose of meeting). I prepared this agenda

(Table 2.3) to keep us focused on several important topics, and I hope each of you will share your perspectives throughout our conversation."

Students' Current Reading Levels

The first agenda item gives teachers a chance to orient themselves to their students' current reading levels and reading goals. Ms. Lopez explains, "each student enrolled in the intervention course has IEP goals related to decoding and comprehension, but their individual reading performance varies." She prompts the teachers to review their individualized communication tool.

Strategy Transfer and Generalization

Next, Ms. Lopez asks Ms. Pack, the school's literacy coach, to give an overview of the intervention and briefly describes a reading strategy that students are currently practicing. Ms. Pack explains, "Through the reading intervention, the students are receiving explicit instruction on the five components of reading: phonemic awareness, phonics, fluency, comprehension, and vocabulary. The main goal is for students to read grade level materials with proficiency. Decoding instruction is a focus because it is a foundational building block for all reading skills. One word attack strategy students are learning helps them recognize phonemes (units of letter sounds), syllables (groups of sound units), and morphemes (word parts with meaning, such as prefixes, roots, and suffixes). As a summary of the strategy, they practice phoneme combinations and break words into syllables or morphemes using a step-by-step process." Next, to facilitate idea-sharing on strategy generalization and transfer from intervention to ELA content, Ms. Lopez asks the teachers to share ideas for how this specific strategy might look with an ELA reading task. She asks them to scan the QR code on their agenda to pull up a Padlet where they can collaboratively answer these questions: What are the reading requirements of your course? What are examples of reading tasks? What are examples of multisyllabic words used in your course?

Collaborative Problem Solving

After they have been working on the Padlet for a while, one of the ELA teachers asks, "I expect students to read certain sections of the short stories for homework, but I realize now that our literature book is several grade levels above the students' reading levels. How will they manage on their own?" Believing that better solutions will come from the group than her alone, Ms. Lopez paraphrases the question and shares: "I'm so glad you brought this up because this is a challenge these students are facing in most of their classes. How will students who are reading around the 4th grade level read their literature book which is written at the 9th grade level? Let's brainstorm together." She hands out a collaborative problem-solving worksheet (Table 2.5) and quickly writes down the problem they identified. Next, they note a few key details: the literature book is five grade levels higher than the students' current reading levels, students read outside of class, and students have reading disabilities related to decoding and comprehension. Ms. Lopez explains the problem-solving process in that they will brainstorm alternative solutions in an open-ended fashion before determining feasible solutions.

One ELA teacher speculates, "I wonder if our school has access to read-aloud software or if the textbook has an audio version." Another teacher asks about the appropriateness of offering a different short story to read that is written with lower readability. Ms. Thoma suggests providing a graphic organizer with some key details filled in and others missing for the student to complete while reading. Ms. Lopez records all ideas on the problem-solving worksheet and adds one more, "Would other students benefit from pre-teaching some of the key vocabulary?"

At this point in the process, Ms. Lopez asks them if they have brainstormed enough ideas to move to deciding which solution to try first. She says, "fortunately, read-aloud software and an audio version of the literature books are available." The ELA teachers are not sure about the availability of audio players to use these accommodations. To keep the meeting on track, Ms. Lopez remembers it is important to consider when to stop, resolve, or move on, so she asks the team, "it seems the issue is about the logistics of making students know how to access their reading accommodations. So, how might we move forward?" One ELA teacher suggests they start with providing scaffolds, and Ms. Lopez offers to speak with the students' case managers tomorrow about their accommodations.

During the last five minutes of the meeting, Ms. Lopez moves to summarize key points and next steps. "We have accomplished several things together: we brainstormed several instructional scaffolds for reading grade-level materials, and I shared introductory information about the intervention so we can prompt students to practice their reading strategies in ELA class. In our next meeting, we will revisit how the scaffolding and accommodations are going as well as reading progress monitoring results. Please share a few specific passages from your class with me that we can practice using our strategies in our intervention class, and it would be helpful if you could complete the bottom half of the two-way communication tool by next Friday, September 2nd."

Reflecting About the Meeting

After the meeting, Ms. Lopez thought about what went well. She was pleased they addressed the meeting purposes and the handouts helped focus the discussion. Overall, everyone seems to feel comfortable expressing their concerns and sharing ideas. Next time, she decides she will invite each teacher to share their student samples or data closer to the start of the meeting. She thought about her own follow-up responsibilities and added them to her calendar.

Case Study Part 2: Leading an Intensive Intervention Meeting

This case study focuses on reviewing Kasey Langdon's progress on a reading intervention. Jamal Williams, Kasey's IEP case manager, will coordinate and facilitate the meeting while the special education teacher, Rosa Lopez, plays an active role, sharing data and engaging in problem-solving and action planning. Additionally, Kasey's 9th grade ELA teacher, Josie Strothcamp, her father, Mr. Langdon, and a paraeducator, Dilicia Thoma, are meeting participants. Two key elements illustrated in this case study are active listening when disagreement occurs and use of data to inform adaptations to the intervention. The meeting is necessary due to the student's non-responsiveness to the team's previously selected validated intervention program.

Preparing for an Effective Meeting

Given the purpose of the meeting and the intended meeting participants, Mr. Williams considers the best timing for the meeting. He schedules the meeting for an hour before school to avoid securing class coverage for the teachers involved and to accommodate the father's work schedule. Ms. Williams pulls the Intensive Intervention Meeting Agenda template, modifies it for the meeting, and sends it along with Kasey Langdon's current Intervention Plan to each participant prior to the meeting (see Table 2.6; Fuchs et al., 2017). The agenda includes the following items:

1. Welcome, Purpose, and Process for Today's Meeting about Kasey
2. Review Intervention Plan
3. Area of Concern/Problem for Dialogue

Table 2.6 Kasey Langdon's Intervention Plan

Description of the Intervention: Explicit instruction phonemic awareness, phonics, fluency, comprehension, and vocabulary.
Logistics:

Person(s) responsible for delivering the intervention, including any adaptations: Rosa Lopez
Additional resources or support needed: Professional development and monthly coaching sessions with school literacy coach
Plan for communication with Mr. Langdon: monthly email progress updates
Plan for communication with other relevant staff supporting the student: overview session at start of year and at semester change; monthly ELA department meeting; every other week emails updates

Data Collection Plan:

Person responsible for collecting progress monitoring data: Rosa Lopez
Progress monitoring measure or tool: school's curriculum-based measurement tool
Frequency of progress monitoring data collection: once per week
How will we know if the intervention is working (is there a clearly defined goal)?

Goals:
By the end of the IEP period, when given a list of 40 multisyllabic words containing closed, open, consonant-vowel-e, and vowel team syllable types, the student will be able to decode 38/40 (95%) words correctly as measured by teacher records.
By the end of the IEP period, when given a grade-level nonfiction passage, Kasey will identify the main idea and provide at least two details related to the main idea with 90% accuracy in three out of four trials.

How will we know if the intervention was implemented as intended?
Fidelity Plan: School literacy coach will visit the class, complete the fidelity checklist, and debrief with Ms. Lopez once per week.

Source: Adapted from the National Center on Intensive Intervention's Taxonomy of Intervention Intensity by Fuchs et al. (2017).

4. Desired Outcome/Goal
5. Potential Reason for not Progressing Toward Expected Performance (hypothesis)
6. Solutions to Implement
7. Wrap Up with Action Plan and Next Steps

In the meeting invitation, Mr. Williams states the meeting purpose is to review Kasey's progress monitoring data and to use the data to modify Kasey's intervention plan as needed. He asks the following team members to bring specific information to share at the meeting.

• Josie Strothcamp (ELA teacher): A work sample from Kasey
• Rosa Lopez (special education teacher): All data available (e.g., spreadsheet of literacy progress monitoring results and student attendance) and initial hypothesis for inadequate progress
• Althea Pack (Literacy coach): Fidelity checks
• Mr. Langdon: Father's perspective about Kasey's needs and progress toward reading goals

Knowing the meeting will require each team member to share, listen to each other's perspective, problem solve, and make instructional decisions, Mr. Williams prepared a set of clarifying questions aligned with the dimensions of the intervention plan from a question bank he found on the National Center for Intensive Interventions (NCII) website for data teaming. These questions included:

1. **Dosage:** Does the group size, duration, and frequency of the intervention provide sufficient opportunities to respond and receive corrective feedback?
2. **Attention to Transfer:** Does the intervention assist the student in generalizing the learned skills to general education or other tasks?
3. **Engagement:** How engaged and involved is the student in this instruction/intervention?
4. **Learner Needs and Background:** Are other factors contributing to the learning or behavior concerns that need to be addressed (e.g., home life, health, vision, hearing, attendance/tardiness, disability, behavior)?
5. **Alignment:** Does the student need additional instruction in a specific skill area?
6. What specific skill deficits may be contributing to the problem?
7. Are the academic tasks on the right level for the student?
8. **Fidelity:** Is there evidence that the intervention was delivered with fidelity? (e.g., adherence, program specificity, duration)?

Facilitating an Effective Meeting

Setting the Stage

Mr. Williams begins the meeting by saying, "Good morning and welcome. I'm so glad we could be here today, and I wanted to mention that Althea Pack can't attend as she is home with a sick child. I think most of you have met Mr. Langdon, but let's introduce ourselves as it might help to share our names again [members introduce themselves]. We are meeting to review Kasey's progress toward her decoding reading goal and consider needed adaptations to the reading intervention plan. Kasey was involved in the IEP meeting a month ago when we developed the reading intervention plan. I want you to know that Kasey is progressing well on her reading comprehension goal, which is why we will not be discussing it today." Mr. Williams projects the agenda on the screen and continues, "Here is an overview of our agenda today. First, let's look at Kasey's intervention plan. We need to confirm if there are any current barriers to implementing this plan. Next, Ms. Lopez will share data about how Kasey is pronouncing multisyllabic words in isolation, but not yet while reading passages. She will also share her initial hypothesis for what might be getting in the way of using it in passages. We'll share data and discuss possible adaptations to the intervention. To support our conversation, I've selected several possible guiding questions" (see above questions).

Core Discussion

Mr. Williams invites Ms. Lopez to share the validated intervention program she is teaching. "Our reading program includes units of instruction for all aspects of reading and includes spiraling components that prompt students to practice active thinking strategies while reading a variety of different texts. We can expect students to gain two to three years of reading growth in one year when the intervention is taught as designed. We do have the proper dosage in place. At the start of the year, Kasey was reading text at the 680 Lexile level, so this means Kasey should be able to read text at approximately 1000 Lexile by the end of the year. Most high school texts are written at the 1100 Lexile (Metametrics)." Mr. Williams thanks Ms. Lopez for the overview of the intervention plan and expected outcomes, and advances the conversation by saying, "This reading program has many strong features, so let's talk about how Kasey is responding to the instruction."

Mr. Williams displays a graphic organizer (see Figure 2.2) and describes how the team will use this thinking process to discuss an area of concern, its possible causes, and potential solutions to try. He explains while drawing a connecting arrow between the causes and solutions, "We can examine each cause to figure out data-informed adaptations needed within the intervention plan. Ms. Lopez,

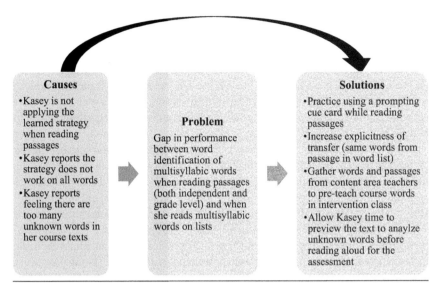

Causes	Problem	Solutions
•Kasey is not applying the learned strategy when reading passages •Kasey reports the strategy does not work on all words •Kasey reports feeling there are too many unknown words in her course texts	Gap in performance between word identification of multisyllabic words when reading passages (both independent and grade level) and when she reads multisyllabic words on lists	•Practice using a prompting cue card while reading passages •Increase explicitness of transfer (same words from passage in word list) •Gather words and passages from content area teachers to pre-teach course words in intervention class •Allow Kasey time to preview the text to anaylze unknown words before reading aloud for the assessment

Figure 2.2 Completed Example of the Thinking Process for Dialogue

will you summarize the problem you noticed and give your initial hypothesis for why this might be happening? Then, we'll each share."

Special educator's perspective. Ms. Lopez states, "We are seeing a mismatch between how successful Kasey is when pronouncing multisyllabic words on a list and when she is reading multisyllabic words in passages, both independent reading passages and course text." Ms. Lopez shares a spreadsheet that shows her strategy pre-test scores on a grade-level passage (48% comprehension, 88% accuracy, and 90 words correct per minute [WCPM]), her practice scores for pronouncing multisyllabic words in lists (90% or higher), and her scores on the progress monitoring measure administered weekly. She shows a graph to display her word list reading accuracy compared to her passage reading accuracy (see Figure 2.1). The progress monitoring tool measures her automaticity when reading an instructional level passage and her comprehension of the text by answering a set of six questions. Her scores remain relatively level, around 95 WCPM and 70% comprehension. Ms. Lopez continues, "My initial hypothesis is that Kasey is not applying the word identification strategy while reading passages. Have others observed this?"

Parent's perspective. Mr. Williams records the problem in the center of the graphic organizer and the first cause shared and waits to hear from others. Her father, Mr. Langdon, adds, "Kasey is frustrated about how long the strategy takes. She says there are too many words in the passages, and it doesn't work for all the words. She's becoming disheartened." Mr. Williams nods and leans in a little, "I understand what you mean. From what I know it takes time to be able to use it automatically. Also, I can imagine how frustrating and overwhelmed Kasey might feel if the reading passages have too many unknown words."

ELA Teacher's Perspective. Mr. Williams encourages Kasey's ELA teacher to share the work sample she brought. Ms. Strothcamp shows an example of a class reading assignment where Kasey answered 65% of the comprehension questions correctly. The passage is an excerpt of authentic literature from the 1800s and has many challenging words. Ms. Lopez exclaims, "Those words are much too difficult, and I didn't know that's what Kasey was reading in class right now." Ms. Strothcamp replies, "I didn't see Kasey using any particular strategy while reading. She just reads and answers the questions." Mr. Langdon, the father, looks surprised, and asks, "Well how did we get this far without her using whatever strategy you are teaching—I'm concerned about what you are saying."

Mr. Williams recognizes some tension in his voice and says, "Mr. Langdon, thanks for sharing that—I understand it is frustrating and this is the reason all of us are here. I'd like to return to your point after we go through the problem-solving process, so you can hear about our plan to address the lack of progress—are you OK with that?" Mr. Langdon says, "yes, I do want to hear what you plan to do." Mr. Williams focuses the conversation on the problem-solving process and hands out the bank of clarifying questions. "This information is important to communicating about Kasey's experiences and making improvements to our instruction. Let's see if any of these clarifying questions will help us develop some solutions and they are tied to the intervention plan."

Paraeducator's Perspective. Noticing that Ms. Thoma, who provides instructional support during the intervention, has not shared yet, Mr. Williams enlists her contribution. Ms. Thoma says, "As the one who administers the progress monitoring tool, I don't see when Kasey could use the strategy since it is a timed assessment." Ms. Lopez builds on this notion, "That's an important observation! The progress monitoring tool has standardized procedures for administration and scoring, and it provides one gauge of her reading performance. Could we create opportunities for Kasey to identify unknown words before the timer begins to find out how much better her scores might be if she applied the word attack strategy first?" The team decides to temporarily modify the testing procedure to provide Kasey the opportunity to show what she can do.

Interactive Dialogue. Ms. Strothcamp draws the team's attention to two of the clarifying questions. She states, "I see these two questions as related, perhaps we can find a solution that will connect them." She reads aloud, "Does the intervention assist the student in generalizing the learned skills to general education or other tasks? Also, are the academic tasks on the right level for the student?" Then, she adds, "I'm thinking we need to strengthen the bridge between what is practiced in the intervention and my class by providing more scaffolded supports and making sure these supports are provided in others' classes as well. I'm thinking we need to use some pre-teaching techniques when we know the academic tasks or when reading assignments are higher than Kasey's current independent reading skills." These questions lead the team to brainstorming several new adaptations to the intervention plan as follows:

- Kasey will make a bookmark with the strategy steps that she can carry in her backpack to all classes;
- Ms. Lopez will gather current course passages and create words lists from these texts for Kasey to practice in the intervention period; and
- Mr. Williams will communicate to all Kasey's teachers to pre-teach key vocabulary words before assigning independent reading.

Mr. Williams documents these decisions on the intervention plan in the adaptation column. Mr. Williams stops for a moment and focuses on Mr. Langdon. "What do you think of what we've planned—how do you feel about this?" Mr. Langdon responds, "It seems you are trying to make this work for Kasey, to support her in the classes where the reading is harder. I think she needs that additional help. But I am also concerned about her level of motivation right now." Mr. Williams responds by saying, "Yes, I think we should consider her motivation as we move forward with these changes. Let's see about how we can work that into our plan today." Mr. Williams asks Ms. Lopez, "How will we know if the intervention and these adaptations are working?" Ms. Lopez responds, "We will see upward trending scores on the progress monitoring measures, representing her performance on increasingly complex text with 80% or greater mastery on strategy use and comprehension, approximately 125 for WCPM. We should also see improved assignment grades in her content courses." Mr. Williams states, "That provides clear criteria for progress and now let's address Kasey's motivation. I do think if she experiences more success with the strategy that will help her motivation. We might try one more thing. Ms. Lopez, since you have such good rapport with Kasey, maybe the two of you can discuss this change and ask Kasey for input as well. Would you also check-in with her weekly to see how she is feeling about the changes and maybe involve her in charting her progress, so she can see how the intervention is working? Then in a month let's go back to the data and she how she is progressing." Ms. Lopez responded, saying, "Yes, I like these ideas, especially getting her involved in charting her progress, and we can do that together." Mr. Langdon seems encouraged by these comments and states, "Yes, she feels very connected to you, Ms. Lopez, so I think this could help."

Review

With only ten minutes left, Mr. Williams prompts the team to create an action plan. He records team decisions on a table to email to team members after the meeting (see Table 2.7). He summarizes: "I think we have a good plan to support Kasey in reaching her reading goals. We reviewed the validated reading intervention, considered Kasey's current levels of responsiveness to the program, and used data sources and observational information to adapt our plan. Ms. Lopez will check with Kasey before we begin these changes and review the plan with her. She will also observe her using the strategy more often and see if Kasey would like to track her progress. Let's meet again in one month to review how these adaptations are working. When Althea Pack, the literacy coach, told me she could not attend the meeting, she also wrote that she didn't see any issues during class visits when she conducted intervention fidelity checks. Next time, she can discuss these checks with us. Does this sound like I captured our discussion?"

Reflecting About the Meeting

In this meeting, the case manager and a special education teacher led an intensive intervention meeting aimed at resolving a student's non-responsiveness to a reading intervention. Before the meeting, the case manager took several steps to create a solution-oriented and inclusive meeting. He shared an agenda prior to the meeting, clarifying what participants needed to bring and share, selected an instructional decision-making process, and used guiding questions to facilitate dialogue. During the meeting, participants used active listening to demonstrate their understanding of varied perspectives. This was particularly important given Mr. Landon's concerns. Everyone was

Table 2.7 Action Plan

Who	Action	When
Ms. Lopez, special education teacher	Check in with Kasey about the changes in her plan and see if she is interested in charting her own data.	Today
	Requests Kasey's teachers to share upcoming course texts and lists of critical vocabulary words	Tomorrow
	Shares reading intervention progress monitoring spreadsheet with Mr. Williams.	In 2 weeks
Mr. Williams, case manager	Summarize Kasey's progress with Mr. Langdon.	In two weeks
Ms. Strothcamp, ELA Teacher	Presents to 9th grade team of teachers about scaffolding supports for grade level text and identify critical vocabulary to pre-teach	Next Monday
Mr. Langdon, father	Share any concerns with the team moving forward	As needed

glad Mr. Langdon shared his concerns because they didn't realize Kasey felt discouraged and unsuccessful using the intervention. The case manager also kept the meeting on track by linking individual contributions to their common goal and frequently reported on their progress toward accomplishing most of the purposes for the meeting. He hoped Althea would have been available to review the fidelity checks, but they will check with her in the next day or two and add to the next meeting agenda.

Wrap Up

In this chapter, we first addressed overall guidelines for leading effective meetings, including how to prepare, lead, and follow-up after meetings. We illustrated the need for a systematic decision-making process as well as the use of data within process. Second, we provided an overview of intensive intervention meetings, and we illustrated the guidelines in Table 2.1. We focused on meetings that address intensive interventions, detailing the work of two high school teachers. We now conclude with tips and key resources.

Tips

1. New teachers may have little preparation for leading meetings; thus, mentors should provide new teachers with information about how to lead meetings and model these practices. Ideally, new teachers will gradually take over these responsibilities under the guidance of a mentor.
2. Teams should consider debriefing after selected meetings to identify what is working well with meetings and what needs improvement. This allows for understanding the local context, as some schools/districts may face unique challenges (Beck & DeSutter, 2021).
3. If unanticipated conflicts arise, it is crucial to take time to listen to family members' concerns without interruption to fully understand their perspectives. If a disagreement occurs and a resolution or consensus does not emerge or seem unlikely to be resolved, then take time to restate family members' concerns, ask if you have fully captured them, and suggest rescheduling the meeting. It is important to consult with the principal and/or special education director for the next steps.
4. Individual Educational Program (IEP) meetings and the resulting documents are the foundation for each student's program. Although we did not focus on IEP meetings in this chapter, there are many online and print sources that address these meetings in detail (see key resources below).
5. Unfortunately, some parents have negative experiences in meetings (Mueller, & Vick, 2019). Facilitated IEP (FIEP) meetings should be considered in disputes that cannot be solved between parents and professionals (Mason & Goldman, 2017). In FIEP meetings, a "facilitator uses procedural practice and skill to support the team throughout the meeting process" to resolve disagreements (Mueller & Vick, 2019, p. 68). District and school administrators should help assess whether a facilitated meeting is needed. For more information, see resources at the end of this chapter.

Key Resources

Articles

Beck, S. J., & DeSutter, K. (2020). An examination of group facilitator challenges and problem-solving techniques during IEP team meetings. *Teacher Education and Special Education, 43*(2), 127–43. https://doi.org/10.1177/0888406419839766

Cavendish, W., & Connor, D.J. (2018). Special series: Parent voice in educational decision making for students with learning disabilities. *Learning Disability Quarterly, 41*(1), 4–6. https://doi.org/10.1177/0731948717692308

Francis, G. L., Register, A., & Reed, A. S. (2019). Barriers and supports to parent involvement and collaboration during transition to adulthood. *Career Development and Transition for Exceptional Individuals, 42*(4), 235–45. https://doi.org/10.1177/2165143418813912

Gershwin, T., Holdren, N., & Aceves, T. C. (2022). Family–professional partnership research: Key methodological considerations for elevating family voices. In *Handbook of Special Education Research, Volume I* (pp. 131–43). Routledge.

Mueller, T. G., & Vick, A. M. (2019). Rebuilding the family–professional partnership through facilitated Individualized Education Program meetings: A conflict prevention and resolution practice. *Journal of Educational and Psychological Consultation, 29*(2), 99–127. doi.org/10.1080/10474412.2018.1470934

Websites

Center for Parent Information and Resources (IEP resources) www.parentcenterhub.org/?s=IEPs

Data Teaming Tools: https://intensiveintervention.org/implementation-intervention/data-teaming

IEP Meeting Facilitation: www.key2ed.com/index.php/facilitation

IRIS Module "IEPs: Developing High-Quality Individualized Education Programs" https://iris.peabody.vanderbilt.edu//iep01/

National Center on Intensive Intervention: https://intensiveintervention.org/

PACER Center: Champions for Children with Disabilities: www.PACER.org/transition

Promoting Progress: https://promotingprogress.org/

Taxonomy Briefs for Intensifying Academic Interventions: https://intensiveintervention.org/tools-charts/academic-intervention-taxonomy-briefs

References

Beck, S. J., & DeSutter, K. (2021). Special education meetings: The role of the facilitator in districts serving rural communities. *Rural Special Education Quarterly, 40*(1), 33–41. https://doi.org/10.1177%2F8756870520972660

Blue-Banning, M., Summers, J. A., Frankland, H. C., Nelson, L. L., & Beegle, G. (2004). Dimensions of family and professional partnerships: Constructive guidelines for collaboration. *Exceptional Children, 70*(2), 167–84. https://doi.org/10.1177/001440290407000203

Cheatham, G. A., & Lim-Mullins, S. (2018). Immigrant, bilingual parents of students with disabilities: Positive perceptions and supportive dialogue. *Intervention in School and Clinic, 54*(1), 40–6. https://doi.org/10.1177%2F1053451218762490

Francis, G. L., Hill, C., Blue-Banning, M., Turnbull, A. P., Haines, S. J. & Gross, J. (2016). Culture in inclusive schools: Parental perspectives on trusting family-professional partnerships. *Education and Training in Autism and Developmental Disabilities, 51*(3), 281–93. www.jstor.org/stable/24827524

Fuchs, L. S., Fuchs, D., & Malone, A. S. (2017). The taxonomy of intervention intensity. *Teaching Exceptional Children, 50*(1), 35–43. https://doi.org/10.1177%2F0040059917703962 \

Knackendoffel, A., Robinson, S. M., Deshler, D. D., & Schumaker, J. B. (1992). *Collaborative problem solving: A step-by-step guide to creating educational solutions.* Edge Enterprises, Incorporated.

Lake, B.J., Billingsley, B. & Stewart, A. (2019). Building trust and responding to parent-school conflict. In Crockett, J., Billingsley, B., & Boscardin, M.L. (Eds.). *Handbook of leadership & administration for special education*, 2nd edition (pp. 265–78). Taylor-Francis.

Lindström, E. R., Gesel, S. A., & Lemons, C. J. (2019). Data-based individualization in reading: Tips for successful implementation. *Intervention in School and Clinic*, *55*(2), 113–19. https://doi.org/10.1177%2F1053451219837634

Mason, C. Q., & Goldman, S. E. (2017). Facilitated individualized education planning: The state of implementation and evaluation. *Journal of Disability Policy Studies*, *27*(4), 212–22. https://doi.org/10.1177/1044207316660828

Mueller, T. G., & Vick, A. M. (2019). Rebuilding the family–professional partnership through facilitated Individualized Education Program meetings: A conflict prevention and resolution practice. *Journal of Educational and Psychological Consultation*, *29*(2), 99–127. https://doi.org/10.1080/10474412.2018.1470934

Washburn, J., & Billingsley, B. (2022). Leading effective meetings with professionals and families. In J. McLeskey, L. Maheady, B. Billingsley, M. Brownell, M., & T. Lewis. *High leverage practices for special education teachers*, 2nd edition (pp. 24–42). Taylor-Francis (co-published with Council for Exceptional Children).

3

Collaborate with Families to Support Student Learning and Secure Needed Services

Grace L. Francis
George Mason University

Colleen K. Vesely
George Mason University

Jihyae Choe
George Mason University

Taneika Tukan
Alexandria City Public School

Krishna Leyva
Alexandria City Public Schools

Introduction

Educator-family collaboration designed to support student learning and securing resources involves "agree[ing] to build on each other's expertise and resources, as appropriate, for the purpose of making and implementing decisions that will directly benefit students and indirectly benefit other family members and professionals." (Turnbull et al., 2021, p. 161). The collaboration strategies in which educators engage differ based on student and family characteristics, preferences, and existing systems of support. Effective collaboration, however, is consistently grounded in equity, respect, communication, advocacy, and commitment (Turnbull et al., 2021). Research indicates that educator-family collaboration results in positive outcomes among students, families, and educators. Examples of positive outcomes include enhanced: (a) student cognitive and language development, academic achievement, and behavior and social-emotional development (Ogg et al., 2021); (b) family connections to important services, community, and social networks (McWayne et al., 2021); and (c) educator efficacy and optimism (Hoy, 2012).

Despite these important outcomes, barriers prevent educators from collaborating with families to support student learning and secure needed services. For example, language and cultural misunderstandings (including limited access to translators and interpreters), the underuse of family-friendly, jargon-free language, and school-centric communication methods (e.g., newsletters, email blasts) present challenges to collaboration (Francis et al., 2018). In addition, while federal special and general education laws (IDEA and ESSA) include requirements for educator and family collaboration, educators are not consistently prepared to engage families in meaningful collaboration that supports learning and access to resources (Kyzar et al., 2019).

DOI: 10.4324/9781003276876-5

Moreover, despite educator efforts, families may experience institutional betrayal, trauma, or further traumatization by harmful practices and policies implemented by institutions designed to support them (Smith & Freyd, 2013). For immigrant families, this layering of trauma can be particularly destabilizing to their family systems (Goodman, et al., 2017) and can result in an inherent distrust of school systems, including distrust of educators. These barriers are exacerbated among marginalized and historically oppressed families, including immigrant families who are less familiar with US policies and systems (e.g., school systems, healthcare, community transportation, Pereira et al., 2012). Still, families and educators share the goal of student success, and collaboration is a powerful practice that benefits all stakeholders over time.

Narrowing the Focus

Meaningful educator-family collaboration can enhance student learning and family access to needed resources. As mentioned, however, collaboration is especially important among immigrant families who are learning English and how to navigate US education systems, services, and supports. This chapter focuses on ways in which educators can meaningfully and respectfully collaborate with diverse immigrant families (see Table 3.1) who have children with disabilities receiving intensive interventions by sharing research-based strategies, brought to life through authentic case study examples.

Chapter Overview

1. Provide three communication-based strategies for educators to engage in meaningful, multifaceted collaboration with families.
2. Describe how educators can serve as agents of change to create just education systems that better serve families and students with disabilities.
3. Provide strategies and tools to bolster educators' collaboration with families via examples of educators collaborating with immigrant families to support student learning and securing needed services.

Table 3.1 Commonly Used Terms Describing Immigrants

Common Terms	Definition
Asylum-seeker	Someone who has fled their home country out of fear of persecution and violation to their human rights. Their own government will not or cannot protect them. They seek safety outside of their country as they wait for their asylum claim to be reviewed.
Refugee	Someone who has fled their home country out of fear of persecution and violations to their human rights. Their own government will not or cannot protect them, so they seek safety outside of their country.
Immigrant	A person living outside of their country of origin who is not an asylee or refugee.
Undocumented Immigrant	A person living outside of their country of origin who does not have legal authorization to be in the new host country. It is not uncommon for undocumented immigrants to have similar reasons as refugees and asylees for leaving their home country; however, they are not recognized as either by the host country.
Migrant Worker	A person who moves temporarily either within their country of origin or across international borders for work. This is especially common among farm workers who move with the crops that need to be harvested.

Using the HLP: Collaboration Strategies

In this section, we highlight the importance of ongoing communication with immigrant families through three key strategies for building educator-family collaboration: (1) identify communication needs and nuances; (2) develop trust; and (3) support home and community learning.

Strategy 1: Identify Communication Needs and Nuances

Investigating communication needs among all families is the foundation for engaging in educator-family collaboration. We detail two ways educators can identify communication needs and nuances among immigrant families.

Consider First Languages and Communication Norm

Investigating the following are critical to collaborating with families: the family's preferred language, the family's ability to access and reciprocate written communication, if the family needs augmentative or alternative communication, and the family's preferences for modes of communication (e.g., in-person, phone, email, text messaging, paper notes). Educators can better understand families' language and communication preferences through a brief conversation with families or by creating a short multilingual survey that can be sent to families electronically or on paper (see Table 3.2).

Educators may also better understand and support verbal, non-verbal, and written communication with families by collaborating with school social workers, family liaisons, cultural brokers, and other families or educators in the school with knowledge of the family's cultural communication norms. In addition, educators may consider connecting with relevant community organizations to learn more about colloquialisms and cultural norms. Examples of non-Western colloquialisms and cultural norms with which many US educators may not be familiar include:

- In some Spanish dialects, tia and tio means "aunt" and "uncle," as well as "lady," "chick" "man," "dude" or "friend."
- There is no "universal" form of Spanish, making it challenging for native Spanish speakers from different countries to communicate fluently.
- There are various dialects of spoken Arabic even though Arabic readers from various countries can read similar text.

These differences in language may require a translator (i.e., individuals to translate one written language to another) from the same region of the world as the family to cross-check translated documents or multiple interpreters (i.e., individuals to interpret one spoken or signed language to another) to support family-educator conversations with families from various countries.

In addition, building relationships with certified school-based interpreters and translators aids in understanding cultural communication norms and nuances and helps ensure that interpreters and translators accurately convey information to families that is consistent with the law (e.g., explaining parental rights). For instance, Table 3.3 provides an example of a brief overview of procedural safeguards that could be translated for families.

Deepen an Understanding of Family Culture

Another critical aspect of communication includes educators deepening their understanding of a family's view of their child's disability. Views of disability vary across culture and disability type. For example, American families may differ in their perceptions of the cause of autism spectrum

Table 3.2 Sample Communication Survey Tool in English and Spanish

Welcome! Communication with families is an important part of our work with you and your child. Given this, we hope to find out from you the best way to communicate with you. Please take a few moments to complete this brief questionnaire about your communication preferences.

Your name(s):   **Child's name:**

Home phone: **Cell phone**   **Email:**

Please circle your selection.

1. **I prefer to be contacted regarding information (non-emergency) about my child via:**
   cell phone call   home phone call   email   text message   other:

2. **I prefer to be contacted regarding information about my child's class (ex: upcoming classroom events) via:**
   cell phone call   home phone call   email   text message   other:

3. **I am interested in receiving information regarding community events and resources.**
   Yes, via email   Yes, via paper   Yes, via classroom website   No, I am not interested

4. **I am interested in having you visit my home to learn more about my child and our family.**
   Yes   No   Not sure, can you tell me more?

Bienvenidos! La comunicación con las familias es una parte fundamental de nuestro trabajo con usted y con su hijo/a. Por lo tanto, esperamos averiguar la mejor manera de comunicarnos con usted. Favor de tomar un momento para llenar este breve cuestionario a cerca de sus preferencias de comunicación.

Su nombre: **Nombre de su hijo/a:**

Número de teléfono fijo: **Número de celular:**   **Email:**

Favor de marcar su preferencia:

1. **Para recibir información a cerca de mi hijo/a, en caso de no emergencia, prefiero que se comuniquen via:**
   llamada celular   llamada a teléfono de la casa   email   mensaje de texto   otro:

2. **Para recibir información general a cerca del grupo o salón de mi hijo (por ejemplo, de algún evento en el salón, etc) prefiero que me contacten via:**
   llamada celular   llamada a teléfono de la casa   email   mensaje de texto   otro:

3. **Estoy interesado/a en recibir infomación a cerca de eventos y recursos de la comunidad:**
   Si, vía email   Si, el papel impreso con la información   Si, via página web del salón
            No, no me interesa

4. **Estoy interesado/a en que visite mi hogar para así aprender más a cerca de mi hijo/a y familia.**
   Si   No   No estoy seguro/a

disorder, with some believing vaccinations cause autism (inaccurate findings from a study that has been scientifically debunked; Eggertson, 2010), whereas others may look to genetic or environmental conditions (e.g., toxins). On the other hand, families from non-Western cultures may consider religion or other sources (e.g., karma, witchcraft) as the source of disability. Further, immigrant families

Table 3.3 Example of a Procedural Safeguards Overview

River Run High School

"Together We Will"

Hello!

This document explains the procedures safeguards, or *you and your child's rights* related to the *special education law*, the Individuals with Disabilities Education Act (IDEA).

This document reviews your *right* to:

- A full explanation of your your rights under IDEA
- Review your child's education records and paperwork and request changes
- Participate in all meeting about your child
- Ask for a professional who does not work at the school to evaluate your child
- Receive a written notice of any special education changes *before* changes are made
- Give permission (or not give permission) to the school about special education decisions about your child
- Disagree with school decisions about special education decisions
- Resolve conflict with schools

Procedures safeguards are lengthy and can be complicated.

If you have any questions, you can ask me (Dr. Volmert, volmert@rr.edu), your child's teacher, River Run's counselor Mr. Lavín (lavin@rr.edu), or River Run's social worker Ms. Jackson (jackson@rr.edu). We are happy to help!

You can also reach out to the *Parent Training and Information Center* at 999-888-7777 or PTI@support.edu. The Parent Training and Information Center supports families of children with disabilities in our community and are experts about special education rights.

Warmly,
Dr. Jancy Volmert
Principal, River Run High School
volmert@rr.edu
999-555-3333
"Together We Will"

with children who have disabilities often experience difficulty transitioning to the US school system. For example, IDEA requires a disability diagnosis for students to receive specialized services. This can become problematic, however, when such diagnoses do not exist in family cultures (Harwood, et al., 1999). Similarly, the US education system emphasizes student independence, especially among students with disabilities (Kalyanpur & Harry, 2012), which is in direct conflict with many non-Western cultures who value family connectedness and interdependence (Francis et al., 2017).

Although understanding traditional cultural norms related to disability is informative, individual families also maintain their own experiences and perspectives related to disabilities that may or may not coalesce with those related to the culture with which they identify. Regardless of a family's views, educators must respect family perspectives by 'meeting them where they are,' or valuing their belief system and building upon their strengths (e.g., social capital, family connectedness). One-way educators can do this is by reflecting on their own views of disability (e.g., expectations for students with differing disabilities, considerations of what is acceptable or unacceptable student behavior). For example, educators may reflect on their expectations for student independence, self-determination, and self-advocacy skills, carefully considering how these expectations may converge or diverge with a family's values, and, in turn, influence collaboration efforts.

Strategy 2: Develop Trust

Trust is the cornerstone of meaningful, effective educator-family collaboration (Turnbull et al., 2021). Educators may develop trust with all families by initiating communication prior to the start of, or early on in the school year by establishing a positive rapport with families. We detail two ways educators can develop trust with immigrant families throughout the year.

Conduct Home Visits

Home visits involve meeting with families on their terms and "on their own turf"; potentially occurring in a family's home or in any community space, outside of the school, like a library or a park, where the family feels comfortable. Home visits provide an opportunity to learn more about the student, the family system, and the family's funds of knowledge (Moll et al., 1992), or the strengths and knowledge the family can offer educators to best work with their child.

Educators can prioritize conducting home visits with immigrant families, as they feel comfortable, given the importance of learning about family culture, their perceptions of disability, and the family's need to understand the US education system. Further, educators may prioritize conducting home visits prior to the school year via "back to school walks," in which education teams make brief visits to family homes during teacher workdays to introduce themselves, meet the family and student, share their excitement about the coming school year, and drop off any information or materials (including back-to-school materials and "school spirit" merchandise). During this time, educators may also schedule an additional meeting within the first week of school to continue to develop trusting relationships.

For longer, more intensive home visits with immigrant families, educators may inquire about the family's daily routine, as well as inquiring about family goals for the student, areas of success and challenge for their family in relation to the student, and how educators and the school might best support the family's and student's needs. During these visits, it is crucial that educators respect family customs (e.g., expectations for gender roles). One cannot ever fully know another culture outside their own; however, ideas of cultural humility teach us that it is important to listen and observe to follow the family's lead regarding interpersonal interactions in their space, as well as to ask respectful and authentic questions (e.g., "I'd love to learn more about the country where you lived, can you tell me a little about it?") to further understand the family and build trust.

Engage in Frequent Communication

Home visits provide educators with an opportunity to spend dedicated time with a family. However, communicating with families efficiently and frequently is also critical to build reciprocal, two-way communication necessary for trusting relationships (Turnbull et al., 2021). Educators may do so by sending brief, individualized emails or texting positive messages, videos, or photos using apps such as Remind (www.remind.com/) with the aid of translation tools (e.g., Language Line) and apps (e.g., Google Translate) to translate information to parents, as needed. In addition, COVID-19 highlighted the potential for educators to meet with families virtually using software platforms such as Zoom.

Virtual meetings provide the flexibility to meet on family-centered schedules and can lessen potential discomfort among families entering school buildings or inviting educators into their homes (Francis et al., 2022).

Another way to engage in frequent communication involves spending time in the community in which students live. Simply shopping, eating, accessing local amenities (e.g., public libraries, community organizations), or attending community events creates opportunities for educators to engage in informal communication with families, as well as become more aware of community culture and organizations that may be of support to families. When families see teachers taking action to learn more about families' experiences, as well as demonstrate knowledge of their family's community, it invokes trust.

Strategy 3: Support Home and Community Learning

Extending learning from school to home and community environments not only enhances student outcomes but can also positively influence family well-being (Turnbull et al., 2021). We provide three ways educators can support home and community learning with immigrant families.

Activate Funds of Knowledge

As educators determine areas and ways in which families desire to collaborate to support student learning, they may simultaneously seek to understand and capture families' funds of knowledge as well as support families' development of navigational capital. Funds of knowledge are the rich expertise and knowledge that a person holds based on their life experiences (Moll et al., 1992). Family funds of knowledge may include community networking, carpentry, painting, building codes, labor laws, sales, accounting, herbal knowledge and folk cures, dance, or storytelling (Moll et al., 1992). Funds of knowledge can serve as a foundation for educators to compare how their current classroom and teaching practices align with families' practices at home and integrate knowledge from families to enhance teaching practices. Maximizing family funds of knowledge at school can ensure that families' rich cultural histories and linguistic knowledge is represented in classrooms and reinforce research-based strategies such as generalization by using similar materials and language in both environments.

Locate Community Resources

Navigational capital includes the knowledge and skills necessary for maneuvering within US systems, including special education. This capital may be constrained among immigrant families by monolingual and monocultural systems as well as anti-immigrant sentiment (Yosso, 2005). Connecting families to community resources enhances student learning and supports families to access various social institutions and policies, necessary to secure needed resources (Vesely et al., 2013). Developing a relationship with school social workers who often have a robust understanding of available resources, services, and supports available in the school and community, allows educators to take stock of organizations, resources, and services available to families. In collaboration with other professionals, educators can research and maintain a list and descriptions of services and resources available to families (see "Key Resources" section for examples of organizations). Educators may also identify existing relationships between their schools and community organizations (e.g., local resettlement agencies, afterschool programming) and consider ways to maximize these relationships in collaboration with families. For example, educators can volunteer for events, invite guest speakers, or engage in mutual professional development activities.

Share Generalizable Strategies

When developing an Individualized Education Program (IEP) or Behavior Intervention Plan (BIP), educators can employ many strategies to enhance at-home learning such as conducting inventories and family interviews to learn about family routines to ensure goals are relevant and consistent with family practices and expectations. Moreover, educators can collaborate with families to create at-home interventions relevant to families (e.g., picture schedules for family routines), prompting strategies (e.g., most-to-least strategies to support students to make choices), or least invasive behavior interventions (e.g., behavior momentum, redirection; Francis & Stanley, 2022).

Educators as Change Agents

Educators experience many competing priorities and constraints on the job. However, educators can serve as change agents in creating more just education systems that better serve families and students with disabilities. For example, educator expectations profoundly influence the expectations of families, thus influencing student outcomes (Mann et al., 2016). By maintaining and expressing high expectations for students, educators may not only enhance the expectations of students and families, but also proliferate high expectations among entire IEP teams during IEP planning and meetings. Another small step educators may take toward change in collaboration with families includes modeling inclusivity by curating a representative classroom library supported by family input (e.g., books featuring diverse characters and histories, books with protagonists who have disabilities) and inviting families to use their funds of knowledge to contribute to the classroom (e.g., reading books of choice in their native/preferred language, teaching students traditional dance). Further, educators may collaborate with administrators to create a dedicated time (e.g., teacher workday, teacher's meetings) to build and share ideas among all school staff to enhance diverse and representative classroom environments and activities.

Educators may also serve as change agents focused on fostering home-school-community collaboration by engaging families, administrators, and invested members of the community in facilitating professional learning on topics. Such topics may include interacting with families via interpreters, teaching families about special education services, and supporting community organizations such as their own places of worship to accommodate children with disabilities. These stakeholders may also help identify and certify interpreters and translators to support families and students, a notable barrier to educator-family collaboration in the field (Pang, 2011). The process of becoming a change agent will evolve over time as educators build their capacity and comfort collaborating with families and other professionals. However, asking for support from administrators and colleagues, seeking out resources, setting personal goals for creating more just education systems, and sharing information with colleagues can result in sustainable change.

Family Case Stories

In this section we share three composite case stories, based on the real experiences of immigrant families. We describe each family's background, as well as the perspectives of the family and their children's educators. We then share strategies teachers may use to enhance collaboration with the families to identify communication needs and nuances, develop trust, support home and community learning, and serve as change agents.

The Hassan Family

Muhammad and Roda grew up in Somalia, meeting at a young age and marrying in their early 20s. Roda's family, owners of a small chain of grocery stores, were openly against the civil war that had been raging in Somalia for years, resulting in the military targeting Roda's family. As a result, Muhammad, Roda, and their young son fled to Kenya, seeking asylum. Muhammad and Roda lived in a Kenyan refugee camp for seven long years, growing their family with the births of Faduma and Amina, and leading community efforts to support young mothers and families with aging family members. While in Kenya, Muhammad and Roda applied for refugee status in the United States. Although it took more than two years, the family of five was resettled in St. Paul, Minnesota in a community with many other Somali refugees.

As the Hassan family adjusted to their new community (e.g., enrolling their children in public school, securing phones and driver's licenses, seeking employment), Muhammad and Roda welcomed their fourth child, Sahra. The Hassan children adapted well to life in the United States, learning English quickly, making friends in the community, and meeting other families at their mosque. Muhammad and Roda were vigilant regarding their children's education, maintaining high expectations for their children to excel academically and respect their teachers. Therefore, it came as a shock when Sahra's teacher asked them to attend a meeting about concerns they held for their six-year-old. During the meeting, Sahra's teacher, the school counselor, and the principal communicated through an interpreter to describe Sahra's difficulty communicating with teachers and peers, sensitivity to sound, and a notable difference between Sahra's exceptional ability to read and her inability to answer comprehension questions. Reluctantly, Muhammad and Roda consented to evaluate Sahra for special education services. They didn't see anything "wrong" with Sahra. She was well-behaved at home, a great reader, and close to her family. Muhammad and Roda, therefore, found themselves in disbelief when the school psychologist diagnosed Sahra with autism spectrum disorder. The Hassans felt rushed by the school to begin the IEP process, especially given their limited experience with the US education system and views of disability in their culture. In Somali culture, disability is often stigmatized, with parents fearing community judgment.

Sahra's special and general education teachers felt frustrated by the Hassans' request for daily email updates on Sahra's progress, given the time it would take to translate and send home a detailed account of the day. Further, the Hassans' insistence that Sahra advance her decoding skills (although she was already reading at a 5th grade level) agitated her teachers. After all, the Hassans agreed to the reading comprehension goals developed during Sahra's recent IEP meeting and know that she does not have a decoding goal.

Strategies for the Hassan Family

The primary barriers experienced by the Hassan family and Sahra's teachers are the Hassan's desire for ongoing communication, as well as conflicting expectations for the focus of Sahra's education. Communication notebooks are a strategy that educators can use to address **communication needs and nuances** and lessen the strain of emailing extensive notes. Educators can use a spiral notebook to send home brief messages, updates, reminders, or questions—even taping or stapling notes, resources, or student work in the notebook. In turn, families can send back notes to educators using the notebook, as needed. If families write in a language not spoken by the educator, the educator can use apps such as Google Translate to translate the writing. Further, as appropriate, educators can include the student in the communication notebook process by ensuring the notebook comes back and forth between school and home every day, students writing their own comments in the book, or by processing the content with the student at school, as appropriate.

To mitigate conflict arising from differing expectations, educators may **develop trust** by validating family beliefs and perspectives. Regardless of differences, educators can highlight shared goals for student happiness and success. Highlighting student and family strengths during communication establishes a foundation for planning how to address student needs. For example, an educator may suggest that Sahar's parents support her comprehension while reading at home by asking her basic "who" questions. In line with this example, educators may engage students in **home and community learning** for families like the Hassans by sharing ways the family may naturally incorporate targeted skills into family routines (e.g., answering "wh" questions while reading recipes). Finally, educators may address differing expectations while also serving as a **change agent** by seeking to understand a family's cultural norms and expectations of children. Through this process, an educator can share information with their colleagues to create a shared appreciation for family wishes for their children. Moreover, if interested, families may elect to formally share about their culture with the school community through a "family spotlight" section of school or classroom newsletters.

The Flores Family

Alejandra and her son's father, Alberto, met while in high school in El Salvador and built a life together as teenagers. After graduation, Alberto became a police officer and Alejandra took care of their son, Ruben. When Ruben was two years old Alberto died in the line of duty. While Alejandra struggled to cope with indescribable grief, her family surrounded her with support, helping her raise young Ruben. During this emotional time, the Flores noted that Ruben was "different" from his cousins. He did not speak, instead grabbing the hands of adults and leading them to what he wanted. He also did not respond to his name and seemed uninterested in playing with other children, preferring to swing, run blades of grass between his fingers, or spin objects with his head laid peacefully on the floor. He often became upset with his family when they interrupted him from playing.

Alejandra worked at a local clinic for nearly two years when the owners of the clinic died in a car accident. The owner's children decided to close the clinic and Alejandra lost her job. Determined to support herself and her son, Alejandra started a small business, buying clothes from the United States and reselling them in El Salvador. Alejandra was able to independently support Ruben as her business grew. Then, another horrific tragedy occurred. Local gang members learned of Alejandra's financial success and began to extort "rent" from her, threatening Ruben's life if she did not pay them. When the gang burned Alejandra's car in the middle of the night she fled for safety, despite an inability to secure a Visa to travel to the United States.

Out of desperation and fear for her and Ruben's lives, Alejandra paid a coyote (a person who secretly supports immigrants to cross the Mexico-US border) a hefty $3,000 to take them through Guatemala and Mexico and into the United States. The trip was harrowing. Alejandra and Ruben "walked for many days" across the desert with limited food and water. Without spoken words, Alejandra knew when her resilient son needed a break, to be held, to have a precious sip of water, all things she tried to provide him at any cost. They reached Mexico and were nearly caught by law enforcement and were forced to remain hidden during the remainder of the arduous journey. In fact, Ruben and Alejandra had to travel in the trunk of a car for hours at a time, in the heat, with limited water. Once they crossed the border into the United States, Alejandra and Ruben continued their trek to meet relatives living outside of Washington, DC.

Alejandra's cousin, Sandra, helped register Ruben for school. Given her documentation status, Alejandra felt gravely concerned about completing school paperwork and providing information such as their address and full name. Sandra assured Alejandra that it was safe to provide the necessary documentation to register Ruben for school, but Alejandra could not escape her haunted past and the perilous journey she took with her son to achieve safety. Sending Ruben to school was the best thing for him, but also the most unimaginable risk Alejandra could take. Ruben was her life. Her whole heart.

Within a week of Ruben attending school, his teacher contacted Alejandra's home. Sandra explained to Alejandra that the school wanted to provide Ruben special services for speaking a different language and to do "some tests" to see if Ruben had a disability. Alejandra cried as Sandra consoled her. Her son had survived so much; the school had no idea what her son had been through. At the same time, Alejandra's stress and fear amplified as Ruben became "obsessed" with spinning things and began biting, hitting, and screaming when asked to stop spinning or when he was told "no." Alejandra yelled at Ruben during a recent meltdown. Afterward she clutched him tightly to her chest despite his scratching and shouting, wracked with guilt for treating her child, a child who had seen too much and kept everything inside, so harshly. She was at a loss.

After Ruben's diagnosis, Alejandra nervously entered the school for Ruben's initial IEP meeting, feeling vulnerable and uncertain. She stepped into a room with no fewer than 10 people talking amongst themselves in English. An interpreter introduced himself in Spanish as everyone settled into seats around a long table. Prior to the meeting, Sandra encouraged Alejandra to talk about her journey to the U.S. from El Salvador with Ruben's teachers, but a fearful Alejandra firmly rejected the idea. The professionals described their observations of Ruben's behaviors, communication, and academics. As the interpreter spoke, Alejandra nodded her head and blinked back tears. Despite asking Alejandra for input throughout the meeting, the IEP team struggled to gather any information about Ruben. As a result, the professionals developed Ruben's IEP and BIP without input from Alejandra.

Strategies for the Flores Family

The primary barriers experienced by the Flores family and Ruben's teachers are Alejandra's fear and isolation and a general lack of resources available to Alejandra to support Ruben's behavior at home and limited communication between Alejandra and Ruben's teachers. Educators may support Alejandra and Ruben by addressing their **communication needs and nuances** by collaborating with a translator to provide translated information to Alejandra ahead of meetings, including simplified information about the education system, Ruben's special education services, and IEP meetings. Educators may also encourage the family to continue to invite family members or other supportive individuals to school meetings to support more effective two-way communication. Encouraging families to invite individuals from their systems of support can also help **develop trust**, as families may be more at ease with their loved ones present during meetings. In addition, a simple gesture such as a team member walking into the IEP meeting with the family can reduce anxiety and demonstrate commitment to family comfort and inclusion.

When working with families like the Flores' who speak a language other than English and have a child with communication and behavior needs, educators may support **home and community learning** by co-developing a low-technology augmentative or alternative communication device using the family's first language for home use. For example, educators may use written words, pictures, or symbols to develop a core word board (words that an individual uses frequently such as "yes," "no," or "help") and fringe word boards (words that are specific to an event or environment such as a restaurant or soccer match). The family and educator can collaborate to determine important words to develop a board, the child's developmental ability to use a board (e.g., determining the size and number of words to include), and discuss key strategies to use a board (e.g., making requests, expressing feelings such as frustration). In addition, educators may serve as **change agents** for families such as the Flores by proactively collaborating with community agencies and organizations to create ready-made school/special education materials specifically designed to support immigrant families who may be unfamiliar with the US education system, as well as a process for referring immigrant families of children with disabilities to available resources and support.

The Park Family

Joyce and Matthew Park noticed their son, Joshua, seemed overly hyperactive and aggressive when excited compared to his sister, Sophia, and other children at their church in South Korea. However, they did not think seriously about his behavior until he was diagnosed autism spectrum disorder by his pediatrician at 10 years old. The family was initially shocked, but quickly came to terms with his diagnosis.

Joshua's family immigrated from South Korea to the United States when he was 14 and his sister was 18 and starting college. The Parks provided his diagnosis documentation to his new school. Joshua's English Language Learning teacher, the school counselor, the vice principal, and the special education teacher met with the Parks to develop Joshua's IEP and placed him in English as a Language Learning class. Joshua knew little English, and, as a result, repeated 7th grade. During this time, his family observed his passion for reading books and memorizing dinosaur and animal facts diminish, as he simultaneously became increasingly shy and isolated at school. As the year progressed, his teachers noted that Joshua rarely expressed himself during class, more often scrolling through his phone. Although Joshua was a polite student who took advantage of accommodations such as extended time and access to a dictionary, he inconsistently submitted homework, telling teachers that he did not understand or forgot directions. This frustrated many of his teachers who spent extra time responding to his frequent requests to re-explain instructions for assignments and exams.

One day, Ms. Jackson, Joshua's math teacher, caught him using his phone during class. Joshua explained that he was trying to search words to better understand the lesson, but Ms. Jackson perceived his actions as disrespectful and inattentive, especially considering Joshua's missing assignments and dropping quiz scores. She emailed Mr. Kyzar, Joshua's special education teacher and the Parks to set up a conference to discuss Joshua's behavior and steadily dropping grades. Joshua's older sister Sophia requests to attend meetings to interpret for her parents and advocate for her brother. However, one of Sophia's college courses overlapped with the conference so Mrs. Kim, the school parent-liaison, served as the interpreter during the conference.

During the meeting Ms. Jackson shared her concerns and deep commitment to Joshua's success. She perceived, however, a disconnect between Joshua's parents' facial expressions and her message as Mrs. Kim interpreted. Also, although they listened attentively as Mrs. Kim interpreted, they seemingly dismissed Mr. Kyzar's efforts to strategize ways to help Joshua stay on task at home to complete his assignments by continuously shaking their heads and responding that Joshua is "a good kid who has troubles." Puzzled by the Parks' responses and reactions during the meeting, Ms. Jackson and Mr. Kyzar consulted with Mrs. Kim after the meeting. Mrs. Kim said that the Parks felt that Joshua was doing the best he could and that "his autism" prevented him from meeting teacher expectations.

A week later, Ms. Jackson was surprised to receive an email from Sophie on behalf of her parents, who were also copied on the email. The email began by thanking Ms. Jackson and Mr. Kyzar for their time, as well as for the updates on Joshua's grades. They also thanked the teachers for understanding how Joshua's depression and self-blame for falling behind make it nearly impossible to keep him motivated at home. They shared that they would "do better" by supporting Joshua to translate his homework into Korean and back into English and sit next to him until he finished his homework each night. Sophie also added that she typically interprets and translates for her family, that she has been involved in Joshua's education for many years, and that she would also like to attend IEP meetings. The teachers met after school, both stunned by this new, critical information. The Parks did not believe that Joshua was "too disabled" to do well in school. It was Joshua's depression and emerging English that were barriers. They were not "blowing off" Mr. Kyzar's strategies to stay on task, but rather contemplating what skills they possessed to help Joshua translate homework and stay motivated at home.

Strategies for the Park Family

The primary barriers experienced by the Park family and Joshua's teachers are miscommunication and limited strategies for the Parks to support their son. Joshua's teachers may prevent miscommunication with families such as the Parks through a communication preference document such as the one included on Table 3.1 to identify the Parks' **communication needs and nuances**. With this knowledge in mind, Joshua's teachers could schedule meetings around the entire family's schedule, including Sophie's college and work schedule. It is important, however, that teachers never assume or expect siblings to serve in the role as interpreter or advocate for their families or siblings with disabilities. In fact, teachers should be sure to inform families of the availability of school-based interpreters and translators to support equal access. Further, educators may send the family follow-up emails reviewing key take-aways and next steps after meetings to clarify any misinformation. In addition, in cases such as the Parks it is essential that all important educators, including English as a second language teachers, participate in education planning and problem solving. Additionally, educators may **develop trust** during meetings with families similar to the Parks by: (a) emailing the family with their concerns before the meeting so families have time to process and prepare; (b) starting all conversations with positive information and stories about the student; and (c) asking families to share their perspectives and feelings about the student before discussing their own concerns. Importantly, educators can also develop trust by integrating information families provide to enhance instruction (e.g., collaborating with the English as a second language teacher and the school translator to translate Joshua's materials, connecting Joshua with the school counselor).

Educators may support **home and community learning** for the Park family by crafting IEP goals that reflect student needs at school and home and co-planning strategies that can be generalized across both settings such as time management strategies and the use of technology to support translation or to dictate answers. Moreover, educators can share screen captures or video models of academic strategies (e.g., a video of an educator demonstrating a math skill) with the family to mitigate barriers the Parks experienced through visuals. Additionally, IEP teams may consider adding IEP accommodations to support at-home learning, such as a reduced amount of homework so that families and students experience reduced stress and are able to focus on the quality of work instead of quantity work. Finally, educators may serve as a **change agent** by collaborating with other professionals (e.g., school counselors) to develop student groups or mentoring programs designed to facilitate sustainable peer supports and student well-being.

Wrap Up

Families are powerful advocates, but also need support to learn how to navigate school systems and support their children with disabilities. This is especially true among immigrant families. This chapter focused on the ways in which educators can meaningfully and respectfully collaborate with diverse immigrant families. The authors described strategies to identify communication needs and nuances, ways in which to develop trust among immigrant families, and strategies to support home and community learning. The chapter also provided ways in which educators can begin to serve as agents of change such as building relationships with community organizations and sharing lessons learned from family funds of knowledge with other educators within the school. Educators can use strategies described in this chapter as a "jumping off point" to continue exploring different cultures and optimize community resources.

Tips

1. Develop cultural humility, or the ability to remain empathic, non-judgmental, and open to learning from others regarding their cultures and experiences. This requires on-going critical self-assessment and reflection to understand how your own cultural values, beliefs, and behaviors influence the relationships you build with families.

2. Recognize the diversity of immigrant and refugee families. Immigrants and refugees migrate from a multitude of countries with diverse education, employment, and familial experiences. Take time to get to know each family to gain information that will promote greater alignment and attunement of services for the child and family.
3. Notice moments of discomfort as you navigate supporting children and their families. Use these as opportunities to critically reflect, take perspective, and build empathy regarding discomfort immigrants and refugees may face as they navigate a new culture and language.
4. Embrace opportunities to be an ambassador to US culture. Support families' development of navigational capital to connect to resources both within and outside of the school.
5. One of the most critical ways to serve as a change agent involves sharing information related to effective strategies, "lessons learned," and key resources with colleagues, as well as asking for support to better serve diverse families and students.

Key Resources

Center for Parent Information and Resources/Parent Training and Information Centers: www.parentcenterhub.org/find-your-center/
Bridging Refugee Youth & Children's Services: https://brycs.org/
USA for UNHCR, The UN Refugee Agency: www.unrefugees.org/
Parent to Parent USA: www.p2pusa.org/

References

Chu, S., & Wu, H. (2012). Development of effective school-family partnerships for students from culturally and linguistically diverse backgrounds: From special education teachers and Chinese American parents' perspectives. *Scholarlypartnershipsedu*, 6(1). Retrieved July 26, 2022 from www.semanticscholar.org/paper/Development-of-Effective-School-Family-Partnerships-Chu-Wu/916ce97e21964138c8d2a07e6d20810c7cf1a19b

Eggertson, L. (2010). Lancet retracts 12-year-old article linking autism to the MMR vaccination. *Canadian Medical Journal*, 182(4), E199–200. https://10.0.5.223/cmaj.109-3179

Francis, G. L., Gross, J. M. S., Lavín, C. E., Casarez Velazquez, L A., & Sheets, N. (2018). Hispanic caregiver experiences supporting positive postschool outcomes for young adults with disabilities. *Intellectual and Developmental Disabilities*, 56(5), 337–53. https://doi.org/10.1352/1934-9556-56.5.337

Francis, G. L., Haines, S. J., & Nagro, S. A. (2017). Developing relationships with immigrant families: Learning by asking the right questions. *Teaching Exceptional Children*, 50, 95–105. https://doi.org/10.1177/0040059917720778

Francis, G. L., Reed, A. S., Strimel., M., Raines, A., & Kinas-Jerome, M. (2022). "You're the experts figure it out:" Experiences of teachers of students with significant support needs during the COVID-19 pandemic, under review.

Francis, G. L., & Stanley, J. L. (2022). Preparing families for age of majority: Five considerations. *Inclusive Practices*. https://doi.org/10.1177/27324745211039748

Goodman, R. D., Vesely, C. K., Letiecq, B. L., & Cleaveland, C. L. (2017). Trauma and resilience among refugee and undocumented immigrant women. *Journal of Counseling and Development*, 95, 309–21. https://doi.org/10.1002/jcad.12145

Harwood, R. L., Schölmerich, A., Schulze, P. A., & Gonzalez, Z. (1999). Situational variability in the instantiation of cultural belief systems among middle-class Anglo and Puerto Rican mother-infant pairs. *Child Development*, 70, 1005–16. https://doi.org/10.1111/1467-8624.00073

Hoy, W. (2012). School characteristics that make a difference for the achievement of all students: A 40-year odyssey. *Journal of Educational Administration*, *50*(1), 76–97. http://dx.doi.org/10.1108/09578231211196078

Kalyanpur, M., & Harry, B. (2012). *Cultural reciprocity in special education: Building family-professional relationships*. Brookes.

Kyzar, K., Mueller, T. G., Francis, G. L., & Haines, S. J. (2019). Special education teacher preparation for family-professional partnerships: Results from a national survey of teacher educators. *Teacher Education and Special Education*, *42*, 320–337. https://doi.org/10.1177/0888406419839123

Mann, G., Moni, K., & Cuskelly, M. (2016). Parents' views of an optimal school life: Using Social Role Valorization to explore differences in parental perspectives when children have intellectual disability. *International Journal of Qualitative Studies in Education*. Retrieved April 26, 2022 from https://eric.ed.gov/?id=EJ1102120

McWayne, C. M., Hyun, S., Diez, V., & Mistry, J. (2021). "We feel connected… and like we belong": A parent-led, staff-supported model of family engagement in early childhood. *Early Childhood Education Journal*, *50*, 445–457. https://doi.org/10.1007/s10643-021-01160-x

Moll, L. C., Amanti, C., Neff, D., & Gonzalez, N. (1992). Funds of knowledge for teaching: Using a qualitative approach to connect homes and classrooms. *Theory into Practice*. https://education.ucsc.edu/ellisa/pdfs/Moll_Amanti_1992_Funds_of_Knowledge.pdf

Ogg, J., Clark, K., Strissel, D., & Rogers, M. (2021). Parents' and teachers' ratings of family engagement: Congruence and prediction of outcomes. *School Psychology*, *36*(3), 142–154. https://doi.org/10.1037/spq0000379

Pang, Y. (2011). Barriers and solutions in involving culturally linguistically diverse families in the IFSP/IEP process. *Making Connections*, *12*(2), 42–51.

Pereira, K. M., Crosnoe. R., Fortuny, K., Pedroza, J. M., Ulvestad, K., Weiland, C., & Yoshikawa, H., & Chaudry, A. (2012, May 24). *Barriers to immigrants' access to health and human services programs*. Assistant Secretary for Planning and Evaluation (ASPE). Retrieved April 26, 2022 from https://aspe.hhs.gov/reports/barriers-immigrants-access-health-human-services-programs-08

Smith, C. P., & Freyd, J. J. (2013). Dangerous safe havens: institutional betrayal exacerbates sexual trauma. *Journal of Traumatic Stress*, *26*(1), 119–124. https://doi.org/10.1002/jts.21778

Turnbull, A., Turnbull, R., Francis, G. L., Burke, M., Kyzar, K., Haines, S. J., Gershwin, T., Shepherd, K.G., Holdren, N., & Singer, G. (2021) *Families and professionals: Trusting partnerships in general and special education* (8th edition). Pearson.

Vesely, C. K., Ewaida, M., & Kearney, K. B. (2013). Capitalizing on early childhood education (ECE): Low-income immigrant mothers' use of ECE to build human, social, and navigational capital. *Early Education & Development*, *24*, 744–65. doi: dx.doi.org/10.1080/10409289.2012.725382

Yosso, T. J. (2005) Whose culture has capital? A critical race theory discussion of community cultural wealth. *Race Ethnicity and Education*, *8*(1), 69–91, https://doi.org/10.1080/1361332052000341006

Section II
Assessment High Leverage Practices
Mary T. Brownell

To implement effective intensive interventions for students with disabilities, special education teachers must be adept at collecting and using assessment data and information that allows them to design and evaluate interventions that address students' needs while capitalizing on their assets (e.g., personal interests, areas of strengths, family and community supports, and students' home culture). Collecting and interpreting this information depends on special educators' facility in using the collaboration high leverage practices, as they must work with other professionals and family members if they are going to collect the information and assessment data they need. Such assessment data and information are used by special education teachers to determine what a student knows regarding a content area, and the skills, strategies, and assets students possess to support their learning. Armed with this information, special education teachers can guide the planning and implementation of intensive intervention that builds on students' assets while addressing their needs. Additionally, special education teachers need to know how to continuously collect and interpret assessment data to determine if instruction is effective and determine how to adapt it when it is not. (Note that these assessment practices are equally applicable to addressing social and behavioral issues for students with disabilities and are further addressed in section 3 of this book).

The assessment high leverage practice chapters in this section address key aspects of the roles and responsibilities of special education teachers in the assessment process. This process begins with the development of a comprehensive learner profile for each student that is used to analyze and understand both a student's assets and needs. To develop a comprehensive learner profile, special education teachers work with other professionals and families to collect, aggregate, and interpret assessment data from a range of sources (e.g., observations, work samples, curriculum-based measures, functional behavior assessments, interest inventories, family interviews) and ensure that these data are used in a way that is responsive to each student's language and cultural background and experiences, his or her interests, and families' expectations and goals for their child. Information generated in the development of this comprehensive profile is then used to design a student's intensive intervention plan. This plan must specifically address students' needs while drawing on their assets to support implementation.

Once assessment data are used to determine goals for intensive intervention, special education teachers identify and implement the intervention plan. The intervention plan should be comprised

DOI: 10.4324/9781003276876-6

of effective instructional practices, including social and emotional and instructional HLPs, to accelerate student learning. Special education teachers should then collect ongoing progress monitoring data to make needed adjustments in the intervention plan. These adjustments might include providing more practice opportunities, increasing duration of the intervention, and reducing instructional group size. They might also include integrating more instructional or social emotional research-based practices. Skills related to collecting ongoing data to make intervention decisions for individual students (i.e., data-based decision making) are at the core of effective practice for special educators. Special educators must have skills managing and engaging in on-going data collection (or formative assessment). They need to learn how to use curriculum-based measures, informal classroom assessments, observations of student performance and behavior, self-assessment of classroom instruction, and information gleaned from discussions with key stakeholders (students, families, and other professionals) if they are to plan intensive interventions that draw on students' assets while meeting their needs.

Throughout the process of collecting data to plan intensive interventions, and using data to evaluate those interventions, special education teachers should be gathering information from families and sharing data about students' progress with them. Families' perspectives on their children, the community in which they live, the assets they bring, and goals they hold for their children are important in designing intensive interventions. Further, helping families understand data and how their child is responding to interventions in clear and friendly language is important for engaging them in their child's educational program.

4

Use Multiple Sources of Information to Develop a Comprehensive Understanding of a Student's Strengths and Needs

Margaret P. Weiss
George Mason University

LaRon A. Scott
Virginia Commonwealth University

Kelly Durso
George Mason University

Joshua P. Taylor
The University of Maine

Introduction

Effectively educating students with disabilities requires collection, aggregation, and interpretation of multiple forms of data. This chapter describes the use of multiple sources of information to develop a comprehensive understanding of a student's strengths and needs—something that is critical to this endeavor. That is, assessing student strengths, interests, and needs is vital for teachers seeking to properly plan instruction and monitor student performance, particularly when providing intensive intervention. In this chapter, we use the National Center for Intensive Intervention (NCII) definition of intensive intervention as supporting "students with severe and persistent learning and behavioral needs, including students with disabilities" (NCII, 2022). Intensive intervention is based upon the use of data to individualize and intensify interventions to meet student needs. Knowledge gathered from assessment data can be used to decide what critical supports and services are required for students and what strengths and interests can be incorporated into those services to engage students and their families (Overton, 2016). This assessment process is dynamic and is an integral part of decision making. More specifically, assessment of students with disabilities for intensive intervention is focused on data-based decision making, using data to continuously inform instruction (National Center for Intensive Intervention, 2022).

Narrowing the Focus

The Individuals with Disabilities Education Act (IDEA) clearly states that teachers and school teams must use multiple sources of information to develop a comprehensive understanding of a student's strengths and needs when planning programs and specially designed instruction. For example, IDEA (2004) requires teams to "use a variety of assessment tools and strategies to gather relevant functional,

DOI: 10.4324/9781003276876-7

developmental, and academic information about the child, including information provided by the parent" (IDEA, 2004, Subpart D, §300.304(b)). In addition to providing guidance on the assessment process, IDEA (2004) also states that "assessments and other evaluation materials used to assess a child under this part—are selected and administered so as not to be discriminatory on a racial or cultural basis" (§300.304(c)(1)). Today, it is more important than ever before to acknowledge that racial, linguistic, social class, gender, culture as well as other forms of identity can influence the gathering and interpretation of student assessment data. Students' and their families' intersectional identities must be front and center when evaluating preferences, interests, strengths, and needs, particularly for historically marginalized students and families who have often been negatively impacted by high-stakes standardized assessments (Au, 2010; Dworkin, 2019). Gathering data from multiple sources to identify needs and strengths, acknowledges the talents, gifts, and skills that a student has to offer and the resources, talents, and skills within the community that support the student (Lubbe & Eloff, 2004). Without data about both needs and assets, teachers may operate from a deficit perspective, focusing school resources and instruction only on the needs of the student and never recognizing and encouraging their strengths. Teachers who make decisions from a deficit-focused perspective are left to make decisions about instruction and support without adequate evidence which can lead to wrong assumptions, ineffective instruction, and isolation (Snider et al., 2020).

Chapter Overview

This chapter has three purposes:

1. The first is to describe an iterative process of data collection that teachers can use to develop a comprehensive understanding of student's strengths and needs for intensive intervention.
2. The second purpose is to provide a description of how this process might be used by teachers to design, implement, and monitor intensive interventions and how these interventions can be integrated and supported across settings and services.
3. The final goal is to provide tips and key resources for teachers to use in their practice.

Ensuring asset-based decision-making about assessments for all students, especially those from historically marginalized backgrounds, is a crucial focus throughout the chapter.

Using the HLP: Assessment as a Process

As noted previously, this chapter is essential for understanding effective assessment practices in special education. We define *assessment* as a continuous process of evaluating a student's strengths and needs, using a variety of sources, to guide decision-making. Within this definition of assessment are several critical points:

1. Assessment is a continuous process.
2. Effective assessment requires multiple sources of data.
3. Assessment guides instructional decision-making.

Table 4.1 includes assessment terms, definitions, and examples for use in this chapter.

Special educators are involved in many decisions regarding students identified to receive special education and intensive intervention. The Individual with Disabilities Education Act (IDEA) of 2004 describes procedures for teams seeking information about students with disabilities, including information about their participation in formal state assessments, procedures for determining eligibility, and participation in special education programs (IDEA, 2004). For example, regulations for IDEA require agencies seeking to evaluate a student for special education to:

Table 4.1 Common Assessment Terms and Definitions

Term	Basic Definition	Examples
Formal assessment or measure	A measure that is administered in a standardized way with standardized scores and/or outcome indicators	Could be a standardized test but could also be a questionnaire or survey with a Likert scale. All formal measures are summative assessments
Standardized test	A test that is administered in the same way by anyone who administers it, to anyone who takes it, and the items are the same	An example would be the Scholastic Aptitude Test (SAT) or the Woodcock-Johnson Tests of Achievement. Performance on these tests is always indicated by a standard score.
Informal measure	A measure that does not include formalized procedures or scores; also known as non-standardized	An observation, interview, essay, or the like
Formative assessment	A measure that is used to target growth and understanding of content across time	An exit ticket is an example of a formative assessment that assesses student understanding of material taught each class session. It is then analyzed and used to determine additional instructional needs. Progress monitoring measures, such as oral reading fluency, are also formative assessments.
Summative assessment	A measure that is used to target mastery, usually at the end of an instructional period like a unit, semester, or school year	A unit test is an example of a summative assessment that assesses student mastery of content. A final exam is also a summative assessment. These are also formal assessments.
Standard score	A derived score from standardized test results; usually based on 100 as average and a 15-point standard deviation	Melanie had a standard score of 92 on the reading comprehension subtest. This puts her in the average range for students her age.
Percentile	Number where a certain percentage of scores fall below that number	If Nancy scored at the 65th percentile of students aged 8year 6 months, she had a raw score the same as or better than 65% of the students who took the test who were 8 years 6 months old.

(1) Use a variety of assessment tools and strategies to gather relevant functional, developmental, and academic information about the child, including information provided by the parent, that may assist in determining:
    i.   Whether the child is a child with a disability under §300.8; and
    ii.   The content of the child's IEP, including information related to enabling the child to be involved in and progress in the general education curriculum (or for a preschool child, to participate in appropriate activities);

Procedures and requirements established in IDEA are important factors that must be considered during key stages of the special education process. In Table 4.2, we highlight some of the major decision points and guiding questions related to intensive intervention.

Table 4.2 Key Special Education Processes and Guiding Questions for Measures

Special Education Process	Overarching Question of Special Education Process	Guiding Questions in Selecting Measures
IEP Services (including intensive interventions)	What services and supports should the student be provided?	Where should instruction begin for the student? What accommodations and modifications does the student need? How will student goals be determined?
Progress Monitoring (including in intensive intervention)	Is the student making progress on goals?	How will the student's progress be evaluated? What information has the student learned? What additional measures are needed to further evaluate a student's progress? How could the students' interests and assets (e.g., strengths, culture, language, family supports) be used to support their progress?
Transition/Functional Evaluation	What are the student's preferences/interests for adult life?	What does the student want to do after high school? What are the student's career goals? Where does the student want to live after high school?

In this chapter, we focus on the decision making required for intensive interventions. With this focus, teachers may ask multiple questions such as: While designing intensive intervention, how can the students' assets and strengths be used? Is the student benefitting from the use of culturally responsive teaching (nourishing a student's culture in teaching) and assessment methods? Are assessment instruments and procedures reliable and/or valid considering student's sociocultural identities? Is the student making progress to meet their goals? How can I communicate student progress to others? The key to collecting and using relevant and high-quality data to answer these questions is understanding the purpose of assessment, evaluating the data already available, and determining what data is needed to make good decisions for students. Special educators and school teams can think of assessment and data collection as an iterative cycle. This cycle is represented in Figure 4.1.

The first step in the cycle (what do we know?) is collecting and reviewing all of the data that is already available for a student. This might mean reviewing a confidential file, examining student work, reading an IEP, or getting documents from parents. The second step (what do we want to know?) is critical. This step is about setting a purpose for assessment. Why are we gathering data? What decisions are we going to make with the data? Without a clear purpose and objective, assessment becomes a chaotic exercise because there is no end to the data one could collect on a student. Critical to designing intensive interventions is an in-depth knowledge of both a student's areas of need and interests and assets. By definition, intensive intervention will focus on an area of academics or behavior in which a student does not currently feel successful. Multiple formal and informal measures will provide evidence for the specific areas to target intensive intervention and detail specific goals for this instruction. Teachers who are designing intensive interventions with an asset-based mindset will also collect data that will identify areas of strength (e.g., spends time after school or during break drawing, creating comic book characters, writing rap lyrics or riding a bike all

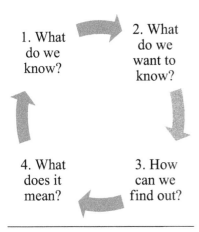

1. What do we know?

2. What do we want to know?

3. How can we find out?

4. What does it mean?

Figure 4.1 The Iterative Assessment Cycle

over town), support (e.g., works with favorite uncle in garden, participates with friends in events at local boys club, works after school in butcher shop), and interests (e.g., athlete, musician, caretaker). An asset-based mindset means that a team is not limiting the purpose of assessment to identifying areas of need but is also including understanding areas of strength and motivation for students.

Once a purpose is set, step three (how can we find out?) becomes clear. If the purpose is to evaluate the effectiveness of a service or intervention, the team will need data from repeated measures for progress monitoring, repeated observational data, and a broad range of repeated teacher (or other) reports across time. Again, multiple sources of data capture patterns of strengths and needs from many vantage points. These multiple sources also allow teachers and teams to make decisions based on input from variables that are both directly related to student performance (e.g., number of words read per minute when investigating a student's reading performance) and variables that may seem indirectly related (e.g., student and parent report that student hates to read; does not pick up books at home but "looks at" everything they can find on skateboarding). In making instructional decisions for intensive intervention, multi-disciplinary teams that always include a special education teacher, use a combination of measures to document a student's need for and their progress in intensive intervention. Particularly critical to this decision making is the use of both summative and formative assessments.

Summative assessments, as described in Table 4.1, are measures used to target mastery, usually at the end of an instructional period like a unit, semester, or school year. These measures provide teachers with information related to how a student stands in comparison with other students or how much or little a student has mastered of curriculum content. For example, a unit test after a teacher has completed instruction on solving one variable equations in an Algebra course will help the teacher determine whether a student has mastered the content or not. The test itself can provide an opportunity for the teacher to do an error analysis of student responses to determine content for reteaching in the next unit or the need for supplemental instruction/intervention. A student who earned a 56 percent correct on a unit test shows evidence of not mastering the content and will need some form of supplemental instruction. Similarly, a student who earns a "proficient" score on an end-of-year, statewide test in Biology has shown overall mastery of the content and will not need supplemental instruction in that topic.

Formative assessments, also described in Table 4.1, include measures that are administered repeatedly over time to monitor a student's progress so that a teacher can respond with changes to instruction while it is occurring, if necessary. Formative assessment is different from summative and is most often classroom- or curriculum-based. This means the measure is a direct representation of what the student is expected to do in a classroom situation. For example, a formative, classroom-based measure might be words read correctly per minute in a grade level piece of text. If collected weekly and a student's rate does not improve across weeks, the teacher should make the decision to alter instruction in some way. It might be the number of steps a student completes in an appropriate attempt to gain teacher attention, gathered using observation and a checklist. If measured daily and the student is progressing toward their goal, supports and prompts can be slowly reduced. It could be measuring a student's engagement in class as culturally relevant teaching is practiced. If the teacher sees increased participation across time, she might share that with colleagues who are not seeing engagement with this student. The critical features of this type of assessment are (a) that it guides instructional decision making and (b) is collected frequently to assess progress toward instructional goals.

Once data is collected, the team must complete step four: what does it mean? In this assessment step, the special educator or team looks across data sources for patterns. These patterns are usually evident across measures, time, domains, and/or environment. The descriptions of Finley and Fatima provide examples of this iterative assessment process.

An Example: The Assessment Process for Finley

Finley Murphy is a nine-year-old, white third grader who has been at the same elementary school since Kindergarten. She lives with her mother and father who are of Irish descent and her younger brother. Mrs. Murphy is one of eight siblings and they all live in the area with their families. Both Mr. and Mrs. Murphy work afternoon and night shifts, so Finley rides the bus to her aunt and uncle's home in a nearby neighborhood. This way, Finley is able to spend time with her cousin, Meredith, who is Finley's age, and complete her homework with support from Mr. and Mrs. Kelly. Mrs. Murphy, Finley's mother, always attends IEP meetings with the school team, and is usually joined by Mrs. Kelly, Finley's aunt who is a former elementary school teacher. Finley is currently receiving intensive intervention in the areas of reading and writing due to an identified learning disability and other health impairment. In her most recent eligibility meeting, the team collected the data in Table 4.3.

What Do We Know?

The school team made the decision that Finley needs intensive intervention in reading and writing based on data from multiple standardized assessments (e.g., CTOPP), developmental inventories (e.g., DRA and DSA), curriculum-based measures, and classroom-based measures (e.g., writing samples, parent reports). As described in Table 4.3, these measures indicated a pattern of significant variation in her performance in the areas of reading and writing. In addition to the information, teachers report that "Finley is able to brainstorm ideas for her stories and enjoys sharing them verbally. However, she requires support editing for casing, punctuation, and spelling." Using a writing sample as a data source, teachers can understand both Finley's interests (art) and her needs in the area of writing. In a short paragraph that is hardly legible and full of erasures, Finley wrote about when she realized she was good at art. Her paragraph includes statements such as "It was 2015 my cusin Roxie Balithday She turning 6 She asks me I waned to draw and I said yes. I drawed and she it is so good I look I said it is. Some people say my art is bad but I do not need thafu pfupl to know it is good. If someone has a pashun and oth do not like it that is no reson to give up." Finley concludes her paragraph with "life whod be boring with out art and this is what I think of art." (The misspellings are intentional to illustrate the student's actual writing.)

The patterns in her writing sample correspond to her standardized scores in that she has ideas and structure in the content of her writing but other aspects such as letter formation and using writing conventions are areas of need. Her teachers also noted a clear strength in math, particularly solving problems, and that corresponds to her standardized assessments. Teacher and parent/family reports

Table 4.3 Finley: What Do We Know?

Type of Measure	Specific Name of Measure	Performance/Scores
Standardized Intelligence, Achievement, or Diagnostic tests	Comprehensive Test of Phonological Processing (2nd edition) Kaufman Test of Educational Achievement (3rd edition) Wechsler Intelligence Scale for Children (5th edition) Test of Visual Perception Skills (4th edition)	Finley's composite scores (groups of tests) were in the average range (standard scores ranged from 84–113); however there was variability within scores. On the CTOPP, Finley was in the 9th percentile for blending words and the 16th for blending non-words. On the WISC, Finley was at the 92nd percentile for fluid reasoning and 88th for verbal comprehension index.
Questionnaires, surveys, inventories	Developmental Reading Assessment (DRA) Developmental Spelling Analysis (DSA)	Finley's accuracy rates on the DRA and DSA were appropriate for beginning 2nd grade.
Classroom-based measures	Writing samples Math word problem samples Class grades	
Curriculum-based measures	Third grade text decoding accuracy	Currently at 26%
Teacher/other report	Family (Mrs. Murphy and Mrs. Kelly) Teacher Discipline data	Consistent reports of strengths in math; interests in art, science, and animals. Difficulty staying engaged in reading and writing focused assignments and homework. Overall happy and friendly student who gets along with peers.

describe Finley's love of art and desire to do well. Parent report also describes how both Mr. and Mrs. Murphy encourage Finley in academics and arrange for her to attend after school art classes and camps. She draws every opportunity she gets during the school day. She would like to go to art school when she graduates from high school. Finley's current IEP goals include: (a) Finley will read 3rd grade leveled text passage with 90 percent accuracy on three of four opportunities and (b) when given a writing prompt, Finley will compose at least five connected sentences with fewer than three grammatical errors.

What Do We Want to Know?

As one aspect of her intensive intervention, Ms. Taylor is implementing a multi-sensory, structured reading program that includes a dictation/spelling component. This program is sequential in its lessons and requires that Ms. Taylor do an initial assessment of specific reading and spelling skills with Finley to place her in the program. This data source provides information about where to place Finley in the program—answering *what do we need to know* about where to start the intensive intervention. Ms. Taylor will administer this assessment and place Finley as directed by program materials. Though the program also has brief checkpoints to assess progress within the lessons, they only provide her with information about how Finley is progressing in the program materials. Ms. Taylor has many additional questions about Finley, including: (a) how is she progressing toward her IEP goals? (b) are the skills being taught in intensive intervention generalizing to the general education classroom? (c) how can Finley's strengths in math and interests in animals and drawing help support her improving her reading and writing skills? And (d) how can Finley's family and community support her learning?

How Can We Find Out?

There are multiple ways to answer the questions that Ms. Taylor has about Finley. The key for Ms. Taylor is to choose a variety of measures to understand as much as she can about Finley and her progress. First, to determine whether Finley is progressing toward her IEP goals, Ms. Taylor can use oral reading fluency, a curriculum-based measurement (CBM; a progress monitoring system; Lembke & Busch, 2004). To determine her accuracy in third-grade text, Mrs. Taylor can have Finley read passages in connected text at grade level each week. She can count the number of words Finley reads correctly per minute and graph that information so that it can be easily communicated to Finley and her family. The graph will be easy to understand because Ms. Taylor will include a goal line that connects Finley's current performance to her goal for the end of the year. If the points on the graph are progressing upward toward that goal line, then Finley is making the progress that intensive instruction is meant to provide. If not, Ms. Taylor will know pretty quickly and she can change her instruction accordingly. Ms. Taylor can also use CBM for her sentence writing. Mrs. Taylor finds there are many resources on the internet (e.g., easyCBM; see Resources) where she can find probes and free graphing programs.

Ms. Taylor understands that Finley loves art, thrives in math problem solving, and has support from her family. Thus, Ms. Taylor arranged with Mrs. Murphy to send a packet of materials home each week that can be used to help reinforce what Finley is learning in her intensive instruction sessions. These packets include short passages about famous artists, paintings, and techniques as well as a list of chapter books that Finley might find interesting. In addition, Ms. Taylor includes a template for Finley to use to write one takeaway or thought about what she has read. After she put together the first packet, Ms. Taylor met with Mrs. Murphy and Mrs. Kelly to talk about how they could use and support Finley with these materials. At the end of each passage, whoever reads with Finley is to write some notes about whether she read fluently or with difficulty, words they had to identify for her (including notes about how she pronounced words), and the degree to which her written retell matched her oral retell. Ms. Taylor uses this information to understand how Finley is generalizing skills learned in intensive intervention.

What Does It Mean?

As Ms. Taylor collects data from these sources and others, she will be able to make her intensive intervention instruction responsive to Finley's academic and behavioral needs. From the home/school packet, Ms. Taylor is hoping to understand how well Finley is generalizing her skills and is building on the strengths of her family and interests.

Learning More from a Comprehensive Approach: The Assessment Process for Fatima

Ms. Acuna, a high school special education teacher, is learning about her new student, Fatima. Fatima is a 16 year-old student. Her family emigrated from Somalia to a culturally diverse, mid-sized city in a rural, predominantly White New England state when she was nine years old. At home, she and her family converse primarily in Somali and Arabic, though her parents try to speak English as

Table 4.4 Fatima: What Do We Know?

Type of Measure	Specific Name of Measure	Performance/Scores
Standardized Intelligence, Achievement, or Diagnostic tests	Woodcock Johnson-IV Wechsler Intelligence Scale for Children-IV WIDA (World Class Instruction Design Assessment)	Fatima's standard scores were all well below average, ranging from 65–80 (ranging from the 5th to 20th percentile). Her English reading comprehension and oral language scores were the lowest.
Observations	Teachers	Teachers noted her slow processing of oral information and that she often "tuned out" Fatima attends classes and often tries to engage but never seeks out interactions with teachers or peers. She does poorly on tests.
Interviews	Parents	Parents reported that Fatima struggled in both English and Arabic. They wanted her to succeed in school and would do anything to assist that.
Classroom-based tests	Class grades/GPA	Teachers report that Fatima has a 2.3 GPA but she is currently failing English. Ecology is her highest grade.

much as possible based upon a middle school principal recommendation. Fatima is the youngest of three siblings and enjoys hiking and fishing with her father and brothers. She would like to learn to read and write in Arabic in order to participate in the broader Somali community. Data collected in the eligibility evaluation is included in Table 4.4. According to the standard assessment protocol for initial eligibility, Fatima was identified as having an intellectual disability.

What Do We Know?

Ms. Acuna reviewed data collected by Fatima's previous teachers. Fatima has a 2.3 GPA but tends to perform inconsistently across all content areas. She exhibits severe anxiety around test-taking. Her favorite subjects are art, science, and English but only when she gets to write or talk about animals and other topics in which she is interested. According to her previous teachers, Fatima is making very little progress in reading and writing, and Ms. Acuna noted that Fatima was never evaluated in Arabic or Somali, the two languages spoken in the home. There are few reports of school-home interaction and little information about Fatima's goals for postsecondary. Thus, Ms. Acuna has several questions about Fatima: (a) what are her language skills in English, Arabic, and Somali? How might these skills be affecting her evaluation and progress? How can these skills be used to support development in each? (b) What are the interests Fatima has now and the goals she has for postsecondary? (c) What is the family involvement? What are her support systems/communities? Ms. Acuna believes these questions could guide her decisions in services and instruction for Fatima.

How Can We Find Out?

Ms. Acuna works with the school team and Fatima's family to gain support for a reevaluation of Fatima a year before it is officially due. In this reevaluation, instead of a standard assessment protocol, Ms. Acuna advocates for additional assessments and more individualized assessments to better understand how Fatima performs in her home language and she will use the data to guide

Fatima's program. First, Ms. Acuna advocates for an evaluation of Fatima's language skills, using the standardized measure WIDA Model (Measure of Developing English Language; WIDA, 2022). This will guide instruction in ESOL (if necessary), provide a better starting point for her English reading and writing instruction, and assist with discussions regarding language use in the home. Second, Ms. Acuna advocates to administer an intelligence measure that is not language-based to get a true sense of Fatima's capabilities. Additionally, since the previous evaluation showed a moderate level of autism-related behaviors, the school psychologist suggests the Naglieri Nonverbal Intelligence Index (3rd ed; Pearson, 2022) and the Autism Diagnostic Observation Schedule (ADOS; 2nd ed; Western Psychological Services) and administers both. Third, Ms. Acuna wants to know more about Fatima's interests and desires for postsecondary. She recommends to the team that career assessments and interest inventories be completed. Finally, Ms. Acuna asks Mr. and Mrs. Ali, Fatima's parents, if they would be willing to meet with her for a brief interview about Fatima, her previous school experiences and their hopes and dreams for the future. They agree and also provide permission to Ms. Acuna to talk with Fatima individually.

What Does It Mean?

Fatima's re-evaluation assessment data provided several insights that led to changes in her IEP and postsecondary goals. Results of the Naglieri indicated that Fatima's IQ was in the average range overall, with several areas of above-average performance. The ESOL teacher assessed Fatima on the WIDA and reported that Fatima scored as a Level 4 (Expanding), meaning she should receive language services delivered through collaboration and consultation between her ESOL teacher, special education case manager, and her general education teachers. Results of the ADOS showed behaviors typical of an autism diagnosis—an area not discussed in previous evaluations. Career assessment and interest inventories revealed a preference for working outside, with animals, and using her strengths in attention to detail. Fatima shared her vision of living on her own or with a roommate, and working as a park ranger or data analyst with the National Park Service as her ideal career. With the help of her team, she mapped out goals for identifying college programs that would allow her to achieve career goals and skills needed for living on her own. Mr. and Mrs. Ali agreed that she could begin taking more responsibility at home related to independent living. Fatima also shared how she valued her family's language and culture, and with the help of the team, decided to take a course in Arabic to strengthen her speaking proficiency and to learn to read and write in it. Her parents were relieved and chose to speak Arabic with her at home.

In addition to this new information, Fatima's achievement scores indicate below average performance in reading comprehension and vocabulary. In addition to her ESOL services, Ms. Acuna provides intensive intervention in reading comprehension in English. Fatima's IEP goals include increasing her ability to retell stories/information read in grade level material and increase general English vocabulary. Both of these IEP goals can be measured using curriculum-based or classroom-based measurement probes administered once a week. Ms. Acuna works with the team to gather data on Fatima's performance in her ESOL class and consults with Fatima and her parents monthly about her progress in an after-school Arabic class.

Wrap Up

For special educators and teams to develop a comprehensive understanding of students' strengths and weaknesses, they must collect data from multiple sources, guided by the assessment purpose. Critical to this aspect of assessment is understanding the information a data source can provide and matching that information to the purpose of assessment. Table 4.5 provides information about many common sources of data for intensive intervention. As one can see, there is a variety of sources

Table 4.5 Sample Data Sources for Intensive Intervention

Type of Assessment	Example	Information Given	Uses	Considerations
Observations	• Narrative • Using an observation guide	• Student action in routine environments • Teacher action in routine environments	• Provides data on student and teacher behavior within routine environments • Can be collected repeatedly across time • Can be collected by multiple individuals • Can be collected across multiple settings	• Context, timing, and relationship of observer to situation of observation are all critical to understand • Qualitative measure that is affected by the bias/beliefs/understandings of the observer • Multiple observations across time, settings, and individuals are best • Observer should be trained in observation techniques • Determine format of the observation with purpose of assessment
Interviews	• Unstructured discussion between student and teacher/between teacher and other stakeholder • Structured discussion between individuals using question protocol	• Reflections from the individuals involved • Thoughts and ideas about situations from individuals involved • Beliefs, assumptions, definitions about situations from individuals involved	• Can provide insight into the thinking of the individuals involved in situation about which decisions are being made • Can be collected repeatedly across time • Can be collected by multiple individuals • Can be collected across multiple settings	• Qualitative measure that is affected by the bias/beliefs/understandings of the interviewer • Best if student or other interviewee is comfortable with interviewer • Interviewer should be trained in interview techniques • Determine format of the interview and reporting format before interview with purpose of assessment
Classroom-based assessments	End of unit test Projects Essays Work Samples	• Grades • Level on a rubric • Complete/incomplete • Percent correct • Errors	• Determine mastery of content taught • Determine ability to apply content taught • Determine errors related to content taught	• Variable between teachers • Reliability and validity of assessment and its evaluation/scoring not established • May be idiosyncratic based on who developed, who taught, who analyzed

(continued)

Table 4.5 Cont.

Type of Assessment	Example	Information Given	Uses	Considerations
Curriculum-based measures	• Oral reading fluency • Maze • Math computation • Math problem solving • Written expression	• Words read correctly per minute • Correct word choice/ completion per time given • Digits correct per time given • Correct letter sequences per time given	• Efficient standardized approach to gathering indicators of broader skill • Probes given repeatedly across time to monitor progress	• Use of nationally-available probes increases likelihood of equivalent difficulty • Users must graph data and understand graph components • Multiple data points across time are required
Teacher/ other report	• Written description of student progress and behavior in courses/ classrooms	• Often narrative with grades or other descriptors of performance	• Provides opportunity for teachers to indicate student performance in their classroom • Gives insight into teacher interpretation of student behavior AND expectations of the class/teacher	• Qualitative measure that is affected by the bias/ beliefs/understandings of the interviewer • Data provided is often different when provided by different teachers or other sources

that may overlap in the information they provide. This is not something to be avoided. Overlapping information from multiple data sources provides an opportunity for the special educator and multi-disciplinary team to triangulate data. In other words, using multiple sources to evaluate similar aspects of student performance allows a teacher or team to determine if the multiple sources display a pattern of performance that is similar across sources or not. Furthermore, a range of assessment sources offers additional opportunity to gather and value perspectives from groups (e.g., historically marginalized families/communities) who have voiced concerns about being ignored during this process (Scott et al., 2021).

Knowledge of students' and their families' backgrounds can provide relevant information that help teachers be informed when selecting and interpreting assessment data. A teacher who does not understand the goals families have for their children or know how to recognize and value families' cultural background and students' views of their background is in danger of misinterpreting information regarding the challenges students face and may miss critical information about students' motivations and interests that can help interpret assessment results and design instruction. Thus, Montenegro and Jankowski (2017) recommend that teachers move toward more responsive assessment planning by: (1) understanding student preferences and strengths and involving students in deciding the multiple ways in which they are assessed and (2) evaluating measures to ensure that they are student-focused and affirming of the student's culture, including language. In noting these recommendations, we emphasize the importance of responding to the needs of developing a comprehensive understanding of students, families, and the assets they bring to intensive intervention of their cultural background.

Tips

1. Use the assessment cycle to identify what is known about a student, what the team wants to know, how to find out, and what it means.
2. Identify specific types of data to gather, including multiple sources and types that will provide information about strengths, culture, identities, and interests.
3. Keep an asset-based mindset in assessment and use those student strengths to address areas of weakness.
4. Collect data about student performance continuously. Use that data to make instructional decisions frequently.
5. Look broadly and across multiple environments for patterns of student behavior.
6. Understand the types and quality indicators of measures. Use only those of high quality and integrity.

Key Resources

Culturally responsive assessment tools and strategies (https://education.wm.edu/about/diversity/diversityresourcelist/faculty-resources/assessment/index.php)
IRIS Modules related to progress monitoring, data-based decision making
  https://iris.peabody.vanderbilt.edu/module/rti02/
  https://iris.peabody.vanderbilt.edu/module/pmr/
  https://iris.peabody.vanderbilt.edu/module/pmm/
  https://iris.peabody.vanderbilt.edu/module/dbi2/
  https://iris.peabody.vanderbilt.edu/module/ebp_03/
easyCBM for resources related to curriculum-based measurement (easyCBM.com)
Teaching Tutorial for step-by-step guidance on implementing CBM (TeachingLD.org)
National Center on Intensive Instruction (intensiveintervention.org)

References

Au, W. (2010). *Unequal by design: High-stakes testing and the standardization of inequality.* Routledge.
Dworkin, A. G., & Quiroz, P. A. (2019). The United States of America: Accountability, high-stakes testing, and the demography of educational inequality. In Peter A. J. Stevens and A. Gary Dworkin (Eds.), *The Palgrave Handbook of Race and Ethnic Inequalities in Education* (pp. 1097–81). Palgrave Macmillan.
Individuals with Disabilities Education Act (2004). https://sites.ed.gov/idea/regs/b.
Lembke, E., & Busch, T. W. (2004). *Teaching Tutorial 4: Curriculum-based measures in reading: Oral fluency.* www.teachingld.org/wp-content/uploads/2019/04/cbmtutorial.pdf
Lubbe, C., & Eloff, I. (2004). Asset-based assessment in educational psychology: Capturing perceptions during a paradigm shift. *The California School Psychologist, 9,* 29–38.
Montenegro, E., & Jankowski, N. A. (2017). Equity and assessment: Moving towards culturally responsive assessment. *National Institute for Learning Outcomes Assessment Occasional Paper, 29.* www.learningoutcomesassessment.org/wp-content/uploads/2019/02/OccasionalPaper29.pdf.
National Center for Intensive Intervention (NCII) (2022). *What is data-based individualization?* https://intensiveintervention.org/data-based-individualization
Overton, T. (2016). *Assessing learners with special needs: An applied approach.* Pearson.

Pearson (2022). Naglieri Nonverbal Ability Test (3rd Ed.). www.pearsonassessments.com/store/usassessments/en/Store/Professional-Assessments/Cognition-%26-Neuro/Non-Verbal-Ability/Naglieri-Nonverbal-Ability-Test-%7C-Third-Edition/p/100001822.html#

Scott, L.A., Thoma, C.A., Gokita, T., Taylor, J., Ruiz, A., Brendli, K., Bruno, L., & Vitullo, V. (2021). I'm trying to make myself happy: Black students with IDD and families on promoting self-determination during transition. *Inclusion, 9*(3), 170–88. https://doi.org/10.1352/2326-6988-9.3.170

Snider, L. A., Talapatra, D., Miller, G., & Zhang, D. (2020). Expanding best practices in assessment for students with intellectual and developmental disabilities. *Contemporary School Psychology, 24*, 429–44. https://doi.org/10.1007/s40688-020-00294-w

Western Psychological Services. (2022). *Autism Diagnostic Observation Scale* (2nd ed.) www.wpspublish.com/

WIDA. (2022). *WIDA Measure of Developing English Language.* https://wida.wisc.edu/assess/model.

5
Interpret and Communicate Assessment Information with Stakeholders to Collaboratively Design and Implement Educational Programs

Terese C. Aceves
Loyola Marymount University
Julie Esparza Brown
Portland State University

Introduction

An essential role of the special education teacher involves interpreting and communicating results from a range of assessments in a language and manner comprehensible to all stakeholders. Specifically, special education teachers share assessment information regarding student progress with the multidisciplinary team including family/caregivers, general educators, school leaders, English language development specialists, individual students, and other related service providers. Special educators keep stakeholders informed on student progress to adjust intensive instruction and support as needed, in school and at home, and to coordinate service delivery. Such communication practices require strong partnerships and an integrated support system to enable students to reach intended annual goals and experience success across settings.

To this end, special educators work to establish strong alliances with families whose contributions are key to interpreting and using assessment information to inform intensive instruction and support. Families specifically provide valuable insights on their children's interests, backgrounds, home and community life, language development, multilingual abilities, and behavior. The Individuals with Disabilities Education Act (IDEA), special education law, clearly confers families the right to participate in the decision-making process related to their child's special education eligibility and programming, and contribute to the development of Individualized Education Program (IEP) goals. However, too often families are provided with complex or incomplete information, and not meaningfully involved in discussions about their child. Furthermore, families who come from diverse communities or cultures and/or speak a language other than English face additional barriers when communicating with schools. These include having limited access to adequate or available interpretation services for phone calls and meetings, and lacking information regarding their rights and responsibilities in decision-making, hindering home-school communication and contributing to their overall distrust of professionals.

The current chapter provides special education teachers guidance with how to establish culturally responsive, multidirectional communication with key partners when sharing and interpreting

DOI: 10.4324/9781003276876-8

assessment information to design and implement intensive intervention. Such communication is ongoing and intentional, valuing all members' expertise, and empowering stakeholders to contribute equally in the decision-making process.

Narrowing the Focus

Specifically, the chapter identifies important considerations when interpreting and communicating assessment information with stakeholders to inform instruction and facilitate individual student progress. These include (1) engaging in multidirectional communication; (2) regularly communicating with stakeholders; (3) providing information in user-friendly formats; (4) considering other factors to explain student progress and inform intensive instruction; (5) making appropriate comparisons to true peers; and (6) using clear language to ensure understanding. Each of these considerations are further described and illustrated within a three-part vignette.

Chapter Overview

1. Provide important considerations when communicating with stakeholders regarding assessment information, student progress, and instructional intervention.
2. Illustrate important considerations within a three-part vignette including an initial special education teacher–parent meeting and two subsequent IEP meetings.
3. Present considerations for specific stakeholders.

Using the HLP: Vignette (Part 1)

Important Considerations

Special educators engage in *multidirectional communication* with important stakeholders regarding intensive instruction so that all voices are included in educational decisions and support. The various stakeholders include parents and caregivers, administrators, general and special education teachers, service providers, paraprofessionals, counselors, and students when appropriate. Multidirectional communication may involve confirming essential team members and their roles and responsibilities, identifying key questions for the team to consider, and sharing data sources and the frequency of data collection and review methods. Figure 5.1 illustrates this concept through the Multidirectional Communication Wheel which highlights equity among all stakeholders and their interconnections. The process requires building strong and trusting partnerships that flow back and forth between stakeholders where anyone can initiate conversation. The spokes of the wheel show that each stakeholder can connect with any or all members of the team. Interpreters enable non-English speaking stakeholders to ensure comprehensible communication across the spokes. Such a model facilitates the information flow respectful of each individual's knowledge base, cultural/social capital, and availability. Processes are established in advance regarding the multiple communication methods available (e.g., phone calls, emails, video chats, in-person meetings at or outside of school) and the available times for communication that may include nontraditional hours to accommodate each partner's schedule. Through active listening and equity for each stakeholder, strong and trusting partnerships essential to supporting each student with an IEP can be created (Ko et al., 2021).

Special educators must engage in *regular communication* with essential stakeholders to ensure that necessary adjustments are made to instruction and support as needed and in a timely fashion. Specifically, communicating with families regarding students' progress on annual goals "such as through the use of quarterly or other periodic reports, concurrent with the issuance of report cards" (Sec. 300.320(a)(3)(ii)) must be provided as required by special education law. The frequency of communication may increase, particularly in areas related to intensive instruction. For instance, families

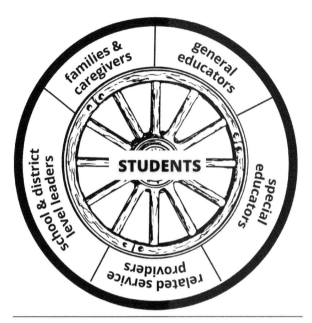

Figure 5.1 Multidirectional Communication Wheel

may be satisfied receiving a monthly or quarterly report on IEP goals yet request a weekly, or even daily, more informal update related to their child's progress in areas of greater concern (e.g., behavior, language). The team may choose to hold an IEP meeting to discuss and possibly adjust services (e.g., frequency, intensity, methods) and share recommendations for how to address specific areas at home and/or in the community. Additionally, when families are not proficient in English, special educators must schedule either school or district interpretation, or for less common languages, request such services through an agency or other community resource. Finally, all agreements should be documented in the student's IEP, specifically the method, language, and frequency of these communications.

The special education teacher provides information in *user-friendly formats* when summarizing a student's documented progress on IEP goals. Table 5.1 in the upcoming vignette provides an example of such a format or template for IEP team members to consider. The template provides the team with brief documentation of quantitative and qualitative information related to IEP goals and recommendations regarding how goals could be supported in other settings as appropriate. Designing a communication template involves active and collaborative discussions with those who will be using the information to inform important decisions regarding progress and instruction. Team members should be reminded to reference the actual IEP document for more specific and complete information regarding a student's agreed upon goals. For families, receiving documentation of their child's progress could better equip them to support their child's specific needs at home. Such tools should be provided in the family's home language and with the option to review the summary in person, over the phone, or virtually (e.g., Zoom) to ensure their understanding.

These considerations are illustrated in the following vignette involving Mrs. Chavez and her son Benny, a ninth-grade student who has recently transferred to Horizon High School.

Using the HLP: Discussing Progress with Families/Caregivers

Benny Chavez immigrated from Mexico at the beginning of eighth grade. During his eighth grade year he was found eligible for special education services under the category of Other Health Impairment due to a previously documented seizure disorder. Benny receives intensive intervention

Table 5.1 IEP Goal Progress Report

Student Name: Benny Chavez	ID Number: 123456		School: Horizon High School
Current Program: General Education	Current Services: Learning Support		Date of Progress Report: 10/15/2022
Grade: 9th grade	Language of Instruction: English		English Proficiency: Level I
Last IEP Date: 5/20/22	Next IEP Due Date: 5/20/23		Number of Months Until Next IEP: 7 months

Please reference the active IEP dated **5/20/22** for additional information regarding services, goals, and supports. For the purposes of this Progress Report, progress toward overall annual goals and most recent/relevant objectives will be discussed.

Goal Number, Area, & Person Responsible	Goal	Progress	Additional Information	Connections Between Home & School	Recommendations for other Settings (i.e., General Education)
Goal #1 *Area:* English Reading Comprehension *Team Member Responsible:* Special Education Teacher	By May 2023, when given a grade/instructional level passage (currently kinder), Benny will read/ listen to the passage and answer comprehension questions (short answer, fill in the blank, or multiple choice) with 80% accuracy as measured by student performance on classroom CBMs and recorded on teacher made data sheets one time per month by the special educator.	Benny's comprehension level is at 60% on a kinder grade text and he can answer 6/ 10 questions.	Benny's listening comprehension continues to be stronger than his reading comprehension. Benny has a positive attitude and is attentive in class and enjoys being paired with peers for additional support. At this time Benny is unable to complete any tasks independently.	Benny should read, at home; he has access to books in the library and in English class.	Continue providing Benny with opportunities to work with strong peers. Continue English language development services and translations on his Chromebook.
Goal #2 *Area:* Writing *Team Member Responsible:* Special Education Teacher	By May, 2029, Benny will be able to write three sentences about a given topic using appropriate capitalization, phonetic spelling, and ending punctuation in 4 out of 5 writing samples.	Benny is currently unable to write a complete sentence independently in English.	Benny can copy a sentence that he has dictated to a teacher or peer in English.	Benny may benefit from participating in the after school Creative Writing Club.	Continue using speech to text application in all settings.

(specially designed instruction) in English and English Language Development (ELD) services since he is a non-native English speaker. As a new parent at Horizon High School, Mrs. Chavez previously attended a beginning of the year parent meeting on the topic of family-school partnerships. The school team discussed the importance of multidirectional communication as a means of ensuring equal partnership with families and communities. The Multidirectional Communication Wheel (Figure 5.1) was presented and discussed with families along with various strategies for keeping the lines of communication open across team members.

At the end of Benny's first quarter at Horizon, Mrs. Chavez received a progress report on his IEP goals (see Table 5.1) from Mr. Drake, Benny's special education teacher. The IEP progress report was provided in the parent's native language of Spanish. Benny's IEP progress report listed an IEP goal for reading a kindergarten grade-level English passage and answering comprehension questions. Although this was developed at the eligibility meeting Mrs. Chavez attended three months prior at his previous school, she now wondered if the teachers were aware that Benny was a good reader in Spanish. She was also concerned about his recent report card which said that Benny was unable to complete tasks independently in his classes. After reviewing the progress report with her family, Mrs. Chavez calls the school's cultural navigator/interpreter to request a phone conference with Mr. Drake to discuss the report and her concerns that the school may not be taking Benny's Spanish skills into account. Soon after, Mrs. Chavez and Mr. Drake communicate over the phone using the interpreter. To begin the conversation, Mr. Drake thanks her for reaching out and confirms that both she and the interpreter have a copy of the progress report in front of them for reference. Mrs. Chavez shares that she is concerned about the low expectations of the goals and adds that Benny is a reader and writer in Spanish. Mr. Drake realizes he needs to have input from the team and particularly someone knowledgeable in Spanish literacy. Therefore, he suggests they meet in person for an IEP meeting to which Mrs. Chavez agrees and provides her availability. Mr. Drake reminds her that she can bring someone familiar with Benny and his literacy skills to the meeting and any examples she has of his work in Spanish.

Part one of this vignette illustrates how providing updates on IEP goal progress creates opportunities for multidirectional communication with stakeholders. During these interactions, special education teachers can discuss additional factors with stakeholders that may influence a student's progress and inform intensive intervention, as we highlight in part two of the vignette.

Vignette (Part 2)

Important Considerations

Special educators should remember that research suggests that culturally and linguistically diverse students' learning environments are often not sensitive to their unique backgrounds (Blazer, 2021; Gershenson, Hansen & Lindsay, 2021; Redding, 2019; Yamasaki & Luk, 2018). Since *multiple factors* may influence students' performance, teachers can use the following questions to guide the team's thinking. Has instruction been consistent over the past few weeks? Has there been a change of teacher, intervention program, or instructional material? Has the location of instruction changed recently or was there a shift in grouping practices? How much has the student's culture, language, and family background been tied to the content or structure of instruction, if at all? For instance, if instruction is focused on improving students' writing performance, do students have opportunities to write about meaningful events and content relevant to their home and daily life? In sum, recent or significant changes in a student's school or home environments could account for changes in their progress and should be reviewed.

When interpreting progress monitoring data, it is also essential for special education teachers to consider how a student's performance and rate of progress compares to local norms or with *true peers* (Brown & Doolittle, 2008). True peers include students having a similar background to the student being assessed including in "developmental, linguistic, cultural and experiential dimensions" (Brown & Doolittle, 2008, p. 69). For example, a second-grade student who has been in the country for only six months and is at a beginning level of English proficiency should not be compared to a second-grade US-born, English-speaking peer to determine adequate progress. True peer comparisons can support teams in monitoring the progress of true peer groups to identify when shifts in general instruction are required to support the group in meeting grade level benchmarks. Conversely, such an analysis can also highlight individual students who need additional support. On those occasions when a true local peer may not exist, educators should make the most appropriate comparisons as possible and consult with district partners as needed for further assistance.

Both of these considerations are illustrated in the next meeting with Benny's IEP team to discuss Mrs. Chavez's concerns about his progress and the team's expectations regarding his skills and abilities.

Using the HLP: IEP Progress Meeting with Team

The team holds an IEP meeting one week later after Mr. Drake and Mrs. Chavez's initial phone call. Additional time is scheduled knowing that meetings with interpreters sometimes take twice the amount of time. Members of the team include Mr. Drake, the interpreter, the English Language Arts (ELA) teacher, the ELD specialist, the counselor, the principal, Mrs. Chavez, her sister, and Benny. Mr. Drake also invited the school psychologist to review the initial eligibility assessment with the new team. Given that IEP meetings are often complex and families have the right to fully understand the content, the team made sure that they used an interpreter trained in the special education process.

To begin the meeting, Mr. Drake shares the agenda. He indicates the purpose of the meeting is to respond to Mrs. Chavez's concerns regarding Benny's IEP goals and progress. Mrs. Chavez shares that the goals seem too basic for his age and grade level, and since he's a reader and writer in Spanish, wonders if his current classes could build on these skills. Benny's aunt nods in agreement and states Benny likes to read sports magazines and comic books in Spanish at home. The ELD specialist thanks Mrs. Chavez for bringing this critical information to the team's attention as it was not

Table 5.2 Levels of English Language Proficiency (Speaking Domain)

Level 1	Level 2	Level 3	Level 4	Level 5
Students use words, phrases, or chunks of language with many errors that can interfere with meaning.	Students speak in phrases or short sentences. There are many errors that can interfere with meaning.	Students speak and write in longer sentences with fewer errors and can carry on conversations.	Students understand and use complex language with minimal errors.	Students use increasingly complex communication and language is approaching comparability to English-proficient peers.
Can respond to yes/no and WH questions. And recognize basic vocabulary and high-frequency words and expressions.	Able to use general vocabulary and everyday expressions.	Use of standard grammar is inconsistent.		

documented in his file. She shares that Benny's current English-language proficiency level (obtained in spring of his eighth-grade year) is at a Level 1 on a rubric of 1 to 5 in all four language domains (listening, speaking, reading, and writing) (see Table 5.2).

The ELD teacher emphasizes that the team also has high expectations for Benny and wants him to receive the most appropriate support that leverages the strengths and assets he brings with him. Mr. Drake agrees and comments that it has been hard to determine if Benny has been making adequate progress because, while there are other Spanish speakers, there are no newcomers, or true peers like Benny in his school. The team then asks Benny to share his progress with the team. Benny describes he loves coming to school, enjoys his classes and is making new friends but that he finds it difficult to communicate in English, preferring Spanish-speaking peers. Benny's ELA teacher chimes in, sharing that Benny gravitates to working with Spanish-speaking peers to support him. The counselor asks Benny about his goals after graduation and Benny reports he plans to attend the local community college and maybe work in the family business.

Next, Ms. LeRoy, the school psychologist, reviews the original eligibility data. Knowing that it is important for all to understand the tasks used in assessments, she explains that the middle school IEP team measured Benny's abilities using the Wechsler Nonverbal Scale of Ability (WNV, Wechsler & Naglieri, 2006). This test measures the general cognitive ability of individuals who are culturally and linguistically diverse as the directions minimize verbal requirements. To help the team better understand what Benny was asked to do, she provides a handout with descriptions of the tasks and a link with pictures (Table 5.3). She then shows the team tables of the scores (Tables 5.4 and 5.5) along with a graphic (Figure 5.2) to illustrate the range of Benny's performance on each of the tasks. Ms. LeRoy reports that while Benny performed in the below average range on the WNV, she notes that the assessment team had not administered a Spanish-language cognitive test. She suggests that the high school team obtain this information in order to gather a more complete profile of his abilities and Mrs. Chavez gives her permission. In the meantime, while the team collects additional information, they agree to identify a bilingual instructional assistant to provide added support for Benny in the classroom. With Benny's input, they determine more assistance may be needed, especially during his ELA block.

This portion of the vignette illustrates how stakeholders tapped critically relevant information from the student, family members, and other providers. Information should be shared ongoing and understood by all members of the team as described in the final considerations and the vignette's conclusion.

Table 5.3 Description of Subtests from the Wechsler Nonverbal Scale of Ability (WNV)

Matrices: The student looks at a set of items arranged in a row and uses it to solve a logic problem. (Measures fluid reasoning or the ability to solve novel problems.)

Coding: The student uses symbols to pair simple shapes or numbers to complete the task within a specified time limit. (Measures processing speed or the quickness with which the student can think.)

Spatial Span: The examiner taps on different blocks and the student has to tap on them in the same order either forward or tapping them in a backward sequence. (Measures short-term memory or memory span.)

Picture Arrangement: The student is asked to arrange cartoon pictures into a sequence that makes logical sense. (Measures visual processing, comprehension knowledge, acculturative knowledge.)

The following link contains pictures of the subtests that can be shared with stakeholders.
Link: https://lesacreduprintemps19.files.wordpress.com/2012/11/wechsler-nonverbal1.pdf

Table 5.4 Full Scale IQ from WNV

	Wechsler Nonverbal Scale of Ability			
	Standard Score	**Percentile Rank**	**Confidence Interval 95%**	**Classification**
Full Scale IQ	65	1	61–72	Extremely Low – Low

Table 5.5 Subtest Scores from WNV

Subtest	Standard Score
Matrices	68
Coding	60
Spatial Span	78
Picture Arrangement	60

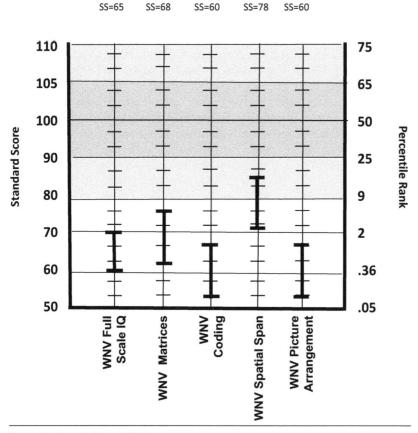

Figure 5.2 Graphic of Benny's WNV Scores

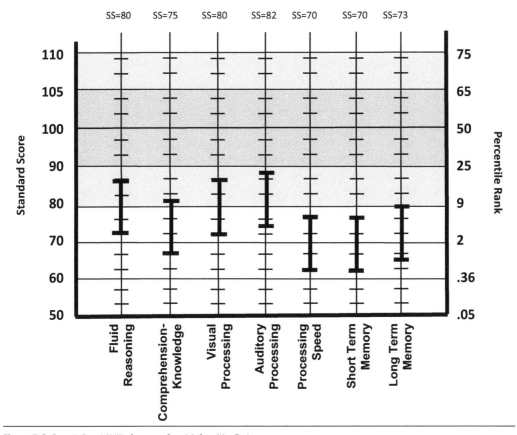

Figure 5.3 Benny's Broad Ability Scores on Spanish Cognitive Test

Vignette (Part 3)

Important Considerations

Regular communication should be *concise, clear, and free of jargon* as much as possible. As indicated previously, teachers should use the family's preferred language when sharing information about ongoing progress. Language preferences should be documented in the IEP since non-English speaking families may be reluctant to ask for language interpretation and translation. Additionally, special educators should be well-versed in concisely communicating progress and assessment procedures that could easily be translated into another language. This is particularly important as many essential documents often use complex language for complicated concepts and yet families are expected to understand them with little explanation. For example, most special education procedural safeguards produced by departments of education in the USA are written at a graduate reading level (Gray, Zraick & Atcherson, 2019). In sum, families need important information related to their child's progress and written in a language they can understand and access without difficulty.

This consideration is illustrated in a subsequent meeting with Benny's IEP team as they review new information to help strengthen his current intensive services.

Using the HLP: Follow Up IEP Meeting with Additional Assessment Information

After Benny was administered a Spanish-language cognitive test and academic testing in both English and Spanish, an additional IEP meeting was held to share the results. Ms. LeRoy reviews the cognitive testing results using a similar process as in the previous meeting to fully describe the tasks and score ranges. The cognitive measure selected included native Spanish speakers in the normative sample who are similar to Benny. Results show that while Benny continues to perform in the below average range, he scores higher on the Spanish test with relative strengths in the areas of visual and auditory processing and fluid reasoning (Figure 5.3).

Mr. Drake reiterates his appreciation to Mrs. Chavez for letting the team know more about Benny's abilities in Spanish reading. He then shares the reading fluency data he has collected in collaboration with a Spanish-speaking paraprofessional. Benny was able to read a fourth-grade passage in Spanish with 97% accuracy while correctly answering comprehension questions and read a second-grade passage in English with 95% accuracy answering a series of comprehension questions correctly. Mr. Drake explains that since the last meeting Benny has made stronger progress in English reading because the team has built upon his Spanish skills. Together, the team develops a new reading goal:

> After reading an English passage at the third-grade level, Benny will be able to correctly answer comprehension questions about the passage with 80% accuracy in 4 out of 5 opportunities by (date) as measured by a curriculum-based measure.

To ensure that Benny stays on track with his reading goal and Mrs. Chavez has more consistent feedback regarding his progress, Mr. Drake explains he will use easyCBM (Alonzo et al., 2006) for monitoring his reading progress. Mr. Drake then shares a sample passage and multiple-choice comprehension questions for reference with Mrs. Chavez and the team (see Table 5.6). He explains that Benny, and all his students, graph their progress by hand or on the computer each Friday. Mr. Drake will check how Benny is doing every eight weeks (as part of his typical cycle of teach, assess, teach, assess) and determine whether any additional adjustments are needed to better support Benny's

Table 5.6 Portion of easyCBM Passage and Questions

The Twenty-Dollar Kite

Kendra lived by the beach. She spent most summer days there with her friends. They played in the sand, building castles and burying each other. And if a parent was with them, they went swimming in the ocean.

One day Kendra went to the beach by herself. Her friends were on vacation with their families. Kendra walked along the shore. She didn't know what to do all by herself.

Kendra looked around. Everyone seemed to be having fun. But not Kendra. She wished she could go swimming. But her Mom was too busy working at home to watch her. "The beach is not fun when you're along," Kendra thought.

Then Kendra saw something beautiful in the sky. It was a colorful kite shaped like a bird! Kendra wondered what it would be like to fly such a kite. She asked the kite owner where he got it. "At the store around the corner," the man told her.

1. What time of year did the story take place?
   A. Spring.
   B. Summer.
   C. Fall.

2. What did Kendra want to do when she saw a colorful kite in the sky?
   A. Sit on the beach and watch it.
   B. Tell her friends about it.
   C. Buy a kite and fly it.

Source: Printed with permission Alonzo, Tindal, Ulmer, & Glasgow (2006).

Table 5.7 Transferable and Nontransferable Sounds Between English and Spanish

Differences between English and Spanish Vowels	
Aa	Only 1 sound in Spanish, 4 different sounds in English, and 7 spelling forms (cat, chair, saw, haul, made, stay, art)
Ee	Only 1 sound in Spanish, 4 different sounds in English and 7 spelling forms (elephant, beat, bee, be, eve, fern, shrew)
Ii	Only 1 sound in Spanish, 5 different sounds in English and 6 spelling forms (fit, sing, high, pie, first, ice, brief)
Oo	Only 1 sound in Spanish, 7 different sounds in English and 14 spelling forms (load, hold, boil, toy, boot, short, cloud, own, not, ocean, robe, toe, owl, soup)
Uu	Only 1 sound in Spanish, 4 different sounds in English and 5 spelling forms (cut, burn, unicorn, cute, blue)

Consonants with Different Sounds in English and Spanish

v, ll, j, h, z, g, rr

reading. Mr. Drake asks Benny whether he could share his progress graph with his mother each week and Benny agrees. The ELD specialist chimes in that she could also provide a brief update on Benny's language development.

Given the new information, the team discusses how to better leverage Benny's literacy skills in Spanish. The ELD teacher suggests that Benny receive explicit instruction on the transferable and non-transferable sounds between the two languages and provides the team a handout on some basic information on transferable sounds (see Table 5.7) (Haas & Brown, 2019).

After the team reviews and adjusts the remaining IEP goals, they discuss how to better support Benny's progress and classroom engagement. Specifically, the ELD teacher shares that since Benny's English proficiency is currently at the beginning level, his listening comprehension in English is below grade level and recommends the use of audiobooks for content text while using strategies such as previewing difficult vocabulary words or sentence structures and providing opportunities to initially discuss texts with general education peers in Spanish. The Language Arts teacher asks Mrs. Chavez about Benny's hobbies and interests at home. They brainstorm ways to capture Benny's interests and make more connections so his teachers could capitalize on this information when selecting his reading material. Mrs. Chavez eagerly shares Benny's home interests that included reading graphic novels. Mr. Drake comments that he could include graphic novels within his instructional program. While the family encourages Benny to read at home, she acknowledges that there is not a designated daily time when he is expected to read. The team asks that Mrs. Chavez provide a quiet space and set a schedule for Benny to read each night at home.

As the meeting comes to a close, several final suggestions and comments are made by team members. The ELD teacher suggests that she change her ELD support to a push-in rather than pull-out model since this would help Benny become more engaged with his classes and peers. Benny's aunt asks Mr. Drake to review the changes made to the IEP with the team to confirm everyone's understanding. Finally, Mr. Drake thanks Mrs. Chavez for requesting the team to consider Benny's Spanish language skills, strengths, and interests to increase the academic expectations in his goals and for assisting the team to create the new plan.

In this three-part vignette, we illustrate how strong collaboration amongst IEP team members leads to a better understanding of assessment information and a more cohesive instructional program for students receiving intensive intervention. Students benefit most when special education teachers are "on the same page" with other stakeholders related to students' progress toward individual IEP goals and their ability to successfully access grade level expectations. Additional considerations should be made when working with families and involving students in this process. These are briefly discussed in the next section.

Special Considerations for Specific Stakeholders

Assisting Families to Participate in Progress Meetings

The previous three-part scenario demonstrates how important families are in helping the IEP team better understand a student's progress during intensive instruction while considering their cultural and linguistic assets and background. Mrs. Chavez knew it was important to reach out to Mr. Drake and provide critical information in the hopes of making adjustments to her son's goals and intensive services. However, not all families know how to or feel comfortable engaging with educational professionals particularly when there are clear cultural and linguistic differences present. As was highlighted, when schools establish multidirectional communication processes that invite all stakeholders to engage and provide readily available interpretation for families and caregivers, schools can create strong and lasting partnerships. Special educators can further multidirectional communication processes by preparing families and caregivers to participate in important conversations. Table 5.8 displays question prompts special educators can share with families in advance when engaging in discussions around monitoring their child's progress, sharing information, and understanding the team's intensive intervention plan. Such questions may also serve to prompt the team to make important adjustments to their own process and planning that reflect necessary cultural and linguistic considerations.

Table 5.8 Question Prompts for Families

Participating in My Child's IEP Progress Meeting	
Questions parents and families can ask when talking with their child's school about intensive intervention	*Preguntas que los padres y las familias pueden hacer al hablar con la escuela de sus hijos sobre la intervención intensiva*
Monitoring Progress • How and when will the team be monitoring my child's progress? • How will I be informed about my child's progress? • What happens when my child is not making enough progress? • Will the team share a report of my child's progress with me in my native language?	**Monitoreando el progreso** • ¿Cómo y cuándo supervisará el equipo el progreso de mi hijo/a? • ¿Cómo seré informado sobre el progreso de mi hijo/a? • ¿Qué sucede cuando mi hijo/a no progresa lo suficiente? • ¿El equipo compartirá conmigo un informe del progreso de mi hijo/a en mi idioma nativo?
Sharing Information • What information should I share about my child? • Will I be invited to meetings where my child's assessment results will be discussed? • Can the team provide options when the suggested meeting days/times conflict with my work or other schedules? • Are there other ways to be involved if I can't be there in person?	**Compartiendo Información** • ¿Qué información debo compartir sobre mi hijo/a? • ¿Seré invitado a participar en reuniones cuando resultados de evaluaciones de mi hija/o serán revisados? • ¿Puede el equipo brindar opciones cuando los días/horas de reunión sugeridos entran en conflicto con mi trabajo u otros horarios? • ¿Hay otras formas de participar si no puedo asistir en persona?

Table 5.8 Cont.

Participating in My Child's IEP Progress Meeting	
Questions parents and families can ask when talking with their child's school about intensive intervention	*Preguntas que los padres y las familias pueden hacer al hablar con la escuela de sus hijos sobre la intervención intensiva*
Understanding the Intervention Plan • What is my child's intervention plan? How long will it last? • Who is responsible for implementing the plan? • Does my child's intervention plan consider my child's language proficiency in the language of instruction, culture, knowledge, strengths and interests? • Is the intervention plan based on practices that have worked with other children with similar needs and from a similar language and cultural background as my child?	**Entendiendo el Plan de Intervención** • ¿Cuál es el plan de intervención de mi hijo/a? ¿Cuánto tiempo duraría? • ¿Quién es responsable de implementar el plan? • ¿El plan de intervención de mi hijo/a considera el dominio del idioma de mi hijo/a en el idioma de instrucción, la cultura, el conocimiento, las fortalezas y los intereses? • ¿El plan de intervención se basa en prácticas que han funcionado con otros niños con necesidades similares y de un idioma y antecedentes culturales similares a los de mi hijo/a?
Supporting my Child's Progress • How can I support my child's progress at home? • How can I keep the team informed of my child's observed progress at home and in the community? • How can I use my child's language, culture, strengths and interests to support my child's progress at home? • How can I help my child understand his/her progress?	**Apoyando el progreso de mi hijo/a** • ¿Cómo puedo apoyar el progreso de mi hijo/a en casa? • ¿Cómo puedo mantener informado al equipo sobre el progreso observado de mi hijo/a en casa y en la comunidad? • ¿Cómo puedo usar el idioma, la cultura, las fortalezas y los intereses de mi hijo/a para apoyar el progreso de mi hijo/a en casa? • ¿Cómo puedo ayudar a mi hijo/a a entender su progreso?
Additional Considerations • How can the team increase the intensity of the plan if my child is still struggling? • How will team members collaborate to support my child's intervention? • How can my child's current IEP reflect the proposed intervention plan? • How can the team involve my child in the development and implementation of the intervention?	**Consideraciones adicionales** • ¿Cómo puede el equipo aumentar la intensidad del plan si mi hijo/a todavía tiene dificultades? • ¿Cómo colaborarán los miembros del equipo para apoyar la intervención de mi hijo/a? • ¿Cómo puede el IEP actual de mi hijo/a reflejar el plan de intervención propuesto? • ¿Cómo puede el equipo involucrar a mi hijo/a en el desarrollo e implementación de la intervención?

Source: Based on Infographics developed by the *National Center on Intensive Intervention* and the *Rhode Island Parent Information Network*. [Translation by Ana Gomez-Soto].
https://intensiveintervention.org/sites/default/files/17-3324_NCII-Family-Questions-508.pdf
https://intensiveintervention.org/sites/default/files/NCII_Family_Questions_Spanish-508.pdf

Involving and Supporting Students to Participate

We must not forget that students with disabilities are critical stakeholders as well when discussing assessment information about their own performance and progress during intensive instruction. In the previous scenario, Benny spoke about his interests and agreed to share his progress with his mother. Similarly, special educators can invite students to monitor their own progress on specific goal areas as appropriate. Such a practice would encourage independence and increase student engagement. The IRIS Center's module, *SOS: Helping Students Become Independent Learners*, provides a specific resource page on the topic. The process involves (1) selecting a behavior to self-monitor; (2) collecting baseline data; (3) obtaining willing cooperation; (4) teaching self-monitoring procedures; and (5) monitoring independent performance (The IRIS Center, 2008). Allowing students to present their progress toward goals and make recommendations to the IEP team is very empowering, and important for becoming self-directed learners (Youjin, Wehmeyer, Palmer, & Little, 2015).

Wrap Up

The special education teacher is knowledgeable of and experienced in the assessment process, and is charged with sharing this information with stakeholders in a comprehensible fashion. Once services begin, teachers regularly monitor students' progress to ensure they make expected and sufficient improvement on IEP goals and objectives. Progress data informs the special education teacher about their instruction and adjustments needed to enhance a student's learning. The cycle of teach, assess, teach, assess, is the foundation of special education service delivery. This cycle, however, is incomplete without the active contributions of other service providers, families, the student, and school leaders who independently and uniquely contribute to a more accurate understanding of a student's strengths and needs. Ongoing communication amongst essential stakeholders is multidirectional, allowing each IEP team member to improve the support they provide and enhance students' learning experience. The special education teacher can contribute to this process by assisting with the development of tools and procedures around monitoring students' progress on IEP goals and objectives.

Tips

1. Prioritize families' expertise, participation, cultural, and linguistic resources by providing continuous opportunities for families and educators to learn about their roles and responsibilities in contributing to decision-making related to their students' progress within intensive instruction.
2. Create information for families in collaboration "with" families in multiple formats and languages (e.g., modules, videos, in-person meetings, digital newsletters, parent co-facilitated workshops, expert speaker series).
3. Provide training for educators regarding how to work with interpreters as ancillary examiners and engaging effectively with them during progress meetings.

Key Resources

- The *Center for Parent Information & Resources* provides multiple resources including guidance on measuring and reporting students' progress. www.parentcenterhub.org/iep-progress
- The *National Center on Intensive Intervention* has several tools to assist with developing procedures to discuss data with stakeholders https://intensiveintervention.org
- The *Progress Center: Promoting Progress for Students with Disabilities* https://promotingprogress.org includes tip sheets, videos, instructional practice briefs, presentation slides, podcasts, and other useful material for educators and families.
- The *US Office of Special Education Programs* developed a toolkit for meaningful communication with families of English learners. www2.ed.gov/about/offices/list/oela/english-learner-toolkit/chap10.pdf

References

Alonzo, J., Tindal, G., Ulmer, K., & Glasgow, A. (2006). easyCBM® online progress monitoring assessment system. http://easycbm.com. University of Oregon, Behavioral Research and Teaching.

Blazar, D. (2021). *Teachers of color, culturally responsive teaching, and student outcomes: Experimental evidence from the random assignment of teachers to classes.* EdWorkingPaper No. 21-510. Annenbberg Institute for School Reform at Brown University.

Brown, J., & Doolittle, J. (2008). A cultural, linguistic, and ecological framework for response to intervention with English language learners. *Teaching Exceptional Children, 40*(5), 66–72.

Gershenson, S., Hansen, M., & Lindsay, C.A. (2021). *Teacher diversity and student success: Why racial representation matters in the classroom.* Harvard Education Press.

Gray, S., Zraick, R.I., & Atcherson, S. R. (2019). Readability of IDEA Part B Procedural Standards: An update, *Language, Speech, and Hearing Services in Schools, 50*, 373–84.

Haas, E., & Brown, J. E. (2019). *Supporting English Learners in the classroom: Best practices for distinguishing language acquisition from learning disabilities.* Teachers College Press.

The IRIS Center (2008). *SOS: Helping students become independent learners.* Retrieved from https://iris.peabody.vanderbilt.edu/module/sr/

Ko, D., Mawene, D., Roberts, K, & Hong, J. J. (2021). A systematic review of boundary-crossing partnerships in designing equity-oriented special education services for culturally and linguistically diverse students with disabilities. *Remedial and Special Education, 42*(6), 412–25.

Redding, C. (2019). A teacher like me: A review of the effect of student-teacher racial/ethnic matching on teacher perception of students and student academic and behavioral outcomes. *Review of Educational Research, 89*(4), 499–535.

Wechsler, D., & Naglieri, J.A. (2006). *Wechsler Nonverbal Scale of Ability (WNV).* NCS Pearson, Inc.

Yamasaki, B.L., & Luk, G. (2018). Eligibility for special education in elementary school: The role of diverse language experiences. *Language, Speech, and Hearing Services in Schools, 49*, 889–901.

Youjin, S., Wehmeyer, M. L., Palmer, S. B., & Little, T. D. (2015). Effects of the self-directed individualized education program on self-determination and transition of adolescents with disabilities. *Career Development and Transition for Exceptional Individuals, 38*(3), 132–141.

6
Use Student Assessment Data, Analyze Instructional Practices, and Make Necessary Adjustments that Improve Student Outcomes

Abigail A. Allen
Clemson University

Introduction

Using student assessment data to analyze instruction is an essential component of special education. Although most special educators know they use assessment data to develop long-term goals for a student's Individual Education Program (IEP), they should also continually assess their students' learning and progress to determine if their instructional approach is effective and if the student is making adequate progress toward their goals. Recent research has concluded that students with disabilities whose teachers regularly monitor their progress and use data for making decisions learn more and have better outcomes (Jung et al., 2018).

The Every Student Succeeds Act requires that each state assess student learning, including that of students with disabilities, yearly with a series of outcome assessments. While this testing may indicate what grade-level material a student has learned, it does not help teachers determine if their instruction is effective as it unfolds weekly or monthly. Likewise, the Individuals with Disabilities Education Act (IDEA) requires IEP teams to provide periodic reports of student progress. However, to truly determine if a student is on track to meet their goals, it is necessary to assess their learning more than 2–3 times per year. A more nuanced way to capture student growth and progress is with *formative assessment*, or regularly assessing students during instruction. Formative assessment can help educators decide if their instruction is effective in time for them to make appropriate changes to increase student learning. This chapter will explain how to implement evidence-based practices in assessment and progress monitoring to adapt and individualize instruction for students with disabilities.

Narrowing the Focus

To collect and use assessment data effectively for intensive intervention, teachers must be fluent in three major components: principles of progress monitoring, curriculum-based measurement, and data-based individualization.

DOI: 10.4324/9781003276876-9

Chapter Overview

1. Definitions of the HLP elements
2. Progress Monitoring
    a.   Purpose and Rationale
    b.   Examples of Progress-Monitoring Measures
3. Curriculum-Based Measurement
    a.   Purpose and Rationale
    b.   Examples of Curriculum-Based Measures
4. Data-Based Individualization
    a.   Purpose and Rationale
    b.   Steps in the Process

Using the HLP

Definitions

Progress monitoring means systematically assessing students on critical skills at regular intervals to evaluate whether they are on track to meet IEP goals and if an instructional change is needed. Without specialized instruction, students receiving special education services usually demonstrate growth slower than typical peers, so educators need to monitor student progress with tools that can detect small increments of progress.

Curriculum-based measurement (CBM) is an evidence-based standardized method for observing and scoring a student's performance on a critical grade-level skill like reading aloud (Hosp et al., 2016). CBM data can be used for progress monitoring.

Data-based individualization (DBI) is an evidence-based process for systematically collecting and analyzing student assessment data to make instructional changes (Zumeta Edmonds et al., 2019). The DBI process requires regular progress monitoring and use of *decision rules* to determine if the student is on track to meet their long-term goal.

Evidence-based practice (EBP) refers to methods, strategies, and frameworks in instruction and assessment that have been evaluated in multiple experimental studies and there is enough research evidence to show the practice influences desired outcomes. Evidence-based practices are the "gold standard" and should be used whenever possible.

In Depth: Progress Monitoring

Progress monitoring is a type of formative assessment designed to predict a student's proficiency in a skill; it is used to determine how a student is responding to instruction (Deno, 2003). Progress monitoring measures are brief, capture important skills, produce scores that are reliable and valid, and can be administered repeatedly. When educators use progress monitoring assessments, their students learn more and their instructional decision making improves (National Center on Intensive Intervention [NCII], 2013). Progress monitoring is a critical component of special education for many reasons. First, teachers must keep track of how a student is progressing toward their IEP goals. If a student is not making the desired amount of progress, the teacher should further individualize instruction to help the student learn. If teachers wait until the end of the year or IEP cycle to assess student learning and find instructional goals have not been met, it is too late to intervene. Second, students with disabilities often make slow and inconsistent progress compared to peers without disabilities unless they have access to instruction tailored to their specific needs. A one-time measure may not give an accurate picture of their learning; thus, special educators should use progress monitoring assessments at regular intervals to accurately estimate student performance. Third,

Mastery Measure: Short /a/ Words	General Outcome Measure: Reading Fluency
1. hat 2. and 3. map 4. hand 5. cat 6. lamp 7. apple 8. crab 9. pan 10. mat	One day I was walking home from school and I saw a black and white cat. It was sitting in the sun on the sidewalk. It had yellow eyes and a cute pink nose. I wished I could take it home with me. I would pet it and brush it! I wanted to name it Fluffy. Then I saw it had a collar. The tag said the name, "Spot". It probably had a home already. I waved at the cat and went home.

Figure 6.1 Examples of Mastery and General Outcome Measures

Created by A. Allen (2022).

progress monitoring lets teachers compare the effect of different interventions and select those that benefit students most.

Special educators may wish to monitor student progress using a mastery measure or a general outcome measure. *Mastery measures* assess one narrow, specific skill at a time, like reading words with short /a/ vowels. One advantage of a mastery measure is the ability to track short-term growth and the effect of instruction on specific skills or benchmarks. One disadvantage is teachers cannot compare performance or instruction on measures that predict overall reading achievement. For example, a teacher cannot make a statement about how a student is progressing toward an IEP goal in reading fluency with data from just a short /a/ word assessment.

General outcome measures, in contrast, assess a broader scope of skills that represents overall achievement in a subject sampled across an academic year, like reading fluency passages. One advantage of general outcome measures is they help teachers decide if instruction is impacting overall achievement. One disadvantage is that performance on general outcome measures does not necessarily help teachers plan instruction. There are usually not enough test items on a specific skill for teachers to identify what the student should focus on during instruction. See Figure 6.1 for examples of a mastery and general outcome measure in reading.

It may be beneficial for teachers to use both mastery and general outcome measures to monitor student progress and to inform instruction and the IEP. One common measure used for progress monitoring is curriculum-based measurement.

In Depth: Curriculum-Based Measurement

Curriculum-based measurement (CBM) is a type of standardized assessment where teachers directly observe a student performing a skill and quickly score their performance (see Table 6.1 for examples of CBM assessments). Student performance is timed and measures are administered, scored, and interpreted the same way each time. CBM tools may contain both mastery and general outcome measures. Additionally, student scores are benchmarked according to how students in the general student population at each grade level might perform. This allows teachers to compare student progress to same-age peers and to determine how much a student needs to grow to function closer to peers. Further, because CBM reflects grade-level curricular content and tasks, low-inference decisions can be made about a student's instructional needs. Research has shown that scores from CBM tasks are *reliable* (i.e., consistent), *valid* (i.e., test the skills they claim to test), and *sensitive to growth* (i.e., able to detect small increments of progress) (Deno, 2003). Using assessments with these

Table 6.1 Common CBM Tasks

Task	Skill Targeted	Description	Administration	Scoring	Grade
Early Literacy					
Letter Naming or Letter Sound Fluency	Knowledge of letter names and/or sounds	Student names upper and lowercase letters or provide the sound of each letter randomly distributed in rows across a page.	Individually for 1 minute	Total letters named or sounds said correctly	K-1
Phoneme Segmentation Fluency	Knowledge of sounds in spoken language	Student hears a word read aloud and repeats back each individual sound in the word.	Individually for 1 minute	Total sounds said correctly	K-1
Nonsense Word Fluency	Letter-sound correspondence	Student reads a series of pseudowords printed on a page.	Individually for 1 minute	Total sounds or nonsense words said correctly	K-3
Reading					
Oral Reading Fluency	Reading fluency	Student reads a printed passage aloud.	Individually for 1 minute	Total words read correctly	1+
Maze	Reading comprehension	Students read a passage silently and selects the correct words to fill in missing words in the passage.	Group for 3 minutes	Total items correct	2+
Early Numeracy					
Number Identification	Knowledge of printed numbers	Student names numbers randomly distributed in rows across a page.	Individually for 1 minute	Total numbers said correctly	K-1
Oral Counting	Ability to count orally in sequential order	Student orally counts as high as they can without making an error.	Individually for 1 minute	Total numbers counted without error	K-1
Quantity Discrimination	Ability to distinguish between numbers	Student identifies which number in a pair is larger.	Individually for 1 minute.	Total items correct	K-1
Missing Number	Knowledge of number order	Student presented with a series of 3–4 number sequences with one missing number each. Student identifies the missing number in each set.	Individually for 1 minute	Total missing numbers correctly identified	K-1

(continued)

Table 6.1 Cont.

Task	Skill Targeted	Description	Administration	Scoring	Grade
Mathematics					
Computation	Ability to solve mathematical statements and equations	Students complete a series of mathematic calculations on paper.	Group for 3–8 minutes	Total items correct and Total digits correct	2+
Concepts and Application	Ability to apply numerical and mathematical concepts to problems	Students complete a series of word problems on paper.	Group for 3–8 minutes	Total items correct and Total digits correct	2+
Writing					
Spelling	Single word spelling	Student writes single words from oral dictation.	Individually for 3 minutes	Words spelled correctly and Correct letter sequences	1+
Picture Word	Sentence-level writing	Students write a series of sentences for pictures paired with single words.	Group for 3 minutes	Words written, Words spelled correctly, and Correct word sequences	1+
Story Prompt	Paragraph-level writing	Students write a story to complete a given prompt.	Group for 3 minutes	Words written, Words spelled correctly, and Correct word sequences	1+

Source: Created by A. Allen (2022).

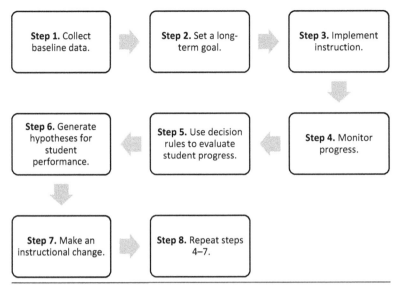

Figure 6.2 Data-Based Individualization Process

three elements is necessary to ensure data accurately represents student learning. CBM is useful for progress monitoring because it is brief and relatively easy to administer and score, so implementation is not burdensome and is designed to be given frequently, which is important for monitoring the progress of students receiving special education services (NCII, 2013).

Putting it All Together: Data-Based Individualization

Even when teachers use evidence-based instructional practices, every strategy does not always work for each student. Teachers need to use assessment data to determine whether a particular strategy is working for an individual student. This is where *data-based individualization* (DBI) can be useful (see Figure 6.2). DBI is a process for systematically and regularly taking assessment data, evaluating student progress and instructional effectiveness, and making sound, reasoned decisions about a student's instruction. DBI is appropriate for students receiving special education or other intensive interventions.

Step 1: Collect Baseline Data

The DBI process starts with collecting **baseline assessment data** on how the student is currently performing, much like the present level of performance on an IEP. Baseline data should be taken over three sessions within one week. To do this, teachers can give the student three different forms, or versions, of one CBM task and score immediately. Then, teachers put the student's three baseline scores in order from smallest to largest. The score that falls in the middle of the three, or the *median*, represents the student's overall baseline score.

Step 2: Set Long-Term Goal

Based on the student's baseline score, set an **ambitious but reasonable long-term goal**. This goal may serve as an IEP goal for the student. There are three basic methods used for goal setting in the DBI framework. The first is the *benchmarking method*. The benchmarking method is most appropriate for

Table 6.2 Benchmark Chart Example

		Total Words Read Correctly per Minute			
Grade	Percentile	Fall	Winter	Spring	Support Level*
3	90	134	161	166	Negligible
	75	104	137	139	Minimal
	50	83	97	112	Low
	25	59	79	91	Moderate
	10	40	62	63	High

Source: Created by A. Allen (2022).

Note: This table is for instructional purposes only. The data is *not* intended to be an accurate representation of reading fluency rates. Please refer to published benchmark charts for use in classrooms.

*Support Level = The likelihood that students performing at a level will need intensive instruction and supports. Some CBM products offer "cut scores" or "risk levels" associated with certain score bands.

students who are performing close to grade-level expectations. In this method, teachers use a table of national benchmarks associated with the CBM they are using to identify a score that may be used to set an appropriate long-term goal. National benchmark tables are typically provided with published CBM tests and often indicate expected scores by grade level and time of year (see Table 6.2). It is crucial to use the benchmarks provided by the publisher of the CBM materials. Benchmarks from one publisher are not generalizable to another.

Using the benchmarking method can help students "close the gap" with their peers and perform near or at grade-level expectations. There is debate about whether students performing below grade level should be assessed using grade-level CBMs. Using grade-level CBMs enables teachers to compare a student to their same-grade peers and whether they are getting close to grade-level expectations. However, using CBMs on a student's instructional level, or below grade level, enables teachers to detect growth for low-performing students. Solely relying on grade-level CBMs may overlook progress students are making at their instructional level because the tests are too difficult to be valid indicators of progress. It may be helpful to use grade-level and instructional-level CBMs to compare a student to grade-level peers and detect progress.

The second method for setting goals is the *ROI (rate of improvement) method*. Instead of selecting a total score for the student to achieve, a teacher will use a predicted ROI for the student and use that to calculate a goal score. National ROI norms are available with certain CBM products while local ROI norms can be calculated using CBM performance data for a school or district. The ROI method is best for students who learn at a slower than typical rate. To use the ROI method, a teacher would use the formula: *Goal = (ROI x weeks in instructional period) + baseline score*. First, identify the projected ROI for the student's grade level. Then, count the total number of weeks left in the instructional period, either the academic year or when the next IEP cycle starts. After multiplying the ROI by the number of weeks, add that result to the baseline score to get a total long-term goal score. Advantages of the ROI method are that it produces an ambitious long-term goal for students who do not learn at a typical rate. A disadvantage of the ROI approach is that it may not close the gap between the student and their grade-level peers; it effectively ignores grade-level proficiency. One would need to use an ambitious ROI if the goal is to "catch up" to grade-level expectations.

The final goal-setting method is the *intra-individual framework*. The intra-individual framework compares a student's past performance to their current performance to derive a student rate of improvement (SROI) to calculate a goal. This approach is most appropriate for students performing well below grade level expectations. To use the intra-individual method, first calculate the individual's

SROI over *at least* 8 data points by subtracting the lowest from the highest score and divide by the number of weeks of data collection. Then, calculate a goal with the formula *Goal = (SROI x 1.5 x weeks left in instructional period) + baseline score.* The advantage of the intra-individual framework is that it produces an individualized goal and provides a systematic way of selecting goals for students who are well below grade level. The disadvantage is that it is the least ambitious of the three methods and will widen the gap between the student and peers unless the student is already making average or better progress.

Step 3: Implement Instruction

The next step in the DBI process is to **implement high-quality instruction.** Instructional strategies should meet the student's immediate needs in a subject area and should be evidence-based whenever possible. Teachers may plan instruction by using mastery monitoring results to determine specific skills a student lacks. The intervention or instructional strategies should be appropriate for the student's disability, current performance, and long-term goals.

Step 4: Monitor Progress

Students receiving special education services should be **progress monitored** at regular intervals (e.g., every week). Teachers should use assessments sensitive to small increments of growth that produce reliable and valid scores (e.g., CBM). It is also critical that teachers score and graph their data soon after administration. Many teachers designate one day a week to giving, scoring, and graphing progress monitoring data. Graphing assessment data is critical for several reasons. Having a visual representation of the student's performance and their long-term goal provides a relatively easy way of assessing their performance. Graphed data can also provide a clear method of presenting student data to other stakeholders like families, other teachers, and administrators.

Progress monitoring data can be easily graphed in a computerized spreadsheet like Microsoft Excel or Google Sheets. The x-axis, or the horizontal line at the bottom of the graph, represents each time the teacher gave the assessment. The y-axis, or vertical line on the left side of the graph, represents the scores a student can achieve on the measure. Next, plot the student's baseline score and their goal on the graph and connect the two dots forming the student's *goal line.* This line represents the student's required trajectory to achieve the goal. Then, as the progress monitoring assessment is given each week, enter the student's score into the graph.

Step 5: Use Decision Rules to Analyze Data

To make sound, reliable decisions about instruction, special educators should **use decision rules** to determine if a student is on track to meet their goal. A decision rule is a method for consistently and fairly evaluating student data. Two basic decision rules are used in DBI.

The *four-point rule* states that once a teacher has *at least* six data points collected over three weeks of instruction, they should look at the four most recent data points. If those four points are all above the goal line, the student is on track to meet their long-term goal and instructional change is necessary. If the four most recent points are all below the goal line, the student is not on track to meet their goal and an instructional change is warranted. If the four most recent points do not meet either criterion, meaning some are above and some are below the goal line, continue to take data each week until one of the criteria is met (see Figure 6.3).

The advantage of the four-point rule is that it is clear and easy to follow. Evaluation of the data points is relatively objective; educators can clearly count how many data points fall above or below

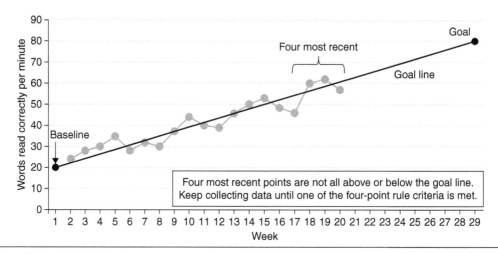

Figure 6.3 Four-Point Rule Example

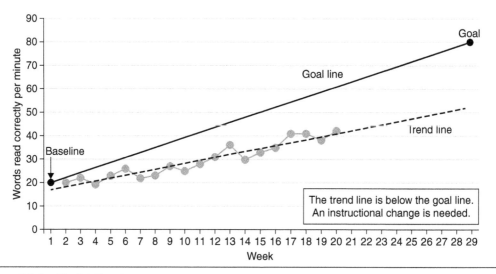

Figure 6.4 Trend Line Rule Example

the goal line. The disadvantage is that teachers are taking relatively little data into account before evaluating student progress and their instruction. Teachers may wish to consider other evidence of progress like mastery measures, work samples, and classroom observations to inform educational decisions.

The *trend line rule* states that once teachers have *at least* eight data points collected over four weeks of instruction, they should compare a student's trend line to their goal line. If the trend line is above the goal line, students have met their goal. The goal should be raised, and instruction should continue as planned. If the trend line is even with the goal line, students are on track to meet their goal and instruction should continue. If the trend line is below the goal line, students are not going to meet their goal and an instructional change is needed (see Figure 6.4).

The advantage of the trend line rule is that it takes a considerable amount of data into account and is likely an accurate representation of a student's progress. When more data is used to make decisions, decisions are likely sound and reasonable. The disadvantage, however, is that it may take longer to collect enough data to apply this rule and sometimes one influential data point, like when a student has a great or bad day, can influence the trend line inappropriately.

A key point to emphasize with decision rules is that if a student is not making adequate progress, the resulting decision should *never* be to lower the long-term goal. If a goal is truly too ambitious for a student, the IEP team can discuss appropriate goals moving forward. Additionally, teachers should use one decision rule consistently with a student. To measure change and effectiveness, the measure and decision rule needs to be consistent.

Step 6: Generate Hypotheses

The next step in the DBI process is **generating hypotheses** for why a student may not be on track to meet their goal. Progress monitoring graphs can tell us *when* it is time to make an instructional change, but it cannot tell us *what* the change needs to be or *why* a student is not making progress. Special educators must use progress monitoring data along with observations, notes, and student work samples to make an educated guess about why a student is not on track to meet their goal.

To generate hypotheses in a systematic way, teachers should first ask themselves if the intervention or instructional strategy was designed for students with similar needs. Was the instructional strategy delivered with *fidelity*, or the way it was meant to be delivered? If the instruction was appropriate and delivered as designed, then teachers may want to think about the focus or content of instruction. If a student made progress on a specific skill but is not demonstrating progress overall, perhaps a new skill or target is necessary. Teachers may wish to give their students additional mastery measures to explore specific skills or concepts that need to be introduced during instruction. The teacher's hypotheses will inform the specific instructional change they choose to make.

Step 7: Make an Instructional Change

Once a hypothesis is made about a student's lack of progress, a teacher must **make an instructional change** to intensify and individualize instruction. If instruction is appropriate and delivered as designed, teachers may wish to explore changes in instructional *quantity* or instructional *quality*. A change in instructional *quantity* might mean longer sessions, more sessions per week, or more weeks total. These changes are often easier said than done, particularly when instructional minutes are written into IEPs. Other ways to indirectly increase the quantity of instruction is to decrease group size, decrease the heterogeneity of group members (i.e., group students of similar ability), or increase the number of practice opportunities in a session. These strategies indirectly increase the amount of instruction a student receives by providing more opportunities to participate or to receive more focused instruction.

A change in instructional *quality* may entail changes to lesson *format*, *focus*, or *content*. Adjustments to the lesson *format* may involve changing the way instruction is explained and delivered to students, such as providing more explicit modeling, clearer directions, more frequent opportunities to respond, and/or more explicit feedback. Changes to lesson *focus* may involve addressing a related or different skill that will spur additional learning toward the long-term goal, like introducing spelling and handwriting work with a student working on writing paragraphs. Changing lesson *content* could entail working on the same target skill but providing different examples, words, problems, or texts, like explicit instruction on writing persuasive essays instead of paragraphs. Consider making one instructional change at a time to better evaluate the effectiveness of that change.

Step 8: Repeat Steps 4–7

Once a teacher has decided on an instructional change, they should implement that change and continue monitoring student progress toward the goal, looking at data, and making decisions. On the progress monitoring graph, a vertical line can represent when the instructional change was implemented and enable teachers to evaluate the new instruction.

Culturally Responsive Assessment Practices

Research on progress monitoring tools and the DBI process with culturally and linguistically diverse (CLD) students is emerging, however most resources have likely not been validated with CLD populations (Sacco et al., 2021). The process of individualizing instruction may have benefit for CLD students, but only if teachers provide linguistic and cultural supports during the DBI process.

Choosing Assessments

Teachers must be careful and thoughtful when choosing measures for CLD students. There are numerous progress monitoring tools that assess basic academic skills such as phonemic awareness, reading fluency, and mathematics calculation that do not involve complex academic language and may be appropriate for CLD students (Sacco et al., 2021). English language acquisition and fluency, however, play a role in how students perform on more complicated tasks like reading comprehension, writing, and mathematics problem solving. Teachers must have knowledge of a student's educational and language background to determine a student's dominant language at the time of testing. It would be helpful to collaborate with the student's English language (EL) teacher if possible. If a student's dominant language is not English, then assessments should be provided in the student's dominant language. If the student is receiving instruction in multiple languages, assessments should be provided in those languages.

Additionally, it may be useful to compare CLD students to other peers at similar levels of English fluency and educational experience rather than grade-level peers to capture their baseline performance and progress (Esparza Brown & Sanford, 2011). It may not be appropriate to set a long-term goal based on benchmarks or predicted rates of growth derived from an English-only speaking population. CLD students with an underlying disability will likely demonstrate slower rates of improvement compared to CLD students without disabilities. Likewise, CLD students struggling academically because of a lack of English fluency will likely start making significant progress when they are provided with quality instruction and language supports (Project ELITE, Project ESTRE2 LLA, & Project REME, 2015).

Choosing Interventions or Instructional Strategies

Teachers must choose strategies aligned with a CLD student's academic needs while also providing language and vocabulary support during instruction. Again, it is essential that teachers collaborate with the student's EL teacher whenever possible. They have a wealth of knowledge about linguistic supports and can offer insights into the student's individual fluency level. If instruction validated with CLD populations is not available, teachers can select instruction validated with students who have similar academic or behavioral needs and then adapt instruction to meet the specific learning and linguistic needs of their student (Sacco et al., 2021). This may mean providing instructional support in the targeted area of need while also providing vocabulary and oral language support during the intervention lesson, such as providing brief, explicit instruction in specific academic terms, or providing additional modeling.

Using Data to Make Decisions

When an educator has enough progress monitoring data to evaluate a CLD student's progress, it is critical they interpret the data with the student's linguistic and cultural influences in mind. For example, a student might sound conversationally fluent in English but does not have enough academic language fluency to make sufficient progress. They may need additional language supports during instruction, like simpler directions or direct instruction on key vocabulary terms in the lesson, to fully benefit from the intervention. Progress monitoring data can help teachers understand how a CLD student is performing, as long as educators use multiple sources of data to develop a completed understanding of a student's performance or behavior.

Once a teacher has a sound hypothesis about why a CLD student is performing in a certain way, they can make reasoned instructional changes. If instruction was provided with fidelity, teachers might choose to increase time or number of sessions (change in quantity), provide more explicit directions and examples during instruction, provide more practice opportunities, change the lesson focus or content, or increase vocabulary and oral expression support during instruction (change in quality).

Case Study Example

Mr. Sanders is working with an eighth-grade student, Marisol, on her writing. Marisol is a bilingual Spanish and English speaker. She was born in the United States and speaks Spanish at home with her parents and English at school and with her younger siblings. Her instruction at school has been in English- only since kindergarten. Mr. Sanders notes that Marisol tends to use simple sentence structures repeatedly in her writing and simple, non-specific vocabulary. Mr. Sanders decides to give Marisol a series of CBM writing prompts to establish her baseline performance. Mr. Sanders knows that he needs to choose writing prompt subjects that are culturally sensitive and likely to be familiar to Marisol. He decides to stick to topics related to school experiences (e.g., One day, at lunch…) or open-ended questions (e.g., If I had a million dollars, I would…). He scores her work using correct word sequences which considers spelling, grammar, and word usage. He also decides to score her writing prompts with a rubric mastery measure to pinpoint specific skills he needs to target during instruction. Marisol's results confirm Mr. Sanders' hunch about Marisol needing support with sentence structure and vocabulary. He sets a long-term goal for her total correct word sequences based on other CLD students in her grade.

Mr. Sanders knows that CLD students often need language supports during instruction and that writing is the last literacy skill to fully develop. He concludes that although Marisol is conversationally fluent in English, she likely needs support to use more sophisticated academic language, especially in writing. He decides to provide Marisol with explicit instruction in sentence combining to help her create more complex, advanced sentences. He uses very clear directions, models how to complete the instructional activity, provides numerous models of compound and complex written sentences and frequent corrective feedback during practice sessions. He also provides her with sentence stems as a visual support. Mr. Sanders continues to give Marisol one story prompt CBM each week as a progress monitoring measure.

After eight weeks of data collection, Mr. Sanders notes that Marisol is not on track to meet her long-term goal. When looking at Marisol's writing prompts, he notices that her sentences are becoming longer and more complex, but her word usage is still lagging, which negatively affects her correct word sequences score and makes her writing seem less sophisticated. Mr. Sanders decides to incorporate more explicit vocabulary instruction into his sessions with Marisol using key academic vocabulary from her classes. He provides simple definitions for vocabulary words and clear examples and non-examples. He asks Marisol to read the words and explain them in her own words. They then practice using the key words during practice writing activities, maintaining the use of sentence stems and support for writing compound and complex sentences. Mr. Sanders also provides explicit instruction in how to use their practice strategies and Marisol's new skills in sentence structure and vocabulary in her other classes and assignments. After eight additional weeks of data collection, Mr. Sanders notes Marisol's writing has improved. She is continuing to use more sophisticated sentence structures and advanced vocabulary in writing prompts and starting to generalize writing skills to other classes.

Wrap Up

Using assessment data for instructional planning is an important skill. Teachers must be proficient with progress monitoring students regularly on key skills using curriculum-based measurement tools. Once a baseline level of performance has been identified, teachers should select evidence-based interventions when available. If evidence-based practices are not available, then teachers should select instructional strategies that meet their students' immediate needs and have at least some supporting research evidence. While providing instruction, educators must continually monitor student progress and use decision rules to analyze student data. By regularly and systematically evaluating student performance and progress, special educators can make sound, reasoned decisions about their students' instruction and ultimately improve student learning. If students are not progressing from instruction, consider making quantitative changes to instruction before qualitative ones.

Tips

1. Use a combination of standardized mastery and general outcome measures for progress monitoring and instructional planning.
2. Score and graph data as soon as possible after giving an assessment.
3. Make sure the y axis on your graph starts at zero and increases in consistent increments.
4. If using published measures, always use their published benchmarks or norms/ROIs.

Key Resources

Hosp, M., Hosp, J., & Howell, K. (2016). *The ABCs of CBM* (2nd ed). Guilford.
Intervention Central CBM Warehouse: www.interventioncentral.org/curriculum-based-measurem ent-reading-math-assesment-tests
IRIS Center Collecting and Analyzing Data for Data-Based Individualization: https://iris.peabody. vanderbilt.edu/module/dbi2/#content
National Center on Intensive Intervention Progress Monitoring Tools Charts: https://intensiveinter vention.org/tools-charts/overview
Zumeta Edmonds, R., Gruner Ghandi, A., & Danielson, L. (2019). *Essentials of Intensive Intervention*. Guilford.

References

Deno, S. L. (2003). Developments in curriculum-based measurement. *The Journal of Special Education*, *37*(3), 184–92. https://doi.org/10.1177/00224669030370030801
Esparza Brown, J., & Sanford, A. (2011). *RTI for English language learners: Appropriately using screening and progress monitoring tools to improve instructional outcomes.* US Department of Education, Office of Special Education Programs, National Center on Response to Intervention. https://mtss4success.org/sites/default/files/2020-07/rtiforells.pdf
Fuchs, L. S., Fuchs, D., Hamlett, C. L., Walz, L., & Germann, G. (1993). Formative evaluation of academic progress: How much growth can we expect? *School Psychology Review*, *22*, 27–48. https://doi.org/10.1080/02796015.1993.12085636
Hasbrouck, J., & Tindal, G. (2017). *An update to compiled ORF norms* (Technical Report No. 1702). Behavioral Research and Teaching, University of Oregon.

Jung, P. G., McMaster, K. L., Kunkel, A. K., Shin, J., & Stecker, P. M. (2018). Effects of data-based individualization for students with intensive learning needs: A meta-analysis. *Learning Disabilities Research & Practice, 33*(3), 144–55. https://doi.org/10.1111/ldrp.12172

National Center on Intensive Intervention (2013). *Using academic progress monitoring for individualized instructional planning.* American Institutes for Research: https://intensiveintervention.org/resource/using-academic-progress-monitoring-individualized-instructional-planning-dbi-training

Project ELITE, Project ESTRE2 LLA, & Project REME (2015). *Effective practices for English learners: Brief 2, Assessment and data-based decision-making.* US Office of Special Education Programs. www.mtss4els.org/files/resource-files/Brief2.pdf

Sacco, D. M., Hoover, J. J., & Spies, T. (2021). *Implementing data-based individualization for English learners.* American Institutes of Research: National Center on Intensive Intervention. https://intensiveintervention.org/sites/default/files/EL_DBI_Brief.pdf

Section III
Social/Emotional/Behavioral High Leverage Practices
Timothy J. Lewis

An on-going challenge for all special educators is learning to effectively manage problem behavior and create a learning environment to increase the likelihood students learn appropriate social, emotional, and behavioral skills. While some disability categories include challenging behavior as part of the symptomology, such as Emotional/Behavioral Disorders, problems of attention under Other Health Impaired, or Autism, there is a high degree of likelihood that when any student with a disability manifests intensive support needs, challenging behavior will be present. Fortunately, there is a large body of research supporting the identified High Leverage Practices (HLP) within this section. As outlined in previous editions of the *High Leverage Practices for Inclusive Classrooms* text, special educators are encouraged to use these HLPs as foundational practices within their classrooms. However, as noted across the four chapters and elsewhere in this text, special educators should use the noted HLPs in concert with the academic and other instructional strategies presented in this text. Research has also demonstrated that the effective instructional strategies outlined in this text significantly increase the likelihood of student success, thereby reducing the likelihood of student misbehavior. Likewise, core HLPs are appropriate for use with students who display mild to more intensive needs. The key is increasing the intensity of implementation (i.e., amount, duration, and frequency of intervention) to match the intensity of the social, emotional, and behavioral challenges.

This section provides four essential HLPs to promote appropriate student social behavior. Chapter 7 provides an overview of essential classroom practices and procedures to create environments to support appropriate student behavior. State and colleagues stress the need for establishing clear and consistent behavioral expectations and procedures, explicitly teaching those expectations and routines, and providing multiple opportunities to practice with feedback. Chapter 8 expands on the critical need to provide differentiated feedback following appropriate and inappropriate student behavior. Rila and Estrapala outline several strategies to support student mastery of social skills as well as using corrective feedback that provides instruction and additional practice opportunities to promote student success when problem behavior is present. In addition, the authors provide specific recommendations to address cultural variations across student groups. Chapter 9 focuses on the ongoing need to continually teach appropriate social behavior. Scott outlines the essential features of explicitly teaching social skills through a multi-step process that guides mastery and generalized use of critical social behaviors. The first three chapters in this section outline the foundational practices

DOI: 10.4324/9781003276876-10

that increase the likelihood students with disabilities demonstrate appropriate social behavior that will foster social, emotional, and behavioral growth and enhance their ability to benefit from academic instruction. However, foundational practices alone are not always sufficient to address all behavioral challenges. Chapter 10 provides the logic and essential features of using Functional Behavioral Assessments (FBA) to guide individual behavior plans. As Pollack and Lloyd explain, challenging (and appropriate) behavior "functions" to meet students' needs. Knowing the function of problem behavior leads to more efficient and effective behavior support plans that incorporate all of the foundational skills provided in Chapters 7 through 9.

Similar to all of the high leverage practices described in this text, the brief chapters alone will not be sufficient to build fluency. Readers are strongly encouraged to focus on the key tips offered at the conclusion of each chapter and review the additional resources provided, many of which can be accessed on the web at no charge. Also, as highlighted throughout this text, special educators are strongly encouraged to differentiate HLPs to reflect the cultural context of the school and community. This is especially important when addressing social behavior given the variations of what is viewed as "appropriate" or "acceptable" across cultural groups and contexts (see Chapter 8). Engaging in conversations around race, religion, or language often makes us uncomfortable when the teaching staff and the students they serve do not share common learning histories. Our advice is to focus on key and important outcomes valued by all groups, such as being "respectful" or being "responsible" and work backwards to discuss how students who come from varied backgrounds have been taught to display social behavior related to common values. Finally, key to all effective behavioral support strategies is to focus on building appropriate student behavior and not simply trying to remove or reduce a problem behavior. A key question to ask yourself when faced with a challenging behavior is "what do you want the student to do instead?" Build your classroom environment, use high rates of positive specific feedback, explicitly teach and practice social skills, and identify functional outcomes that all focus on increasing appropriate social/emotional skills among your students.

7
Establish a Consistent, Organized, and Respectful Learning Environment

Talida M. State
Montclair State University

Barbara S. Mitchell
Kansas State University

Imad Zaheer
St John's University

Introduction

Effective teachers prioritize creating and maintaining a consistent, organized, and respectful classroom environment for all students. To create this environment, teachers focus on establishing, teaching, and reinforcing clear class-wide expectations, rules, routines, and procedures. Attention to these foundational strategies ensures universal prevention is in place such that most students successfully navigate the classroom environment without any additional support. For detailed recommendations on establishing a proactive, positive, and supportive classroom environment we refer the reader to Chapter 7 in *High Leverage Practices for Inclusive Classrooms (2nd Edition)*.

Consider the following scenario. Prior to the start of a new school year, a classroom teacher mentors a "new to the field" first year teacher. As part of the mentoring process, the veteran teacher reflects on and shares the most common problems that occurred the previous year. In anticipation of the same problems, and perhaps others as well, the veteran teacher describes adjustments that will be made to strategically prepare for a consistent, organized, and respectful learning environment. Specifically, the teacher identifies clear classroom expectations as "Be Here, Be Ready, Be Responsible." Next the teacher creates rules to show "Be Here, Be Ready, Be Responsible," at minimum, means (a) arrive to class on time, with needed materials; (b) follow directions the first time asked; (c) use polite and inclusive language and gestures; and (d) ask for or provide help when needed. The teacher plans to share the drafted expectations and rules with students and families during the first week of school to ask them for input and ideas, additions or revisions. In this way, the expectations would reflect the collaborative efforts of the full learning community of teacher, students, and family. Third, the teacher identifies relevant activities and tasks that commonly occur in the classroom and transforms each one into structured procedures that could be taught and reinforced to develop classroom habits or routines (e.g., accessing a hall pass, asking for help, turning in completed work, getting caught up after an absence, lining up to transition out of the classroom, and storage of materials).

After designing the classroom expectations, rules, and routines the teacher also develops a plan to deliver specific positive feedback at much higher rates than had been given to students the previous

DOI: 10.4324/9781003276876-11

year. The teacher decides to try a class-wide point system that would allow the whole class to be awarded one or more "points" when meeting classroom expectations, adhering to rules, or using the designated routines. Use of clear classroom expectations such as "Be here," "Be ready," "Be responsible" is an easy way to categorize points awarded and, in turn, serve as an informal monitoring system. If students earn fewer points in one or more classroom expectation categories this may indicate the need to clarify or reteach a particular rule or procedure, provide additional practice opportunities, and/or offer higher rates of specific feedback. To support the point system, the teacher organizes a survey for students to rate their preferences regarding exchange of points for simple, fun, no-cost celebrations such as eating lunch in the classroom, or playing music during an independent work period.

Finally, the teacher also reconsiders strategies that had been used the previous year for responding to problem behavior that occurred. Rather than repeatedly sending students out of the classroom, taking away privileges, or giving stern lectures followed by a phone call home, the teacher makes plans for an instructional approach to managing problems. Specifically, the teacher organizes a range of responses that would provide additional instruction, practice, and feedback when a behavioral error occurs (i.e., a student breaking a rule). For the upcoming year the teacher aims to make better use of non-verbal gestures and cues, brief and private redirection, short reteaching and practice of rules and routines, and student conferencing for situations that require more discussion.

As the school year begins and students engage in the initial days of instruction, the teacher makes an effort to consistently implement the redesigned classroom plan. In fact, more so than in previous years, the teacher carves out time each day to teach and/or review the classroom expectations, rules, and routines with students. As the mini-lessons continue the teacher notices a generally positive response from students. That is, most students met the classroom expectations and rules and earned points in recognition for their appropriate behavior. Students commented that they enjoyed the celebration activities they earned from the point exchange. In addition, the overall tone and climate of the classroom felt better because the teacher did not spend so much time responding to and correcting problems. By strategically attending to organization, structure, and consistency in delivery of planned practices the teacher created a learning environment that was respectful of all members and facilitated high rates of success for a majority of the students.

Although the teaching plans were implemented and an increasing number of points were awarded and exchanged, indicating most students were responding positively to these efforts, the teacher increasingly becomes aware of a few students who are not thriving to the same degree as the others. For example, one student is tardy to class every day and a few students still have trouble rotating from station to station in a timely and orderly fashion. As a starting point, to address these concerns, the teacher considers what elements of the expectation or routine could be retaught, modified, or further reinforced. Next, the teacher considers what elements of the existing learning environment could be intensified to better address the needs of students who would benefit from just a little more support. For this teacher, who had worked hard to master several effective management and instructional practices, intensifying these practices would be an efficient way to support some students with greater need. Rather than jumping to individual behavior plans or seeking out a special education evaluation, the teacher determines the best approach would be to intensify some of the strategies that were already contributing to the successful teaching and learning environment.

Narrowing the Focus

Despite a teacher's best efforts to establish a maximally effective learning environment, a small number of students, in any given classroom, are likely to need extra support beyond the universal support provided for all students. This chapter describes the application of "functional contextual thinking" (FCT), which is a framework for teachers to consider the function of a student's behavior, and problem solve to identify strategies for students who need additional help to be successful in the classroom (see Chapter 10 for additional information on function of behavior). Using this FCT logic enables teachers to better select strategies that align with individual student challenges. All too often educators use intervention techniques before considering the context in which the problem is happening and what the "function" of students' behavior is. In these cases, one or more interventions may be selected and used correctly but will not actually lead to expected change in student behavior. Or, worse yet, they are implemented and, unintentionally, make problem behaviors more severe. These experiences are frustrating for teachers, students, and families alike because rather than seeing improvement, problem behavior continues or may increase in frequency or intensity. Learning to think about "function" and context first saves time, effort, and frustration for all involved because this approach increases the likelihood selected interventions will address presenting problems and that desired, appropriate school behaviors will be adopted and regularly used.

Chapter Overview

This chapter describes how to engage in functional contextual thinking (FCT) so that selection of more intensive interventions is tailored to the individual student and their particular learning environment. Chapter content is designed for educators to better understand the types of additional in-class supports required by some students and how to implement these practices. Accordingly, the chapter is organized to address the following major topics:

1. Describe the FCT logic.
2. Provide a menu of strategies teachers can use to prevent problem behaviors, teach appropriate replacement behaviors, and consistently respond to appropriate or inappropriate behaviors.
3. Explain one strategy, with accompanying implementation examples, from each category of the intervention menu. The following strategies are included:
   a. *Prevent* using precorrection & choice.
   b. *Teach* skills using task analysis and self-monitoring.
   c. *Respond* using an individualized point chart with problem solving.
4. Summarize key content and offer tips for using foundational practices that intensify consistency, organization, and respect within the learning environment.

Using the HLP: Functional Contextual Thinking

In any context, when a student does not consistently follow the classroom expectations and routines (e.g., a student is consistently tardy for class), the teacher can consider the degree to which a contextual mismatch, between the students' needs or skills and the learning environment, is responsible. The following line of questioning can help a teacher consider the influence of context.

1. Is the expectation or routine age appropriate?
2. Does the student actually have the skills required to perform the routine?
3. If the student has the skills, is the student sufficiently motivated to follow the expectation or routine?
4. Are there specific data patterns that indicate the student is struggling to follow expectations during specific times of the day, in specific locations, or around certain people?
5. Are there barriers in the environment that prevent the student from meeting the expectation or following the routine?

Thinking about the context in which a student does not meet the expectation or routine is a critical next step for identifying additional instruction and support that will match student needs. For example, support for a student who is consistently tardy because they look after younger siblings each morning will differ from support provided to a student who regularly chats with friends in the hallways instead of getting to class on time.

The FCT framework takes into account the "context" in which behavior occurs and the "function," or reason, why the behavior occurs (Allday, 2017; Walker, et al., 2018). The first step of FCT is to clearly define the behavior and skills of interest (e.g., the student is off-task by doodling on his paper instead of solving the required math equation during independent seat work). Next, identify the context in which problematic behaviors, externalized or internalized, take place including the setting events (e.g., motivating factors, such as lack of sleep), antecedents that trigger the behavior (e.g., work demand), and consequences that maintain it (e.g., sent out of the classroom) in order to determine the function of the behavior (e.g., escape from demand). Functions that maintain behavior generally include *access* to attention, preferred tangible items, activities, and/or sensory experiences, or *avoidance* or *escape* from attention, demands or undesired situations, and in some cases, aversive sensory stimulation. Knowing the function of behavior leads to selection of strategies that modify the context, teach or re-teach desired replacement behavior, and support use of appropriate replacement behaviors. Effective interventions seek the dual goal of increasing desirable behaviors and decreasing problematic behaviors by understanding these variables that trigger and maintain behavior.

When using FCT logic, teachers will draw from the ABCs of behavior, where A stands for antecedents (i.e., events that prompt/trigger the behavior), B stands for behavior (i.e., measurable and observable actions that describe exactly what the student is doing), and C stands for consequences (i.e., what happens right after the behavior is performed). Accordingly, teachers can apply FCT logic, using the following prompts, to identify the student's behavior, its context and function, and necessary supports:

(1) Identify the *setting events* and *antecedents* that triggered the problem *behavior.*
   - A student comes to class upset from *a fight they had on the bus* (i.e., setting event). When the *teacher gives a prompt* to open the textbook (i.e., antecedent), the student refuses by yelling "I don't feel like it" and throwing the textbook (i.e., behavior).
(2) Identify immediate *consequences* following the behavior.
   - In response, the *teacher sends the student to the principal's office* to be disciplined (i.e., consequence).
(3) Hypothesize the *function/s* of the behavior.
   - The student goes to the office thus, *escaping* the teacher's demand and classroom environment.
   - The student prefers to go to the office as they enjoy spending time with the administrator thus, *obtaining attention* from a preferred adult.
(4) Identify appropriate *replacement behavior* linked to the identified function.
   - Instead of acting upon his frustration by throwing the book, the student should ask for a break and use a previously taught strategy to calm down when feeling frustrated. Once calm, the student will then be able to follow the teacher's direction.
(5) Select strategies that prompt and encourage use of the replacement behavior
   - When the teacher recognizes the student is frustrated, the teacher will give the student a 5-minute break and remind the student to use a breathing strategy to calm down and refocus (e.g., this breathing strategy has been previously taught to the student as an appropriate replacement behavior when feeling frustrated). The 5-minute break allows the student to temporarily escape the teacher's demand, thus honoring the function of the student's misbehavior. The breathing strategy serves as an appropriate replacement behavior to throwing textbooks and yelling.
   - If the student uses the breathing strategy and successfully calms down and participates in class, as a reward, they can stop by the principal's office for a brief chat at the end of day (i.e.,

student obtains the desired attention for the appropriate behavior instead of inappropriate behavior).

(6) Select strategies that discourage the use of inappropriate behaviors and minimize reinforcement of the inappropriate behavior.

- If the student continues to be disruptive, they will "owe" the teacher the time spent disrupting the class and they will not be allowed to stop by the principal's office for a chat at the end of the day.

Once a teacher identifies the necessary ABC-related information and formulates a hypothesis about the function of the student's misbehaviors, strategies can be identified to address the questions below:

(1) How can I change my classroom environment to promote appropriate behaviors and prevent inappropriate behaviors for my students?
(2) What else do I need to teach my students to perform instead of the problem behavior, and how will I teach it? What would it look like to teach expectations, rules, procedures on a more intensive and individualized level?
(3) When students perform the appropriate replacement behavior, how do I respond to ensure the students will perform that behavior again in the future? How do I respond to the problem behavior to make sure I reduce the probability it will happen again in the future?

How many and what combination of strategies to select depends on what is feasible and most likely to lead to desired change for the student. For example, brief re-teaching of a focus skill followed by consistent use of precorrection may be sufficient for a student whose behavior has not yet become too frequent or severe. In other cases, for students with higher needs, several strategies may need to be selected and combined to have the desired impact on student behavior. Regardless of which and how many, the selected support must be applied with integrity, often referred to as "fidelity," which means the strategy is delivered correctly or as designed. In addition, data collection to monitor impact of the provided support on student behavior also must continue. Reduction in tardy events or increase in class-wide points awarded are simple data-based monitoring examples (see Figure 7.1 for further function-based examples).

Pre-correction

Pre-correction, often referred to as pre-corrects, is a simple strategy that sets students up for success. To use pre-correction, a teacher provides a statement that tells students the expected or desired behaviors *prior to* any activity, routine, or transition that may be associated with problem behavior (Ennis et al., 2017). For example, right before a transition from the classroom a teacher might say:

"Class, we are getting ready to go to lunch. As you walk through the hallway please remember to stay on the right, keep hands by your side, and walk quietly so we don't disturb other classrooms."

By using a pre-correction, the teacher reminds students of expected behaviors as a way to encourage desired behavior. These simple reminder statements are easy to deliver and serve as a proactive positive support because students are told what *to do* in advance of situations that have potential for problems. When pre-correction is followed by behavior-specific praise, students are more likely to repeat behaviors that were prompted. Using this cycle of pre-correct, monitor, and praise, teachers can shape student behavior to become routine or automatic.

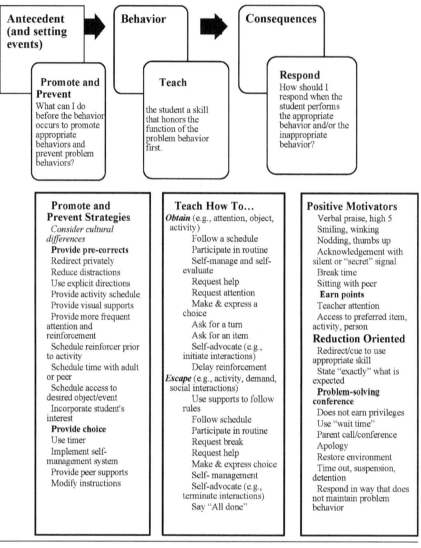

Figure 7.1 Example of Problem Solving for Elementary Students

Often pre-correction is used with an entire class of students. For students with more intensive needs, a pre-correction can be delivered individually prior to activities or transitions identified as most problematic for that student. Providing positive adult attention in the form of a friendly reminder is one powerful way to address the needs of students whose problem behavior is maintained by adult attention. For example, a teacher might say:

> Hey Dion, during the writing workshop yesterday I noticed you got your materials out right away, started the work as soon as I finished giving instructions, and continued working until I checked on you. That was a great way to demonstrate our classroom expectations "Be Here, Be Ready." See if you can do the exact same thing today. I'll be watching, and I will check on you in a few minutes.

Alternately, for students with behavior maintained by avoidance or escape, pre-correction statements can be designed to explicitly tell them what behaviors to engage in to access desired outcomes or preferred conditions.

> Tamika, we are getting ready to start our writing workshop which I know is not your favorite activity. Remember, if you become frustrated or need a break you have two break cards you can use that will let you do something else for a minute. Using your break card is a nice way to step back from work that is difficult, regroup, and then get a little more writing done.

To implement pre-corrections that are designed with particular students in mind teachers can use the following steps:

1. Identify conditions that tend to be problematic for the students with more intensive needs. For example, think about transitions, routines, or instructional settings in which a student most often engages in problem/unwanted behavior.
2. Next, determine what you want the student *to do* instead (e.g., desired or expected behavior). Identify replacement behaviors that will serve the same purpose or function of the problem behavior (e.g., obtain or avoid/escape).
3. Write a brief but clear statement to use just before the desired behavior is needed. Make connections with classroom expectations and rules when relevant (e.g., "Be Here, Be Ready").
4. Verbally deliver the pre-correct statement.
5. Watch the student perform the expectation or routine, then provide specific feedback.

Particularly for students with more intensive needs, pre-corrects should directly align with existing classroom expectations and rules. In addition, pre-corrects may need to be provided more frequently and target specific routines in which the student is most likely to experience challenges. For example, aim to match the frequency of precorrection with the frequency of problem behavior. Finally, although teachers may be frustrated by behaviors a student demonstrates, pre-corrects should always be delivered in a respectful manner and tone. Pre-correction statements offer an opportunity to set a student up for success even though the student may have a significant history of challenging behavior.

Choice

Providing students with choice is one of the easiest to use strategies in the classroom. Allowing students to make choices is a great preventative strategy to promote cooperation and task engagement, and reduce disruptive behaviors (Bambara et al., 1995; Kern et al., 2001; Kern et al., 1998). Providing students with opportunities to make choices enables students to more easily navigate their environment, leading to improved teacher-student interactions (Jolivette et al. 2001). Although teachers may want routines to be set ahead of time, providing students opportunities for choice within and across routines will lead to increased cooperation (see Table 7.1). Teachers who want to incorporate choice can follow these easy steps to get started:

1. Create a range of choice options you would be willing to provide students within the routines you have established in the classroom.
2. Look through the list of options prior to implementing a particular routine/procedure.
3. Decide which choices can be offered for the specified routine/procedure.
4. Decide where choice-making opportunities fit best with your routine/procedure.
5. Provide the choices as planned while implementing the routine/procedure.

Table 7.1 Examples of Embedded Choice in Routines

Area of choice	Examples	
	Elementary Routines	**Secondary Routines**
Choice of routine	Would you like to start working now and take a break after you are finished, or take a break first and then complete the task?	Would you like to take out your materials and finish on your phone until we get started with instruction, or finish on your phone and then take out materials before instruction begins?
Choice of order of routine activity/step to be completed	Would you like to first put your bookbag away or remove your coat?	Would you like to first mark yourself present or first take materials to your desk?
Choice of materials to complete routine/ expectation	Would you like to use the red pen or blue pen to complete your writing?	Would you like to participate by answering out loud or writing down your answer?
Choice of whom to work with to complete routine/expectation	Would you like to work with Johnny or Paul?	Would you like to complete the assignment with a peer or independently?
Choice of place to complete routine	Would you like to read your book at the desk or on the carpet area?	Would you like to do your work at your own desk, or at the open desk close to me?
Choice of time to complete routine	Would you like to have a snack now or wait for the next snack break?	Are you ready to submit the assignment now, or would you rather hand it in at the end of class allowing you more time?

See Table 7.1 for some examples of choices teachers can incorporate with elementary and secondary students within and across routines.

Task Analysis

When students struggle to follow a classroom routine, teachers can use task analysis to identify components of the routine that might be difficult for the student and determine where additional scaffolding is needed. Task analysis is a process of identifying specific steps required to perform a task. Using task analysis, the teacher can examine carefully how a student performs a certain routine or procedure by breaking it down into a series of observable behaviors. In this way a complex routine becomes manageable, with discrete steps that teachers can use to provide individualized, explicit instruction. To further individualize a routine and incorporate supports, the teacher can add visual aids or turn the routine into a visual schedule. Teachers can follow several simple steps when using task analysis:

1. Identify the expectation, procedure or routine that is difficult for the student.
   • E.g.: Classroom entry routine
2. Identify the prerequisite skills and materials needed to teach the task.
   • Be able to sit quietly and wait
   • Cue card to prompt student to sit quietly and wait

3. Break expectation, routine, procedure into discrete steps:
   - Come into the classroom quietly
   - Find your seat
   - Sit down
   - Take out necessary material
   - Keep hands and feet to self
   - Stay quiet and wait for teacher's directions
4. Teach the task analyzed routine by modeling each step to the student.
5. Implement routine and monitor progress.
6. Reteach each step as necessary until the student is able to independently complete the routine.

The teacher can also turn the task-analyzed routine or procedure into a tool for monitoring student progress toward independence (see Table 7.2). In addition, if age and ability levels allow, the student can learn to self-monitor their own performance of the task-analyzed skill.

Depending on the level of support a student needs to learn a routine, the teacher can use different levels of prompting such as the ones described in the example below. Prompts can be actions, gestures, verbal instructions, visuals teachers can use to support students in their learning. There is a wide range of prompting procedures from which teachers can choose depending on the level of assistance a student requires. For example, full physical prompts require physical contact from the teacher throughout the activity, such as hand over hand to help the student clean the table. Partial physical prompting requires some physical contact and assistance through part of the activity to be completed, such as gently touching the hand to nudge the student to clean the table. A verbal prompt could be a verbal reminder of the next step or activity to be completed; a visual prompt could include an image or drawing of the next step of the routine; while a gestural prompt could be the teacher pointing to the next step. Teachers should always use the least amount of prompting necessary for a student to complete a task. Over time, as the student becomes competent in completing the steps, the teacher steps back and uses the least intrusive level of prompting until the student can complete the entire routine independently.

Individualized Point Chart

Reinforcing students is often a very effective strategy to increase motivation for students who have the skill but lack the motivation or incentive to engage in the skill. This is especially true if the skill in question is a non-preferred task (i.e., complete undesired academic work) or requires a considerable

Table 7.2 Example Progress Monitoring Sheet for a Task-analyzed Morning Routine

Step of Routine	March 1st	March 2nd	March 3rd	March 4th	March 5th
Hang up bag	**Yes**/No	**Yes**/No	**Yes**/No	**Yes**/No	**Yes**/No
Take off coat	**Yes**/No	**Yes**/No	**Yes**/No	**Yes**/No	**Yes**/No
Open bag	Yes/**No**	**Yes**/No	**Yes**/No	**Yes**/No	**Yes**/No
Take out books	Yes/**No**	Yes/**No**	**Yes**/No	**Yes**/No	**Yes**/No
Close bag	Yes/**No**	Yes/**No**	Yes/**No**	**Yes**/No	**Yes**/No
Sit in desk	Yes/**No**	Yes/**No**	Yes/**No**	Yes/**No**	**Yes**/No
Total steps mastered	2/6	3/6	4/6	5/6	6/6

amount of response effort (i.e., writing a three-paragraph essay, starting with planning, drafting, and editing). Delivering reinforcement effectively can be challenging as whatever reinforces the student may not be easily accessible or deliverable to the student. For example, the student may value quality time with a peer but the task requires independent work. One effective solution to this challenge is an individualized point system that can bridge the time and logistic gap by using points as placeholders for the promise of receiving the reinforcer (Boniecki & Moore, 2003). For the student who values peer attention, the system allows the student to earn points for each step completed in the writing process until they reach a pre-established threshold where they can earn a brief fun break with their peer partner.

Many teachers already use some type of class-wide point or token system that allows all students to earn points for following the expectations or completing the routines. For students who have greater or more specific needs a teacher can intensify the use of an existing class-wide approach. For example, consider a class-wide point system that awards 1 point to students who arrive to class before the second bell rings (e.g., Be Here, Be Ready, Be Responsible). For a student who consistently struggles to make it to class at all, the point system may be intensified in a way that allows the student to earn points for demonstrations of behavior that are increasingly closer to the desired outcome. At first, the student would earn one point for showing up any time before the last 10 minutes of class. Next, the student may be further incentivized by earning more points the earlier they show up (e.g., 2 points for arriving within 15 minutes of class beginning). This approach allows the teacher to intensify an existing practice in a way that meets the student's current level of performance. In this way, teacher and student have a systematic plan for moving forward. The use of individualized point systems is appropriate for both elementary and secondary settings.

Over time, as the student develops fluency with the new skill, the intensified point system can be faded. In the example of coming to class on time, once the student consistently demonstrates arrival to class before the second bell (e.g., four out of five school days per week for two consecutive weeks), the intensified point system is no longer needed. Instead, when a specified threshold is met, the teacher can return to simply using the existing class-wide point system for all students, including the student who, for a time, needed additional support.

Problem Solving

While prevention and teaching strategies often minimize the occurrence of many problems, teachers still need to plan for responding effectively when challenging situations arise. One effective strategy is problem solving skills training (PSST), which involves a brief but structured conversation with the student after a problem has occurred (Kazdin et al., 1992). Using this approach, teacher and student (1) discuss the problem that occurred; (2) consider what to do differently; (3) brainstorm possible solutions; (4) select the best solution; and (5) put solution into practice and evaluate its success.

Like other strategies described in this chapter, problem solving can be incorporated class-wide for all students, and be intensified for students who need additional instruction or support. At the class-wide level, a teacher can directly teach a problem-solving process recognizing that many students in class could benefit from such a strategy. Teaching everyone a problem-solving strategy provides defined procedures for students to use when they do encounter a problem. Once the strategy is taught to all students, teachers can prompt for use of the strategy as issues arise.

Intensifying use of problem-solving strategies is typically triggered by a repeated problem that has not been remediated with other strategies. Teachers and/or other school professionals will actively facilitate, direct, and/or lead problem-solving conversations with the student. In fact, this more intensive approach may include a structured format that guides conversation and documentation of plans for moving forward. This additional adult assistance provided for individual students bridges a skill gap for students who have not already learned to successfully problem solve on their own. For many students, the cognitive process of problem solving (what steps to follow), as well as emotional regulation skills required during problem solving, may be new or unknown. An example format is provided in Figures 7.2 and 7.3 to support teacher and school professionals who want to adopt and use a structured problem-solving process.

Problem Solving for Success!

1. What was the problem? _____

_____
_____
_____

Somebody teased me	The noise level was too loud
Somebody told me to do something	Somebody touched/took something of mine
I did something wrong	Somebody was doing something I did not like
I lost control of my emotions	Somebody started fighting with me
I was disruptive and aggressive in class	I didn't like what someone said to me
The work was too hard	I was surprised by _____
Someone was in my personal space	Somebody was not listening to me
I was ignored	Other: (Write below)

What was the expectation?

Be Safe	Be Responsible	Be Respectful	Be a Problem Solver

2. What are some other things you could have done instead?

I could have ignored it	I could have talked it out	I could have focused on myself
I could have asked an adult for help	I could have walked away	I could have counted to 10 to calm myself
I could have talked appropriately	I could have followed the teacher's directions	I could have worked quietly
I could have helped	I could have asked to talk to someone	I could have ignored inappropriate behavior

3. What would have happened if you (insert child's choice from #2 above)?

I would have had a normal day	I would have remained in control
I would have kept things from getting worse	I would have controlled my emotions
I would have resolved the conflict	I would have gotten all my work done
I would have been safe	I would have felt better
I would have maintained a good relationship with_____	I would have been rewarded for following the rules

4. What can you do differently when you return to the (setting/activity)? What can adults do to support you? (Pick based on student response)

Child's strategy:

Adult Support:

Always end with positive praise for working through the problem
Encouragement to do better!

Figure 7.2 Example of Problem Solving for Elementary Students Correct font to Times New Roman

Date_____
Time Started_____   Time Ended_____

Staff_____
Student_____

SAMPLE PROBLEM SOLVING FORM

Student explanation of the event that took place: _____
_____

In a calm voice, tell the student "We are here because you made a choice that led to a problem. We are here to problem solve how you could have handled the situation differently."

1. What was the problem?

Somebody teased me	The noise level was too loud
Somebody told me to do something	Somebody touched/took something of mine
I did something wrong	Somebody was doing something I did not like
I lost control of my emotions	Somebody started fighting with me
I was disruptive and aggressive in class	I didn't like what someone said to me
The work was too hard	I was surprised by _____
Someone was in my personal space	Somebody was not listening to me
I was ignored	Other: (Write below)

Other: _____

2. What was the expectation?

Be safe	Be Responsible	Be Respectful

3. What are some other things you could have done instead?

I could have ignored it	I could have talked it out	I could have focused on myself
I could have asked a teacher for help	I could have walked away	I could have counted to 10 to calm myself
I could have talked appropriately	I could have followed the teacher's directions	I could have worked quietly
I could have helped	I could have asked to talk to someone	I could have ignored inappropriate behavior

Other: _____
_____

4. What would have happened if you (insert student choice from #3 above)?

I would have had a normal day	I would have remained in control
I would have kept things from getting worse	I would have controlled my emotions
I would have resolved the conflict	I would have gotten all my work done
I would have been safe	I would have felt better
I would have maintained a good relationship with_____	I would have been rewarded for following the rules

5. What can you do differently when you return to the (setting/activity)? What can your teachers/staff do to support you? (Pick based on student response)

Child's strategy:

Adult Supports:

6. Problem-solving skills consequences
   a. Give Behavior Specific Praise for completing problem solving process.
   b. Encourage student to make the best choice next time.

Student Signature_____   Adult Signature _____

Figure 7.3 Example of Problem Solving for Secondary Students Correct font to Times New Roman...as used in rest of chapter

Cultural Considerations

Another element of FCT is considering the degree to which expectations, daily routines, and practices are influenced by the teacher's own cultural background and upbringing. The way we interact with other people, show respect, ask for help, holidays and traditions we celebrate, and many other actions we engage in are dictated by our own cultural lens. This unique lens impacts how we operate our classroom, what expectations we prioritize, what procedures we create, what consequences we use. When developing classroom expectations and routines, it is the responsibility of the teacher to learn about the community, the families, and cultural histories students come from. To make connections with the varied circumstances that may be evident in any given classroom, the teacher can intentionally seek out information about family expectations, home language, or family routines. For example, when defining classroom expectations, teachers, students, and families can consider collective values that overlap among home, school, and community settings. This communal approach is particularly important at any grade level or when a new student joins a classroom. Once expectations and routines have been established, continued considerations of cultural relevance should be the norm. For example, when a student struggles to meet an expectation or follow a routine, the teacher can seek to understand whether a cultural mismatch is the potential problem. Below we recommend several variables for consideration:

- Using the FCT approach described in the chapter, examine whether a cultural mismatch serves as a setting event influencing the student's response to the teacher's expectation or prompt to follow a routine. Culture needs to be part of our conversation as culture defines the context where the expected behavior is performed or not performed. For example, if a student is resistant to follow a certain expectation such as keeping shoes on while napping in a preschool setting, a cultural expectation of always removing shoes in the house can be the cause of why the student refuses to follow the expectation for keeping shoes on while sleeping. Mixed messaging between the home and school settings can lead to the student appearing noncompliant. As another example, "Be Here and Be Ready" in school might be defined as being on time to class, before the bell rings. If a student has different expectations at home where being 5 minutes late is considered on time, the student can potentially get in trouble in school when consistently showing up to class after the bell rang. It is important for the teacher to engage in a conversation with the family and the student to understand the possible influence of culture and find a solution that fits for all involved.
- If language is a possible barrier, teachers can use visual reminders of the routines and expectations, incorporate visual aids to exemplify the steps of a routine, or translate the expectations and routines in the student's native language.
- Teachers should communicate with families being mindful of language barriers (e.g., use a translator or parent liaison as needed), using a problem-solving approach where families are recognized as experts and partners in the student's education and encouraged to provide solutions, and using I-messages. For example, a teacher could approach a family by stating *"I noticed this concern, how could we collaborate moving forward? I have lots of experience working with children but limited experience at this point working with your child. You are the experts, could you help me understand your child's strengths and your culture better, so I can embed relevant aspects into my classroom?"*

Wrap Up

In this chapter, we discussed how teachers can use the FCT framework to individualize supports for students. Using FCT along with considerations of culture, teachers are better able to select and implement strategies closely matched with student needs. When determining how to support students who continue to have social, emotional, or behavioral challenges even when effective universal supports are in place, a first step is to intensify one or more of the effective practices that are already in place. To intensify existing supports teachers can draw from a menu of strategies to:

- *prevent* problem behavior, such as pre-corrects and choice;
- explicitly *teach* pro-social behavior using task analysis;
- reinforce desired behaviors using an individualized point program that aligns with an existing class-wide system;
- respond to problem behaviors from an instructional approach using a structured problem-solving process.

For some students a simple adjustment of antecedent, behavioral, or consequence conditions will suffice to reroute the existing pattern of problem behavior. Whereas for other students, alterations within each condition may be needed to solidify prosocial behavioral patterns. Regardless of the intensity needed, thinking from a functional contextual perspective that also examines the influence of culture is an effective approach for supporting students with more intensive needs.

Tips

Despite a teacher's best efforts designed to ensure that the classroom is an organized, predictable, and supportive environment, some students will need additional support to experience success in your classroom. Once the class-wide expectations, routines, and procedures have been explicitly taught to all of the students, and consistently acknowledged, we recommend the teacher identifies, designs and implements more individualized support for students who still struggle in the classroom. Here are some tips for teachers who want to successfully implement additional supports for students:

1. Consider if the expectations, rules, routines, and procedures are contextually appropriate.
2. Think functionally and contextually. Successful identification of effective strategies relies on accurate problem identification with function, context, and culture in mind.
3. Be consistent yet flexible. If a student cannot perform or would not perform the step of a routine, are there alternative ways for the student to perform that routine? Can choice be embedded within and across the routine?

Key Resources

Video Examples

- CIBRS: Behavior Pre-Correction Video Example: www.youtube.com/watch?v=JW1yZNYWs_4
- High Leverage Practice (HLP) #7: Establish a Consistent, Organized and Respectful Learning Environment: https://youtu.be/F-y48KAijbE
- The IRIS Center Video Collection: Choice Making Elementary School Example & Non-Example: www.youtube.com/watch?v=dWN__65eoN4
- The IRIS Center Video Collection: Differentiating Instruction, 6–12, Part I: Student Choice and Multiple Modes of Learning: https://youtu.be/akvDT9KFZPw

Information Briefs and Publications

- IRIS Center Fundamental Skill Sheet: Choice Making: https://iris.peabody.vanderbilt.edu/wp-content/uploads/misc_media/fss/pdfs/2018/fss_choice_making.pdf
- National Center on Intensive Intervention: Behavior Strategies to Support Intensifying Intervention: https://intensiveintervention.org/implementation-intervention/behavior-strategies

- High Leverage Practices in Inclusive Classrooms (2nd edition) https://exceptionalchildren.org/store/books/high-leverage-practices-inclusive-classrooms-2nd-ed

Training Modules

- National Center on Intensive Interventions: https://intensiveintervention.org/training/course-content/behavior-support-intensive-intervention
- Classroom Behavior Management (Part 1): Key Concepts and Foundational Practices. https://iris.peabody.vanderbilt.edu/module/beh1/cinit/#content
- Classroom Behavior Management (Part 2, Elementary): Developing a Behavior Management Plan. https://iris.peabody.vanderbilt.edu/module/beh2_elem/#content
- Classroom Behavior Management (Part 2, Secondary): Developing a Behavior Management Plan. https://iris.peabody.vanderbilt.edu/module/beh2_sec/#content

References

Allday, A. R. (2017). Functional thinking for managing challenging behavior. *Intervention in School and Clinic, 53*, 245–51.

Bambara, L.M., Koger, F., Katzer, T., & Davenport, T. (1995). Embedding choice making in daily routine. *The Journal of the Association for Persons with Severe Disabilities, 20*, 185–95.

Boniecki, K. A., & Moore, S. (2003). Breaking the silence: Using a token economy to reinforce classroom participation. *Teaching of Psychology, 30*(3), 224–7. https://doi.org/10.1207/S15328023TOP3003_05

Ennis, R. P., Royer, D. J., Lane, K. L., & Griffith, C. E. (2017). A systematic review of precorrection in PK-12 settings. *Education and Treatment of Children, 40*(4), 465–95.

Jolivette, K., Wehby, J. H., Canale, J., & Massey, N. G. (2001). Effect of choice-making opportunities on the behavior of students with emotional and behavioral disorders. *Behavioral Disorders, 26*(2), 131–45. https://doi.org/10.1177/019874290102600203

Kazdin, A. E., Siegel, T. C., & Bass, D. (1992). Cognitive problem- solving skills training and parent management training in the treatment of antisocial behavior in children. *Journal of Consulting and Clinical Psychology, 60*(5), 733–47. http://doi.org/10.1037/0022-006X.60.5.733

Kern, L., Mantegna, M. E., Vorndran, C. M., Bailin, D., & Hilt, A. (2001). Choice of task sequence to reduce problem behaviors. *Journal of Positive Behavior Interventions, 3*(1), 3–10. https://doi.org/10.1177/109830070100300102

Kern, L., Vorndran, C. M., Hilt, A. A., Ringdahl, J. E., Adelman, B. E., & Dunlap, G. (1998). Choice as an intervention to improve behavior: A review of the literature. *Journal of Behavioral Education, 8*, 151–69.

Walker, V. L., Chung, Y. & Bonnet, L. K. (2018). Function-based interventions in inclusive school settings: A meta-analysis. *Journal of Positive Behavior Interventions, 20*, 203–216.

8
Provide Positive and Constructive Feedback to Guide Students' Behavior

Ashley Rila, PhD
University of Iowa
Sara Estrapala, PhD
University of Missouri

Introduction

Providing students with feedback is a core responsibility for teachers. Feedback is considered a low-intensity strategy (Gable et al., 2009) which can increase academic achievement and improve socially appropriate behaviors (Wisniewski et al., 2020). Delivering consistent, well-articulated feedback is considered one of the strongest predictors of student success, and scholars argue that feedback is essential for learning to occur (Hattie & Timperley, 2007). That is, a student is more likely to make academic, social, emotional, and behavioral gains if they receive effective feedback on their performance (Stronge, 2002).

Feedback is information provided to a student that they can use to improve their academic and behavioral performance. Students typically receive large amounts of feedback in a given day. Feedback can be verbal, written, or gestural, and can come from a variety of sources like general and special education teachers, administrators, support staff, peers, and books. Feedback serves to affirm or correct a demonstration of student behavior or academic knowledge. Affirmative feedback informs the student that they are correct, whereas corrective feedback informs the student that they have a flawed or inaccurate understanding (Archer & Hughes, 2011). While simple affirmative or corrective feedback may generally be useful, students are more likely to demonstrate growth when feedback includes an instructional component related to an achievable goal (Wisniewski et al., 2020). When an instructional component is included, it provides information students can use to make informed decisions in the future regarding their performance of the concept or skill. This type of feedback promotes student motivation, engagement, and independence (Stronge, 2002).

Feedback is critical for all students, regardless of age, ability, or background. The way feedback is delivered can have a variety of effects on student motivation and performance. For example, positively stated, behavior-focused feedback can improve academic performance and enhance student self-worth, whereas overtly harsh or critical feedback can cause emotional distress and decrease motivation (Harbour et al., 2015). Thus, it is imperative for teachers to understand how to provide students with high-quality, instructional feedback to promote academic, social, emotional, and behavioral growth. Specifically, feedback should be timely, outcome focused, positive, individualized, and constructive (Jenkins et al., 2015).

DOI: 10.4324/9781003276876-12

Narrowing the Focus

Feedback is a broad concept and therefore we narrow the focus of this chapter on the essential aspects of instructional feedback to enhance student learning and promote socially appropriate behavior. Specifically, we will describe (a) the essential components for delivering effective feedback; (b) methods for delivering feedback equitably and in a culturally responsive manner; and (c) strategies for intensifying feedback.

Chapter Overview

1. Describe essential components of effective, instructional feedback: timely, outcome focused, positive, individualized, and constructive.
2. Describe how to deliver feedback equitability and in a culturally responsive manner.
3. Describe strategies to intensify feedback for students who struggle academically or behaviorally.

Using the HLP: What Are the Essential Components of Quality Feedback?

Timely

First, effective feedback must be timely. It is best practice for teachers to provide students with feedback immediately following their performance. Immediately providing students with feedback is especially important when correcting misconceptions or inappropriate behaviors. When teachers provide immediate feedback to correct student behavior it reduces the number of times the student will practice the behavior incorrectly. The more times a student practices a skill incorrectly, the more difficult it can be for the behavior to be corrected. Thus, the immediacy of feedback is important to improve outcomes (Archer & Hughes, 2011). However, providing immediate feedback to students every time they perform an error may not be feasible. Teachers may be working with other students, the student may not be near the teacher when the error occurred, or the error may have occurred on a homework assignment. If immediately providing feedback is not possible, teachers should provide feedback as soon as they are made aware of the error and when the teacher is able.

Relatedly, when students are first learning new concepts or skills, providing students with continuous feedback on their performance is necessary to help ensure students learn the skill or concept correctly (Cooper et al., 2020). This means that when introducing a new concept, the teacher should provide numerous opportunities for the student to engage and practice the skill. When students are engaged in these learning opportunities, the teacher must pay close attention to their students' performance and provide them with continuous feedback. Continuous feedback means that the teacher provides feedback after every opportunity the student has practiced the skill. In a classroom with numerous students learning the new concept, this feedback can be delivered to a group so long as the feedback represents how *all* students in the group are performing. Once students have demonstrated skill accuracy, the teacher can reduce the amount of feedback to an intermittent schedule. Meaning, the teacher provides feedback to students occasionally. Intermittent schedules of feedback are one of the most powerful schedules of feedback to ensure student behaviors continue at mastery levels (Cooper et al., 2020). Figure 8.1 depicts approximately how much feedback a teacher should provide based on the novelty of the skill being learned.

Outcome Focused

Second, effective feedback must be outcome focused. To be outcome focused, the feedback statement must follow instruction, and include a direct link between how the student performed related to the desired academic or behavioral outcome. When feedback is outcome focused, it provides the student

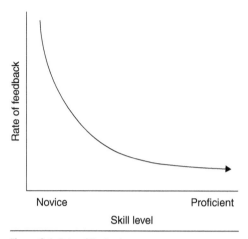

Figure 8.1 Rates of Feedback

with useful information on how they should proceed toward the desired outcome or goal. That is, has the student met the goal and can move on, or has the student not met the goal and must continue adjusting their performance to meet the goal? The goal will differ based on the learning activity, student developmental level, or behavioral expectation. Goals can also be individualized for specific student needs, such as a student who over-participates in class, frequently forgets to bring their assistive technology device to class, or has specific instructional needs described in their individualized education program (IEP). Regardless of the domain, feedback that is outcome focused is an ongoing process. Students should continue receiving feedback until they have reached the goal. For example, if all students are to line up quietly by the door before going to lunch, all feedback should relate explicitly to components of this goal. The teacher might provide affirmative feedback related to this goal, such as, "Great job Priscilla for standing in line quietly, and holding your lunchbox at your side." This goal-oriented feedback also provides a reminder of the behavioral expectation for students who have not yet achieved the goal.

When students have a gap in their understanding, they need outcome focused feedback. This feedback will inform them that they have not achieved the goal and that they need to adjustment their performance to improve their academic skill or socially appropriate behaviors (Hatti & Timperley, 2007). If the desired outcome is for students to be prepared for small group instruction, and a student displays a gap in their performance, the outcome focused, corrective feedback may sound like this:

> Rubye, thank you for coming to group on-time. Remember our expectations are for you to be prepared for group and you are missing a couple items. Please look at the poster of what you need to have at your seat to be prepared and go grab your materials.
>
> [Teacher provides affirmative feedback when Rubye comes back with appropriate materials.]

When a student does not have a gap in their understanding or performance, outcome focused feedback is essential initially because it informs the student that they have an accurate understanding of the goal. Once students have demonstrated mastery and they have received effective feedback, students know they then can move on to new goals. If the desired outcome is for a student to correctly set up a multidigit math calculation problem and the student performed the skill correctly, the outcome focused, affirmative feedback may sound like this:

Nice job setting up your math problem correctly, Juan. You aligned all the ones in the one's column and all the tens in the ten's column. Now, you are ready to find the solution. Use your reference sheet to solve this problem starting with step 2.

[Teacher then provides effective feedback on the new goal—correctly solving the problem.]

Positive

Third, effective student feedback must be positive. Positive feedback is multidimensional. First, feedback is positive when the statement is respectful and genuine. Respectful means that the statement is considerate of the student receiving the feedback and provides encouragement. Genuine means the statement is sincere and avoids condescending or sarcastic tones. Although the intent may be encouragement, statements that compare the student's performance to their previous performance (e.g., "You did this last week, I know you can do it.") or to the performance of a peer (e.g., "Shaun's already halfway done, see if you can beat him.") should be avoided. Comparative statements can demotivate a student from engaging in a task, particularly for students who struggle behaviorally or academically (Covington, 2000).

Second, positive feedback describes what the student should be doing rather than what they should not be doing. Centering the feedback on what students should be doing helps students focus their attention on the desirable behavior. Which then can lead to increases in student performance (Simonsen & Myers, 2015). For example, a teacher may say "Remember respect is one of our classroom expectations. During whole group instruction, that means we listen with our voices off, unless it's your turn, so everyone can learn together," rather than saying "no talking."

Third, positive feedback is process-centered and not person-centered. Processed-center feedback focuses on the specific behaviors the student performed. Person-centered statements focus on the student themselves and should be avoided as they are seldom effective. Person-centered statements such as, "you're so smart," or, "wow, you're so creative," have been found to decrease student motivation and persistence on a difficult task (Black & Wiliam, 1998). Instead, process-centered statements focus on the student progress such as "nice job using the distributive property strategies to solve that problem" or "the words you used in your story to describe the characters, captured my attention."

Finally, students should receive more positive feedback than negative, or corrective, feedback. Some experts recommend a positive to negative ratio of 3:1 or 4:1 (Scott et al., 2011). This recommended ratio applies to the individual receiving the feedback, and not to the overall feedback the teacher provides to all students. If a teacher provides an overall high ratio of positive to negative feedback, but they provide higher rates of positive feedback to a few students and predominately negative feedback to others, then the teacher is not meeting the recommended ratio. In which case, the teacher should provide more positive feedback to the students who were receiving predominately negative feedback. Teachers may consider collecting data on the number of positive and negative feedback statements they provide and to whom they were delivered (see self-monitoring below).

Individualized

Fourth, effective feedback is individualized. For feedback to be individualized, teachers must get to know individual student preferences on how they want to receive feedback. Some students may respond to feedback in different ways. Remember, the goal of effective feedback is for students to use the information to improve skills and delivering feedback to students in ways they do not prefer may be counterproductive. It is possible some students may feel embarrassed when they receive feedback publicly where it can be overheard. In this situation, these students may become uncomfortable and avoid the behavior which prompted the feedback, resulting in lower achievement (Hattie, 2009). The best way to get to know individual preferences is to ask students. Then, teachers should use this

1. Is it acceptable for a teacher to give you positive feedback out loud in front of other students?
_____ Yes _____ No

2. Is it acceptable for a teacher to give you positive feedback so only you know (verbal or written)?
_____ Yes _____ No

3. Is it acceptable for a teacher to provide you with a correction out loud in front of other students?
_____ Yes _____ No

4. Is it acceptable for a teacher to provide you with a correction so only you know (verbal or written)?
_____ Yes _____ No

5. I prefer when my teacher provides me with:
_____Feedback that is group focused
_____Feedback that is individual focused
_____Both group and individual focused

6. Is it acceptable for a teacher to communicate to your parent or caregiver when you are doing well in school?
_____ Yes _____ No

7. Is it acceptable for a teacher to communicate to your parent or caregiver when you are not doing well in school?
_____ Yes _____ No

8. Is it acceptable for your classmates to give you positive feedback about your work?
_____ Yes _____ No

9. Is it acceptable for your classmates to give you corrective feedback about your work?
_____ Yes _____ No

10. Is there anything else you would like me to know about providing you with positive or corrective feedback?

Figure 8.2 Student Preference Questions

Note: Adapted from Fefer et al. (2015).

information and strive to provide students with feedback in their preferred way. Figure 8.2 includes some possible questions to ask students (adapted from Fefer et al., 2015). Teachers are encouraged to add additional questions or adjust the options to fit their classroom needs. If teachers decide to have classmates provide one another feedback (as seen in one of the options in Figure 8.2), it is essential for teachers to instruct students on how to provide one another with effective feedback.

Constructive

Finally, effective feedback must be constructive. To be constructive, feedback must provide the student with information to support the mastery achievement of the goal. This information can include suggestions or guidance the student can use to independently correct their errors or misconceptions. A teacher may refer the student to a resource such as class notes, an example in a textbook, or a poster on the classroom wall. Constructive feedback may also focus on a specific area where the error occurred, such as the second sentence in the paragraph. When provided with this information, students have a better understanding of how to adjust their performance independently and leading to sustained, improved outcomes (Hatti & Timperley, 2007).

When a performance gap exists, constructive feedback should allow the student to identify and correct their error independently, as opposed to teachers providing the correct answer. Students independently correcting their misconceptions promotes self-evaluation and motivation to continue working on the task (Hattie, 2009). If the intended outcome is for students to write a complete sentence and a student has written an incomplete sentence, constructive feedback may sound this:

> Ayra, you're close to writing a complete sentence. You have appropriate spacing and capitalized the proper noun. Go back to the example we did together and pay attention to the beginning and end of the sentence to see if you can correct the errors to make a complete sentence.
>
> [Teacher provides affirmative feedback when Ayra corrects the errors to create a complete sentence.]

Providing constructive feedback to a student who has accurately performed a goal, again, is necessary initially. It provides the student with information about why and how they obtained mastery. Students knowing the how and why they obtained mastery is necessary so they know the specific behaviors they can continue using to maintain performance mastery. This feedback can be particularly beneficial for students who have previously struggled to demonstrate content mastery. If the desired outcome is for students to be safe while entering the classroom, the constructive feedback may sound like this: "Remi, thank you for using your walking feet while keeping your hands to yourself. You showed how to be safe when entering the classroom. Keep up the good work!" This statement is helpful for Remi, who previously struggled with safety, as it affirms that he mastered the goal of entering the classroom safely and tells him exactly how he demonstrated mastery.

In summary, effective feedback includes five component parts. Effective feedback must be timely, outcome focused, positive, individualized, and constructive. To conclude this section, we provide you with a table (Table 8.1) of examples and non-examples of effective feedback.

How to Deliver Feedback Equitably and in a Culturally Responsive Manner?

Culturally responsive teaching means that *all* students receive an education that reflects and respects their individual culture, identity, and beliefs, and that it is essential for *all* students to "experience academic success" (Ladson-Billings, 1995). This means that *all* students must receive effective feedback, since effective feedback is essential to student learning. Given that minoritized students such as students of color, students who are LGTBQ+, or students with disabilities experience dismal school outcomes (Demie, 2022; Robinson & Espelage, 2011; Wang et al., 2018), it is essential for these populations of students to receive high rates of effective feedback. However, research indicates that minoritized students often receive lower rates of effect feedback than their counterparts (Scott et al., 2019). Thus, it is imperative for teachers to equitably provide feedback to all students, regardless of race, ethnicity, sexuality, or disability status. In the following section, we highlight two specific aspects of essential feedback which promote culturally relevant teaching and providing equitable feedback across student populations: **promoting high expectations** and **individualization** (Eriksson et al., 2020; Wang et al., 2018).

First, teachers must hold *all* students to **high expectations**, especially when feedback is outcome focused, and most importantly when working with minoritized students. Unfortunately, research indicates that teachers of minoritized students have lower expectations that result in reduced achievement (Wang et al., 2018). Thus, to be culturally responsive, teachers need to believe *all* students can achieve at high levels and provide *all* students with outcome focused feedback that

Table 8.1 Examples and Non-examples

Component	Type	Non-example	Example
Academic Feedback			
Outcome focused	Affirmative	Excellent.	Excellent Jing! <u>You wrote a capital letter J</u>. You started at the top, then went down and around to the middle, and put a line on top. <u>That is a capital J.</u>
	Corrective	Work harder.	Class, remember to <u>turn in a complete draft of your paper by the end of the class. Your paper needs to include all paragraphs which are an introduction, three supporting paragraphs, and a conclusion.</u>
Constructive	Affirmative	You're so smart!	Jonah, you are completing great work. You have <u>created a correct map of the United States with the correct states and capitals.</u>
	Corrective	Your paragraph is not long enough.	Ahmed, a complete paragraph needs to have at least 5 sentences. <u>Come up with one more detail sentence that supports your topic sentence to add in</u> to make a complete paragraph.
Positive	Affirmative	A+ work!	<u>I like how you are showed your work</u> on this division problem <u>you are correctly using all the steps</u> we learned today.
	Corrective	Nope.	<u>You are on the right page</u> to find the answer. Look at the second column.
Timely	Affirmative	*Note delivered after one month.*	Sam's solar system model is an excellent representation of how the planets, sun, and moons are in our galaxy. You should be proud. [*<u>Email sent to Sam's parents the day after the Science Fair</u>.*]
	Corrective	Not quite.	You set your problem up correctly but let's look back at our notes starting with step two to see if we can spot the error in your solution together. [*<u>Feedback provided immediately after teacher spotted the error</u>.*]
Individualized	Affirmative	*High five.*	Great job, <u>Violetta</u>, on your short story. I enjoyed reading the vivid description of the enchanted forest. [*<u>Written note to honor student preference</u>.*]
	Corrective	No. Pay more attention.	I can see why you think the answer is Marxism, but take another look at the first paragraph on page 43. See if you can find a different answer. [*<u>Feedback provided privately in one-on-one conversation to honor student preference</u>.*]
Behavioral Feedback			
Outcome focused	Affirmative	Jose, you're such a good kid.	Jose, I noticed you invited Ellen to read with you during partner reading time. Thank you for showing the class <u>how to be cooperative!</u>
	Corrective	No running!	Remember class, the <u>expectation is to be safe in the hallway with walking feet. Show me your walking feet.</u>

Table 8.1 Cont.

Component	Type	Non-example	Example
Behavioral Feedback			
Constructive	Affirmative	Nice work!	Tim, thank you for putting the caps on each of the markers before you put them away!
	Corrective	Go to the office.	Sam I need you to be safe right now by having all six feet on the floor, four chair feet and your two feet.
Positive	Affirmative	*Thumbs up to class.*	Class, excellent job quietly lining up at the door! Way to show how to be responsible fifth graders!
	Corrective	*Glare at Team Blue.*	Team Blue, thank you for being in the appropriate location to work on your project. The expectation is for you to be on-task with cell phones put away.
Timely	Affirmative	Thank you.	Thank you for putting your library book away when asked. [*Feedback provided right after student put book away after morning silent reading*.]
	Corrective	Stop that!	Sarah, our expectation is to respect our peers with our hands to ourselves. Look at our expectations poster and show me where your hands go. [*Feedback provided immediately after teacher saw Sarah's hands on peer*.]
Individualized	Affirmative	*Gold star.*	Maria, thank you for being kind to Sam when you helped him pick up his books. Here is a gold star for being kind.
	Corrective	*Head shake.*	Table 1, make sure you are working together and listening to one another. [*Group feedback when one student who prefers group feedback was not meeting expectations*.]

Note: Italics represent actions. Underlines highlight specific feedback component.

supports high achievement. Teachers who struggle to equitably distribute outcome focused feedback across all students might benefit from a simple intervention (described below).

The second component to highlight is **individualized**. Teachers must take time to get to know their students individually. Students will come from a host of backgrounds that shape their values, performances, and how they interact with their environments. Some students may come from cultures that promote the collective progress of a larger group and calling out individual performances may not be helpful (Knochel et al., 2021). Whereas others may come from cultures that may prefer individually calling attention to their specific progress (Hammond, 2015). As mentioned previously, teacher feedback is essential to promote student achievement. If teachers deliver feedback to students in ways in which they feel embarrassed or alienated, the feedback may be counterintuitive to student progress. One study found that when teachers in Ghana provided individual students with affirmative feedback student engagement decreased, but engagement increased when the teachers altered their feedback to be group focused (Knochel et al., 2021), which improved student outcomes.

Feedback can be delivered in numerous ways (public, private, group-based, individual-based, etc.) and not all students may respond well to certain types of feedback. The questions outlined in Figure 8.2 is one tool a teacher can use to learn which types of feedback a student may response best to. As mentioned above, minoritized students often experience poorer academic outcomes, thus, these students may need intensified feedback to help close the achievement gap. This too requires teachers to learn about their students to identify possible achievement gaps in addition to their students' feedback preferences. Thus, to be culturally responsive, teachers need to get to know their students' individual preferences and learning histories to provide all students with feedback in a way that will promote achievement.

How to Intensify Feedback?

Students who struggle academically or behaviorally may benefit from intensified feedback prior to referral for more intensive interventions. Whether the student is struggling because their teacher is delivering less than optimal rates of effective feedback, or the student needs more feedback, teachers should implement a simple strategy to increase the delivery rate and quality of the feedback they provide. First, the teacher should consider increasing the frequency and specificity of the feedback, with respect to the student's individual needs, using the essential components described above. If a teacher continues to struggle to provide quality feedback with increased intensity, the following strategies can be applied, individually or in combination with one another, to support teachers in increasing effective feedback for both class-wide and individual student needs.

Visual Cues

Placing visual cues is one simple strategy teachers can use to intensify effective feedback. A visual cue serves as a reminder for the teacher to deliver feedback. A simple visual cue has been found to be an effective intervention used to increase behaviors across multiple disciplines (Geller et al., 1973; Ford et al., 2014; Meis & Kashima, 2017). A visual cue can be a short, written note in the margin of a lesson plan or on a sticky note, or a detailed poster placed on walls throughout the classroom. To aid in providing students with all components of effective feedback, teachers are encouraged to use the TOPIC acronym, as seen in Figure 8.3. Each letter in the acronym represents the five component parts of effective feedback: timely, outcome focused, positive, individualized, and constructive. When writing a visual cue, the note could say "deliver TOPIC feedback." Teachers are encouraged to use numerous types of visual cues throughout their classroom and lesson plans. The more times a teacher sees a visual cue, the more likely it is that the teacher will deliver effective feedback to students.

T	**Timely** • Immediately delivered after student performance
O	**Outcome Focused** • Links performance to learning or behavioral goal
P	**Positive** • Focuses on success, respectful, and genuine
I	**Individualized** • Student preferences taken into account
C	**Constructive** • Guides students to continue performance or correct errors

Figure 8.3 Visual Cue of Components for Effective Instruction

Regardless of the visual cues used, the visual cue needs to be strategically placed. Strategic placement of the visual cue would be in an area the teacher frequently sees when they deliver a lesson. When selecting a placement, teachers may select an area to post the visual cue where they teach students struggling academically or in a place where they deliver less than optimal rates of feedback. If a teacher frequently delivers small group instruction at a kidney-shaped table, posting a visual cue in front of the teacher's seat would be an example of a strategic placement, since the teacher frequently sees this spot when instructing. If a teacher frequently delivers whole group lessons using a whiteboard in front of the class, a TOPIC poster (Figure 8.3) could be hung on the whiteboard or on an adjacent bulletin board where the teacher can easily see the poster throughout the lesson. When placed in visible areas, the teacher can easily reference the cue if they need a reminder of the component parts of effective feedback.

Another strategic placement of a visual cue would be within a lesson plan or a scripted curriculum, placed at integral points of student learning. If the lesson asks for students to practice a newly learned skill, the visual cue, such as a note in the margin or on a sticky note, should be placed at the point where the teacher asks students to practice the skill. At which point, the teacher monitors students' accuracy of their skill performance and provides them with effective feedback. If using a scaffolded teaching approach (i.e., I do [teacher models skill], we do [students practice skill with teacher supports], you do [students practice skill independently]; Archer & Hughes, 2011), a visual cue would be included in the lesson where the students are asked to practice the skill with teacher guidance (i.e., we do) as well as when the teacher releases students to practice the skill independently (i.e., you do). Additionally, teachers could strategically place a visual cue in the lesson plan where they anticipate students to perform poorly. If students have had a break from engaging in an activity such as lab experiments, centers, or partner work, or the students have demonstrated a pattern of not meeting expectations, or assessments (formative or summative) indicate students have an inaccurate understanding, the teacher should include a visual cue in the lesson when the students transition to the activity to engage in the setting or with the skill.

Audio and Tactile Prompts

Another simple strategy for teachers to use to increase their delivery of effective feedback is through audio or tactile prompting. Research has found audio and tactical prompting can increase the rates of evidence-based teacher practices (Markelz et al., 2019). An audio prompt is a prompt a teacher hears, like a chime or ringer. A tactile prompt is something the teacher feels, such as a vibration on the wrist. Teachers can use prompting mechanisms individually or in conjunction with one another like a vibrating ringer. Regardless of the mechanism, when the prompt is activated the prompt serves as a reminder for the teacher to deliver effective feedback.

Prior to using a prompting system, the teacher needs to determine when they will use the device. Often, teachers will select the time of day where they deliver low rates of effective feedback or a time of day where students may struggle. Initially, teachers should select only one, short period (e.g., math instruction) to implement a prompting system. Then, after the teacher becomes familiar and comfortable with the process, they can increase the length of time they use the prompting system (e.g., math instruction and student math seatwork) or add in another time of day (e.g., math and reading instruction). Second, the teacher needs to determine the amount of time they want to lapse between each prompt (e.g., 3 min, 5 min, 10 min). This amount of time is going to depend on the novelty of the student skill, student performance, and the types of activities the teacher will be doing. The more novel the skill and poorer student performance, the more effective feedback the teacher needs to deliver, consequently, the shorter the interval a teacher may select. See Figure 8.1 for how much feedback should be delivered based on skill novelty. However, teachers should take into consideration the types of activities they will be doing during this time. If the teacher is delivering whole group math instruction, a prompting device alerting the teacher every 3 minutes may be disruptive to the flow of instruction and therefore the teacher may consider the device to go off every 5 minutes.

Remember, when setting up a prompting system, the more often effective feedback is delivered, the faster students will master content.

A variety of prompting devices exist that include a range of features. A simple and cost-effective prompting device is a kitchen timer. With a kitchen timer, the teacher manually sets the timer, hits start, delivers effective feedback when the timer sounds, and then manually restarts the timer to be alerted for another prompt. Remembering to reset the timer manually can easily be forgotten given the large number of demands a classroom teacher has at any given point in the day. Therefore, using an interval timer that automatically resets after the alarm is sounded can be beneficial. Numerous physical and app-based interval timers exist that include a variety of features, such as options for both auditory and tactile prompting to trigger simultaneously (e.g., Gymboss [physical timer]), programming when the interval timer will stop going off (e.g., after 60 min) or adding in a visual, light reminder when the timer lapses (e.g., Time Tracker [physical timer]), or features allowing a teacher to self-monitor implementation (e.g., Be Positive [BE+] app). A common style of interval times are applications that teachers can download to a smart device (e.g., smartphone, table, smartwatch, smartboard) that can be free or require payment. When determining which application to download, teachers are encouraged to assess the types of technology they have readily available. If the teacher regularly uses a smartphone for a token economy or student response system, downloading an interval timer application onto the same smartphone may be a viable option. If a smart device is not available or will not mesh well with the teaching style, physical interval timers are also available (e.g., Gymboss, MotivAider, Time Tracker). Regardless of the type of interval timer, the teacher will set the length of time they want to lapse between each prompt, deliver effective feedback when prompted, and then continue this cycle until the teacher stops the timer or the pre-programmed amount of time has lapsed.

Self-monitoring

Related to a prompting system, another strategy for teachers to use to increase their rates of effective feedback is self-monitoring. Self-monitoring is the act of an individual observing and recording a particular behavior at a given time. Research has shown that self-monitoring can increase desired behaviors while reducing undesired behaviors for both students and teachers (Simonsen et al., 2014). Self-monitoring can help teachers increase their delivery rates of effective feedback by developing a simple self-monitoring plan whereby they count the number of times they deliver feedback during a given timeframe. First, the teacher needs to select a specific activity or time of day to self-monitor. Teachers may select the most problematic time of day, either when they struggle to provide effective feedback or when a particular student or group of students struggles the most. Second, teachers create a simple self-monitoring form where they track their data (see Figure 8.4). Third, the teacher begins tracking their feedback statements for 2–3 days to establish a baseline average, or the number of feedback statements they give on a typical day. Fourth, using their baseline data, teachers write an appropriate goal for increasing the rate in which they provide feedback. Although there is no consensus on how many feedback statements are ideal, teachers could try increasing their goal by one or two statements per day until they notice a change in student performance. To help teachers review their performance, they graph their data daily.

This type of self-monitoring can improve feedback delivery in a couple of ways. First, teachers will concentrate on delivering feedback during a time when it is needed most. Second, they will have a record of their feedback delivery rates with their self-monitoring data. Teachers can then use these data to determine whether their delivery rates have improved.

At-Home Caregiver Involvement

Many academic and behavior interventions use home caregiver involvement to increase student learning or appropriate behaviors, and many of these interventions include providing feedback. For

Mr. Bradford's Self-Monitoring Form

Setting: Reading Rotations (10:00–10:30)
Behavior: Effective feedback—outcome focused, constructive, timely, positive, individualized

Directions: Mark a tally in today's row every time you deliver effective feedback. Total your feedback statements for the day and determine whether you met your daily goal.

Goal: 15 effective feedback statements

Date	Statements	Total	Did I meet my goal?	
4/3/22	|||||||||||||||||	16	(Yes)	No
4/4/22	|||||||||||	11	Yes	(No)
4/5/22	|||||||||||||||||||||||||	25	(Yes)	No
			Yes	No
			Yes	No
			Yes	No

Figure 8.4 Self-monitoring Form

example, Check-In/Check-Out (CICO; Hawken et al., 2020) is an evidence-based behavior intervention where students receive structured feedback throughout the day from their teachers, and teachers structure this feedback using a daily progress report. Specifically, teachers rate the student on behavioral expectations, provide feedback to the student about their ratings, and the student takes this daily progress report home to review with their parents or caregiver. Then, at home, parents can see how their student is performing at school and provide them with additional feedback. Although CICO is a Tier 2 intervention, teachers can implement components from this intervention to (a) communicate home regarding student academic and behavioral performance and (b) provide an opportunity for parents/caregivers to deliver effective feedback. That is, teachers could regularly schedule communication home via email, text message, or phone calls to relay student progress, and ask that parents talk about this progress with their student. This also provides an opportunity for parents to receive increased communication about the student's performance more frequently than quarterly report cards.

Wrap Up

Providing students with regular effective feedback is an evidence-based practice shown to improve student outcomes. Teachers should ensure they are providing all students with timely, outcome focused, positive, individualized, and constructive feedback. Providing students with effective feedback is a culturally relevant practice when teachers provide feedback that is individualized and with high expectations. When students struggle to meet behavioral or academic expectations, or when a teacher delivers low rates of feedback, teachers should implement a simple strategy to increase their rates of effective feedback they provide to students.

Tips

- Provide all students with timely, outcome focused, positive, individualized, and constructive feedback.
- Practice incorporating all components of effective feedback.
- Use effective feedback for both behavioral and academic domains.

- Deliver a rich schedule of effective feedback when students are learning a new skill and thin to an intermittent schedule after the skill is mastered.
- Implement simple strategies to increase the delivery of effective feedback.

Key Resources

- https://iris.peabody.vanderbilt.edu/wp-content/uploads/misc_media/fss/pdfs/2018/fss_behaviro_specific_praise.pdf
- https://highleveragepractices.org/hlps-8-and-22-provide-positive-and-constructive-feedback-guide-students-learning-and-behavior
- https://pbismissouri.org/media/educators-blueprint-podcast/
- www.pbis.org/resource/supporting-and-responding-to-behavior-evidence-based-classroom-strategies-for-teachers

References

Archer, A., & Hughes, C. A. (2011). *Explicit instruction: Effective and efficient teaching.* Guilford Press.

Black, P., & William, D. (1998). Assessment and classroom learning. *Assessment in Education: Principles, Policy & Practice, 5*(1), 7–74. https://doi.org/10.1080/0969595980050102

Cooper, J. O., Heron, T. E., & Heward, W. L. (2020). *Applied behavior analysis* (3rd ed.). Pearson Education.

Covington, M. V. (2000). Goal theory, motivation, and school achievement: An integrative review. *Annual Review of Psychology, 51*, 171–200. https://doi.org/10.1146/annurev.psych.51.1.171

Demie, F. (2022). Tackling teachers' low expectations of Black Caribbean students in English schools. *Equity in Education & Society, 1.* https://doi.org/10.1177/27526461211068511

Eriksson, K., Lindvall, J., Helenius, O., & Ryve, A. (2020). Cultural variations in the effectiveness of feedback on students' mistakes. *Frontiers in Psychology, 10.* https://doi.org/10.3389/fpsyg.2019.03053

Fefer, S. A. (2015). *Adolescent praise preference survey* (Unpublished measure). University of Massachusetts.

Ford, E., Boyer, B., Menachemi, N., & Huerta, T. (2014). Increasing hand washing compliance with a simple visual cue. *American Journal of Public Health, 104*(10), 1851–56.

Gable, R. A., Hester, P. H., Rock, M. L., & Hughes, K. G. (2009). Back to basics: Rules, praise, ignoring, and reprimands revisited. *Intervention in School and Clinic, 44*, 195–205. https://doi.org/10.1177/1053451208328831

Geller, E., Farris, J., & Post, D.(1973). Prompting a consumer behavior for pollution control. *Journal of Applied Behavior Analysis, 6*, 367–76. https://doi.org/b9xbqr

Hammond, Z. (2015). *Culturally responsive teaching and the brain: Promoting authentic engagement and rigor among culturally and linguistically diverse students.* Corwin.

Harbour, K. E., Evanovich, L. L., Sweigart, C. A., & Hughes, L. E. (2015). A brief review of effective teaching practices that maximize student engagement. *Preventing School Failure, 59*, 5–13. https://doi.org/10.1080/1045988X.2014.919136

Hattie, J. (2009). *Visible learning: A synthesis of over 800 meta-analyses relating to achievement.* Routledge.

Hattie, J., & Timperley, H. (2007). The power of feedback. *Review of Educational Research, 77*(1), 81–112. https://doi.org/10.3102/003465430298487

Hawken, L. S., Crone, D. A., Bundock, K., & Horner, R. H. (2020). *Responding to problem behavior in schools.* Guilford Press.

Jenkins, L., Floress, M., & Reinke, W. (2015). Rates and types of teacher praise: A review and future directions. *Psychology in the Schools, 52*(5), 463–76. https://doi.org/f68mtp

Knochel, A. E., Blair, K. C., & Sofarelli, R. (2021). Culturally focused classroom staff training to increase praise for students with autism spectrum disorder in Ghana. *Journal of Positive Behavior Interventions, 23,* 106–17. https://doi.org/10.1177/1098300720929351

Ladson-Billings, G. (1995). But that's just good teaching! The case for culturally relevant pedagogy. *Theory Into Practice, 34,* 159–65, https://doi.org/c7gt92

Markelz, A., Scheeler, M. C., Riccomini, P., & Taylor, J. C. (2019). A systematic review of tactile prompting in teacher education. *Teacher Education and Special Education, 43*(4). https://doi.org/10.1177/0888406419877500

Meis, J., & Kashima, Y. (2017). Signage as a tool for behavioral change: Direct and indirect routes to understanding the meaning of a sign. *PloS one, 12*(8). https://doi.org/gbtb7f

Robinson, J. P., & Espelage, D. L. (2011). Inequities in educational and psychological outcomes between LGBTQ and straight students in middle and high school. *Educational Researcher, 40*(7), 315–30. https://doi.org/10.3102/0013189X11422112

Scott, T. M., Alter, P. J., & Hirn, R. G. (2011). An examination of typical classroom context in instruction for students with and without behavioral disorders. *Education and Treatment of Children, 2011,* 619–41. https://doi.org/10.1353/etc.2011.0039

Scott, T. M., Gage, N., Hirn, R., & Han, H. (2019). Teacher and student race as a predictor for negative feedback during instruction. *School Psychology, 34*(1), 22. http://dx.doi.org/10.1037/spq0000251

Simonsen, B., MacSuga-Gage, A. S., Briere, D. E., Freeman, J., Myers, D., Scott, T. M., & Sugai, G. (2014). Multitiered support framework for teachers' classroom-management practices: Overview and case study of building the triangle for teachers. *Journal of Positive Behavior Interventions, 16,* 179–90. https://doi.org/10.1177/1098300713484062

Simonsen, B., & Myers, D. (2015). *Classwide positive behavior interventions and supports: A guide to proactive classroom management.* Guilford Press.

Stronge, J. H. (2002). *Qualities of effective teachers.* Association for Supervision and Curriculum Development.

Wang, S., Rubie-Davies, C. M., & Meissel, K. (2018). A systematic review of the teacher expectation literature over the past 30 years. *Educational Research and Evaluation, 24.* https://doi.org/10.1080/13803611.2018.1548798

Wisniewski, B., Zierer, K., & Hattie, J. (2020). The power of feedback revisited: A meta-analysis of educational feedback research. *Frontiers in Psychology, 10.* https://doi.org/ggk3gb

9
Teach Social Behaviors

Terrance M. Scott
University of Louisville

Introduction

When queried, every teacher can name students whose chronic and intense bickering, name calling, extreme shyness, inability to share, physical aggression, and/or withdrawal has disrupted their ability to form and maintain positive peer relationships. Reported by teachers to be among their greatest challenges, these most challenging students can be characterized as displaying deficits in social competence. That is, when interacting with others, they have deficits in terms of the critical skills that typically predict positive social outcomes. While social skills is often captured under the more global term of social-emotional learning (e.g., Collaborative for Academics, Emotional, and Social Learning (CASEL), 2021), the teaching of social skills using the tenets of effective instruction has been identified as a high-leverage practice.

Though supported inclusion should be a goal, simply placing these children with social deficits in typical school settings will not be sufficient to foster appropriate behaviors (Colvin & Scott, 2015). These children require instruction in appropriate social behaviors which, when practiced in combination with training, will facilitate positive interaction with peers. In response to these concerns, several curricular programs are commercially available for training social skills. However, such programs often suffer from three distinct shortcomings. First, teachers are often hesitant to address these problems, citing lack of training, difficulty with curriculum set-up, and associated logistical concerns (American Psychological Association, 2006). Second, commercially available programs are generally not tailored to the specific and unique social skills issues affecting students with identified deficits (McDaniel et al., 2021). To be effective, social skills instruction must teach functional replacement behaviors that fit the culture, age, and norms of the environments in which they are expected to be used (Colvin & Scott, 2015). Third, evidence generally supports the notion that, in the absence of specific programming strategies, social behaviors do not generalize from training to other settings or circumstances (Gunning et al., 2019).

Narrowing the Focus

While challenging, these shortcomings can be overcome with thoughtful planning to increase the likelihood of success. The focus of this chapter is on the planning, development, and delivery of

DOI: 10.4324/9781003276876-13

specific social skills instruction to students with more intensive needs. As we consider students with more intense and individualized needs, it's important to acknowledge the necessity of multi-tiered systems and the necessity of additional supports for some students. While effective social skills instruction for all students at tier 1 is critical, this broad level of instruction will likely be insufficient to meaningfully affect those students with larger deficits. These students will require instruction to be more explicit, more direct, and to offer more opportunities for practice with teacher feedback. Because social skills are by nature interactive, it makes sense that students with more intense needs be taught in small groups.

The concept of "skill deficits" connotes a need for instruction. For any given student, a social skills deficit may be the result of skill deficits such as unfamiliarity (i.e., doesn't know how) or a lack of fluency (i.e., forgets). However, some deficits may be more performance in nature in which the student knows how but prefers another way because it is more reinforcing. In any case, effective intervention involves teaching and reinforcing appropriate behaviors. In the case of a skill deficit, instruction will focus on what to do and why. In the case of a fluency deficit, instruction will focus on repetition and practice. When the problem involves a competing function, the focus of instruction is mainly on consequences—what will happen when desired skills are and are not used. But in every case, instruction involves planning for the arrangement of environments to facilitate success. Regardless of why the deficit exists, consideration of prompts, reminders, arrangements, routines, and consequences is crucial to the success of instruction.

Chapter Overview

Teaching social behaviors is described in terms of a sequential set of planning considerations, leading up to the actual delivery of instruction. The following key considerations will be described.

1. Scheduling and Logistics: Decisions about when to teach, what students are involved, who will teach the group, where groups will meet for instruction, how often groups will meet, and the total duration of training.
2. Generalization Strategies: The development of strategies before, during, and after instruction to help students maintain and use skills in settings and conditions outside of training.
3. Group Management Strategies: Consideration of strategies for maintaining a positive learning environment during instruction.
4. Teaching: Step-by-step instructions for delivering instruction and assessment, including the selection and sequencing of teaching examples and formative assessment for mastery.

Using the HLP

As these considerations are discussed, there is an assumption that students have been identified either through a school-wide screening or referral process and that their deficits are sufficiently similar to justify inclusion in the same small group for instruction. As will be described, each group is specific to a particular skill. However, while school-side screening may broadly identify students with suspected social deficits, these students will require more individualized observation and assessment to determine the extent and nature of such deficits.

Scheduling and Logistics

The first considerations with planning for any instruction are typically logistical in nature. In most schools, decisions regarding scheduling and space are among the most challenging and must be a first consideration. To simplify, it's typically easiest to first identify the faculty or staff member who will be delivering the instruction, and to then use his or her schedule and location as a first option. While there are few hard-and-fast requirements, it is generally preferable that social skills instruction takes place in a setting away from other students. Group instruction involves active engagement and role play activities that are best done without an outside audience. Further, it is best to avoid advertising the nature of the group skills for fear of creating a spectacle that may serve to ostracize participating students.

The content of social skills instruction is dictated by the needs of the students and instruction is developed to teach specific and individualized skills rather than a more generic and broad set of social skills as are often the focus of commercial curricula. As such, groups will be comprised of students for whom specific skills have been identified as deficit, and the focus of the group will be on those specific skills. For example, if multiple students are identified as having difficulty handling criticism, that may be the basis for a social skills group and the focus of instruction with those students. Other groups formed as skill deficits are noted, and some students may be involved in multiple groups. Because in a typical school there are most likely not sufficient resources to run multiple groups at once, instructional topics are generally taught consecutively, with student need prioritizing decisions around content and participation.

Due to the highly interactive nature of social skills, instructional activities will naturally be interactive and engaging. For this reason, the social skills instruction literature (e.g., Carter & Sugai, 1988; Elliott & Grasham, 1993; Gresham, 2015) has generally recommended that there be no fewer than four students and no more than six, allowing the teacher to maximize the amount of time that students spend actively engaged with the content and one another. Further, the literature recommendations that groups meet twice a week for at least 30 minutes, and that this continue until all students have reached mastery with a skill. Because instruction involves, practice, role plays, and assessments for all participants, it's best to plan that any particular skill group will continue for at least four weeks. Clearly, some skills may take longer to teach than others, and planning for future groups will always be somewhat tentative as mastery must be achieved with one skill before moving to another.

Generalization

Simply teaching social skills will not be sufficient to predict that students will use them once they leave the instructional setting. In fact, research has continually shown this not to be the case (Kazdin, 2013). Specific steps must be planned and implemented in order to enhance the probability that students will generalize these skills to novel settings, other people, and different circumstances.

Poor generalization is an instructional problem and one that requires specific strategies. For instance, consider that a teacher has been working with a student, Roberta, to greet others appropriately. He has become frustrated because every real-life opportunity to practice this skill seems to be just enough different from training examples to confuse Roberta. At other times she has performed an appropriate greeting response, but at an inappropriate time. The teacher has come to feel that there are just too many possible scenarios to efficiently train Roberta to mastery.

Another teacher has been teaching social skills to a group of students who have been disruptive on the playground. This second teacher has become similarly frustrated because the students in the group always seem to engage in an activity on the playground that was not specifically covered during training. The students were taught how to wait in line for a basketball rather than to run into the middle and disrupt a game. The next day one of the students, James, disrupted a soccer game while trying to become involved. The teacher talked with James and reminded him of the previous day's lesson. James replied, "But that was basketball, not soccer!" This teacher is now wondering whether it will be necessary to train every possible game and activity that conceivably could occur on a playground.

In actuality, both teachers are correct in their judgment of the problem behind their students' failure to generalize trained social behaviors. Their frustration likely comes, in part, from the relative successes they've achieved in teaching academic lessons. Knowing when a story problem requires addition or determining when to add a question mark to the end of a sentence are relatively concrete and objective. Simple "if-then" statements often suffice as a rule to prompt behaviors across academic examples. However, when dealing with the social realm, the key events that should prompt appropriate behavior are often subtle, may vary greatly across people, and can change in the presence or absence of different individuals or groups. Thus, students often fail to recognize environmental cues and act in undesirable ways or at undesirable times. But there are specific steps that can be taken to enhance the probability of generalization.

Generalization Strategies: Before Teaching

Prior to teaching, there are several things that can be planned to enhance generalization. First, as a simple rule of thumb, the more the training setting looks and feels like the natural settings in which they would be expected to be used, the better. For example, when considering skills on the playground, bringing in playground sounds (e.g., tape recording of playground) and physical features (e.g., tape lines on the floor to approximate 4-square lines) help to enhance generalization of new skills to the actual playground. Of course, taking instruction directly to natural settings such as the hallway, playground, or locker area is best, although often not logistically feasible.

Generalization can also be enhanced by teaching social skills that are relevant in the natural environment. Relevant skills can be considered by asking the question, "what do successful students do under these circumstances?" Thinking in this way helps to consider factors related to age and culture. Because social skills may vary greatly across cultures, teachers must take care to consider cultural relevance as one of the key factors affecting what is deemed to be social competence. This also reinforces the importance of surveying the natural environment to determine the culturally relevant behaviors of socially competent students. Clearly, what a college-educated middle-class Caucasian teacher considered to be an appropriate way for people to greet one another may be far from relevant for his or her students. It is important for each school to determine a set of agreed upon social expectations necessary to maintain safe. When there is a conflict between these expectations and social norms for a particular culture, a rationale for maintaining safety take precident, without passing judgement on those culturally relevant behaviors that may be in practice outside of school.

In general, the more the behaviors being taught are relevant (what important others deem important and appropriate) in the natural setting, the more likely they are to be used and reinforced. In addition, involving a number of adults in training and practice sessions helps students to understand that these new skills are not attached just to one adult, but are appropriate with all. While the same can be said of involving a number of students, it is tricky to use peers as confederates during instruction because of issues related to confidentiality and logistics of having large groups. However, practice with a wider range of students should be planned as part of school-wide instruction. This should happen as a part of both school-wide and classroom instruction regarding behavioral expectations.

Generalization Strategies: During Teaching

During instruction teachers can engage students in ways that significantly enhance generalization. While surveying the natural environment for key features to bring into the instructional setting, the teacher can also observe naturally occurring examples that might be useful. As part of these examples, teachers should take note of age appropriate and culturally relevant language—bringing this into instruction to maintain relevance. Taking this a step further, it's helpful to query those who

Role-Play Examples 1-5 for each student in group

Skill: Responding to others when you feel you've been disrespected

Student	Role-Play	Done
Bob	Thought someone in 4-square was cheating - argued Others laughed because he cried and he yelled and threatened Got low grade on test – felt others were laughing and yelled Thought teacher mispronounced his name on purpose and yelled Others making faces at him during lunch and he threw food	
Cindy	Student made rude comment about her shoes and she struck Teacher accused her of cheating and she cursed at teacher In low reading group, accused teacher of trying to embarrass her Fell on playground, thought others were laughing and cursed Someone wrote about her on bathroom wall and she pulled hair	
Aaron	Arguments about cheating in games on playground - threats Arguments about cheating in games in classroom - yelling Thinks others are looking at him to bug him - threats Felt teacher moved him to new seat unfairly – yelled at teacher Punched student who told him he was short	
Sam	Ridiculed for wearing "girls" boots and threw boots at others Couldn't answer math question and yelled at teacher Accused of copying by another student and threatened harm Disagreement about place in line and pushed peer Threw pencil at boys that looked and laughed at him	
Ruth	Comment about her eating "like a pig" and she punched girl Accused by other girls of farting – tore student's coat Pushed younger students in hallway for being in her way Called names at bus stop, pulled hair and broke girls lunch box Was not asked to join a group and broke their project	

Figure 9.1 Individualized Student Role-Play Examples

know the students participating in group and ask for specific examples of circumstances in which they had difficulty with a targeted skill. These help to personalize instruction, but teachers can still alter these example scenarios and present as hypothetical so as not to make it obvious that they represent a past failure. Figure 9.1 presents an example of what these teacher-generated authentic examples might look like. For example, consider Bob in Figure 9.1. The teacher was provided with each of these as examples of circumstances in which Bob has difficulty with managing his emotions in the past. The teacher may present role-play 3 to him by saying, "What if something happened that embarrassed you a little bit in class and maybe others laughed?" So, the gist of the example is inherent in the role-play but it is not obvious to others in the group that the example is real.

Teaching social skills should always involve teaching a range of possible solutions because it's unlikely that any single strategy will work in every possible situation. For example, walking away from a conflict may work with peers but is likely to cause larger problems if a student walks away from an authority figure. Consideration of the range of possible strategies can be accomplished through observations of natural environments and discussions with both the students and other people familiar with the circumstances under which the skills are necessary. Finally, it's important to show students why these skills are more effective, and this is done by directing their attention to functional consequences. If students use inappropriate behaviors to solve a conflict, they need to see that using problem solving also provides this same outcome, but without negative consequences. Making these connections is facilitated by immediate teacher feedback, providing positive affirmations to help students discriminate right from wrong and recognize that reinforcement is available for appropriate social behaviors.

Generalization Strategies: After Teaching

As with any skill, teachers must define mastery. In terms of social skills, mastery is typically defined by a number of appropriate unprompted demonstrations in training. Once students understand the new skill and have mastered its use during instruction, there are several strategies teachers can use to further enhance generalization. First and foremost, prompts and reminders are among the most effective strategies available to promote students' use of new skills. But the most important part of getting students to continue using these new skills in generalized settings is to make sure that they are appropriately reinforced in those settings. That is, when a student demonstrates a newly learned social skill, it should be met with specific verbal praise describing exactly what the student did that was appropriate and, to the extent possible, natural reinforcement (i.e., function). As social skills instruction continues, the teacher should continuously communicate with other adults in the school, alerting them to the new skills and asking them to prompt, encourage, and praise students who use them. For those students who are resistant or forgetful, individual contracts and other contingencies may be useful as a means of facilitating demonstrations of skills so that more naturally maintaining reinforcers may be accessed. For example, a student may have demonstrated mastery during instruction but does not seem to remember to practice the skill naturally. A simple contract might be used as a manner of incentivizing the student to remember to practice at key opportunities.

Group Management Strategies

In many ways, effective instruction is the key to behavior management in either group or individual instructional settings. When students are interested, engaged, and successful during instruction, the probability of problem behaviors is greatly diminished (MacSuga-Gage & Gage, 2015). However, maintaining 100% engagement is unlikely with any students and, remember, these groups involve students who have been identified as having significant difficulties engaging with others. For these reasons it's important for teachers to plan for group management. Perhaps the most important aspect of management is the development and teaching of a clear set of expectations to maintain a focus on active participation. In the social skills group, this typically involves rules that put the focus on listening and participating. These may be stated as "listening means when someone else is talking we look at them and hear what they're saying" and "participating means to do what the teacher asks and do your best." Because these are to be taught, teachers will want to discuss, demonstrate, and facilitate practice with these rules the same as they would any other important content. Other rules may be relevant for specific groups when teachers foresee other potential problems.

Once expectations have been taught, some basic strategies for effective management can be easily implemented. First, teachers should provide frequent reminders of the expectations, providing prompts to both the group and individuals throughout the lesson and immediately preceding circumstances that are particularly challenging for students. Second, teachers must acknowledge appropriate behavior with specific praise so that all students are aware of exactly what behaviors are being affirmed. Praise should occur regularly throughout the lesson and focus on both the group as a whole and individual students. In addition, praise can be used as an initial strategy in response to misbehavior. For example, when one student is not participating or has drifted off task, the teacher may very obviously praise a student who is participating, "wow, thank you, Jon, for really being present and participating!" This is often enough to prompt other students back to task without the use of corrective statements. Third, it may be useful to develop some type of point system and use it during at least the first few group meetings. Ideally, point systems involve only the awarding of points and not the loss. In this way, the focus of the points is on positive behavior and encourages students to act appropriately.

Points can be earned by either individuals or the group for demonstrating the expectations and can be withheld when the expectations are not being met. Points can then be used toward desired activities during group such as an individual student selecting a role play partner or the entire group selecting a song to be played at the end of group. Finally, points can be used as part of a competition between the teacher and the group. When the group is following expectations, they receive a point and when they are not, the teacher receives a point. This type of modified interdependent group contingency creates a teamwork among the participants, which may enhance discussions of social skills.

Teaching

Once logistics have been addressed, generalization strategies planned, and group management systems considered, it is time to put it all together as a teaching plan. The specific skills to be taught were determined as part of planning for generalization and are deemed to be appropriate and relevant replacements for deficit areas. Teaching social skills is done in exactly the same manner as any other instruction. First, teachers provide a rationale for the new skill and provide a clear rule for when it should be used. They then model and demonstrate in an interactive manner, asking students to take on more and more of the practice with initial guidance, culminating with novel role-play scenarios for all participants.

Set-Up

During the first meeting, the teacher welcomes the students and tells them that they are there to learn some new skills for interacting with others. This typically involves a couple of stories, detailing why the new skills are necessary and some poor outcomes that occur when not used. These skills are not specifically tied to any specific social skill and are used only as a rule for helping group to run smoothly. This opening rationale needn't specifically refer to any of the students as having had problems, only that there are some skills that we all need to practice. The following is an example of a teacher's introductory story.

When I was in school there was this boy named Roger who was a real bully and he just said mean things to hurt people's feelings. I watched him hurt people's feelings and it really bugged me. One day I was already mad because I got a bad grade on a test and he walked by and called me a dummy. I got so mad, so fast, that I just yelled at him to shut up. The whole class looked at me and when the teacher came over I yelled at her that is wasn't my fault. But she made me stay in at recess and I remember thinking, he's the bully but I'm the one that got in trouble; there must be a better way to deal with people like him. And that's really what we want to talk about in this group.

Next, the teacher provides an advance organizer, describing what will happen during that session and a general agenda for every session. A typical agenda might begin with a discussion of where we've been and any homework, followed by discussion of a key skill, some facilitated practice, and as time goes by, more and more role-play practice.

As with any new group, the teacher should try to engage students positively from the very beginning. This involves finding ways to compliment students and make the group session a fun way to talk about social skills. During the first session, the expectations are taught as a lesson, with the teacher describing and modeling, engaging the students in discussions, and moving to guided and then independent practice. If a point system of any kind is being used, it also needs to be introduced at the same time.

Lesson Components

Each skill is introduced with a clear rule for why it is important for the student. This involves some consideration of the function of behavior and, because functions may vary with individual students, teachers need to provide a rationale for both access and escape functions. For example, when introducing skills for handling a conflict, the teacher can describe how aggression may both gain attention and make an annoyance go away (i.e., have two functions), there are other negative outcomes that come along with it (e.g., punishments) and there are better ways of handling it that can provide the same attention or escape but without the other negative outcomes. Next, the teacher provides a rule for when to use the skill. This is important because most social skills are effective under specific circumstances but not all. For example, if we teach a student to raise her hand to get the teacher's attention, we need to make clear that this only works in the classroom. If the student were to attempt hand raising on the playground it likely wouldn't work and it likely would make the student less likely to try that skill in the future. Students need to understand the circumstances under which specific skills are effective.

Model and Demonstrate Skills. After introducing a skill and describing the key rules for when and why to use it, the teacher moves to modeling and demonstration. Importantly, these steps are not always distinct and often overlap. For example, while describing why stopping to think before acting when frustrated is an important skill, the teacher can be modeling a skill and calling attention to the key steps with statements like "Notice how I'm taking deep breaths to help me calm down before making a decision." Immediately after introducing a skill, the teacher should engage the students with questions. Asking if they've ever seen anyone use the skill, how they think it would work, or what concerns they may have are all ways of helping them think about how the skill might be applicable in their lives. While some of the key components involve a student taking inventory of their emotions, this is done only as a specific step in the sequence and is not intended to be a cognitive exercise. Rather, students are taught to identify a feeling or sensation and to engage in a specific set of behaviors.

At this point instruction becomes more precise as the teacher breaks skills into specific component behaviors. This deconstruction helps students to focus on the key components of a complex skill and develop success with each piece before putting them together. For example, anger control might be parsed into four component behaviors: stop and think, pick an action, go with it, and self-assess. Each component may be taught and practiced independently and then joined later, or each may be added consecutively across lessons in the form of a chain.

Selection and Presentation of Teaching Examples. One of the most important aspects of effective instruction is the selection and presentation of teaching examples. The natural world contains all the examples necessary to teach a skill. However, not all natural examples are teaching examples and it's the teacher's job to sort through the available natural examples to find those that are most instructional. As a part of considerations for generalization it was recommended that the teacher solicit actual examples of times when other adults observed the students having difficulties in a social circumstance. Because these examples are authentic, they will be more salient for students. The teacher can use these examples as problems to be solved and then model the "solution" as a set of skills within a single lesson.

Once selected, teachers should present these examples in a sequence that demonstrates the range of circumstances under which they are to be used. For example, when teaching a request to borrow, examples might be sequenced to vary the playground/classroom, games/academics, and groups/individuals. If all examples were to be of individual games on the playground, it's not as likely that students would understand the full range of circumstances in which the skill is warranted and useful. Examples must be selected to sample the full range of variations in the natural environment (Horner et al., 1984; Stokes, 2004). Once a range of examples for demonstrating the appropriate use of the skill has been presented, the teacher moves to a negative example, or one in which the response is not quite correct. The juxtaposition of positive and negative examples is critical in teaching students to discriminate the specific features of an appropriate response. When presenting negative examples, the teacher must keep the circumstances of the most immediately preceding examples the same, simply showing a different, incorrect response. For example, "when Betty walks by and calls me a name when I'm getting a drink and I ignore, I have not allowed her to bait me and I win. But if she walks by and calls me a name when I'm getting a drink and I call her a name back, I'll get in trouble." If the second part of this were to have shifted from getting a drink to being on the playground, "But if she calls me a name on the playground and I ignore…," it would not have been as obvious to students that it was the response that made it correct or incorrect.

Finally, because social skills are used in complex social situations, it's very likely that there will be exceptions to the rule, times when the skill will not work as trained. Rather than attempting to address these throughout instruction, exceptions should be taught after students have mastered the basic rule. A summary of these basic recommendations for the selection and sequencing of teaching examples is presented in Table 9.1.

This discussion of the effective presentation of teaching examples has focused solely on the teacher's considerations and actions. However, throughout this presentation process the teacher is continuously engaging students. Once a skill has been described, each example presents the teacher with opportunities to ask questions or prompt other student responses. With the introduction of each example the teacher can ask students if they've encountered such a circumstance and what they think should be done. As the skill is modeled for a given example, students can be questioned about whether the skill is correct, what would happen if it was done differently, or what skill variations might also work. As instruction progresses, these interactions can begin asking students to demonstrate skills. This step represents the initiation of student practice and the teacher is involved, providing guidance and feedback as part of a discussion.

Facilitate Role Play Activities. The guided practice that began during modeling and demonstration eventually leads to role-plays in which students actually stand up and practice skills in authentic circumstances. But even during role-plays, teachers begin with reminders and coaching that will fade out as students demonstrate success. This level of guidance is important because the idea is to create as much success as possible. Because these students have failed with these skills in the past, failures during instruction may lead to student's giving up, refusing to participate, or even becoming defiant. The concept of "errorless learning" does not mean that there will be no errors, but it does mean that teachers attempt to create instruction in which errors are rare (Markham et al., 2020). In this sense,

Table 9.1 Recommendations for Sequencing Teaching Examples

1	Present multiple examples within individual training sessions.
2	Present a wide range of positive examples one right after the other.
3	Present maximally similar negative examples, changing only the key behavior
4	Teach the basic rule before teaching exceptions..

Source: Adapted from Horner et al. (1986).

student success is dependent upon the teacher's instruction, including generalization strategies and the effective use of positive reinforcement to promote that success.

Initial role-plays may involve asking students to think aloud or to describe what they are thinking as they behave. In such cases it's reasonable to have a student walk through the situation multiple times, with open discussions throughout. Because this repetition can potentially mean longer down time for some students, it's important to give tasks to the students not involved in a role play. For example, different students can be asked to monitor how many times a student used a correct word, how they looked, whether there were other possible positive responses, and even to judge whether the role-play was acted out in the correct way.

The selection of role-plays for each student goes back to the personalized examples solicited prior to instruction. Each role-play should be as different as possible from the previous so that the student keys in on the key features of the circumstances in which the skill is appropriate. As students demonstrate success, the teacher provides less and less coaching until at some point the students are performing in a completely independent manner.

Assess for Mastery. While assessing for mastery connotes a more summative assessment, student performance should be monitored in a formative manner. To keep track of this, teachers often track student performance in each of their individual role-plays. A sample of what this monitoring form might look like is presented in Figure 9.2. After each lesson the teacher notes the level of guidance and coaching that was necessary, and this is then used in planning for the level of guidance to be provided in the next session. But there is a more summative assessment of mastery that is saved for the end of instruction. Once a student has demonstrated success in modeling an appropriate skill in multiple role-plays without teacher prompting or guidance, the teacher makes a determination as to whether the student's performance warrants trial with an untrained mastery probe example. This requires the teacher to hold back one of the personalized role-play examples for each student to use as an end assessment.

Students who are able to appropriately demonstrate skills in novel role-play scenarios without teacher guidance can be deemed to have mastered the skill during training. However, because generalization requires such purposeful planning, it's often the case that mastery is dependent upon a more natural example, often set up with a confederate actor to test the student. While these tests are to be naturalistic, students should be told that a test is coming so that they are ready and thinking about it. For example, a teacher may ask another adult to acuse a student of something later in the day. The student would be told that this accuasation is coming so that he or she may be prepared and continue thinking about appropriate responses.

Wrap Up

While social competence is an important component of success for students and should be taught school-wide, some pick up the key skills more readily than others. For these students, effective social skills instruction relies heavily on the teacher's ability to develop plans that are individualized to both the students' actual lives and their identified deficit areas. Through thoughtful programming for generalization and adherence to the tenets of effective instruction, teachers can maximize the probability of success for students with identified social skills deficits.

Tips

The following tips should be considered when teaching social skills to small groups of students:

1. **Build Curriculum in Response to Student Need**. While it's much easier to simply adopt a published social skills curriculum and follow the lesson guides, when dealing with students who

Social Skills Group

Skill: Responding to others when you feel you've been disrespected

Student	Bob	Cindy	Aaron	Sam	Ruth
3/11	No role play	No role play	No role play	Role play 1 2	No role play
3/13	Role play 1 2	Role play 1 2	Role play 1 3	Role play 1 3	Role play 1 T
3/18	Role play 1 3	Role play 1 3	Absent	Role play 1 mastery	Role play 1 1
3/20	Role play 1 M	Role play 1 M	Role play 1 M	Role play 2 2	Role play 1 3
3/25	Role play 2 2	Role play 2 3	Role play 2 3	No role play	Role play 1 M
3/27	Role play 2 3	Role play 2 M	Role play 2 M	Role play 2 M	Role play 2 3
4/1	Role play 2 M	Role play 3 3	Role play 3 M	Role play 3 3	Role play 2 M
4/3	Role play 3 2	Role play 3 M	No role play	Role play 3 M	Role play 3 2
4/8	Role play 3 3	No role play	Mastery probe M	Role play 4 3	Role play 3 3
4/10	Role play 3 M	Role play 4 3	No role play	Role play 4 M	Role play 3 M
4/15	Role play 4 3	Role play 4 M	No role play	Mastery probe M	Role play 4 3
4/17	Role play 4 M	Mastery probe - error	No role play	No role play	Role play 4 M
4/22	Absent	Mastery probe M	No role play	No role play	Mastery probe M
4/24	Mastery probe M	No role play	No role play	No role play	No role play
Generalization probe date	5/1	5/2	4/22	4/26	

Figure 9.2 Teacher Monitoring Form for Student Mastery

T = Talk through Only

1 = Heavy Guidance

2 = Moderate Guidance

3 = Minimal Guidance

M = Mastery

have been identified with specific social deficits, the curriculum must be focused on teaching the specific skills that students will need to be successful. Further, grouping students around common skills allows for more guided practice.

2. **Consider and Plan for Generalization**. Because it is well-established that behaviors learned in a training setting are unlikely to automatically generalize to natural settings, teachers must attend to and develop plans for enhancing generalization before, during, and after instruction. Strategies such as soliciting authentic examples from those who know the students increase the likelihood of student success outside of training.

3. **Attend to the Principles of Effective Instruction**. Teachers should consider instruction for social skills in the same light that they would consider instruction for any academic content. Introductions to the content, explicit description of rules for using skills, engaging lessons, and the effective selection and sequencing of examples are all critical features of effective instruction.

Key Resources

Center for Instructional and Behavioral Research in Schools (2022, April 1). *Social Skills Instruction*. https://cibrs.com/restraint-and-seclusion-videos/

Positive Action (2020, October 19). *13 Evidence-Based Ways to Teach Social Skills in 2021*. www.positiveaction.net/blog/ways-to-teach-social-skills

Talking With Trees (2022, April 1). *Social Skills Videos*. https://talkingtreebooks.com/category/social-skills-teaching-resources/social-skills-videos-best-of-web.html#politeness

References

American Psychological Association. *Coalition for Psychology in Schools and Education* (2006). Report on the teacher needs survey. American Psychological Association. Center for Psychology in Schools and Education.

Carter, J., & Sugai, G. M. (1988). Teaching social skills. *Teaching Exceptional Children*, 20(3), 68–71.

Collaborative for Academics, Emotional, and Social Learning (2021). *What is SEL?* Retrieved from https://casel.org/what-is-sel/

Colvin, G., & Scott, T. M. (2015). *Managing the Cycle of Acting Out Behavior* (2nd Ed). Corwin Press.

Elliott, S. N., & Gresham, F. M. (1993). Social skills interventions for children. *Behavior modification*, 17(3), 287–313.

Gresham, F. (2015). Evidence-based social skills interventions for students at risk for EBD. *Remedial and Special Education*, 36(2), 100–4.

Gunning, C., Holloway, J., Fee, B., Breathnach, Ó., Bergin, C. M., Greene, I., & Ní Bheoláin, R. (2019). A systematic review of generalization and maintenance outcomes of social skills intervention for preschool children with autism spectrum disorder. *Review Journal of Autism and Developmental Disorders*, 6(2), 172–99.

Horner, R. H., Bellamy, G. T., & Colvin, G. T. (1984). Responding in the presence of nontrained stimuli: Implications of generalization error patterns. *Journal of the Association for Persons with Severe Handicaps*, 9(4), 287–95.

Horner, R. H., McDonnell, J. J., & Bellamy, G. T. (1986). Teaching generalized behaviors: General case instruction in simulation and community settings. In R. H. Horner, L. H. Meyer, and H. D. B. Fredericks (Eds.), *Education of learners with severe handicaps: Exemplary service strategies* (pp. 289–315). Paul H. Brookes.

Kazdin, A. E. (2013). *Behavior modification in applied settings* (7th ed.). Waveland Press.

MacSuga-Gage, A. S., & Gage, N. A. (2015). Student-level effects of increased teacher-directed opportunities to respond. *Journal of Behavioral Education*, 24, 273–88. doi:10.1007/s10864-015-9223-2

Markham, V. A., Giles, A. F., Roderique-Davies, G., Adshead, V., Tamiaki, G., & May, R. J. (2020). Applications of within-stimulus errorless learning methods for teaching discrimination skills to individuals with intellectual and developmental disabilities: A systematic review. *Research in Developmental Disabilities*, *97*, 103521.

McDaniel, S., Zaheer, I., & Scott, T. M. (2021). Teaching social behaviors. In J. McLeskey, L. Maheady, B. Billingsley, M. T. Brownell, & T. J. Lewis (Eds.), *High Leverage Practices for Inclusive Classrooms* (2nd ed). Routledge.

Stokes, J. V., Cameron, M. J., Dorsey, M. F., & Fleming, E. (2004). Task analysis, correspondence training, and general case instruction for teaching personal hygiene skills. *Behavioral Interventions*, *19*, 121–35.

10
Conduct Functional Behavioral Assessments to Develop Individual Student Behavior Support Plans

Marney S. Pollack
Peabody College at Vanderbilt University

Blair P. Lloyd
Peabody College at Vanderbilt University

Introduction

Students who engage in challenging behavior—including behaviors that pose safety threats to themselves or others—face an increased likelihood of exclusionary discipline (Smith et al., 2011). This is particularly true for certain groups of students (e.g., students with disabilities, male students, Black students, Hispanic or Latino boys), for whom national rates of suspension and expulsion exceed their relative shares of total student enrollment in K-12 schools (Office for Civil Rights, 2021). It should come as no surprise that these reactive and punitive responses to challenging behavior are ineffective. After all, they represent the very opposite of intervention, in that students are removed from the educational settings intended to teach them the skills they need to progress academically and socially. Indeed, multiple forms of exclusionary discipline have been linked to low academic achievement, school dropout, and contact with the justice system (Noltemeyer et al., 2015).

Establishing student support teams to conduct functional behavior assessments (FBAs) and develop individualized behavior support plans (BSPs) is an alternative to exclusionary discipline that is proactive, collaborative, and responsive to students' strengths and needs. First, a student support team is formed, often including a special education teacher, a behavior specialist and/or school psychologist, an administrator, and other personnel who support the student (e.g., general education teacher, school counselor). The team partners with the student and their family to identify and define the behaviors of concern that are interfering with the student's progress at school. Then, they work to assess which aspects of the school, classroom, and home environment are contributing to these behaviors. Based on results of the FBA, the student support team then develops a BSP to modify aspects of the student's classroom environment that are contributing to challenging behavior, and teach and promote new skills that make these behaviors irrelevant (Sugai et al., 2000).

A large and growing body of evidence supports the use of FBAs and individualized BSPs for students with persistent challenging behavior. The promise of this approach to intensive behavioral intervention has been documented across a variety of student profiles, including students with or at risk for emotional/behavioral disorders, students diagnosed with attention deficit/hyperactivity

DOI: 10.4324/9781003276876-14

disorder, and students with autism (Goh & Bambara, 2012). Positive effects of individualized behavior interventions informed by FBAs also have been demonstrated across inclusive general education and self-contained special education classrooms, as well as across a range of interventionists (e.g., paraeducators, general and special education teachers; Goh & Bambara, 2012).

Based on its highly individualized nature, the FBA and BSP process can include a wide variety of assessment and intervention strategies (Collins & Zirkel, 2017). In this chapter, we focus on students with mild/moderate disabilities who engage in severe and complex challenging behavior. By severe, we mean the behavior poses safety threats to the student or others. By complex, we mean that multiple factors (within and outside the classroom) are likely contributing to challenging behavior. We describe three FBA/BSP strategies that are especially relevant for these students. First, more rigorous assessments are sometimes warranted to incorporate in the FBA, including ones that allow *testing*, as opposed to merely *generating*, hypotheses about when and why behaviors of concern are happening. Although they require advanced planning and support from a Board Certified Behavior Analyst (BCBA), hypothesis testing can lend more certainty to assessment results relative to interviews and classroom observations; Hanley, 2012). Second, students with severe and complex challenging behavior often have needs and skill deficits across multiple domains, including academics, language, and social/emotional functioning (Chow & Wehby, 2018; Fowler et al., 2008; Hukkelberg et al., 2019). For this reason, their BSPs should prioritize skill-building interventions to equip students with the skills they need to succeed behaviorally, academically, and socially. Third, given the complexity of these students' behavior and diversity of their prior learning experiences, their BSPs often require further individualization after the initial plan is developed and implemented. Data informing student responsiveness to intervention should be collected and monitored to inform if, when, and how the BSP should be adapted.

Narrowing the Focus

In Chapter 10 of *High Leverage Practices (HLPs) for Inclusive Classrooms,* we identified and described essential components that should be included in every FBA and BSP and focused on beginning special educators as the primary audience (Lloyd, Pollack, et al., 2022). Importantly, those essential components are still relevant for students with severe and complex challenging behavior. The current chapter is intended for special educators and other members of student support teams (e.g., behavior specialists, school psychologists) who are responsible for completing the FBA and BSP process for students who may require more intensive and interdisciplinary intervention. Given this focus, we begin by identifying three critical principles that should drive individualized assessment and intervention for these students: safety, interdisciplinary collaboration, and family and student partnership. Next, we describe a method for systematically testing hypotheses as part of the FBA. Though hypothesis testing is not warranted in all FBAs, it can be a useful addition when initial assessment data are difficult to interpret or when behavior is dangerous, increasing the urgency of designing an effective intervention (Hanley, 2012; Lloyd, Torelli, et al., 2022). In the rest of the chapter, we focus on the development and implementation of individualized BSPs, with an emphasis on skill building and progress monitoring. Effectively teaching relevant skills is critical not only to address challenging behavior, but also to position students to access and benefit from instructional and social learning opportunities at school (McKenna et al., 2016). To illustrate critical components of the FBA and BSP process for students with severe and complex challenging behavior, we embed a hypothetical case example throughout the chapter.

Mateo is a fifth-grade student who receives special education services in a self-contained classroom under an emotional disturbance eligibility category. He and his family primarily speak Spanish, and they recently moved to the United States from Honduras. Though Mateo's records indicate he communicates verbally using full sentences, he has shown limited expressive language since joining his new school. His student support team includes a special educator (Ms. Cole), a one-on-one paraeducator, a school social worker, and an English as a second language (ESL) teacher. Mateo was referred for an FBA after his physical aggression escalated to the point of requiring physical restraint to keep him and others in the classroom safe.

Chapter Overview

1. Consider three guiding priorities (i.e., safety, interdisciplinary collaboration, and family and student partnership) throughout individualized assessment and intervention.
2. When warranted, incorporate hypothesis testing to increase confidence in FBA outcomes.
3. Use FBA results to design an individualized BSP focused on skill acquisition.
4. Create a progress monitoring system and use data to adapt and refine the BSP over time.

Using the HLP

Guiding Priorities

When it comes to designing and implementing FBAs and BSPs for students with severe and complex challenging behavior, support teams should consider three guiding priorities. First, because these students' challenging behavior often includes some form of physical aggression toward others, self, or property, safety must be a top priority. Safety includes both actual, physical safety (i.e., prevention of injury) as well as perceived safety, or the extent to which the student and others involved *feel* safe and out of harm's way. Second, meaningful interdisciplinary collaboration among professionals with distinct and complementary areas of expertise (e.g., instructional, behavioral, and mental health support) should be prioritized throughout the FBA and BSP process, as students with severe and complex challenging behavior often need supports across multiple domains. Interdisciplinary collaborators (in addition to those who are already part of the student support team) will vary by team according to each student's unique needs, but might include school counselors, school social workers, trauma specialists, occupational therapists, speech-language pathologists, or school nurses (Jolivette et al., 2000). Third, team members must prioritize partnership with the student's family, and the student themselves. Beyond formal requirements to obtain permission from legal guardians to conduct FBA/BSP, key members of the students' family or support system should be involved to ensure multiple perspectives on the students' strengths and needs are carefully considered and factored into the assessment and intervention process. These partnerships are especially important for students from diverse backgrounds, to ensure assessment and intervention goals and procedures are responsive to their cultures.

Incorporating Hypothesis Testing as a Component of FBA

In Chapter 10 of the *HLPs for Inclusive Classrooms* textbook (Lloyd, Pollack, et al., 2022), we outlined descriptive FBA methods (e.g., record reviews, interviews, direct observations) that can be used to generate a hypothesis, or best guess, about the relationship between a student's challenging behavior and their learning environment. The hypothesis describes: (1) *when* challenging behavior is likely to happen (antecedents); (2) *what* behavior(s) are of primary concern; and (3) *why* challenging behavior likely occurs (consequences). For example: *When his teacher initiates a transition from break to work, Josiah tantrums, and delays or avoids the transition.* Hypotheses generated from descriptive FBA methods can also be tested directly using a strategy called functional analysis.

Overview of Functional Analysis. A functional analysis can be used to test and confirm when and why a student engages in challenging behavior (Lloyd, Torelli, et al., 2022). This information is subsequently used to design a safe and effective context for intervention. During a functional analysis, school staff—under the guidance of an experienced BCBA—systematically arrange a student's environment to evaluate whether the hypothesized antecedents trigger, or turn on, challenging behavior, and whether the hypothesized consequences turn it off. A hypothesis is confirmed if challenging behavior reliably occurs when hypothesized antecedent events are presented and does not occur when hypothesized reinforcing consequences are provided. For example, if Josiah engaged in property destruction each time his paraeducator initiated a transition from breaks to work, but stopped engaging in property destruction once the transition was delayed, this pattern of behavior would confirm the corresponding hypothesis.

Systematically testing hypotheses about when and why a student engages in challenging behavior is not a required component of FBA. However, it can be beneficial under certain conditions. For example, sometimes data collected from other assessment tools (e.g., interviews, classroom observations) are difficult to interpret, especially for students with complex challenging behavior. Results of an interview might point to one hypothesis of when and why challenging behavior happens, yet data from classroom observations point to another hypothesis. In such cases, a functional analysis can be used to test one or both hypotheses and gain more conclusive and interpretable results. Hypothesis testing can also be warranted for especially severe cases of challenging behavior, when there might not be time to schedule a series of classroom observations with potential for missed opportunities to observe these behaviors (Hanley, 2012). In these cases, completing a functional analysis in a single visit can actually save time while simultaneously increasing the trustworthiness of assessment outcomes.

By confirming a hypothesis, the student support team learns two important things, each of which has direct implications for intervention. First, by confirming the environmental conditions that trigger challenging behavior, the team can use these antecedent events to create a motivating context for intervention. For example, if diverted teacher attention evoked disruptive behavior in the functional analysis, the teacher can divert their attention during intervention to motivate the student to practice using a replacement skill (e.g., raising hand to request help) instead of engaging in disruptive behavior. Second, by confirming the environmental conditions that reinforce challenging behavior, the team can reserve these consequences for pro-social replacement behaviors during intervention. Additionally, they can use these consequences as needed to "turn off" challenging behavior when any safety concerns arise. Taken together, using functional analysis to confirm a hypothesis can help student support teams design a motivating and safe context for intensive intervention.

Maximizing Acceptability in Schools. Importantly, a functional analysis should be supervised by a BCBA with experience using this assessment strategy in schools. This is because completing a functional analysis from start to finish requires a series of clinical judgements, like determining when and how to modify assessment conditions or when to end the assessment. Additionally, there is always some degree of risk involved when assessment procedures require triggering challenging behavior.

In recent years, researchers and expert practitioners have made much progress in developing practical variations of functional analysis that make them safer and more feasible to complete in schools (Hanley, 2012; Lloyd, Torelli, et al., 2022). For example, precursor or "warning" behaviors can be targeted along with the primary behaviors of concern. Precursor behaviors are those that precede or co-occur with challenging behavior but do not present a safety threat (e.g., whining, stomping feet, putting head down on desk). Responding to precursor behaviors during the assessment means that teams don't have to wait for a student's behavior to escalate to more severe forms to confirm a hypothesis. Additionally, brief trials can be run that begin with a single presentation of the antecedent(s), and end at the first instance of challenging (or precursor) behavior. This format minimizes the time the student is exposed to potentially stressful antecedents, and minimizes the number of times precursor or challenging behavior has to occur to be able to interpret results.

Because functional analysis involves triggering and reinforcing challenging (or precursor) behaviors, transparency with caregivers is critical. Before completing a functional analysis, the student support team should contact the child's caregivers and explain (a) why this assessment is important before beginning intervention and (b) what the procedures will entail. If caregivers have questions about the procedures, the supervising BCBA should provide answers, and if caregivers express discomfort with procedures, the plans should change accordingly.

Additionally, it is important to maintain transparency with the student around the functional analysis. Before starting the assessment, a trusted adult might engage in a "pre-brief" conversation, during which they broadly describe the goal of the activity (e.g., "to find out what will help you at school") and clarify that typical school routines will be suspended during the activity. At the end of the assessment, a trusted adult could "debrief" with the student, pointing out which parts of the assessment seemed frustrating, which parts they seemed to enjoy, and communicating that the team will use this information to figure out how best to support the student at school. These procedures not only promote transparency, but can help practitioners bolster or repair their relationship with the student throughout the assessment process.

After collecting initial descriptive FBA data, the student support team convened to review the information and generated the following hypothesis about when and why Mateo engages in aggression: When transitioning from free time to one-on-one instruction with the special educator, Mateo engages in physical aggression toward adults to avoid instruction and access preferred activities with teacher attention. Given the severity of Mateo's aggression, and the recent use of restraint, the team consulted the district BCBA who suggested conducting a functional analysis to confirm the hypothesis and increase the likelihood of developing an effective BSP. The team met with Mateo's father to review planned procedures and ask his permission to proceed. An interpreter was present to facilitate the conversation. When Mateo's father asked how the team would respond if behavior escalated, the school social worker shared her recommendations for a safety plan, given her expertise in behavior de-escalation. The support team, in collaboration with Mateo's father, decided it was safe to proceed with a functional analysis after choosing to complete the analysis in an empty class-room without peers present, and target precursors to aggression (e.g., swiping materials off the table, stomping feet) to prevent Mateo's behavior from escalating.

Before the assessment began, Ms. Cole and the interpreter pre-briefed with Mateo to give him a heads up that the morning instructional block was going to be different that day. Under the supervision of the BCBA, Ms. Cole conducted a series of 5-minute sessions, alternating between two conditions: "test" and "control." During test sessions, she initiated a transition from free time (with preferred activities) to one-on-one academic instruction. As soon as Mateo engaged in precursor behavior or aggression, she stopped the transition, told Mateo he could have a few more minutes of free time, and ended the session. During control sessions, Mateo had uninterrupted access to free time with preferred items and Ms. Cole's high-quality attention. The BCBA graphed the time that elapsed between the start of each session and the first instance of precursor or aggressive behavior (see top panel of Figure 10.1). After six sessions, she noted a clear pattern that confirmed their hypothesis: precursors happened quickly in test sessions and did not happen in control sessions. The team ended the assessment and Ms. Cole debriefed with Mateo by telling him—with the help of the interpreter—that the goal of the activity was to help her learn about things that were hard for him and things that he liked so she could help him succeed in school. Ms. Cole solicited questions and answered them honestly.

Individualized Behavior Support Plans Focused on Skill Building

Just like the FBA process, the development of an individualized BSP must be collaborative. All members of the student support team, a family member or caregiver, and the student themselves should have an opportunity to weigh in on both the intervention goals and procedures. That is, they should have a say in which behaviors are targeted for reduction, which skills are targeted for acqui-sition, and the methods used to pursue these goals.

Particularly when designed for students with severe and complex challenging behavior, individualized BSPs should include multiple components. As discussed in Chapter 10 of the *HLPs*

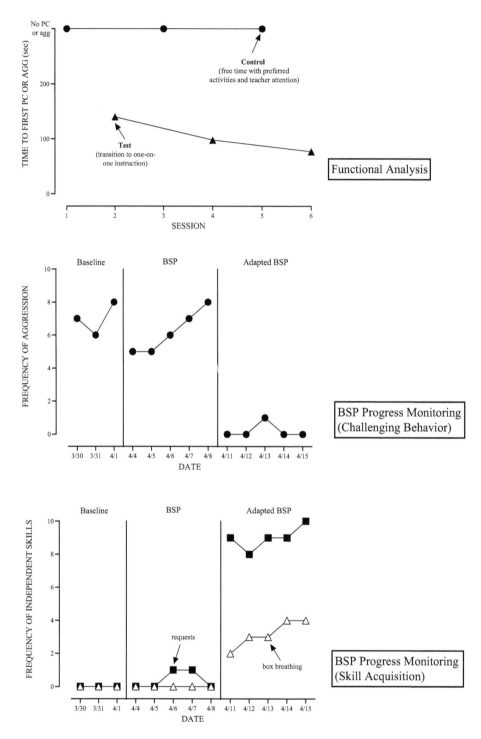

Note. BSP = behavior support plan; PC = precursor; agg = aggression.

Figure 10.1 Mateo's Hypothetical Functional Analysis and Behavior Support Plan (BSP) Outcomes

for Inclusive Classrooms textbook (Lloyd, Pollack, et al., 2022), components include environmental modifications to prevent the occurrence of challenging behavior (e.g., adjusting task difficulty, increasing teacher proximity); teaching a replacement behavior that meets the same need as challenging behavior (e.g., asking for help when the function of challenging behavior is attention); and arranging consequences in ways that favor replacement behavior over challenging behavior (e.g., providing breaks with preferred activities following appropriate requests, providing breaks without preferred activities following challenging behavior).

In this chapter, we take a deeper dive into aspects of the BSP that focus on skill acquisition. This component of a BSP is arguably most critical, as the persistence of challenging behavior can almost always be linked to skill deficits. The skills targeted in a BSP are designed to replace challenging behavior. For example, instead of engaging in challenging behavior, we might expect students to communicate their wants and needs, cope with stressful situations, participate and engage in academic instruction, or interact in ways that will build, not strain, relationships with teachers and peers. Additionally, interventions that focus on teaching and reinforcing relevant skills (as opposed to focusing only on environmental modifications or behavior reduction strategies) will be more likely to generalize across contexts, and have longer lasting impacts.

Identifying What Skills to Teach. Individualized BSPs can be designed to target a range of skills. First and foremost, a BSP should target a replacement behavior that serves the same function as the student's challenging behavior. This type of replacement behavior is called a functional communication response, and represents an appropriate way to request the consequences linked to challenging behavior. For example, if a student had historically engaged in challenging behavior to escape from instruction and access preferred activities, they might be taught to ask for a "break" or to "play" instead. Alternatively, a student whose challenging behavior is maintained by access to teacher attention might be taught to raise their hand to recruit attention. Regardless of the exact form of the request, the functional communication response should be less effortful than the challenging behavior it's designed to replace. This difference in effort increases the likelihood that the student will choose to engage in the replacement behavior instead of challenging behavior, creating a safer context for intervention.

Once the student reliably uses the initial functional communication response, a more complex request can be taught that is more likely to produce the desired consequences outside of the intervention context (Ghaemmaghami et al., 2018). For example, after learning to request a "break" to escape from instruction and access preferred activities, a student might be taught to raise their hand, wait for a teacher to acknowledge them, and then ask for a break politely (e.g., "can I please have a break?"). This complex response might align more closely to classroom expectations than simply requesting "break," and would be more likely to be reinforced in the classroom. Increasing the complexity of the communication response should happen gradually, such that expectations increase only after the student has demonstrated success with the current requirement.

Importantly, skill instruction does not stop here. The primary goal of an individualized BSP is to equip students with the skills they need to be successful, thereby rendering challenging behavior unnecessary. While communication is an important first step, student support teams must consider deficits in other skills (e.g., emotion regulation, academic skills, social skills) that could be contributing to challenging behavior. Returning to the outcomes from a functional analysis can help teams identify which additional skills to teach. In some cases, students might benefit from learning skills that will help them tolerate events that triggered challenging behavior in the analysis. For example, students whose challenging behavior was triggered by stressful social situations (e.g., loud or chaotic classroom environments) might benefit from learning coping strategies (e.g., deep breathing, mindfulness practices) to use in these scenarios. As another example, students whose challenging behavior was maintained by escape from difficult academic tasks might benefit from targeted academic skill instruction. The purpose of this instruction would be to make the tasks less challenging and increase students' motivation to attempt them. The form of challenging behavior targeted during the functional analysis might also indicate potential targets for skill acquisition. For example, appropriate social interactions might be an important instructional target for students who have a history of engaging in peer-directed aggression. While not exhaustive, these examples are intended to demonstrate the range of skills that teams might consider when developing the BSP.

How to Teach Skills. Once target skills are identified, the team must then determine how to teach them (see Chapter 9 for additional information on teaching social skills). With respect to the context for skill instruction, one option is to schedule structured sessions with repeated opportunities to practice skills. For example, in some applications of intensive intervention, practice sessions are held a few days per week in an empty classroom or instructional area for a specified block of time. Alternatively, or in addition to structured sessions, teams might elect to program naturalistic opportunities to practice skills throughout the school day. In this case, practice opportunities are embedded into instructional routines that already occur in the classroom. The most appropriate context depends on several factors, including the targeted skill, severity of challenging behavior and skill deficits, available resources, and the phase of intervention. For example, a functional communication response might be best taught and practiced with a teacher in a special education classroom. Alternatively, a private counseling session might be a more appropriate context for a student to practice mindfulness. Regardless of the intervention context, it's critical that teams promote generalization to the naturalistic setting. This can be done by practicing across people, contexts, and materials during pull-out intervention sessions; implementing supplemental practice sessions in the classroom; or programming naturalistic practice opportunities after structured sessions conclude.

Depending on the skill domains targeted, different members of the student support team might take on increased responsibility in planning and/or implementing a particular skill-building intervention. For example, an instructional specialist would be best equipped to lead planning and implementation of explicit instruction to shore up academic skills that will make work less difficult for the student. A school counselor, on the other hand, would be better equipped to plan and implement procedures focused on teaching coping skills. Leaning on the unique strengths and areas of expertise represented on the student support team will make for a more comprehensive and impactful BSP.

Regardless of the intervention context and provider, many students with severe and complex challenging behavior will require explicit instruction to learn new skills. Explicit instruction is a systematic approach to teaching that involves a gradual shift from interventionist-led instruction to independent student practice opportunities during learning trials (Archer & Hughes, 2011). Throughout the explicit instruction process, the structure of each learning trial remains the same: (a) an antecedent condition designed to motivate the student to use the target skill is put in place; (b) some level of prompting is provided to show the student how to use the target skill; and (c) consequences are delivered to reinforce the use of the target skill.

Each part of a learning trial serves a specific purpose. The first part—the antecedent condition— should be motivating enough to warrant use of the skill, but not too stressful that it causes behavior to escalate. For example, a teacher might announce the transition from break time to work time, without immediately restricting the student's access to their toys. The second part of the trial— prompting—varies depending on the phase of intervention. When first teaching a new skill, the interventionist might model the skill for the student, or provide a level of prompting likely to ensure a correct response (e.g., "If you want more time to play, you can say *I need more time*"). As the student successfully demonstrates the skill following prompts, the interventionist gradually fades the level of prompting provided, until the student uses the skill independently. The third part of the trial—the delivery of reinforcing consequences—matches the consequence condition confirmed to reinforce challenging behavior in the functional analysis. That is, the skill must produce the same desired outcome (e.g., delaying a transition to work) that previously followed challenging behavior.

Mateo's student support team identified two skills to teach: a functional communication response to request "free time" and a deep breathing strategy to use during difficult transitions. Before moving ahead, the team called a meeting with Mateo's father to ask for his input. He agreed the skills were important to prioritize but wanted the functional communication response to be taught in both English and Spanish. He noted it would only be a helpful skill for Mateo to use at home if he could make the request in Spanish. When asked, Mateo's father suggested "tiempo libre" as a Spanish phrase similar to "free time." To incorporate Mateo's input, the school social worker provided him with a menu of effective deep breathing strategies and asked him to choose one he wanted to learn. He chose the "box breathing" technique; he drew a square with his finger in the air, breathing in and out as his finger slowly traced each side.

Due to the severity of Mateo's aggressive behavior, the team decided it would be safest to initially teach these skills during structured "pull-out" sessions. Given the team's decision to teach the functional communication response in both English and Spanish, Mateo's ESL teacher suggested teaching the request during English language intervention sessions. The school social worker volunteered to teach the box breathing skill during one-on-one therapy sessions. In both contexts, interventionists began by modeling the target skill during teaching trials: each team member initiated a transition from free time to instruction (antecedent condition), modeled the target skill (requesting "free time" or "tiempo libre" in the language intervention context or practicing box breathing in the therapy context), and then returned to free time (reinforcing consequence) when Mateo used the skill. After several trials, they gradually faded the model prompt, allowing opportunities for independent skill use.

Once Mateo started practicing these skills independently in the one-on-one settings, opportunities for practice were also embedded in Mateo's special education classroom routines. During transitions from free time to work, Ms. Cole occasionally granted his appropriate requests for free time. Of course, he couldn't always have free time without stalling his academic progress, so when Ms. Cole followed through with transitions to work, she reminded him to use the box breathing technique. When he successfully used the technique, she provided him with high-quality attention before continuing the transition to instruction.

Progress Monitoring and Data-Based Decision Making

To inform next steps after initiating an individualized BSP, progress monitoring is essential. Regular collection and evaluation of progress monitoring data helps student support teams determine whether to continue, modify, intensify, fade, or discontinue the BSP. For students who engage in severe and complex challenging behavior, refinements of initial BSPs are often necessary to bring about meaningful changes in behavior, and sustain them over time.

To create a progress monitoring system, a student support team first determines which behaviors should be measured, then determines how to measure them. Chances are, teams will already have a measurement system in place for challenging behavior, based on data collected as part of the FBA. Common methods of measuring challenging behavior include counts (e.g., tallying the number of times challenging behavior happens) or durations (e.g., using a stopwatch or timer to determine how long challenging behavior lasts, or what percentage of time challenging behavior happens). In addition to challenging behavior, of course, teams must also collect data on appropriate replacement behaviors, and additional skills targeted as part of the BSP. With respect to measuring new skills, teams will likely want to collect data on how often these skills are displayed (counts), and, particularly when skills are first being taught, whether skills were prompted by an adult or engaged in independently.

When designing systems for progress monitoring—especially when BSPs involve multiple skill acquisition components—the team must also ensure the system is feasible. Importantly, progress monitoring data need not reflect the entire school day. Rather, data collection periods can be limited to specific contexts prioritized for intervention (e.g., independent work during reading/language arts block). Additionally, as is the case for FBA and BSP implementation, progress monitoring responsibilities should not fall on any single team member. Ideally, progress monitoring tasks should be divided among team members according to their distinct roles, skillsets, and capacities. For example, it's likely not feasible for a special educator to count each and every instance of challenging behavior while also teaching and implementing behavior supports. Instead, a behavior specialist would be better positioned to collect count data on challenging and replacement behaviors during intermittent focused observation visits. The specialist might also train another staff member, such as a paraeducator, on procedures so they can collect data on days observation visits aren't scheduled. Additionally, a school counselor may be responsible for collecting data on skills to be practiced outside the classroom, during one-on-one therapy sessions. As is the case throughout assessment and intervention, considering and leveraging the unique capacities of each support team member will help maximize the amount, quality, and relevance of data to inform progress monitoring.

In addition to collecting data on student behavior, it is also important to collect data on staff implementation of the BSP, or fidelity data (Conley et al., 2019). Especially when a BSP is not producing its intended effects on student behavior, knowing the extent to which components of the BSP are being implemented as planned provides teams critical information on what to do next. For example, if the plan was not yet showing effects on student behavior, and fidelity was low, efforts should focus on re-training implementers, or adapting intervention procedures to make them easier to implement consistently. However, if the plan was not yet effective, and fidelity was high, efforts should focus on changing the intervention itself. There are multiple ways to collect fidelity data, depending on which aspects of fidelity are of interest and what resources are available. For example, intervention implementers might complete treatment logs or self-checklists to document how often they implemented intervention, and which intervention components they used. Additionally, behavior specialists or school psychologists might collect direct observation data on the frequency and quality of implementation during classroom visits.

The purpose of collecting progress monitoring data is to help the team identify when changes to the BSP might be warranted based on student responsiveness, or lack thereof. If data show consistent reductions in challenging behavior and frequent, independent use of newly acquired skills (or trends in these directions), the team should continue with implementation. If data do not show a reduction in challenging behavior, nor evidence of skill acquisition, after 1–2 weeks of consistent implementation, a variety of adaptations should be considered. Adaptations might include the addition of preventative strategies (e.g., changes to seating, incorporating student choices into assigned tasks), modifications to teaching or prompting procedures for skill acquisition, adjustments to consequences for appropriate and/or inappropriate behavior (e.g., reserving highest quality consequences for appropriate behavior), or increasing the dosage of one or more intervention components. In cases where it is difficult to determine which adjustments might be most effective, a team member might start by asking the student what they think about various aspects of the BSP, using this information to further tailor the intervention. Regardless of what patterns progress monitoring data reveal, they equip student support teams with the information needed to determine the best next steps for the student.

Prior to referring Mateo for an FBA, Ms. Cole asked the paraeducator to track the frequency of aggressive behavior during morning math instruction, the period that tended to be most challenging. Mateo's team decided the paraeducator should continue to count the number of instances of aggressive behavior during the math period once the BSP was implemented. They also asked that she count the times he independently (a) requests "free time" or "tiempo libre" and (b) uses the box breathing technique. In addition, the BCBA offered to visit the pull-out intervention sessions in each context at least once per week to collect data on the fidelity of implementation. The team agreed that collecting fidelity data would be helpful in interpreting progress monitoring data and making decisions about the effectiveness of the BSP.

The student support team called a meeting to review progress monitoring data on challenging behavior and target skills after the first week of intervention implementation (see middle and bottom panels of Figure 10.1, respectively). Data showed that when intervention was first implemented, the frequency of Mateo's aggressive behavior decreased slightly, but began to rise around the third intervention day. In addition, while the frequency of independent requests increased slightly, it dropped back to zero at the end of the week, and Mateo never used the box breathing technique independently. Fidelity data indicated the intervention was being implemented as planned by both the ESL teacher and the school social worker. These patterns suggested to the team that Mateo was not responding to the BSP as intended, and an adaptation was warranted.

The ESL teacher asked Mateo about the things he liked and didn't like about the new intervention. Mateo shared that he liked their one-on-one sessions, and his sessions with the social worker. He expressed frustration with practicing the skills in the classroom context because sometimes he "got free time" when he asked, but other times he "still had to work" even if he asked politely for more free time. The ESL teacher offered to create a visual schedule that would signal to Mateo the transitions during which he could ask for more free time versus those during which he needed to begin work after practicing box breathing. Mateo liked this idea, and asked if he could help make the schedule. After this adaptation was made, the progress monitoring data showed a positive response (decrease in aggression, increase in frequency of both skills).

Wrap Up

The stakes are high for students who engage in severe and complex challenging behavior. To avoid restrictive disciplinary approaches that place blame on the student, FBAs—including hypothesis testing strategies like functional analysis—allow student support teams to draw strong conclusions about the interaction between student behavior and their learning environment. With this understanding, and in partnership with students and families, support teams can develop individualized BSPs focused on skill building to equip students with the skills they need. Subsequently, teams can monitor student progress and use data to inform adaptations to BSPs. In this chapter, we emphasized three priorities that should guide student support teams through the FBA/BSP process: safety, interdisciplinary collaboration, and family and student partnership (see Table 10.1 for a summary of hypothesis testing, skill building, and progress monitoring components aligned with each priority). With these priorities at the forefront, students with severe and complex challenging behavior can learn skills that empower them to advocate for what they need, meaningfully engage with the academic curriculum, and develop positive, supportive relationships with peers and adults at school.

Tips

1. **Develop a plan to maximize safety during assessment and intervention**. A safety plan is a critical component of both FBAs (especially those incorporating hypothesis testing) and BSPs. The plan outlines what procedures to follow in the event of behavior escalation that poses danger to the student or others. When creating safety plans, be sure to identify (a) how team members should know when to enact the plan (e.g., student-specific signs of imminent physical harm or emotional distress); (b) the specific actions to be taken (e.g., evacuating the classroom, calling an administrator, removing dangerous items); and (c) who is responsible for each action (e.g., teacher takes peers across the hall, paraeducator calls the principal).

2. **Promote interdisciplinary collaboration by proactively learning about your teammates**. A common barrier to effective interdisciplinary collaboration is a lack of understanding around the roles, responsibilities, and skillsets of team members. Before beginning the FBA/BSP process, bring the student support team together to ensure everyone knows who is on the team, what roles they are best suited to play, and what unique training backgrounds, professional experiences, and skills they bring to the table.

Table 10.1 Components of FBAs and BSPs Aligned with Guiding Priorities

Guiding Priority	FBA Hypothesis Testing Components	BSP Skill Building Components	Progress Monitoring Components
Safety	• Identify and target precursors in addition to severe challenging behavior • End sessions after the first instance of challenging or precursor behavior • Have a trusted adult pre-brief and debrief with the student • Develop a safety plan for use in the event behavior escalates to dangerous levels	• Provide a safe way to "opt out" of intervention sessions • Create antecedent conditions that are sufficiently motivating, but not stressful beyond what is reasonably expected in school • Explicitly review expectations before intervention sessions • Revisit the safety plan to ensure alignment with intervention context and procedures	• Use data to inform adaptations or intensification of the BSP if challenging behavior persists or worsens
Interdisciplinary Collaboration	• Ask all members of the student support team to contribute information about student behavior to inform hypothesis • Partner with a BCBA who can oversee planning and implementation of hypothesis testing	• Collaboratively identify critical skills to teach across domains • Collaboratively identify appropriate context(s) for teaching trials • Distribute responsibilities for intervention implementation across student support team members	• Distribute responsibilities for progress monitoring across student support team members • Share data among team members
Family and Student Partnership	• Seek input from the student and their caregivers about factors affecting challenging behavior • Ask for permission and feedback from caregivers before testing hypotheses	• Solicit feedback from caregivers about intervention goals and procedures • Solicit feedback from the student about intervention goals and procedures	• Share intervention progress with caregivers • Share and celebrate intervention progress with students • Incorporate family or student input to adapt intervention procedures

3. **Prioritize partnerships by empowering caregivers and students to share input**. For caregivers whose familiarity with the FBA and BSP process might be limited, offer choices among viable alternatives when seeking their input. For example, instead of asking an open-ended question about aspects of the BSP they might like to change, share examples of potential adaptations, noting relevant pros and cons for each option. For students who are reluctant or unable to share input on their intervention, give them an option to "pause" or "opt out" of intervention at any time. Whether and how often students choose to opt out of the intervention context can inform the acceptability of intervention procedures.

Key Resources

1. www.practicalfunctionalassessment.com This website provides free access to a variety of resources (e.g., journal articles, video tutorials) for conducting "practical" functional assessments for children with severe and complex challenging behavior.
2. www.lab.vanderbilt.edu/lloyd-lab/sffa These free video modules outline the steps for planning and implementing a "school-friendly functional analysis." Sample role-played assessment videos and planning templates are also included.
3. https://afirm.fpg.unc.edu/prompting This free module provides a deep dive into prompting procedures, including how to select and use various prompting strategies. The module includes opportunities for practice with scenario-based activities.

References

Archer, A., & Hughes, C. (2011). *Explicit instruction: Effective and efficient teaching*. Guilford Publications.

Chow, J. C., & Wehby, J. H. (2018). Associations between language and problem behavior: A systematic review and correlational meta-analysis. *Educational Psychology Review, 30*(1), 61–82. https://doi.org/10.1007/s10648-016-9385-z

Collins, L. W., & Zirkel, P. A. (2017). Functional behavior assessments and behavior intervention plans: Legal requirements and professional recommendations. *Journal of Positive Behavior Interventions, 19*(3), 180–90. https://doi.org/gbmkpq

Conley, K. M., Everett, S. R., & Pinkelman, S. E. (2019). Strengthening progress monitoring procedures for individual student behavior support. *Beyond Behavior, 28*(3), 124–33. https://doi.org/10.1177/1074295619852333

Fowler, L. T. S., Banks, T. I., Anhalt, K., Der, H. H., & Kalis, T. (2008). The association between externalizing behavior problems, teacher-student relationship quality, and academic performance in young urban learners. *Behavioral Disorders, 33*(3), 167–83. https://doi.org/gh2xcd

Ghaemmaghami, M., Hanley, G. P., Jessel, J., & Landa, R. (2018). Shaping complex functional communication responses. *Journal of Applied Behavior Analysis, 51*(3), 502–20. https://doi.org/10.1002/jaba.468

Goh, A. E., & Bambara, L. M. (2012). Individualized positive behavior support in school settings: A meta-analysis. *Remedial and Special Education, 33*(5), 271–86. https://doi.org/10.1177/0741932510383990

Hanley, G. P. (2012). Functional assessment of problem behavior: Dispelling myths, overcoming implementation obstacles, and developing new lore. *Behavior Analysis in Practice, 5*(1), 54–72. https://doi.org/10.1007/bf03391818

Hukkelberg, S., Keles, S., Ogden, T., & Hammerstrøm, K. (2019). The relation between behavioral problems and social competence: A correlational meta-analysis. *BMC Psychiatry, 19*(354), 1–14. https://doi.org/ggxbwd

Jolivette, K., Barton-Arwood, S., & Scott, T. M. (2000). Functional behavioral assessment as a collaborative process among professionals. *Education and Treatment of Children, 23*(3), 298–313.

Lloyd, B. P., Pollack, M. S., Wills, H. P., & Lewis, T. J. (2022). Conducting functional behavior assessments to develop individualized behavior support plans. In J. McLeskey, L. Maheady, B. Billingsley, M. Brownell & T. Lewis (Eds.), *High leverage practices for inclusive classrooms* (2nd ed.). Routledge.

Lloyd, B. P., Torelli, J. N., Pollack, M. S., & Weaver, E. S. (2022). Piloting a decision tool to guide individualized hypothesis testing for students with severe and complex challenging behavior. *Journal of Behavioral Education.* https://doi.org/10.1007/s10864-022-09478-1

McKenna, J. W., Flower, A., & Adamson, R. (2016). A systematic review of function-based replacement behavior interventions for students with and at risk for emotional and behavioral disorders. *Behavior Modification, 40*(5), 678–712. https://doi.org/10.1177/0145445515621489

Noltemeyer, A. L., Ward, R. M., & Mcloughlin, C. (2015). Relationship between school suspension and student outcomes: A meta-analysis. *School Psychology Review, 44*(2), 224–40. https://doi.org/10.17105/spr-14-0008.1

Office for Civil Rights (2021). *An overview of exclusionary discipline practices in public schools for the 2017–18 school year.* U.S. Department of Education. www2.ed.gov/about/offices/list/ocr/docs/crdc-exclusionary-school-discipline.pdf

Smith, C. R., Katsiyannis, A., & Ryan, J. B. (2011). Challenges of serving students with emotional and behavioral disorders: Legal and policy considerations. *Behavioral Disorders, 36*(3), 185–94. https://doi.org/gh2xg5

Sugai, G., Lewis-Palmer, T., & Hagan-Burke, S. (2000). Overview of the functional behavioral assessment process. *Exceptionality, 8*(3), 149–60. https://doi.org/bhf2cc

Section IV
Instruction High Leverage Practices
Lawrence Maheady, James McLeskey, and Sheila R. Alber-Morgan

Effective special education teachers are strategic, flexible, and data-based decision-makers. They use exemplary instructional materials, interactive teaching practices, and formative assessment data to design, deliver, and assess their teaching performance. They make instructional decisions based on the use of evidence-based practices, professional wisdom, and a thorough understanding of student needs and important contextual variables. Special education teachers value diversity, embed knowledge of student culture and language into instructional planning, and use this knowledge and decision-making competence to improve student outcomes across multiple curricula and varied educational settings.

Effective special educators also know how to deliver intensive interventions to students with disabilities when they are not responsive to existing instruction. They intensify instruction by expanding student opportunities to practice and receive positive and corrective feedback, strengthening alignment within target skills, facilitating learning transfer, and increasing student engagement and motivation.

Developing and delivering effective instruction starts with well-designed lessons. Effective special education teachers integrate their knowledge of general education and contextually relevant curricula (e.g., culturally responsive, universally designed) to plan lessons. They link these understandings to relevant learning standards and benchmarks, align them with Individualized Education Program (IEP) requirements, and prioritize long- and short-term learning goals. Special educators then systematically design instruction and adapt curriculum tasks and materials to support student learning.

After learning goals are identified and lessons are designed, effective special educators use interactive teaching practices to deliver well-planned instruction. Their instruction actively engages *all* students in meaningful learning activities, includes and fades scaffolded supports to help those in need, shapes student learning with positive and constructive feedback, and promotes generalization of learning across time and settings. Special educators use instructional technology, culturally responsive instruction, and a Universal Design for Learning framework to plan, deliver, and differentiate instruction that addresses a range of important student learning goals.

Effective special educators use multiple flexible grouping arrangements and instructional strategies to deliver varied and differentiated instruction. They use teacher-led practices like explicit instruction to increase the intensity of instruction for small groups of students with similar learning

DOI: 10.4324/9781003276876-15

needs. Special education teachers augment teacher-led instruction with a variety of peer-assisted teaching practices to enhance learning and promote prosocial interactions. They also teach students to use strategies to regulate their own learning.

Effective special education teachers are instructionally diverse. They use teacher-led, peer-assisted, student-regulated, and technology-enhanced instruction and know when, where, and how to apply these practices. They monitor student progress using appropriate formative assessment measures and maintain, adapt, and/or discard practices that do not sufficiently improve student learning. Effective instructional practices are defined ultimately by their impact on student learning. When students make acceptable progress, effective special educators sustain and expand the use of these practices. When formative data indicate less progress, they intensify instruction and continue to monitor student performance. This section describes how effective special education teachers, design, implement, and evaluate teaching practices and intensify their instruction when students do not progress as expected.

11
Identify and Prioritize Long- and Short-term Learning Goals

Alana Telesman
The Ohio State University

Amanda Yurick
Cleveland State University

Sheila R. Alber-Morgan
The Ohio State University

Introduction

Teachers are responsible for providing high-quality instruction and grade-level content that will contribute to their students' future success. Special education teachers should take additional steps to evaluate grade-level content and adapt their instruction to meet learners' unique needs by identifying and prioritizing long- and short-term learning goals. Goals should be individualized, appropriate, and contribute to student gains in the classroom.

Results from the Supreme Court's 2017 ruling of the Endrew F. v. Douglas County School District case have emphasized the need to ensure students are not simply *advancing* from grade to grade, but making *meaningful* academic progress based on their individual circumstances (Yell, 2017). To determine long- and short-term goals that support students with *intensive* academic needs, educators should plan to complete the following steps: (a) selecting grade-level standards; (b) unpacking standards; (c) getting to know your student(s); and (d) designing long- and short-term goals. Once goals are identified, the next steps for determining if goals need to be further refined are (e) adjusting the intervention and (f) monitoring progress.

Narrowing the Focus

Teachers are responsible for programming goals that will lead to academic gains for all learners, including those with intensive learning needs. In this chapter we provide steps teachers can follow to identify and prioritize appropriate short-term and long-term goals for students who require intensive instruction. Guidelines are presented for evaluating student performance and, from there, creating goals that meet students' unique needs while still addressing grade-level standards. Figure 11.1 shows a flowchart that will help guide teachers through the process of effective goal design. Each step in this flowchart will be discussed in detail throughout this chapter. Finally, this flowchart will be applied to a case study for a student in need of intensive academic support.

DOI: 10.4324/9781003276876-16

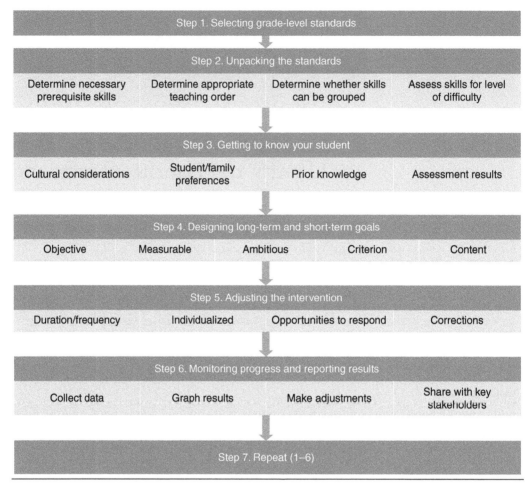

Figure 11.1 Flowchart for Long and Short-term Goal Design

Chapter Overview

1. Identify factors that should be considered when selecting and prioritizing goals for learners who need intensive academic support.
2. Explain a process for identifying and prioritizing academic goals that are aligned with grade level standards and individual learning needs.
3. Apply the goal design process to a student case example.

Using the HLP: Steps for Designing Goals for Students Who Need Intensive Academic Support

Step 1: Identifying Standards to Support Goal Design

Before teachers can create individualized student goals, they need to have a clear understanding of grade-level content and standards. Standards are designed to identify the knowledge and skills students should master by the end of their current grade level. Teachers should use local or state standards to learn *what* content should be covered for each grade level. Although standards are used to support teacher planning, they do not specify *how* teachers should deliver instruction and bridge gaps for struggling learners. They also do not reveal the intermediate instructional steps required to transition students from acquisition to content mastery. Rather, teachers can use state or local standards as a broad template or preliminary outline from which they can begin to tailor learning goals for their individual students. Teachers can also refer to standards from specific professional organizations such as the National Reading Panel, National Council on Teachers of English, International Reading Association (IRA), National Mathematics Advisory Panel, National Science Teaching Association, and National Council for the Social Studies.

Reading and Language Arts Standards. The National Reading Panel (2000) identified five instructional priorities for early reading instruction including phonemic awareness (hearing and manipulating sounds in spoken words), alphabetic principle (understanding the correspondence between phonemes and letters to decode print), fluency (reading with speed and accuracy), vocabulary (understanding content area words in context), and comprehension (understanding reading passages for literal and inferential main ideas and details).

A set of 12 English language arts standards were developed jointly by the National Council on Teachers of English (NCTE) and the International Reading Association (IRA) in 1996. These standards were reaffirmed in 2012. The NCTE and IRA collaboratively identified and described standards that include goals for understanding literature, language structure, language conventions, written expression, communication, research, using resources, and understanding diversity. For example, the first standard addresses literature, "Students read a wide range of print and nonprint texts to build an understanding of texts, of themselves, and of the cultures of the United States and the world; to acquire new information; to respond to the needs and demands of society and the workplace; and for personal fulfillment. Among these texts are fiction and nonfiction, classic and contemporary works" (p. 19).

Math Standards. The National Mathematics Advisory Panel (2008) identified priorities for elementary and secondary students such as the base ten numeration system; equivalence, comparison, operation meanings and relationships; properties, basic facts and algorithms, estimation, equations and inequalities, shapes and solids, measurement, and data collection.

Science Standards. The National Science Teaching Association standards (2022) provides objectives for each grade level that are designed to build upon previous learning. Students in kindergarten through fifth grade focus on physical sciences; life sciences; earth and space sciences; and engineering, technology, and applications of science. Middle and high school standards include using scientific practices such as planning and conducting investigations, analyzing and interpreting data, using mathematical and computational thinking, and constructing explanations.

Social Studies Standards. The National Council for the Social Studies (2010) recommends standards that center on ten themes including culture; time, continuity, and change; people, places, and environments; individual development and identity; individuals, groups, and institutions; power, authority, and governance; production, distribution, and consumption; science, technology, and society; global connections; and civic ideals and practice.

Step 2: Unpacking the Standards

When unpacking the standards for students with intensive learning needs, structuring learning goals in an explicit and sequential manner will be critical to ensuring academic success. Teachers should examine the standards and identify the learning progressions needed for students to achieve their goals related to each standard. Learning progressions are carefully selected and sequenced subskills or prerequisite skills that enable students to progress from basic skills to more advanced knowledge and understanding (Furtak et al., 2018). Carefully selected and sequenced prerequisite skills allow students to achieve their long term goals which should be aligned with the academic standards described in the first step. For example, if students are struggling with reading comprehension, it is important to break down the skill into its component parts and critical foundational skills. Some considerations may include looking at the students' overall vocabulary knowledge and their ability to decode text at the word, sentence, and paragraph level. If students can decode words, can they also interpret the meaning of the word using context? These are just a few examples of types of learning progressions that should be considered when designing goals.

Step 3: Knowing Your Student(s)

Most teachers would agree that knowing your students is crucial for facilitating successful learning. But knowing your students goes well beyond their likes, dislikes, hobbies, and academic strengths and challenges. In addition to knowing a student's levels of academic performance, selecting appropriate goals requires teachers to understand the culture and context which helped to shape this learner.

According to recent data collected in 2017–2018 by the National Center for Education Statistics (NCES, 2018), the teaching population in the United States is overwhelmingly White and female. By contrast, the most recent data available from NCES in 2018 reveals that of the 50.7 million students enrolled in K-12 public schools, 47% are White, 27% are Latinx, 15% are Black, and the remaining 11% represent other racial demographics. Taken together, it is apparent that while White females are strongly represented in the teaching profession, the student population is majority non-White students. This has important implications for addressing the unique needs of individual learners in their cultural context. When identifying culturally responsive goals, teachers should consider communication styles and language of the students and their families, design and examine instructional materials for cultural relevance, and identify their students present levels of academic performance. Note that selected goals may need to be further modified to include more culturally relevant references and connections to the learner.

Communication modes. Collaboration between school professionals and families are facilitated through communication modes, styles, preferences, and even language itself, so it is important to know your student's language and cultural background (McWayne et al., 2022). This is true not only for ELL students, but also English-speaking students as they can have varying expectations and norms within their home that may differ from those of their teachers. For example, is the student and family comfortable with collaborating in a way that encourages co-equal communications among all parties? Teachers should be aware that communication is not only verbal. Nonverbal communication such as eye contact, hand gestures, and facial expressions will influence how the verbal communications are delivered and received.

Instructional Materials. Of equal importance to communication styles is the selection of appropriate instructional materials used to teach and evaluate identified goals. Engaging students with instructional materials that reflect their cultural identity will likely result in increased motivation, deeper connections to academic content, and meaningful learning. By using culturally relevant instructional materials, teachers can deliver instruction that reduces stereotypes (lowered performance in evaluative situations that do not reflect students' identities), increases identity safety (affirmed high expectations for students' identities), and capitalizes on students' existing background knowledge (Cartledge et al., 2016). Teachers should consider students' unique identities, strengths, and challenges at every stage of the instructional process: before, during, and after instruction (Roofe, 2015).

Present levels of performance. In addition to having familiarity with learners' background, culture, and communication styles, teachers should have a clear understanding of their students' *present* levels of performance in relation to grade-level standards. Teachers should carefully assess their students' prior knowledge and select or create assessments that appropriately measure student performance such as using pretests, concept maps, and KWL charts a 3-column chart on which the student writes "What I *Know*" in the first column, "What I *Want* to Learn" in the second column, and "What I *Learned*" in the third column).

Types of Assessments. Not all assessments will be culturally reflective of all students, so it is important to gather assessments from a variety of sources to prevent bias and to provide a clear picture about the students' learning needs (Stevenson et al., 2016). Below are common assessments that can be used to measure student performance.

- **State and District Assessments.** Norm-referenced standardized assessments are one way to compare student performance in relation to their peers (Lok et al., 2016). Results from these assessments show student learning disparities compared to peers but do not provide useful information about what skills the student needs to be successful in a particular academic area.
- **Curriculum Based Measurement (CBM).** Curriculum based measures are standardized evaluative tools that compare student performance to a preset grade level standard, rather than to other peers. Teachers use CBMs to monitor student progress toward meeting annual goals (Deno, 2003). Results help teachers select instructional methods that will work best for their students. Dynamic Indicators of Early Literacy Skills (DIBELS) and Achievement Improvement Monitoring System (AIMSweb) are examples of commercial CBMs.
- **Curriculum Based Assessment (CBA).** Curriculum based assessments are teacher-made tests used to measure student acquisition of classroom material. Teachers design these assessments to align with material taught in the classroom so they can see whether students are meeting classroom objectives. An example of a CBA may be a weekly quiz created by the teacher to assess student acquisition of newly taught social studies or science content.

Knowing your student is important for developing meaningful short- and long-term goals. When teachers consider their students' background experiences, interests, preferences, and present levels of performance when designing goals, their students may maximally benefit from the educational process.

Step 4: Designing Long- and Short-term Goals

Teachers can follow a consistent structure to write effective goals by including four key components: conditions, learner, target skill, and criteria for mastery. The term "conditions" refers to the specific materials or environmental circumstances present when working on this goal. Stating the conditions for a goal or objective should start with "When presented with..." For example: "When presented with a science reading passage during small group instruction in the resource room..." or "When presented with ten 2-digit multiplication problems during independent practice in the regular classroom..." The next component is the "learner" for whom the goal is written. For intensive interventions, all goals should be individualized to support each student as they work toward mastery of the target skill. Teachers should ensure that the target skills selected are objective, observable, and measurable to determine how much progress the student is making. Finally, teachers need to specify the "criteria" needed for mastery so they can confirm the goal was met. The criteria may include percentage of correct responses, rate of performance, and/or number of trials completed to reach mastery. The following is an example of a learning goal with each of these components: "When presented with ten 2-digit subtraction problems during one-on-one instruction (*conditions*), Felina (*the learner*) will write the answers (*target skill*) to 90% accuracy (*criterion*)."

It is important to remember that the criteria for mastery should be ambitious enough to promote student gains yet attainable to ensure students stay motivated. Goals should be adjustable. When students have not shown sufficient improvements in their one-on-one or small-group supplemental instruction, teachers should adjust the goals so that they are more individualized (Harvey et al., 2020).

Refer to the flowchart introduced in Figure 11.1. First, the teacher should look to the content standards in the student's current small-group intervention. Utilizing those same content standards, the teacher may begin to unpack a standard more explicitly by writing a step-by-step progression of the skills and sub-skills needed to successfully meet the standard. Next, the teacher should consider the student's personal and cultural characteristics to guide the collaborative process with the family and perhaps incorporate reflective or representative instructional materials. Intensifying short-term goals at this stage may include individualizing the goal to meet features of performance specific to the student, temporarily adjusting the goal criteria or procedures, and increasing the frequency and/or duration of interventions.

Perhaps the work done in a small group intervention was helpful, but simply not sufficient for the learner to make *enough* progress to meet their goal. The purpose of individualization is to draw from specific performance data about the learner that can help identify instructional features for improving outcomes. Another adjustment to intensify the goal is temporarily adjusting the content or the criteria. These adjustments should only be made in the short term, with the long-term goal retaining the original content and criteria for mastery. For example, a student who struggles with reading endurance may benefit from a temporarily adjusted goal such as shorter timed readings with gradual and systematic increases in the timings. The short-term goal may be modified to reflect a reduced rate of performance. If the original goal was to read 110 words in one minute with 90% accuracy, but the student's endurance difficulty was preventing achievement of that goal, the goal may be temporarily adjusted. For example, the teacher can temporarily adjust the goal to 45 correct words in a 30-second timed reading, then gradually build back up to the original goal of 110 words in one minute.

Teachers can also adjust content to intensify a short-term goal. For example, if a student is working on reading fluency using nonfiction passages, it may be beneficial to select materials that match student interests. This may result in more student engagement during reading instruction. Allowing student choice can also facilitate increased interest, motivation, and engagement. Further, the teacher may choose to temporarily lower the difficulty level of the passage to give a boost to performance. Practicing with lower grade reading passages may give students the confidence to increase their fluency without focusing solely on decoding. As students learn to keep pace, the text difficulty can be gradually increased. Again, these content and criterion adjustments should be made in the short term, gradually and systematically moving back to the content and criterion in the original long-term goal.

Step 5: Adjusting the Intervention

Once the teacher has designed and intensified short-term goals that will ultimately facilitate achievement of the long-term goal, interventions may be adjusted to meet those short-term goals. By evaluating practices for their most effective features—keeping what works and eliminating the features that do not work as well for the student—teachers can accelerate student learning to meet the original, long-term goal. Once individualized practice is in place, the teacher should closely monitor the data to determine when to systematically fade these adjustments and to re-introduce the original goals that were not initially achieved. When it comes to intensifying goals and adjusting the intervention, one size does not fit all. The individual student's performance should drive goal setting and decision making.

After the teacher has adjusted the intervention's materials and/or response modalities, changing the duration and/or frequency of the intervention sessions should be considered. Intervention intensity generally suggests that the amount of time engaged with the intervention (duration) increases and/or that the size of the instructional group decreases (Mellard et al., 2010). For example, if the student participates in one-on-one intervention work twice per week, the number of sessions may be increased to three to five times per week. With these adjustments, the student's number of learning opportunities increases. More opportunities to respond and receive feedback will affect the efficiency of instructional progress.

Step 6: Monitoring Progress

Designing relevant and ambitious goals to support student growth is essential. However, teachers should also continuously monitor student data to ensure students are making *meaningful* growth. Teachers should feel encouraged when they see student gains, yet it is important to remember that modest academic gains may not lead to the student achieving their long-term goals. This is particularly true for students with intensive learning needs who must make greater progress to reach grade level benchmarks. Frequent data collection and progress monitoring will help teachers adjust the intensity of goals and intervention as needed.

Communication of Student Progress

Making data-based decisions and adjusting goals should not be a one-person job. Teachers should communicate student goals and progress with the student, their family, and other teachers or staff.

Communicating with the Student. Teachers should use student-friendly language when sharing data with the student. How can data be broken down so the students understand their progress and also take ownership of their learning goals? Teach learners how to interpret their data when it is visually represented on a graph. Ask them what areas they might like to work on next and prepare them for the changes they might see when working on a new goal. Make sure to provide positive reinforcement such as praise statements or a small reward when students reach their goal. Their success should be celebrated!

Communicating with Parents and Caregivers. Before beginning intervention, ask families about their preferred modes of communication and their own communication expectations. Do they want weekly notes sent home? Emails? Phone calls? Do they require a translator or any assistance with communication? Teachers should take the time to carefully explain how data will be collected and what the graphic display means in terms of their child's learning. Data can be intimidating so it is the teacher's job to use understandable language to carefully explain all steps in the process. Teachers should also provide a clear explanation to parents or caregivers about their child's progress compared to past performance and an explanation of the child's next steps toward achieving his or her goals. Make sure to encourage parent participation and feedback during these meetings.

Communicating with other Teachers or Staff. Collaborate with general education teachers and staff by involving them in data-based decision making and goal planning. Explain how they can embed strategies from the intervention into their own instruction to help support learners and their goals. For example, can challenging vocabulary words be reviewed with the learner in advance of providing a class reading passage? Encourage teacher feedback on targeted goals and ask for their opinions about additional areas for which the student may need support. Remember, working as a team will be the best way to support your learner.

Fawzia's Story: Moving from Supplemental Instruction to a More Intensified Goal

The steps for developing and intensifying goals are illustrated in the following example. Fawzia is a hard-working student in Ms. Council's third-grade classroom who moved from Somalia when he was four years old. He is equally proficient at speaking Somali and English. Ms. Council notices that Fawzia often brings in Somali graphic novels or comic books to read during silent reading. She also notices that Fawzia appears to enjoy school and particularly excels in mathematics where he successfully demonstrates his knowledge through class assignments and various curriculum-based assessments. While conducting weekly progress monitoring checks, Ms. Council notices that Fawzia's mathematics performance declines when he is asked to complete word problems rather than basic mathematical equations, which may be related to some reading comprehension issues. She also notices that Fawzia's reading fluency is lagging behind his peers. She conducts several curriculum-based measurements including oral reading fluency probes (e.g., 1-minute timed readings) and finds Fawzia's reading performance to be below the 25th percentile. Additionally, Fawzia is struggling to answer basic comprehension questions aligned to reading passages.

Ms. Council reviews the reading standards and selects a goal that states students should read fluently and accurately enough to support comprehension. She reviews learning progressions for literacy which describes explicit vocabulary instruction as one of the "building blocks" to support comprehension. Targeted fluency instruction is also listed as another method to support comprehension. Next, Ms. Council contacts the school's intervention team to provide Fawzia with additional reading support to improve his reading fluency and comprehension. After conducting additional assessments and discussing interventions with Fawzia's parents, the support team decides to provide Fawzia with supplemental instruction by using a peer-mediated repeated reading intervention twice a week for 10 minutes. Based on Fawzia's need, the team creates a long-term goal that focuses on improving Fawzia's oral reading fluency so he can reach the benchmark for his grade level. *When given a nonfiction third-grade reading passage, Fawzia will read orally with accuracy, appropriate rate, and expression at 110 words per minute with 90 percent accuracy.*

The peer-mediated intervention consists of providing Fawzia and a partner with a grade-level, nonfiction passage. Before beginning intervention, each student completes a 1-minute timed reading of the passage. Then, the dyads alternate repeatedly reading the passage for ten minutes. Data from the peer-mediated repeated reading intervention indicate slight increases in Fawzia's oral reading fluency after ten sessions. His teachers would like to determine whether this intervention is sufficient for Fawzia to achieve his long-term literacy goal by the end of the school year. They look at his three most recent data points (see Figure 11.2) and calculate his average performance level to be about 72 words in a minute, which is below benchmark.

Next, they compare Fawzia's rate of growth to the suggested rate of growth for fluency in third grade. Again, Fawzia is not meeting this benchmark. The team determines Fawzia still requires more intensive instructional support to effectively address his needs and more appropriately aligned short-term goals to help him build to his long-term oral reading fluency goal. They decide to move to a more intensified goal. Figure 11.3 shows the flow chart for designing and adjusting goals and interventions for Fawzia. As indicated in Figure 11.4, intensifying Fawzia's short-term goals in combination with adjusting instructional content and delivery are the changes needed to boost Fawzia's

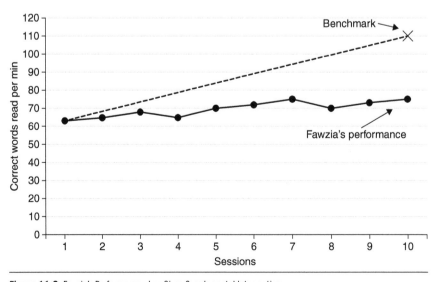

Figure 11.2 Fawzia's Performance when Given Supplemental Intervention

Step 1. Selecting grade-level standards

CCSS.ELA-LITERACY.RF.3. → Read with sufficient accuracy and fluency to support comprehension

Step 2. Unpacking the standards

Determine necessary prerequisite skills	Determine appropriate teaching order	Determine whether skills can be grouped
Letter sounds Decoding words Sight word recognition	Chunk individual sentences, then paragraphs, then passage	Fluency practice with letter sounds Fluency practice with CVC words Fluency practice with sight word deck

Step 3. Getting to know your student

Cultural considerations	Student/family preferences	Prior knowledge	Assessment results
ELL Somali Islam	Mathematics Graphic novels Partner work	Concept maps KWL chart Entrance slips	25th percentile on oral fluency probes

Step 4. Designing long-term and short-term goals

Objective	Measurable	Ambitious	Criterion	Content

Refer to sequenced goals in case study included: condition, Fawzia's target behavior, and goal criterion

Fawzia's short-term goals build upon previous fluency goals. Criterion is temporarily adjusted to enable Fawzia to improve reading endurance and reach long-term goals of 110 words per minute

Step 5. Adjusting the intervention

Duration/frequency	Individualized	Opportunities to respond	Corrections
Increase sessions from 10 to 30 minutes Increase from 2X a week to 3X a week	Play passage recordings Precorrection of challenging words	Build in additional practice opportunities	Provide clear and immediate feedback

Step 6. Monitoring progress and reporting results

Collect data	Graph results	Make adjustments	Share with key stakeholders
See Fawzia's graphs from case study		Increase goal criterion or timing when Fawzia met previous goal	Share data with Fawzia's family Solicit feedback

Step 7. Repeat (1–6)

Figure 11.3 Fawzia's Data for Intensified Goals

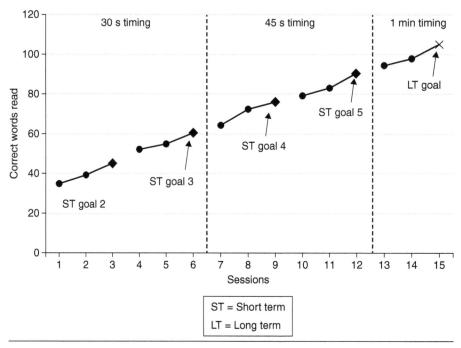

Figure 11.4 Fawzia's Goal Design Flowchart

reading fluency and reach his original long-term goal of 110 words per minute with at least 90 percent accuracy.

Wrap Up

All students deserve an education that meets their learning needs and enables them to make meaningful gains. Effective teachers unpack grade-level content standards while simultaneously incorporating individualized learning progressions to help students build up to achieving both short- and long-term goals. The ability to individualize learning goals is predicated on the idea that teachers "know" their students. What are the academic needs and strengths of their learners and how can goals be arranged to produce the greatest outcomes? From there, teachers tailor instructional goals to meet each student's needs by changing the intensity, frequency, and duration. The process highlighted in this chapter helps teachers individualize long-term and short-term goals for learners with intensive needs while continuing to integrate curriculum standards.

Tips

1. Involve your students in selecting and designing their learning goals. Ask for their input for what skills they would like to target and embed those skills into your planning. By incorporating the learner in their own academic plans, teachers can increase motivation, engagement, and ownership of the learning process. Teach your students how to engage in progress monitoring and self-management. Finally involve your students in sharing their progress with key stakeholders, such as their parents or other teachers. This is a great way to increase their self-advocacy skills and promote independence.
2. Stay connected with the data to determine if students are meeting their goals. It is easy to get excited when seeing student progress, but it is important to make decisions based on objective

data. Collecting data may seem like a daunting task, but it can be as easy as using graph paper and a pencil. Keep your data readily accessible so it can be easily communicated with families, other teachers, and instructional aides.

3. Collaborate with and rely on other content area experts in your school or district for support with goal design. You do not need to reinvent the wheel or operate in a silo. Working as a team will mean better overall support for your learner.

Key Resources

National Council for Teachers of Mathematics
(www.nctm.org/standardspositions/)
Reading Learning Progressions
www.nciea.org/publications/ELA_LPF_12%202011_final.pdf
National Center on Intensive Interventions
https://intensiveintervention.org/).
Center on Teaching Learning
http://oregonreadingfirst.uoregon.edu/inst_curr_review_si.html
Florida Center for Reading Research
www.fcrr.org/student-center-activities

References

Cartledge, G., Keesey, S., Bennet, J. G., Ramnath, R., & Council, M. R. (2016). Culturally relevant literature: What matters most to primary age urban learners. *Reading & Writing Quarterly, 32*(5), 399–426.

Deno, S. L. (2003). Developments in curriculum-based measurement. *Remedial and Special Education, 37*(3), 184–92.

Furtak, E. M., Circi, R., & Heredia, S. C. (2018). Exploring alignment among learning progressions, teacher-designed formative assessment tasks, and student growth: Results of a four-year study. *Applied Measurement in Education, 31*(2), 143–56.

Harvey, J., Farquharson, K., Schneider-Cline, W., Bush, E. & Pelatti, C. (2020). Describing the composition of individualized education plans for students with traumatic brain injury. *Language, Speech & Hearing Services in Schools, 51*(3), 839–51.

International Reading Association and National Council on Teachers of English (1996). *Standards for the English Language Arts.* https://cdn.ncte.org/nctefiles/resources/books/sample/standards doc.pdf

Lok, B., McNaught, C., & Young, K. (2016). Criterion-referenced and norm-referenced assessments: compatibility and complementarity. *Assessment & Evaluation in Higher Education, 41*(3), 450–65.

Mellard, D., McKnight, M., & Jordan, J. (2010). RTI tier structures and instructional intensity. *Learning Disabilities Research & Practice, 25*(4), 217–25.

National Center for Educational Statistics (NCES), McWayne, C., Hyun, S., Diez, V., & Mistry, J. (2022). "We feel connected… and like we belong": A parent-led, staff-supported model of family engagement in early childhood. *Early Childhood Education Journal, 50*(3), 445–57.

National Council for the Social Studies (2010). *National curriculum standards for social studies: A framework for teaching, learning, and assessment.* Retrieved from www.socialstudies.org/standard

National Mathematics Advisory Panel (2008). *Foundations for success: The final report of the National Mathematics Advisory Panel.* US Department of Education.

National Reading Panel (2000). *Teaching children to read: An evidence-based assessment of the scientific research literature on reading and its implications for reading instruction* (National Institute of Health Pub. No. 00-4769). National Institute of Child Health and Human Development.

National Science Teaching Association (2022). The Standards. www.nsta.org/nstas-official-positi ons/next-generation-science-standards

Roofe, C. (2015). The urban teacher: Towards a context-responsive teacher preparation curriculum. *International Studies in Educational Administration, 43*(1), 5–17.

Stevenson, N. A., Reed, D. K., & Tighe, E. L. (2016). Examining potential bias in screening measures for middle school students by special education and low socioeconomic status subgroups. *Psychology in the Schools, 53*(5), 533–47.

Yell, M. L., & Bateman, D. F. (2017). Endrew F. v. Douglas county school district (2017) FAPE and the US supreme court. *Teaching Exceptional Children, 50*(1), 7–15.

12
Systematically Design Instruction Toward a Specific Learning Goal

Moira Konrad
Ohio State University
Kristall J. Graham Day
Ohio Dominican University
Mary T. Peters
Ohio State University

Introduction

Systematically designing instruction toward a specific learning goal is important for all learners, but it is especially important for children who require intensive intervention. Teachers who do not systematically align, design, and refine their instruction run the risk of teaching the wrong skills at the wrong times, and for children and youth with disabilities, in particular, time cannot be wasted (Kame'enui, 2021). Indeed, although all the high leverage practices (HLPs) presented in this book are essential for effective intensive instruction, we contend the HLP presented in this chapter (Systematically Design Instruction Toward a Specific Learning Goal) is the glue that holds many of the others together. That is, without this HLP, the others may be rendered ineffective. For instance, active engagement (see Chapter 18) is critical for success, but if students are actively engaged in activities or content that has not been well aligned to appropriate outcomes, students will not make meaningful progress. Similarly, it does not matter how well a teacher has taught a metacognitive strategy (see Chapter 14) or planned for generalization (see Chapter 21) if the strategies are not aligned to standards and individualized education program (IEP) goals or the instruction is not systematically designed to move learning forward. At the heart of intensive instruction is a recursive process that requires teachers to align, design, and refine their instruction.

Narrowing the Focus

In this chapter we present teachers with Align-Design-Refine, a recursive process that relies on two key tools for planning and delivering intensive instruction. First, "ACCOMPLISH" is a tool for writing standards-aligned IEP goals, objectives, and benchmarks and for systematically designing instruction to help learners reach those goals. Second, we provide a 10-step task analysis to guide teachers through this process. Although intensive instruction can be used to teach a range of goals and objectives, the focus of this chapter is on using goals and objectives from students' IEPs to design instruction. Further, we have narrowed the focus to academic goals. Teachers can readily adapt these

DOI: 10.4324/9781003276876-17

tools to address goals related to social skills, communication, daily living skills, vocational skills, or any other areas of need for their students.

Chapter Overview

By the end of this chapter, readers will be able to:

1. Define important terminology related to the systematic design of instruction, and distinguish among different types and levels of goals.
2. Describe the recursive nature of instructional planning using the Align-Design-Refine framework.
3. Apply ACCOMPLISH to (a) develop clear, standards-aligned goals for students' IEPs and daily lessons, and (b) systematically align instruction to goals.
4. Apply a 10-step task analysis to systemically design and refine instruction.

Using the HLP

Overview of Terminology

What follows is a brief description of key terms that will be important for understanding the concepts in this chapter. Although these definitions may be described or used differently by other authors or in other contexts, the intention here is to make distinctions that correspond with the varying levels of planning and alignment.

- *Standards*: overarching statements (generally state adopted grade level content learning expectations) that describe what all students in each grade should know and be able to do by the end of that grade.
- *IEP goals*: observable, measurable statements that describe the knowledge and skills students with disabilities should acquire by the end of the IEP period (typically one year).
- *IEP objectives*: observable, measurable statements that describe subskills of the larger IEP goal.
- *IEP benchmarks*: observable, measurable statements that represent quantitative steps toward reaching the larger goal and include where students should be performing by set dates in order to reach the final goal.
- *Learning progression*: a sequence of knowledge and skills designed to systematically move students toward a standard or goal.
- *Lesson objectives*: observable, measurable statements of what students should know and be able to do by the end of a given lesson; these are created by breaking down IEP objectives or benchmarks into component skills needed to achieve the larger goal.
- *Student-friendly learning targets*: lesson objectives that have been simplified for students; these should be shared with students to make clear the learning intentions and success expectations for the lesson.

Align-Design-Refine

Planning for intensive instruction should follow an iterative process that can be accomplished by (a) aligning standards, IEP goals and benchmarks, learning progressions, lesson objectives, and learning targets; (b) designing instruction to execute this alignment; and (c) refining alignment and instructional design using data-based decision-making. When tackling this complex task, it may be helpful for teachers to consider using following framework: Align, Design, and Refine (see Figure 12.1).

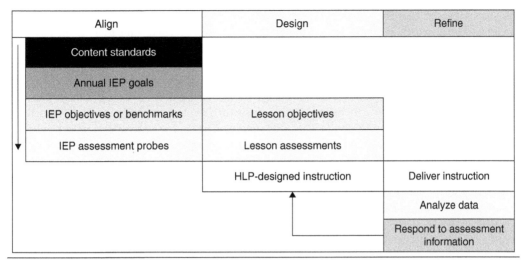

Align	Design	Refine
Content standards		
Annual IEP goals		
IEP objectives or benchmarks	Lesson objectives	
IEP assessment probes	Lesson assessments	
	HLP-designed instruction	Deliver instruction
		Analyze data
		Respond to assessment information

Figure 12.1 Align-Design-Refine Framework

Align. Alignment is a prerequisite for designing effective intensive instruction. First, teachers must align IEP goals to the standards. Specifically, IEP goals must address the student's individual needs in relation to acquisition of the standard; that is, what knowledge or skills does *this* student need to move them toward the grade-level standard? This can be challenging when working with students who need intensive instruction because they are performing below grade level; however, this alignment to grade-level standards helps teachers keep an eye toward what is possible and maintain high expectations (Konrad et al., 2014). Closing the achievement gaps between students with and without disabilities requires this type of alignment and rigor.

After standards-aligned IEP goals have been written, the next step is to write objectives or benchmarks that align with the identified annual goals. Teachers can approach this task in one of two ways. The annual goal can be broken down into smaller component skills and then written as smaller *objectives*, or goals can be organized as *benchmarks*, which include quantifiable snapshots of student progress toward the annual goal at specified points in time. In either case, the purpose is for teachers to identify milestones for their students to achieve throughout the school year to ensure adequate progress toward annual goals.

Another important aspect of alignment is creating probes to measure student progress on IEP objectives and benchmarks; these assessments must be directly *aligned* with the skills they are purported to measure and will provide valuable data during the refining step of the process. Developing these assessments in tandem with identifying IEP benchmarks (i.e., during or immediately after the IEP meeting) will prepare the teacher to engage in frequent, meaningful progress monitoring.

Even with well-aligned IEP goals, benchmarks, and probes, there is still a wide planning gap between the IEP meeting and execution of daily intensive instruction. Logically, the next steps involve breaking down benchmarks even further, into teachable skills and subskills—lesson objectives—and then sequencing those objectives into learning progressions.

Design. The design stage of planning requires teachers to understand learning progressions and how to systematically sequence instruction. This means that teachers need to know where students are currently performing and what skills are needed for students to reach goals and master standards. Well-designed learning progressions begin with main ideas, basic skills, prerequisite knowledge, unambiguous concepts, and higher utility content (Konrad et al., 2022). As students master foundational skills and knowledge, teachers gradually move them to important details, more advanced skills, concepts that require higher level of discrimination, and content that is encountered less frequently. In other words, learning progressions begin with target-related skills that lay the base and then advance with a set of well-defined steps that moves the student closer to the objective or goal.

Once the IEP objectives or benchmarks have been broken down and sequenced, teachers can articulate lesson objectives. Specifically, the lesson objectives state *what* students should know and be able to do by the end of a single lesson as well as *how* teachers will collect evidence of student learning toward meeting the objective. Once the objectives and data collection methods are established, these become the guide for determining the learning activities. That is, lesson activities must be aligned with lesson objectives. In addition, they must be designed to reflect other relevant HLPs discussed in this book.

Refine. As teachers continue in this iterative process, they deliver the planned instruction and use evidence of student learning as a guide for decision-making. By analyzing the data collected in each lesson, teachers can evaluate alignment and instructional design. Indeed, the only true way to know if teachers have been successful in systematically designing instruction toward a specific goal is to measure progress toward that goal. Assuming the goal is appropriate, if the student is making acceptable progress toward that goal, then the teacher's instructional design is achieving its aims. However, it is often more complicated than that.

Special educators must collect periodic data on specific IEP objectives and benchmarks; these progress monitoring measures, required by Individuals with Disabilities Education Improvement Act (IDEA), serve as a gauge of whether or not students are on track to meeting their IEP goals. In addition to gathering data on their IEP objectives and benchmarks, teachers should also be measuring performance on daily lesson objectives. If the daily lesson objectives have been strategically selected and systematically sequenced, then student success on the daily objectives should predict improvement on IEP probes. That is, if students are meeting daily objectives, they should be on target to meet IEP goals. If, on the other hand, students are *not* making adequate progress on IEP goals and objectives, but they *are* making progress on daily objectives, then there is likely a mismatch between instruction and targeted outcomes.

In this case, the teacher should evaluate and ask the following questions: Are my daily targets challenging enough? For instance, do I need to (a) change the conditions to fade supplemental supports; (b) change the target behavior to represent a higher level of learning (e.g., more advanced level on Bloom's taxonomy); or (c) change the criteria to a higher mastery level or fluency rate? Am I targeting the wrong skills altogether (i.e., skills that are *not* in alignment with the IEP goal or skills that are not built on prior learning)? Am I spending too much time on instruction on grade-level standards and not enough time on individualized instruction? Do I need to more explicitly program for generalization and maintenance (see Chapter 21)? Answers to these questions can help teachers better align their instruction to IEP goals. Clearly, frequent, direct monitoring of student progress is an essential component of refining systematically aligned instruction. For more information on assessment and data-based decision making, refer to Chapters 4, 5, and 6.

Tools for Aligning, Designing, and Refining

The Align-Design-Refine framework gives teachers an overarching schema for approaching instructional design. It provides guiding principles—a way to *think about* systematically designing instruction. However, to execute instruction that is carefully and systematically aligned, designed, and refined, teachers need specific tools. Below are two such tools: ACCOMPLISH and a 10-step task analysis for systematically designing intensive instruction.

Using ACCOMPLISH to Set Goals for IEPs and Lessons. Whether the outcome is a goal or objective and whether it is for an IEP or for a lesson, it is important that it be clear (Chappuis et al, 2012; Hattie, 2009; Marzano, 2007). Teachers can use "ACCOMPLISH" and the following guiding questions to ensure the intended learning outcome is appropriate (Konrad et al., 2022). See Tables 12.1 and 12.2 for examples of IEP and lesson objectives that meet ACCOMPLISH criteria. These examples are limited to reading and writing; however, the model can be applied a range of academic and non-academic skills (e.g., social skills, functional skills). The first three letters of this mnemonic (ACC) represent the components of a goal. The remaining seven letters of the mnemonic (OMPLISH) are quality indicators that help make goals most meaningful.

Antecedent conditions. Under what conditions will I expect the student to perform the behavior or task? Examples include settings and situations, materials, directions, prompts and cues, assignments, and time constraints. Often a goal or objective will begin with "when given" or "when presented with" to clarify the antecedent conditions. When selecting antecedent conditions, teachers should also be mindful to select materials that are relevant to their students. Specifically, will my students see themselves reflected in the materials? Is there representation of my students' culture, race, and community? This is essential when implementing culturally responsive pedagogy and will help students feel seen and heard.

Conspicuous behavior. What is the behavior I want the student to perform to demonstrate their learning? This must be clearly defined, or it will be impossible to collect meaningful data that can be used to inform instructional decisions.

Clear criteria. To what degree should my student be able to perform the behavior? The criteria should be challenging for the student so they can be pushed to make progress, yet still achievable with the right instruction. Identifying various measurable dimensions of behavior will help clarify the criteria: count, frequency or rate, duration, and latency.

Observable. Is the conspicuous behavior defined in a way that is observable? Specifically, is the target behavior one that I will be able to see or hear (e.g., writing, speaking, reading aloud)? Or is the behavior vaguely defined as one that can be open to interpretation (e.g., understand, comprehend, analyze)? If the latter, teachers must refine their definition of the behavior to make it observable.

Measurable. Is the conspicuous behavior measurable? Specifically, can it be counted or timed? One approach to making sure the behavior is measurable is to envision how data for progress monitoring will be collected. Using a backward design process (Wiggins & McTighe, 2005) wherein teachers create the actual assessment or data collection sheet before instruction allows them to check if the defined behavior is observable and measurable.

Positive. Is the target behavior defined in a way that states what my students *will do* rather than what they will *not* do? Although in some cases, teachers may want to reduce a specific behavior, it is important that the focus is on teaching a desirable replacement behavior to improve or increase.

Linked to standards. Is the behavior aligned with a standard? When writing unit or lesson goals, it is easy to make this connection because the curriculum is often based on the academic content standards. When writing IEP goals and objectives, teachers must ask themselves if the target behavior will support the student in accessing or moving toward the standards. When setting non-academic goals, the most important link is to the student's individualized needs—what is getting in the way of their success? In many cases, non-academic standards have been adopted by states or are expressed in school board-adopted curricula (e.g., Social-Emotional Learning Standards, developmental milestones for younger children, career and technical education curriculum); however, if there are no published standards, the team should discuss contextualizing the student's need in terms of a longer term outcome.

Individualized. Does the target behavior address a specific, individualized need for the student? Individualization is the priority when writing IEP goals and objectives; therefore, it is essential to consider the student's present levels of academic achievement and functional performance and existing baseline data related to the target behavior. When writing unit goals or lesson objectives, it is important to think about how instruction should be differentiated to support individual students within the group. It is also essential to consider students' cultures and personal assets to leverage students' strengths and make learning experiences relevant.

Socially valid. Is the target behavior meaningful? Given that students who are receiving intensive instruction are already behind, it is essential that teachers prioritize skills they need to learn. Will reaching this goal help the student access higher level content, contact more positive social experiences, or perform important skills in real-world settings? An important component of checking to make sure the selected goals are socially valid is to also assess if the goals reflect cultural values of the student and their family. Gaining input or gathering information from families is an excellent way to get feedback on how well goals align with and honor students' cultural values.

High-reaching. Is the goal going to push the student to make significant progress while still being attainable? It is essential to set up students for success to support motivation while also closing the performance gap. Teachers should use existing performance data to help identify short-term and long-term objectives and benchmarks for progress. Checking in on these benchmarks frequently allows teachers to make ongoing instructional decisions.

Using ACCOMPLISH to Design Instruction. Well-written IEP goals and objectives are only a starting point. ACCOMPLISH can also be used to help teachers plan daily instruction. Specifically, teachers can use each part of the mnemonic to guide their instructional planning, helping them to identify instructional materials (antecedent conditions, linked to standards, socially valid), methods for documenting evidence of student learning (clear criteria, observable, measurable, high reaching), and activities in which students will be engaged (conspicuous behavior, positive). Tables 12.1 and 12.2 provide additional specific examples of how ACCOMPLISH can be used to support instructional planning. Table 12.1 shows how an IEP goal is broken down into objectives and how each part of the ACCOMPLISH mnemonic is used to assist teachers in designing instruction to move students toward accomplishing that goal. Table 12.2 shows how one of the objectives (identified in Table 12.1) is broken down even further into a lesson objective and, again, how each part of the ACCOMPLISH mnemonic can assist the teacher in designing one lesson.

Ten-Step Task Analysis for Systematically Designing Intensive Instruction. There are many ways to implement the Align-Design-Refine framework. One tool is the 10-step task analysis presented in Table 12.3. Note the recursive and overlapping nature of instructional design and the critical role of student data in informing the process. The 10-step process is demonstrated in the applied example below.

Off-Track and On-Track Planning

Teachers who follow the 10-step task analysis are headed in the right direction when it comes to instructional planning, as are those who implement the HLPs discussed throughout this book. However, even these teachers can fall victim to faulty thinking, which will lead to "Off-Track Planning." Table 12.4 shows some off-track ideas teachers may have while planning and guidelines to avoid these faulty ideas or to get planning back on track.

An Applied Example

Systematically designing instruction toward a specific learning goal is complex and can be approached in myriad ways. There is no "one-size-fits-all" approach, particularly given the individualized nature of intensive instruction and special education. Therefore, the example we provide is just that: an example. It is intended to illustrate *one* way a teacher, Ms. Jones, could apply the principles of systematic instructional design to one hypothetical teaching arrangement. Teachers are encouraged to focus on the bigger picture while considering this example as inspiration for tailoring this approach to their own contexts. Jaxson is one of Ms. Jones' students. In this

Table 12.1 Example of a Reading Fluency Goal That Meets ACCOMPLISH Criteria

IEP Goal: When given a 6th grade narrative passage, Jaxson will orally read 140 words per minute with no more than 2 errors across 3 consecutive trials.

Objective #1: When presented with a set of flashcards containing phonemes or morphemes, Jaxson will say sounds (phoneme cards) or meanings (morpheme cards) at a rate of 40 responses per minute with no more than 2 errors across 3 consecutive trials.

Objective #2: When given a list of 20 multisyllabic words, Jaxson will correctly decode (read aloud) or encode (spell) at least 18 words across 3 consecutive trials.

Objective #3: When given a high-frequency sight words within printed lists or narrative passages, Jaxson will read each word within 3 seconds with 95% accuracy across 3 consecutive trials.

Objective #4: When presented with a narrative passage, Jaxson will demonstrate proficiency with three fluency strategies (i.e., prereading, finger tracking, self-graphing), executing 100% of steps identified in the strategy's task analysis across 3 consecutive trials (for each strategy).

Example from the Goal	Explanation of ACCOMPLISH Criteria	ACCOMPLISH-Aligned Instruction
Antecedent conditions: "When given a 6th grade narrative passage" and "per minute"	"6th grade narrative passage" provides a clear explanation of the task given to Jaxson including level (6th grade) and type of passage (narrative). "Per minute" indicates that timing is also part of the context.	Present a variety of narrative passages that are at a 6th grade level. Include fiction and non-fiction text. Be prepared by having a timer and set expectations.
Conspicuous behavior: "orally read"	Having Jaxson orally read is a behavior that is specific and can be observed and measured	Each lesson should be planned to provide Jaxson with opportunities to read aloud.
Clear criteria: "140 words per minute with no more than 2 errors across 3 trials"	The criteria specify the exact number of correct responses (140 words per minute) and allowable errors (no more than 2). Assessors will be able to determine decisively if the student has met the goal.	Having these clear criteria helps with monitoring progress over time. Include Jaxson in documenting his own progress by charting words per minute.
Observable: "orally read"	"Orally read" is a behavior that can be heard and observed.	Again, be sure Jaxson has opportunities to read aloud. Model the appropriate speed, volume, and prosody.
Measurable: "orally read" and "140 words per minute with no more than 2 errors across 3 trials"	"Orally read" can be heard so it can be measured. Number of words read correctly and incorrectly can be counted and represents rate. Noting number of trials adds specific information about how the behavior will be measured across time to show mastery.	Create a data sheet. Use it to graph Jaxson's progress across lessons. Note error patterns as well as qualitative observations.
Positive: "*will* orally read"	Stating that Jaxson "will orally read" emphasizes what he will do and represents an increase in the desirable target behavior.	Start each lesson with an anticipatory set: Connect each lesson to prior learning; share a student-friendly learning target (e.g., "I can read all the words in the story quickly, correctly, and with expression") with Jaxson and challenge him to meet it; and help Jaxon focus on what he *will* do during each lesson by setting positive behavioral expectations and sharing success criteria.

(continued)

Table 12.1 Cont.

Example from the Goal	Explanation of ACCOMPLISH Criteria	ACCOMPLISH-Aligned Instruction
Linked to Standards: "read"	The goal is linked to the following standard: Range of Reading and Level of Text Complexity: CCSS.ELA-LITERACY.RL.6.10 By the end of the year, read and comprehend literature, including stories, dramas, and poems, in the grades 6–8 text complexity band proficiently, with scaffolding as needed at the high end of the range.	Present instruction in a progression of lessons that are organized to increase Jaxson's correct responses though explicit instruction. Each lesson should help Jaxon advance toward meeting the grade-level standard. Provide feedback that includes modeling, error correction, and praise for accurate responses and improvement.
Individualized	Although the goal is linked to the grade-level standards, the specific conditions, behavior, and criteria are set specifically for Jaxson based on *his* needs and *his* baseline performance.	Present passages that are relevant and interesting to Jaxson. Support Jaxson's self-evaluation and self-monitoring of his performance so he can track his success over time. Remind him that his goals were created for *him*, so he need not compare himself to peers but rather to his individualized target.
Socially Valid: "read"	Reading is an essential skill for success in school and beyond. Being a proficient reader is a skill students need to have as they progress through school and for future employment.	Select reading passages that are age-appropriate, culturally relevant, and related to Jaxson's interests. Help Jaxson make connections to the importance of reading in the "real world."
High Reaching: "140 words per minute with no more than 2 errors across 3 trials"	For reading fluency goals, it is helpful to reference published "rates of improvement" (ROIs) to determine appropriate reading growth goals. For Jaxson, the ROI selected was 0.65 x 36 weeks to set an ambitious goal. During the baseline assessment, Jaxson was able to read 98 words per minute; therefore, he needs to gain 10 to 11 additional words per minute for each benchmark to reach the end of the year goal.	Keep expectations high. Encourage Jaxson to "beat" his own scores each time. Use specific praise to reinforce progress. End lessons by recounting Jaxson's success. For example, "Today you were able to read 108 words per minute and only made two errors. You are making progress toward your goal!" Allow Jaxson to document his performance on his own graph.

Note: This example addresses planning related to the overall fluency goal. However, it is equally important to use the ACCOMPLISH criteria to plan for instruction on each objective as well.

Table 12.2 Example of ACCOMPLISH-aligned Instruction

IEP Goal: When given a 6th grade narrative passage, Jaxson will orally read 140 words per minute with no more than 2 errors across 3 trials.

IEP Objective #2: When given a list of 20 multisyllabic words, Jaxson will correctly decode (read aloud) or encode (spell) at least 18 words across 3 consecutive trials.

Lesson 2 of 12

Lesson Objective: When given a list of 10 words containing the newly taught "ea" vowel team, Jaxson will correctly read and spell at least 9 words.

ACCOMPLISH Criteria	ACCOMPLISH-Aligned Instruction
Antecedent conditions When given a list of 10 words containing the newly taught "ea" vowel team	Plan to present examples of the most commonly used words that use the "ea" vowel combination. As much as possible, be sure the other sounds in each word have already been mastered.
Conspicuous behavior: "read and spell"	All lessons should include modeling, guided practice, and independent practice on both reading the words and spelling the words.
Clear criteria: "correctly read and spell at least 9 words"	Be sure the lesson ends with a probe of 10 words containing the "ea" vowel team so Jaxson has the opportunity to demonstrate the skill at the "9 out of 10" level. This is the only way to decisively determine if Jaxson has met the goal.
Observable: "read [aloud] and spell [in writing]"	Be sure the lesson includes multiple opportunities for Jaxson to demonstrate both the reading and spelling skills. Make sure the lesson is designed to elicit the *specific* behavior described in the lesson objective: • Present and have Jaxson read and spell words with "ea" vowel teams • Encoding requires that Jaxson *write* the spelling of the "ea" words (rather than selecting a correctly spelled word, spelling a word out loud, etc.)
Measurable: 9 out of 10 correct	The data sheet should be set up to document the number of "ea" words correctly decoded and encoded. Make sure there is a place to note error patterns as well as qualitative observations.
Positive: "*will* read" and "spell"	To focus on the positive and build momentum, start each lesson by reviewing previously learned words and patterns. Share the student-friendly learning target with Jaxson ("I can read and spell words with the 'ea' vowel team.") and challenge him to meet it. Help Jaxon focus on what he *will* do during each lesson by setting positive behavioral expectations and sharing success criteria ("Yesterday you learned a decoding strategy. Today you'll practice using that strategy with 'ea' words and will meet the goal if you read and spell 9 out of the 10 challenge words. You can do it!") Make sure to align feedback provided throughout the lesson and at the end of the lesson with the lesson objective as well.
Linked to Standards: "read" and "spell"	This lesson and the data collected will document evidence of growth toward meeting the following grade level standards. *CCSS.ELA-LITERACY.L.6.2.B Spell correctly.* *CCSS.ELA-LITERACY.L.4.B Use common, grade-appropriate Greek or Latin affixes and roots as clues to the meaning of a word.*

(*continued*)

Table 12.2 Cont.

ACCOMPLISH Criteria	ACCOMPLISH-Aligned Instruction
I̲ndividualized	Present words that are relevant to Jaxson. Have him self-score and self-graph his performance at the end of the lesson. Remind him that his goals were created for *him*, so he need not compare himself to peers but rather to his individualized target.
S̲ocially Valid: "read" and "spell"	Jaxson is in sixth grade, so select words that are aligned to the grade-level academic vocabulary (e.g., "s*ea*t in Congress," "rep*ea*ting decimals," "b*ea*ker"). Although the goal for this lesson is to read words in isolation, make sure to provide the words in context as well. This lesson might include a reading passage that not only contains "ea" words in context but also gives practice on the larger reading fluency goal.
H̲igh Reaching: 9 out of 10 correct	Some students may exceed the goals that were set for them. Although this is cause for celebration—don't stop! Challenge them to go beyond and then adjust lesson objectives for the next lessons.

Table 12.3 Steps for Systematically Designing Instruction: A Task Analysis for Teachers

The following steps can guide teachers from IEP goal development to systematically designing instruction toward those goals.

1. Set an annual goal that aligns with ACCOMPLISH criteria.
2. Break down the goal into benchmarks or objectives. Deconstruct each benchmark and objective into smaller subskills—teachable steps.
3. Sequence those subskills into a logical learning progression.
4. Gather information about students' strengths, interests, and backgrounds.
5. Create task analyses, data sheets, spreadsheets for graphs, and organization systems for tracking progress toward benchmarks and objectives.
6. Design ACCOMPLISH-aligned and HLP-rich lessons to teach the identified skills.
7. Begin teaching lessons. Use data gathered during and after lessons to make timely decisions about what and how to teach.
8. Gather frequent data on IEP probes.
9. Analyze data gathered in Steps 7 and 8.
10. Continue implementing Steps 5 through 9 to plan daily instruction until the student reaches their IEP goals or the next annual review. Use data to develop new IEP goals (starting back at Step 1).

example, Ms. Jones enacts each of the 10 steps to systematically design instruction toward a specific learning goal for Jaxson.

Step 1: Set an annual goal that aligns with ACCOMPLISH criteria. At Jaxson's IEP meeting, Ms. Jones and the team developed the following reading fluency goal for Jaxson: When given a 6th grade narrative passage, Jaxson will orally read 140 words per minute with no more than 2 errors across 3 consecutive trials. This goal includes the ACCOMPLISH criteria as outlined in Tables 12.1 and 12.2. Looking at Jaxson's individual needs, the team agreed that Jaxson needed to receive direct, systematic instruction in English language arts within a small group in the resource room for one class period per day. Ms. Jones will use this goal as the foundation to plan and implement intensive instruction for Jaxson over the next year.

Step 2: Break down the goal into benchmarks or objectives. Deconstruct each benchmark and objective into smaller subskills—teachable steps. The team decided to break down the fluency IEP goal into objectives. Based on observations of Jaxson's oral reading, Ms. Jones identified the following skill areas needed to help him reach his fluency goal: phoneme and morpheme fluency, decoding and encoding multisyllabic words, sight word fluency, and oral reading fluency strategies. Each of these skills was written into ACCOMPLISH-aligned IEP objectives (see Table 12.1).

For this example, we will illustrate how Objective #2 (decode and encode multisyllabic words) might be broken down further into smaller subskills. Based on several assessments, Ms. Jones identified some basic phonics skills Jaxson needs to work on to be able to eventually read and spell multisyllabic words: vowel teams for long vowel sounds, vowel-r combinations, digraphs, trigraphs, affixes, and Latin roots. In addition, he needs to learn strategies for breaking down multisyllabic words into parts both in isolation and within connected text.

Step 3: Sequence those subskills into a logical learning progression. Based on the subskills aligned to Jaxson's decoding and encoding objective in Step 2, Ms. Jones identified the following learning progression:

1. word attack strategy (basic, single-syllable words)
2. decoding and encoding vowel teams for long vowel sounds
3. decoding and encoding vowel-r combinations
4. decoding and encoding digraphs, trigraphs, and affixes
5. word attack strategy (multisyllabic words in isolation)
6. multisyllabic words in connected text

Again, for this example, we are illustrating the process with only one IEP objective. However, Ms. Jones will target all these objectives throughout her lessons. For instance, each lesson may include fluency practice with sound cards and/or morpheme flashcards (Objective #1), a sight word activity (Objective #3), and repeated passage reading exercises with embedded instruction on fluency and self-management strategies (Objective #4).

Step 4: Gather information about students' strengths, interests, and backgrounds. Although Ms. Jones is informally gathering this information consistently throughout the year for each student, she also gathers this type of information in a more formal manner at least twice per year. Specifically, at the start of the school year and right before the IEP meeting, she interviews each student about their interests and goals; asks families to share information about their backgrounds and interests; and asks for input from the student, family, and other teachers about the students' strengths and motivations. Jaxson has strengths in math and science. He is also good at building things, assembling puzzles, and drawing. He enjoys playing and watching sports (especially golf and basketball), baking and decorating cakes, and spending time with friends. This background information helps Ms. Jones select high-interest instructional materials and activities or tangible items for reinforcement, which will motivate Jaxson to engage in lessons and persist when faced with challenges. Ms. Jones also makes sure to select instructional materials and activities—literature, teaching examples, writing topics, video clips, discussion topics—that reflect Jaxson's cultural background. For example, she knows it is important for Jaxson, who is Black, to read non-fiction pieces about accomplishments of Black historical figures, to read fiction featuring Black characters written by Black authors, to use writing prompts that honor Black history and culture (e.g., to practice writing dialogue with appropriate punctuation, she might have her students write an imagined conversation between Rosa Parks and Claudette Colvin), and use teaching examples that reflect Jaxson's community (e.g., read an excerpt from a local newspaper article about a neighborhood store that is closing and discuss the impact that might have on the community).

Step 5: Create task analyses, data sheets, spreadsheets for graphs, and organization systems for tracking progress toward benchmarks and objectives. As part of the planning and preparation, Ms.

Jones created several data collection and progress monitoring tools to get herself organized. For example, in addition to a curriculum-based measurement graph she uses for tracking oral reading fluency for the annual goal, she also designed a data sheet for each phonics rule she plans to teach Jaxson as well as a task analysis for the word attack strategy.

Step 6: Design ACCOMPLISH-aligned and HLP-rich lessons to teach the identified skills. ACCOMPLISH is a helpful tool for goal development but can also be used to inform instructional planning. Table 12.2 provides a specific example of how Ms. Jones used the ACCOMPLISH criteria to plan a lesson for Jaxson. As she is considering the ACCOMPLISH criteria, she is also designing her lesson to reflect the other HLPs discussed throughout this book (e.g., explicit instruction, feedback, flexible grouping, programing for maintenance and generalization). She is careful to keep her planning "on track" by attending to the suggestions presented in Table 12.4.

Step 7: Begin teaching lessons. Use data gathered before, during, and after lessons to make timely decisions about what and how to teach. Ms. Jones delivers her aligned and systematically designed instruction and uses her instructional data to continue to refine her planning. Specifically, Ms. Jones uses data from prior lessons to inform the current lesson, and then throughout each lesson, she formatively assesses student performance on the lesson objective to inform her instructional decisions

Table 12.4 How to Get Off-track Planning Back on Track

Off-Track Planning	On-Track Planning
"I created IEP goals based on the deficits identified in the multi-factored evaluation."	Although you absolutely should use assessment information to inform your goals, you must set challenging expectations that help each student achieve (or make significant progress toward) grade-level standards. The IEP goals should target skills to fill in the gaps, but they must be aligned to grade-level standards.
"I need to find a standard that is related my lesson."	Be careful not to put your lesson planning before you've identified target standards. If your IEP objectives are aligned to the standards, your lessons should be systemically arranged in a learning progression that builds student proficiency toward meeting the grade-level standards.
"My lessons are based on what's happening in the general education classroom."	It is a good idea to know what the general education teachers are doing in their classrooms, so you can maintain rigor and support your students in the regular classroom. However, your intensive instruction must meet students where they are and then be aligned and designed to move students systematically forward.
"I'm using HLP 6: Progress reports are due this week, so I need to do a quick assessment."	In addition to daily assessments on the lesson objectives, you must be gathering data that is specifically measuring progress on the IEP goals and objectives. These data do not need to be collected every day, but they need to be gathered and analyzed frequently enough to inform your instruction.
"I'm using HLP 11: My IEP objective *is* my lesson objective."	Although you may be collecting data on an IEP objective in a given lesson, the lesson objective(s) should only be targeting a subskill that will help the student make progress toward the IEP objective and that can be met in one lesson. A given IEP objective may take several weeks to a full year for a student to reach.
"My students will reach today's lesson objective with 80% accuracy in 2 out of 3 trials."	When writing a lesson objective, make sure… • success criteria are rigorous/appropriate (e.g., Is 80% a sufficient level of mastery?) • criteria are possible (e.g., A 4-item assessment cannot earn 80%. Are you really going to do 3 trials in today's lesson?)

Table 12.4 Cont.

Off-Track Planning	On-Track Planning
"I'm using HLP 4: I plan to use 'observation' as my assessment method."	Certainly, direct observation is necessary to measure student performance. However, you must be specific about… • what you are observing (What are you looking for?) • the dimension of behavior (Are you counting frequency, timing for fluency/rate, assessing for accuracy, timing for duration or latency?) • how your observations are directly aligned to the lesson objective • your plan for data collection—including development of data sheets—*prior to the lesson* • your plan for providing immediate, specific, objective-aligned feedback to students • your plan for engaging students in reflecting on their own learning in relation to the learning target
"I'm using HLP 11: Today we're going to learn a new skill."	Each day you should be targeting a new skill, but it needs to be clear to students (and you) how it connects to previous learning, how it will move students toward their larger goals, and how it is relevant to their lives. Be culturally responsive by connecting the new skill to the student's interests and experiences.
"I'm using HLP 18: I've designed a spelling lesson with multiple opportunities for students to chorally respond the spelling rules and examples."	This activity may be appropriate, but it is not sufficient if students are practicing… • in the wrong modality (e.g., the planned practice is aloud but assessment requires writing) • skills that are not aligned with standards • in a way that doesn't allow for individual level feedback
"I'm using HLPs 13, 15, and 19: I'm going to adapt and scaffold my lesson with assistive technology by having students select words from a dropdown menu when writing their paragraphs."	Certainly, this type of assistive technology is appropriate for many students, and it may be an excellent steppingstone toward writing proficiency for others. However, teachers must be intentional when identifying ways to adapt their instruction by keeping the goal front and center and then aligning, designing, and refining instruction accordingly. If the goal is for students to "write," then there needs to be a clear learning progression from this adaptation to independent writing.
"I'm using HLP 22: I'll be giving my students lots of praise and corrective feedback throughout my lesson."	Feedback is critical to student learning—it should be delivered with immediacy and frequency. However, the quality of feedback is just as important as the quantity. High-quality feedback is *aligned* with the lesson (or IEP) objective; that is, it informs the student where they are in relation to where they need to be. Additionally, feedback is enhanced when the teacher starts each lesson with clear learning intentions, shares them explicitly with students, and then engages students in reflecting on their own learning.
"I'm using HLP 6: I analyzed my data and 7 of my 12 students made the same the error on the comprehension question."	The error the students made may not be the result of the students' understanding of the text. Instead, errors may be due to the clarity of the prompt or the background knowledge that students need to respond accurately. Teachers should carefully examine their assessments to determine if assessment items give them accurate representation of student knowledge and refine accordingly.

during the lesson. She provides immediate, specific feedback to correct errors and to acknowledge accurate student responding and progress toward meeting the learning objective as part of the formative assessment process. She uses end-of-lesson assessments to evaluate the overall effectiveness of the current lesson to inform subsequent lessons.

In the example outlined in Table 12.2, Ms. Jones knew from the baseline assessments that Jaxson needed instruction on the "ea" vowel team. In the current lesson, she will begin by reviewing the simple word attack strategy she introduced yesterday and a few previously mastered phonemes. Next, she will model the "ea" sound, then she will move to asking Jaxson to read aloud several words with the targeted vowel team and then spell these words. During these activities, Ms. Jones is collecting formative assessment data and will provide systematic feedback to affirm correct responses or provide error corrections for words that are missed. At the end of the lesson, Jaxson will be asked to read 10 words containing the "ea" vowel team while Ms. Jaxson collects data on accuracy. Jaxson will also be asked to spell these words independently as a post-lesson assessment. Finally, Jaxson will evaluate his own spelling test using an answer key and plot his score on a chart to self-monitor his progress.

Step 8: Gather frequent data on IEP probes. Collecting data before, during, and after instruction is a critical step in daily planning. However, to ensure teachers are on-track with achieving the purpose of intensive instruction—student progress on IEP goals and objectives—it is important to gather data on the IEP-aligned probes that were identified as part of the IEP writing process. Frequency of probes should be determined by students' individual needs; keep in mind that students receiving intensive intervention need more frequent progress monitoring.

Ms. Jones has planned to collect IEP probe data on Jaxson's fluency goal on a weekly basis because he is significantly below grade level on fluency benchmark measures. At the end of each week, she tracks the number of words correctly read aloud per minute and notes words that were incorrectly read to investigate error patterns that can later be considered in Step 9. At the same time, she is collecting data on the IEP objectives she is targeting for instruction. To involve Jaxson in the process, he also graphs his own fluency data.

Step 9: Analyze those data gathered in Steps 7 and 8. One of the most important components of checking alignment is to analyze both lesson data and IEP data. If students are reaching lesson objectives, but are not making progress on the IEP goals and/or objectives, there may be misalignment between the IEP and the intensive instruction the student is receiving. As Ms. Jones reviews Jaxson's data, she sees that he has achieved most of the lesson objectives thus far and this is reflected in the most recent IEP probes. Specifically, the direct instruction Jaxson is receiving during individual lessons on phoneme and morpheme fluency, sight words, and word reading strategies is contributing to his overall reading fluency.

Step 10: Continue implementing Steps 5 through 9 to plan daily instruction until the student reaches their IEP goals or until the next annual review. Use data to develop new IEP goals (starting back at Step 1). The goal of intensive instruction is for students to make progress on standards-aligned IEP goals. Ms. Jones continues to engage in the Align-Design-Refine process and sees that Jaxson's reading fluency is steadily improving as are the skills identified in each IEP objective. These outcomes affirm that her intensive instruction is effective, and Jaxson is on track to achieve his annual goal. Because she has been gathering consistent data, she is feeling prepared with adequate baseline data for the next IEP. Additionally, she has been making the learning intentions clear to Jaxson and has invested him by asking him to reflect on his own growth; she is excited to have Jaxson share his progress at the next student-led IEP meeting.

Wrap Up

Effective intensive instruction requires teachers to engage in a continuous process of aligning, designing, and refining their teaching. The Align-Design-Refine framework, the ACCOMPLISH mnemonic, and the 10-step task analysis outlined in this chapter serve as guides to identify, prioritize, sequence, and evaluate instructional goals for each student.

Tips

1. **Work together with colleagues to lighten the load.** Deconstructing standards and goals is a lot of work! Divide and conquer so to avoid duplicating efforts and reduce burn-out.
2. **Look for ways to teach overlapping skills.** Be strategic and use natural alignment rather than forcing things to fit together or trying to connect them with an arbitrary theme. When teaching a reading comprehension strategy, for instance, use content from science or social studies (overlapping with what students are learning in the regular classroom). Then, select passages at the student's independent level to allow them to focus on the content and the strategies. Gradually raise the passage difficulty as they master the comprehension strategies.
3. **Engage students in self-evaluation.** Help students know where they are in relation to their goals and involve them in tracking their progress. This will support the development of their self-determination and help them become active in their own educational planning.

Key Resources

- AFIRM modules (https://afirm.fpg.unc.edu/afirm-modules), specifically the following: "Direct Instruction" and "Task Analysis"
- *Deconstructing Standards* (www.ocali.org/up_doc/Deconstructing_Standards.pdf)
- IRIS modules (https://iris.peabody.vanderbilt.edu/), specifically the following: "Intensive Intervention (Part 1): Using Data-Based Individualization to Intensify Instruction" and "Intensive Intervention (Part 2): Collecting and Analyzing Data for Data-Based Individualization"
- National Center on Intensive Intervention (https://intensiveintervention.org/)
- National Institute for Direct Instruction (www.nifdi.org/)
- *Unwrapping the Standards: A Simple Way to Deconstruct Learning Outcomes* (https://www.edweek.org/education/opinion-unwrapping-the-standards-a-simple-way-to-deconstruct-learning-outcomes/2015/03)

References

Chappuis, J., Stiggins, R., Chappuis, S., & Arter, J. (2012). *Classroom assessment for student learning* (2nd ed.). Pearson Education.

Hattie, J. (2009). *Visible learning: A synthesis of over 800 meta-analyses relating to achievement.* Routledge.

Kame'enui, E. J. (2021). Ode to Zig (and the Bard): In support of an incomplete logical-empirical model of Direct Instruction. *Perspectives on Behavior Science, 44,* 285–305.

Konrad, M., Hessler, T., Alber-Morgan, S. R., Graham-Day, K. J., Davenport, C. A., & Helton, M. R. (2022). Systematically design instruction toward a specific goal. In J. McLeskey, L. Maheady, B. Billingsley, M. Brownell, & Tim Lewis (Eds.). *HLPs for Inclusive Classrooms* (2nd ed.). Routledge.

Konrad., M., Keesey, S., Ressa, V. A., Alexeeff, M., Chan, P. E., & Peters, M. T. (2014). Setting clear learning targets to guide instruction for all students. *Intervention in School and Clinic, 50,* 76–85.

Marzano, R. J. (2007). *Art and science of teaching.* Association for Supervision and Curriculum Development.

Wiggins, G., & McTighe, J. (2005). *Understanding by design* (expanded 2nd ed.). Association for Supervision and Curriculum Development.

13
Adapt Curriculum Tasks and Materials for Specific Learning Goals

Sheila R. Alber-Morgan
The Ohio State University

Marcella M. Gallmeyer
The Ohio State University

Alyxandra Zavodney
The Ohio State University

Introduction

Effective teachers consistently and purposefully adapt curriculum tasks and materials so that students with diverse learning needs can achieve success with their grade-level curriculum. Decisions about which instructional adaptations to use and how to use them must be guided by individual student performance and responsiveness to intervention. Multitiered systems of support are useful for planning and implementing the appropriate intensity of instruction and the types of adapted tasks and materials needed for individual learners. In the response to intervention (RTI) model students who are not responding successfully to whole class instruction (Tier 1) are provided with intensive small group instruction (Tier 2). If students are not reaching their goals with Tier 1 or Tier 2 instruction, they are provided with more intensive Tier 3 instruction which includes one-on-one or small group instructional arrangements (Fuchs et al., 2012; Peng et al., 2019).

Teachers can proactively manage Tier 3 instruction by building in adaptations that remove barriers to learning and structuring individualized lessons that are engaging, motivating, and organized. This chapter focuses on academic adaptations for students with mild to moderate disabilities who need intensive interventions (Tier 3). Well-designed adaptations provide students with the opportunity to experience success with the same academic content as their grade-level peers (Al Hazmi & Ahmad, 2018; Browder et al., 2007). Additionally, when appropriate adaptations are in place, students spend more time actively responding to academic content and less time engaging in off-task behavior (Goodnight et al., 2019; Lee et al., 2010).

Narrowing the Focus

Adaptations that promote content mastery can bridge the gap between a student's current academic level and the level needed to succeed in the general education curriculum (Alber-Morgan et al., 2022). Students who have difficulty remembering multi-step directions, attending to important

DOI: 10.4324/9781003276876-18

details, understanding expectations, working efficiently, and comprehending written text can benefit from adapted materials that simplify task directions, alter the amount and difficulty of material, and/or highlight important points. Curriculum adaptations that help students identify, organize, understand, and remember important concepts or skills are called content enhancements (Curtis & Green, 2021). Content enhancements are based on evidence that students learn more when teachers progress from concrete to abstract presentations, explicitly clarify relationships between ideas, teach students to focus on key points, and incorporate the student's cultural background experiences into instruction (Peterson et al., 2017; Schumaker & Fisher, 2021).

This chapter provides practitioners with strategies for using adaptations and content enhancements that increase the frequency and intensity of academic engagement. Under adaptations, we address: (a) simplifying task directions; (b) altering difficulty level; (c) altering amount of material; and (d) highlighting relevant information. Under content enhancements, we address using (a) graphic organizers; (b) guided notes; and (c) mnemonic strategies.

Chapter Overview

1. Describe how teachers can make adaptations to curriculum tasks and materials for students with mild disabilities receiving intensive Tier 3 instruction including simplifying task directions, altering difficulty of material, altering amount of material, and highlighting relevant material.
2. Describe the design and implementation of content enhancements for Tier 3 instruction, including guided notes, graphic organizers, and mnemonic strategies.

Using the HLP: Material and Task Adaptations

When implementing multitiered interventions, differentiation occurs at all levels. Students with intensive academic needs will require materials that are adapted to their present levels of performance in the different academic areas. Intensive interventions should provide explicit instruction within one-on-one or small group teaching arrangements. When implementing intensive interventions, teachers provide modeling, clear instructions, frequent opportunities to respond, and specific feedback that is immediate, affirmative, and corrective (Heward et al., 2022). Teachers should collect frequent data on individual student progress to inform their instructional decisions for each lesson including level of task difficulty, pace of instructional delivery, and when to begin fading the adaptations.

Simplify Task Directions

Simplifying task directions includes rewriting directions using fewer words, simpler sentences, and less difficult vocabulary. To simplify directions, carefully examine the directions provided in the instructional material and identify vocabulary that may be too complex for the student. Replace advanced vocabulary with simpler synonyms and break down complex directions into short and distinct steps. Then ask the student to repeat the directions to check for understanding. Figure 13.1 shows an example of how to simplify task directions for creating a bar graph. The assignment provides a short list of direct steps with the important words **printed** and a place to check off when each step is completed.

Altering the Difficulty Level of Material

Adapting the difficulty level of material can include providing fewer task steps or requiring the student to complete only a portion of a problem. Students can also be provided with supports such

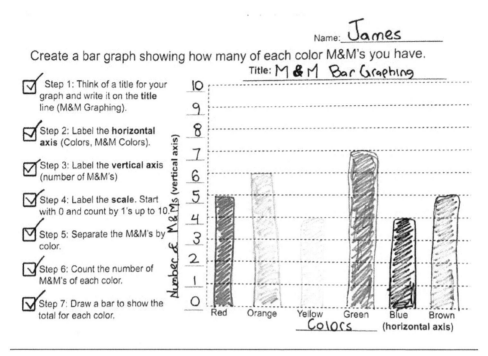

Figure 13.1 Example of Simplifying Task Directions for Creating a Bar Graph

as manipulatives, calculators, or visual prompts. Additionally, teachers can build varying levels of difficulty into the instructional materials so that students can progress from beginning to intermediate to advanced. Figure 13.2 shows an example of how teachers can structure materials that build sequentially in difficulty. Specifically, this is a visual model for building the levels of difficulty into spelling rules for the letter -y based on its position in a written word. Different levels of difficulty are labeled and presented independently of each other based on the student's current level of understanding of the spelling concept as well as what has been explicitly taught. Practitioners can use this adaptation when introducing words with different levels of difficulty and placement of letter -y. Starting from the top of this visual, the spelling of letter -y moves from beginning to intermediate to advanced. Students can also use parts of this visual after a concept is taught as a reference when spelling words with -y as the final letter or vowel within a word. See Leopold (2019) for strategies for teaching spelling patterns. By having students create artwork in reference to spelling rules, teachers can provide culturally responsive opportunities for practice. Specifically, students can select a personally meaningful word that uses the target spelling rule and then create images of the word which they could share with the class.

Teachers can also alter the difficulty level by using a concrete-representational-abstract sequence when teaching mathematical operations. Using this sequence helps students "gain meaning from numbers and the mathematical concepts those numbers represent" (Hinton & Flores, 2019, p. 493). Figure 13.3 shows an example of a concrete-representational-abstract sequence for multiplication and division that students can use when making calculations. To create this adaptation, fold a piece of paper in fourths, then write the relevant information in each column. The students can cover (i.e., fold back) the more complex sections until they are ready to use them to solve problems. When using this strategy at Tier 1, a student may use only the columns that show the abstract examples of how to solve a problem (i.e., Inverse). At Tier 2, a student may need to fold his or her strategy sheet to reference the columns reflecting the representational steps of solving a problem (i.e., Benchmark

Spelling Tip
Final -y and y as a vowel

Mnemonic- My bunny

Beginning

In a one syllable word the final -y = /ī/

by	my	fly	why	try
spy	shy	dry	cry	fry

Intermediate

In a two syllable word the final -y = /ē/

bunny	candy	baby	body
foggy	hungry	ruby	copy

*Important Note- Sometimes -y = /ī/ at the end of multisyllabic words, in an accented syllable (Keep an eye out for morphemes -**fy** & -**ply**)*

lullaby	*deny*	*July*	*occupy*	*rely*
*veri**fy***	*re**ply***	*im**ply***	*classi**fy***	*sup**ply***

Advanced

Investigating -y in words of Greek origin

Mnemonic- What's the hype about Physics all about?

Closed Syllable Words -y = /i/

gym	myth	lynx
crypt	symbol	Physics

Open Syllable Words -y = /ī/

nylon	stylish	python

Vowel Consonant -e (VCe) Words -y (*as a vowel*) = /ī/

type	hype	style

Figure 13.2 Example of Altering Difficulty Level with Spelling

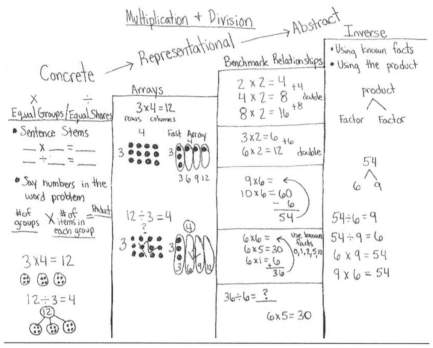

Figure 13.3 Example of Concrete-Representational-Abstract Sequence for Multiplication

Relationships, Arrays). Finally, at Tier 3 students could start with the concrete column (i.e., Equal Groups, Equal Shares) and progress through to representational and abstract solutions with direct instruction and repeated practice. The student and teacher can create this adaptation together as the student progresses through the different levels of difficulty.

Altering the Amount of Material Provided

Too much instructional material presented at once can be overwhelming to the extent that students may give up before they try. A struggling reader might refuse to read a particular text or complete a worksheet because there are too many words on a page and no pictures. When productivity is slow and laborious, teachers should examine various ways of altering the amount of material to best fit individual learners. Teachers should consider altering the amount of material by using any or a combination of the following.

- Reduce the amount of information on a page by using larger font, fewer words, and more blank space. Mayer's Coherence Principle states that we learn best when extraneous, distracting material is not included (Mayer, 2019). For computer-based instruction, this means showing one question at a time on the screen, using simple text and visuals, and using only material related directly to the topic.
- Present fewer learning trials on assignments (e.g., fewer math problems, fewer sentences to write). Have the student complete every other item or question on a math page or provide choices of which answers to complete (e.g., answer any 5 of the 10 questions).
- Use brief and clearly stated questions or response prompts. For multiple choice test questions, provide brief question stems and fewer choices (e.g., 2 instead of 4). Gradually alter the number of choices as students become more proficient.

What is the difference between weather and climate?

Weather is the condition of Earth's atmosphere at a particular time and place. We generally think of weather as the combination of temperature, humidity, precipitation, cloudiness, visibility, and wind. We talk about weather in terms of the near future: "What will it be like today?" "What is the temperature right now?" and "Will we get rain this week?"

Climate describes what an area's typical weather conditions are like over a long period of time—30 years or more. To describe the climate of a place, we might say what the temperatures are like during different seasons, or how much rain or snow typically falls. We talk about climate in terms of years, decades, centuries, even millions of years. When scientists talk about climate, they are looking at averages of precipitation, temperature, humidity, and other weather variables that occur over a long period of time in a particular place. Human activities, such as the release of greenhouse gases from burning fossil fuels, are major factors in the current rise in Earth's mean surface temperature that are influencing changes in climate.

The ☀difference between weather and climate is time. Weather is what is happening right now, and climate is what you typically expect the weather in a specific location to be like for this time of year.

Key: Key Vocabulary   Key Phrases   ☀ Main Idea

Figure 13.4 Example of Passage with Highlighted Text

The extent to which teachers alter material should be based on individual performance and responsiveness to instruction. As students become more proficient, teachers can gradually increase the amount of material until students can achieve mastery of grade-level content.

Highlighting Relevant Information

Many students with intensive learning needs have difficulty identifying important information in their content area assignments. Providing students with highlighted text that identifies key information aids struggling readers in comprehension by helping them focus on the crucial points and decreasing the overall amount of material. Figure 13.4 shows an example of highlighting for comprehension using a reading passage about the difference between climate and weather. The text has been pre-highlighted to direct the student's attention to key vocabulary, phrases, and the main idea. Highlighted text can be gradually faded until the students are able to independently identify the key points. Teachers can build on this adaptation by including examples of weather and climate in various countries around the globe and providing opportunities for their students to be the atmospheric scientists of a specific region. Students can demonstrate their knowledge by creating a newscast video clip.

Content Enhancements

Guided notes, graphic organizers, and mnemonic strategies are three content enhancements that help students identify, organize, and remember important information while actively responding to instruction.

Graphic Organizers

Graphic organizers are clear and concise visual representations of information that aid in organizing and comprehending academic content. Graphic organizers can be used across content areas and grade levels and may assist with the development of crucial cognitive skills such as categorizing,

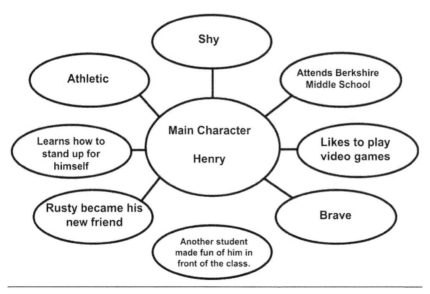

Figure 13.5 Example of Thinking Map for Main Character of a Story

critical thinking, and reflection (Root et al., 2021). Examples of graphic organizers include concept maps, storyboards, problem-solving organizers, timelines, sequence charts, and thinking maps. Students can use thinking maps to assist with reading comprehension, written expression, and studying for tests.

Figure 13.5 is an example of a thinking map that helps the student identify characteristics of a main character in a story. Teachers can guide students through completing thinking maps using modeling, questioning, and guided practice until students are able to complete them independently. An example of culturally responsive teaching is having students demonstrate how they may identify with characters in stories they read. Guiding students to choose reading materials that are relatable to their culture and then using a graphic organizer to compare and contrast their own cultural traits to those of a fictional character may allow deeper cultural connections to academic content.

Figure 13.6 shows a graphic organizer for solving word problems. The graphic organizer provides the following response prompts and placeholders to help the student solve the problem: draw a visual representation, write the steps for solving the equation, and write the solution. Depending on their proficiency level, students can complete a teacher-provided graphic organizer that already has some or most of the sections completed. As students make progress in their level of proficiency, the teacher can have them independently complete more sections of the graphic organizer.

Guided Notes

Many students have difficulty taking notes because they are not able to identify the key information or write it down quickly enough to keep pace with instruction. Providing students with guided notes helps to address these potential challenges. This type of note taking is used alongside a lecture or a presentation of material in a traditional classroom setting. Heward et al. (2022) recommend that guided notes include background information and visual prompts (e.g., blank lines, asterisks) so students know when and where to write key points. Guided notes provide students with opportunities for active responding while creating a standard set of notes for the student to study and can be adapted for all content areas and across grade levels (Heward et al., 2022). Guided notes can be designed by prioritizing what is most important for students to learn, creating a set of notes with all

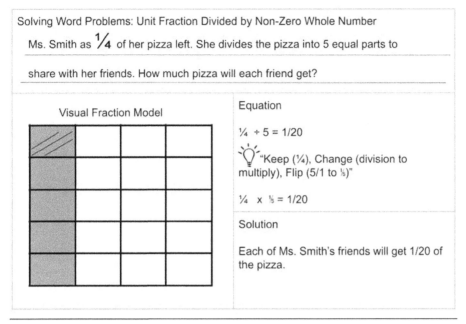

Solving Word Problems: Unit Fraction Divided by Non-Zero Whole Number

Ms. Smith as $\frac{1}{4}$ of her pizza left. She divides the pizza into 5 equal parts to share with her friends. How much pizza will each friend get?

Visual Fraction Model	Equation
	¼ ÷ 5 = 1/20
	"Keep (¼), Change (division to multiply), Flip (5/1 to ⅕)"
	¼ × ⅕ = 1/20
	Solution
	Each of Ms. Smith's friends will get 1/20 of the pizza.

Figure 13.6 Example of Graphic Organizer for Solving Word Problems

essential information that is clearly organized, and then deleting key concepts, facts, or relationships and replacing them with blank lines or other cues for the students to write their notes.

Guided notes that provide frequent and varied response opportunities will likely increase learning and motivation. Figure 13.7 shows an example of guided notes about Ancient Maya Math that includes a variety of appealing activities to keep students engaged and actively responding. The activities include activating background knowledge (e.g., Write your idea), interacting with peers (e.g., Think-Pair-Share), and completing example problems (e.g., TRY IT! Write 3). Teachers can also supplement guided notes with activities using manipulatives or practicing with whiteboards and dry erase markers.

Mnemonic Strategies

By using visual and verbal cues, mnemonic strategies enable students to relate new information to prior knowledge so they can retrieve information more readily (Boon et al., 2019). Mnemonic strategies use meaningful words and phrases to help students remember concepts. Familiar examples include using the mnemonic HOMES to remember the Great Lakes (Huron, Ontario, Michigan, Erie, Superior), or My Very Educated Mother Just Served Us Noodles to remember the planets (Mercury, Venus, Earth, Mars, Jupiter, Saturn, Uranus, and Neptune), and the phrase, "King Henry Died Drinking Chocolate Milk" to remember the metric system prefixes Kilo, Hecto, Deca, Deci, Centi, and Milli. The following are examples of mnemonic strategies for reading, writing, and math.

Reading

- RAP strategy for reading comprehension (Schumaker et al., 1985): Read a paragraph, Ask yourself the main idea and two details, Paraphrase the main idea and details in your own words.
- DISSECT for decoding words (Lenz & Hughes, 1990): Discover the context, Isolate the prefix, Separate the suffix, Say the word's stem, Examine the word's stem and segment into pronounceable

The Basics of Ancient Maya Math

Look at the picture on the right. What patterns do you recognize? What numbers are being represented?

Write your idea: _____

_____

_____

Base 20

The Maya number system is very different from the system we use every day in math class. The Maya used only 3 symbols to represent all numbers! They used a _dot_ to represent 1, a _line_ to represent 5, and a _shell_ to represent 0. The Maya wrote their numbers vertically and used zero as a placeholder.

The Maya used a place value system based on _20s_, not 10s like the number system we use today. So the place values were multiples of 20s: 1s, 20s (20x1), 400s (20x20), 8,000s (20x400), and so on.

Think-Pair-Share: Question, think, share answer with partner.

How is this different from our the Base 10 system we use?

Numbers 1- 4 were written using a row of dots.	The number 5 was written as a horizontal line.	Numbers 6 through 19 were written using a combination of lines and dots, or 5s and 1s. For example: 7 was written as one line with two dots above it: (5+2).
TRY IT! Write 3.	TRY IT! Write 5.	TRY IT! Write 7
Practice		
15 was written using two lines: (5+5+5) TRY IT! Write 15.	18 was written as 3 stacked lines with a row of 3 dots on top of them: (5+5+5+1+1+1) TRY IT! Write 18.	What do you think the numeral is for 20?

Numbers greater than 19

For numbers greater than 19, the symbols are arranged vertically in place values, with the greatest value on top. Each place value was 20 times greater than the one that came before it.

8000	•
400	(shell)
20	(line)
1	• •
What number is represented above? Discuss with your group.	

Figure 13.7 Example of Guided Notes for Ancient Maya Math

parts, Check with another person to see if you are correct, Try finding the word in the dictionary.

Written Expression

- COPS for editing (Schumaker et al., 1985): Capital letters, Overall Appearance, Punctuation, and Spelling
- C-SPACE for writing stories (Harris & Graham, 1996): Characters, Setting, Purpose, Action, Conclusion, Emotion

Math

- Please Excuse My Dear Aunt Sally for order of operations: Parentheses, Exponents, Multiply, Divide, Add, and Subtract.
- FILMS to add and subtract fractions (Ennis & Lozinski, 2019): Find the denominators, Identify the multiples, Locate the least common multiple, Multiply to make new fractions, Solve the problem.

When teaching students to use mnemonic strategies, teachers should use scaffolded instruction that consists of activating the student's background knowledge, discussing the strategy, modeling the strategy, memorizing the strategy, supporting the strategy, and using the strategy independently (Harris, 2021).

Selecting Appropriate Adaptations

When considering which adaptations to use and how to design them, teachers should consider individual strengths and learning needs. The student's individualized education program (IEP) outlines present levels of performance, goals and objectives, and current accommodations and/or modifications. The student's IEP should guide teachers with determining strengths, areas of need, and learning goals. Additionally, teachers should identify their students' individual areas of interest to build into instructional adaptations. This allows the student to make meaningful and culturally relevant connections with instructional material.

Once teachers have determined a student's Preferences, Interests, Needs, and Strengths (use the mnemonic PINS to remember), they should examine the content to be taught and determine what areas may need to be adapted to maximize student performance. For example, a student who has difficulty organizing information may benefit from graphic organizers. If a student has difficulty retaining and recalling information, mnemonic strategies will likely be helpful. Use guided notes for students who write slowly and/or have difficulty identifying the important points. Overall, the intent of adapting curriculum tasks and materials is to increase students' independence, engagement, and skill development.

Wrap Up

Implementing instructional adaptations is critical for students requiring intensive instruction and interventions to meet their individualized goals and to be successful in the general education setting. The adaptations presented in this chapter consisted of: (a) simplifying task directions; (b) altering the difficulty level of material; (c) altering the amount of material provided to students; and (d) highlighting relevant information. Determining the type and intensity of adaptation is carefully guided by the student's present levels of performance, areas of need, and grade-level content requirements. Additionally, this chapter addresses a plethora of high leverage adaptations with specific examples that can be used to increase student learning outcomes and overall performance across a variety of content areas. Finally, practitioners should consider which form of differentiation (providing content enhancements, modifying curriculum and/or providing adaptations) would be best suited as determined by each of their student's unique needs.

Tips

1. **Be culturally responsive**. The best way to be culturally responsive is to get to know your students and their families. Select reading materials, learning goals, and activities that connect with your student's background, family, and culture. Find out what the students are interested in and use their interests in your instructional materials to motivate them to learn important academic skills. Also, examine your instructional materials for cultural bias. Asking questions about not only the language used but also the images can be the starting point of determining the cultural responsiveness of your materials.
2. **Use frequent progress monitoring**. When adapting materials and tasks for intensive interventions, it is important to closely monitor student progress to determine if the adaptations are effective enough or if they need to be adjusted. Frequent progress monitoring will also guide teachers' instructional decisioning-making for determining changes to instruction, such as when to start fading adaptations. Continue monitoring progress after the adaptations are faded to assess maintenance outcomes.
3. **Collaborate with colleagues**. Meet with your grade-level colleagues and support staff to discuss ideas for creating and implementing adaptations. During the meeting, it is important to remember that one role of the special education teacher is to serve as a consultant for what strategies may work best given a student's preferences, interests, needs, and strengths addressed in the IEP. For example, the general education teacher can make guided notes for her class and the special education teacher can adapt those guided notes for the students with intensive learning needs. Both general education teachers and support staff can share in the responsibility of brainstorming, creating, and adapting curriculum.

Key Resources

Blackburn, B. R., & Witzel, B. S. (2018). *Rigor in the RTI and MTSS classroom: Practical tools and strategies*. Routledge.
Orton-Gillingham Academy: www.ortonacademy.org/
The Teacher Toolkit (n.d.). *Graphic organizers*. Retrieved April 19, 2022, from www.theteachertool kit.com/index.php/tool/graphic-organizers
TeacherVision (2020). *Simplifying or supplementing existing materials*. Retrieved April 20, 2022, from www.teachervision.com/curriculum-planning/simplifying-or-supplementing-existing-materials
Wise, M., & Cooper, C. (2019). Increasing the value of graphic organizers. *Edutopia*, www.edutopia.org/article/increasing-value-graphic-organizers

References

Al Hazmi, A. N., & Ahmad, A. C. (2018). Universal design for learning to support access to the general education curriculum for students with intellectual disabilities. *World Journal of Education*, 8(2), 66–72.
Alber-Morgan, S. R., Konrad, M., Harris, A., Sulaimon, T., Telesman, A. O., & Helton, M. R. (2022). Adapt curriculum tasks and materials for specific learning goals. In J. McLeskey, L. Maheady,

B. Billingsley, M. Brownell, & Tim Lewis (Eds.). *HLPs for Inclusive Classrooms* (2nd Ed., pp. 189–200). Routledge.

Boon, R. T., Urton, K., Grunke, M., & Rux, T. A. (2019). Mnemonic strategies in mathematics instruction for students with learning disabilities. *Learning Disabilities: A Multidisciplinary Journal, 24*(1), 49–62.

Browder, D. M., Trela, K., & Jimenez, B. (2007). Training teachers to follow a task analysis to engage middle school students with moderate and severe developmental disabilities in grade-appropriate literature. *Focus on Autism and Other Developmental Disabilities, 22*, 206–19.

Curtis, M. D., & Green, A. L. (2021) A systematic review of evidence-based practices for students with learning disabilities in social studies classrooms, *The Social Studies, 112*(3), 105–119.

Ennis, R. P., & Losinski, M. (2019). SRSD fractions: Helping students at risk for disabilities add/subtract fractions with unlike denominators. *Journal of Learning Disabilities, 52*(5), 399–412.

Fuchs, D., Fuchs, L. S., & Compton, D. L. (2012). Smart RTI: A next-generation approach to multi-level prevention. *Exceptional Children, 78*(3), 263–79.

Goodnight, C. I., Whitley, K. G., & Brophy-Dick, A. A. (2019). Effects of response cards on fourth-grade students' participation and disruptive behavior during language arts lesson in an inclusive elementary classroom. *Journal of Behavioral Education, 30*, 92–111.

Harris, K. R. (2021). SRSD instructional research for students with or at-risk for ld across the content areas: History and reflections. *Learning Disabilities Research and Practice, 36*(3), 235–41.

Harris, K. R., & Graham, S. (1996). *Making the writing process work: Strategies for composition and self-regulation.* Brookline.

Heward, W. L., Alber-Morgan, S. R., & Konrad, M. (2022). *Exceptional children: An introduction to special education (12th Edition).* Pearson.

Hinton, V. A., & Flores, M. M. (2019). The effects of the concrete representational abstract sequence for students at risk for mathematics failure. *Journal of Behavioral Education, 28*, 493–516.

Kettler, R. J. (2015). Adaptations and access to assessment of common core content. *Review of Research in Education, 39*, 295–330.

Lee, S. H., Wehmeyer, M. L., Soukup, J. H., & Palmer, S. B. (2010). Impact of curriculum modifications on access to the general education curriculum for students with disabilities, *Exceptional Children, 76*(2), 213–33.

Lenz, B. K., & Hughes, C.A. (1990). A word identification strategy for adolescents with learning disabilities. *Journal of Learning Disabilities, 23*, 149–58.

Leopold, K. (2019). *Multisensory techniques & mnemonics to keep your lessons effective and fun.* Retrieved from: www.ortonacademy.org/wp-content/uploads/2019/04/6F_Multisensory-Techniques_LeopoldR.pdf

Mayer, R.E. (2019). Thirty years of research on online learning. *Applied Cognitive Psychology, 33*(2), 152–9.

Peng, P., Fuchs, D., Fuchs, L. S., Elleman, A. M., Kearns, D. M., Gilbert, J. K., Compton, D. L., Cho, E., & Patton, S. (2019). A longitudinal analysis of the trajectories and predictors of word reading and reading comprehension development among at-risk readers. *Journal of Learning Disabilities, 52*, 195–208.

Peterson, L. S., Villarreal, V., & Castro, M. J. (2017). Models and frameworks for culturally responsive adaptations of interventions. *Contemporary School Psychology, 21*(3), 181–90.

Root, J., Ingelin, B., & Cox, S. K. (2021). Teaching mathematical word problem solving for students with autism spectrum disorder: A best-evidence synthesis. *Education and Training in Autism and Developmental Disabilities, 56*(4), 420–36.

Schumaker, J. B., & Fisher, J. B. (2021). 35 years on the road from research to practice: A review of content enhancement routines for inclusive subject-area classes: Part 1. *Learning Disabilities Research & Practice, 36*(3), 242–57.

Schumaker, J. B., Nolan, S. M. & Deshler, D. D. (1985). *The error monitoring strategy.* University of Kansas Press.

14
Teach Cognitive and Metacognitive Strategies to Support Learning and Independence

Andrew L. Hashey
SUNY Buffalo State College

Lauren L. Foxworth,
The College of New Jersey

Dane Marco Di Cesare,
Brock University

Tara L. Kaczorowski,
Daemen University

Introduction

Driven by the goal of ensuring their students' success, educators are constantly making instructional decisions in pursuit of the most optimal paths to learning and growth. Designing effective instruction in classrooms serving students with a wide range of strengths and support needs, means that teachers must focus on *what* students should learn and *how* successful students perform and self-regulate throughout the learning process. Much research has been devoted to the importance of teaching cognitive strategies to help students perform important cognitive tasks such as memorization, expression, and comprehension (Pressley & Harris, 2009). Informed by the process of *how* students learn and perform, strong cognitive strategies help learners by equipping them with procedural knowledge (i.e., knowing how to execute the steps involved in a task) as well as conditional knowledge (i.e., knowing under what conditions should the strategy be implemented). A separate and closely related aspect of learning cognitive strategies is the metacognitive skills learners employ as they approach and engage in complex tasks. This chapter articulates the need for teachers to explicitly teach cognitive and metacognitive strategies thereby promoting self-regulation. This better enables students to set goals, regulate attention, monitor their own performance, provide self-direction, and make adjustments to their actions in pursuit of their goals (McLeskey et al., 2018).

Educators who teach their students cognitive and metacognitive strategies during Tier 1 whole-class instruction offer learners the ability to better plan, execute, monitor, problem-solve, and evaluate their strategy use throughout the learning process. Collectively, the development of these strategies can help students develop into self-directed learners capable of achieving success across a wide variety of contexts (Luke, 2006). As expert learners themselves, teachers' deep understanding of the ways cognitive and metacognitive strategies influence student learning should be an essential underpinning of their design of effective instruction.

DOI: 10.4324/9781003276876-19

Some students naturally develop or acquire effective cognitive and metacognitive strategies independently or without extensive teaching. Other students, however, have difficulty developing these skills within the context of Tier 1 whole-class instruction, even when they are overtly introduced to such strategies by their teachers. Still others may not have been taught these types of strategies in the first place—conditions under which learning and performance may become even more difficult for students with significant learning support needs, including those with disabilities. Multi-tiered Systems of Support (MTSS) play a critical role in ensuring all learners make continual progress toward meaningful educational outcomes (Sugai & Horner, 2009).

Teaching students cognitive and metacognitive strategies in the context of supplemental Tier 2 instruction provides a means by which educators can intensify instruction and narrow the performance gap for students with or at-risk of disabilities, and for those with other complex learning needs. For students not responding to Tier 2 instruction, more intensive Tier 3 intervention may be warranted to ensure they meet their grade-appropriate learning objectives. Educators who teach cognitive and metacognitive strategies within Tier 2 services have the potential to empower learners experiencing learning difficulties in the whole-class setting (Harris et al., 2015). They should explicitly and systematically teach learners to self-regulate their thoughts, actions, and feelings throughout a learning task (Korinek & deFur, 2016).

Narrowing the Focus

When learners are introduced to new strategies, they are typically quite intentional as they focus their attention on various kinds of knowledge and skills required by a task, and they benefit from modeling and guided practice to approach proficiency. Over time, however, their support needs should gradually fade as students develop automaticity with a new strategy, and they exert far less conscious control over its use than they did when they were first acquiring the strategy. Helping all students develop into self-regulated and self-directed learners requires differentiated approaches across multi-tiered systems of support. Given schools' ability to provide targeted and well-designed instruction, all learners should be afforded the opportunity to acquire and develop proficiency in essential cognitive and metacognitive strategy usage.

To deliver meaningful instruction in this area, reflective educators must maintain a sharp focus on the extent to which their students are acquiring and applying skills in various domains, and then tailor instruction as needed. This chapter is designed to illustrate how educators who provide supplemental Tier 2 or Tier 3 instruction can deliver high-quality, culturally relevant cognitive and metacognitive instruction that is aligned with the instruction students receive in Tier 1 contexts. With this broad goal in mind, we raise several questions for readers who are becoming familiar with high leverage practices (HLPs) in general, and who want to learn more about implementing supplemental instruction to support cognitive and metacognitive strategy usage: What role can cognitive and metacognitive strategies play in providing Tier 2 and 3 services? In what ways can the alignment of instruction in Tiers 1 and 2 facilitate students' cognitive and metacognitive strategy use? How can teachers individualize and intensify cognitive and metacognitive strategy instruction in Tier 2 and 3?

Chapter Overview

1. Common approaches used to teach cognitive and metacognitive strategies.
2. Guidance and examples for implementing Tier 1-aligned, culturally responsive strategy instruction at Tier 2.
3. Vignettes detailing how to individualize and intensify cognitive and metacognitive strategy instruction for students receiving Tier 2 and 3 services across two classroom settings.

Using the HLP: Common Approaches Used to Teach and Support Cognition and Metacognition

High Leverage Practices (HLP) are those that have been shown to have a positive impact on student achievement and can be used across content areas and grade levels (McLeskey et al., 2018). HLPs differ from Evidence-Based Practices (EBP); while both are research-based, EBPs focus on specific content areas and/or grade levels (McLeskey et al., 2018). Cognitive and metacognitive approaches are HLPs; backed by research and can be taught to students across grade levels and curricular contexts. Cognition is the mental process involved in *learning, acquiring and using knowledge and understanding* through experiences, thoughts, and senses. Metacognition is *thinking about thinking*, using one's thoughts to think about how best to improve learning. Teachers can use cognitive and metacognitive approaches to teach subject matter knowledge (e.g., knowledge of literary elements used in analyzing poetry) or to teach subject matter skills and strategies (e.g., the *counting on* strategy used for calculating sums). In the classroom, there is a variety of common approaches used to teach and support cognition and metacognition, including Cognitive Self-Instruction (CSI), Self-Regulated Strategy Development (SRSD), Schema-Broadening Instruction (SBI), and the Think-Aloud procedure, used during the modeling phase of Explicit Instruction (EI) or modeling in general.

The goals of CSI are for students to develop self-regulation skills to assist in taking charge of their learning, cognition, and behavior (Manning, 1991). CSI is an approach consisting of specific strategies used in both teaching and learning. These strategies can promote memory functions, listening and reading comprehension, general problem solving, and self-management (Manning, 1991). Verbal rehearsal, for example, is a CSI strategy that can be used for both teaching and learning spelling words. An educator would explicitly teach verbal rehearsal to students who would then use this strategy on their own as they learn to spell new words. Other CSI strategies include but are not limited to SQ3R (Survey/Question/Read/Recite/Review), reciprocal teaching, dyadic problem solving, and critical self-questioning.

SRSD is a flexible approach designed to develop student confidence and build self-regulation skills. This approach is often used for teaching strategies, skills, and processes to support student performance. For example, a teacher may use SRSD to teach students to use the mnemonic writing strategies *POW* (*Pick my idea, Organize my notes, Write and say more*) and *STACS* (*Setting, Tension, rising Action, Climax, Solution*) to generate ideas, organize thoughts, and plan before beginning a narrative writing piece. SRSD stages for strategy acquisition include, developing background knowledge, discussing the strategy, modeling it, memorizing it, providing guided practice, and providing opportunities for independent practice. The six SRSD stages are cyclical in nature and each lesson should be repeated to mastery. Embedded within the lesson progression of SRSD are explicitly taught self-regulation strategies for goal-setting, self-monitoring, self-reinforcement, and self-talk, which can be individualized to meet student needs.

Schema-Broadening Instruction is an approach that can be used to teach word-problem solving through the identification of a problem schema, representation using diagrams or equations to represent the schema, and solving the word problem (Peltier & Vannest, 2017). In SBI, a teacher may teach the mnemonic *FOPS* to remind students to follow these steps: *Find the problem type, Organize the information in the problem using a diagram or equation, Plan to solve the problem*, and *Solve the problem*.

A *think-aloud* procedure is used to model thinking, verbalizing the thought processes used to consider, analyze, and solve problems (Van Someren et al., 1994). *Think-alouds* are used during the modeling phase of explicit instruction or when modeling other tasks. For example, in a *think-aloud*, a teacher may verbalize and draw a representation of their thinking about place value when adding two numbers like 34 plus 26. The teacher may say something along the lines of, "I'm going to start by breaking up my numbers into tens and ones. 34 can be written as 3 tens and 4 ones … 26 can be written as 2 tens and 6 ones. If I add together 4 ones and 6 ones, that gives me a group of ten. I can picture that on my tens frame." These approaches also use *questioning* to engage students and help them monitor their own progress while stimulating their thinking (de Boer et al., 2018). In whole or in part, these systematic approaches all contain common features; namely, they empower students to think about their own thinking, help learners build awareness of their knowledge processes, and thereby facilitate learning.

Considerations for Implementing Strategy Instruction Across All Tiers

Aligning Instruction Across the Tiers

Well-aligned instruction across the tiers can assist students in applying what they learn in Tier 2 or 3 in whole-class instructional contexts, and help them generalize metacognitive skills in contexts outside the classroom such as sports, or social contexts, etc. Vital to this goal is how skillfully educators use HLP #1: *collaborate with professionals to increase student success.* This underscores the essential nature of, and practical linkages between, the entire set of high leverage practices. For example, Tier 2 reading comprehension interventions aligned with high-quality Tier 1 instruction, have been shown to result in statistically significant, positive effects when compared to interventions designed without such alignment (e.g., Chambers et al., 2011; Fien et al., 2015; Stevens et al., 2020). Better aligned interventions make more efficient use of the available time typical in many schools' MTSS structures and offer outsized value to all stakeholders (Stevens et al., 2020). Greater alignment across the tiers also offers a way to address teachers' concerns about Tier 3 interventions appearing less effective than those at Tier 2 (Braun et al., 2020). Better alignment to what and how students are taught across the tiers may offer a more fruitful path forward than adding different instruction throughout the tiers. Therefore, the vignettes featured in this chapter are intended to illustrate the strong role such alignment can play in supercharging the instruction students receive across the tiers, and to highlight the specific ways in which cognitive and metacognitive strategies can be used to support learners with more complex learning profiles.

Culturally Responsive Strategy Instruction

When teaching cognitive and metacognitive strategies, educators have a unique opportunity to affirm and leverage students' experiences and identities through culturally responsive pedagogy (Muhammad, 2020). This approach is particularly important for students who are culturally diverse (e.g., multilingual learners; Black, Indigenous, People of Color [BIPOC]), those with disabilities, or those who are gender and sexually diverse; their experiences are not often included or represented in the classroom, and they may therefore see less relevance. For example, when developing positive self-talk statements as part of an SRSD approach to writing instruction, a teacher may choose to identify possible self-talk statements from a range of famous experts who represent a diverse range of people including people of color (i.e., Andre De Grasse, Lizzo), those with disabilities (i.e., Billie Eilish, Chris Rock), and who are representative of the 2SLGBTQ+ community (i.e., Kristen Stewart, Alexander Wang). Further, texts used in this strategy instruction should, in part, allow students to draw upon their funds of knowledge, and help students to see themselves in terms of their cultures, identities, interests, and experiences (Muhammed, 2020). Thus, for students learning a metacognitive strategy to assist with narrative writing (e.g., POW + STACS), texts used within the lessons may include *My Name* (Sandra Cisneros), *How to Be Black* (Baratunde Thurston), *Mixtapes Saved My Career* (Gucci Mane with Neil Martines-Belkin), and excerpts from *The Freedom Writers' Diary* (Erin Gruwell and the Freedom Writers), all texts that critically examine power dynamics and barriers that impede success in communities of color (Muhammed, 2020). By adopting an instructional stance that values students' lived experiences and identities, teachers can deliver cognitive and metacognitive strategy instruction that is both more relevant and more powerful.

Vignette 1: Individualizing and Intensifying Cognitive and Metacognitive Strategy Instruction

General and special educators often provide cognitive and metacognitive strategy instruction as a Tier 1 practice. Despite implementation of high-quality, research-supported strategy instruction, educators may find students who are not responding to instruction at Tier 1. Tier 2 provides an optimal context in which to individualize and/or intensify cognitive and metacognitive strategy instruction to support recall, self-regulation, motivation, persistence, and/or generalization. This individualization is important as it is not appropriate to provide one standardized recommendation for intensified Tier 2 support. The following vignette demonstrates how educators can individualize and intensify supports for different students based on data, as well as observed student strengths and needs.

Mr. Valasa currently uses explicit strategy instruction to support narrative essay writing in his 4th grade classroom. Specifically, Mr. Valasa is teaching the POW + STACS (Pick my idea, Organize my notes, Write and say more + Setting, Tension, rising Action, Climax, and Solution) idea generation, planning, and narrative writing strategies. At Tier 1, he has been careful to develop background knowledge, to expertly model the use of a graphic organizer matched to the narrative writing strategy, and to engage all learners frequently, providing immediate affirmative and corrective feedback with every opportunity to respond. Mr. Valasa has also been keeping data to inform his instruction; he has been counting the number of narrative essay elements included before and during instruction and has also been measuring essay quality through a holistic scoring rubric. However, Mr. Valasa's class data shows that not all of his students are responding to his instruction. Mr. Valasa wonders, since he is already implementing research-supported strategy instruction, how might individualizing and intensifying strategy instruction look at Tiers 2 and 3?

Teachers providing Tier 2 instruction can dive deeper into student data and intensify, adapt, or individualize cognitive and metacognitive strategy instruction. Analysis of Mr. Valasa's classroom essay data revealed three students—Mia, Bryant, and Joey—were not responding at Tier 1: their number of narrative essay elements and essay quality scores before instruction were similar to their scores during guided and independent practice. Careful observation and analysis of student work during the writing process and discussions with each student helped Mr. Valasa to reveal individual strengths and support needs for each student: *Mia is experiencing significant difficulty remembering the mnemonic. She has shared that she loves to think of story ideas but cannot remember what is included in a strong narrative and is not sure where to begin or end the narrative writing process. On the other hand, Bryant, who identifies as non-binary, can successfully remember all strategy parts, but is having difficulty getting started and staying on task. Bryant reports feeling overwhelmed by the writing process and has trouble staying focused on the task. A third student, Joey, says he dislikes writing and does not want to write. Joey said he knows he is not a strong writer, as his teachers have given him low grades on writing tasks many times in the past.*

Mia, Bryant, and Joey's strengths and areas for improvement in their classroom should inform instruction at Tier 2; Self-regulated Strategy Development (SRSD), for example, would pair well with Mr. Valasa's current methods and may help to provide a foundation for individualizing cognitive and metacognitive supports for Mia, Bryant, and Joey. Mr. Valasa can consider several options for individualizing and intensifying strategy and metacognitive strategy instruction within an SRSD framework at Tier 2. First, for Mia, he adds cue cards and a personal mnemonic chart Mia will keep in her writing folder to help build the background vocabulary (e.g., setting, rising action, climax, solution, etc.) necessary for mastering independent strategy use. The cue cards include pictures and examples from narratives that are familiar and culturally relevant to Mia, specifically, and help her quickly understand and recall the strategy. Repeated opportunities for Mia to practice and master recalling the strategy parts using the cue cards help reduce the cognitive load required to success-fully implement the strategy during the writing process, allowing Mia to focus on her strength—her powerful ideas!

At Tier 2, Mr. Valasa will repeat POW + STACS lessons to mastery—something he was unable to do in whole-class instruction. Since Mia often has difficulty remembering where to begin, Mr. Valasa will infuse self-instructions that heavily emphasize the step-by-step process of using the strategy into a think-aloud during his model. For example, during the model, he might say, "*I have to start with the first step … What is the first step in this strategy? Oh yeah, the first step in POW is P, Pick my idea!*" After the model, Mr. Valasa can ask Mia, what were some things she heard him say to get started with the writing process. He might then ask Mia, "*What are some things* you *can say to* yourself *to get started with the process? Let's write down some of your own self-instructions here and keep them in your writing folder! You can refer to these as you need them.*"

In sum, Mia's Tier 2 strategy instruction plan includes: (a) a shift to SRSD framework for lesson design; (b) cue cards with familiar picture-based examples and personal mnemonic chart; (c) oppor-tunities to practice with vocabulary to facilitate understanding and recall; (d) lessons repeated to mastery; and (e) self-instructions infused into the model and creation of personal self-instructions for use during guided practice and beyond.

Bryant's strengths and areas for support are different from Mia's. Bryant can successfully recall strategy parts, but they have difficulty getting started and staying on task. In this case, Mr. Valasa might intensify implementation of metacognitive strategies for building and maintaining motiv-ation and engagement. Bryant would likely benefit from goal-setting, self-monitoring, and self-talk (specific to self-evaluation and focusing on attention). After developing background knowledge and discussing baseline performance, Mr. Valasa might develop a learning strategies contract to set writing goals with Bryant. Following Bryant's lead, Mr. Valasa and Bryant can set goals together using information from Bryant's initial essay. Tier 2 provides space for them to discuss how Bryant and Mr. Valasa can work together to meet Bryant's goals. Bryant can keep a copy of their self-developed goals on their learning strategies contract in their writing folder along with other writing materials.

Because Bryant also has difficulty staying on task, Mr. Valasa models methods for self-monitoring throughout the writing process. Mr. Valasa can create and model how to use a self-monitoring chart matched to POW + STACS elements. Bryant can use the chart to monitor where they are in the process (even if they take a break during the strategy implementation process), chunking a large, complex process into manageable steps. A self-monitoring chart can be tailored to Bryant's interest (e.g., a sports field with spaces to check off for setting, tension, rising action, climax, and solution). In addition to guiding Bryant in utilizing goal-setting and self-monitoring, Mr. Valasa models self-talk specific to self-evaluation and maintaining attention. Mr. Valasa can model his own self-talk in a think-aloud when he is feeling overwhelmed with the process, for example, "*Am I following my plan? I just have to move through the steps and can check them off as I go through each one!*" As with Mia, Mr. Valasa lets Bryant record some statements they can tell themselves when they are feeling overwhelmed with the writing process. Bryant can refer to these as needed during guided and independent practice opportunities. In sum, Bryant's Tier 2 strategy instruction plan includes: (a) learning strategies contract; (b) self-monitoring sheet with high-interest theme; (c) self-talk spe-cific to self-evaluation and attention infused into the model and creation of personal self-instructions for use during guided practice and beyond.

As demonstrated above, self-talk can be individualized to strengthen positive metacognition. While Bryant may need self-talk support specific to self-evaluation and focusing on attention, Joey, Mr. Valasa's third student in need of Tier 2 support may need greater emphasis on self-talk that builds self-efficacy, as he currently holds a negative view of himself as a writer. For example, Mr. Valasa will

Figure 14.1 Joey's Self-Statements

model and support development of positive self-statements such as, "*I know this is tough. I can take time to think of a good idea and start there*" or self-reinforcing statements such as, "*I checked off all the steps on my chart! This is a strong essay!*" Mr. Valasa can use a self-monitoring chart in tandem with self-reinforcement self-talk to model and support positive metacognition. Figure 14.1 provides a sample of Joey's self-statements sheet for supporting development of positive metacognition, linked to his interest in dinosaurs.

After noticing Joey's progress in guided practice, Mr. Valasa will also show Joey his baseline essay compared with his current essay using the self-monitoring chart to further build confidence. Additionally, high-interest writing prompts and themed culturally relevant writing folder materials matched to his interests/strengths can help to make the writing process more approachable and encourage Joey to engage in the learning process. As with Bryant, Mr. Valasa will create a learning strategies contract with Joey to foster motivation and engagement with writing. And, as with Mia, ensuring lessons are carefully scaffolded for Joey and repeated to mastery can help ensure Joey's success with difficult content. In sum, Joey's Tier 2 strategy instruction plan includes the following: (a) self-talk supports specific to building self-efficacy; (b) high-interest writing prompts; (c) themed, culturally relevant writing folder materials matched to his interests/strengths; (d) self-monitoring chart and self-reinforcement supports; (e) learning strategies contracts or goal-setting sheets; and (f) lessons repeated to mastery.

Tier 2 instruction can be individualized and intensified to address students' strengths and needs as revealed through classroom assessment data and observations of and discussions with the student. As demonstrated above, SRSD offers a strong foundation for carefully scaffolding strategy instruction and for bolstering self-regulation skills. Using SRSD, Mr. Valasa can continue to teach the same content, POW + STACS strategies, yet design specialized supports for students in Tier 2 to highlight strengths and intensify instruction around student needs, in an engaging and culturally relevant manner.

Vignette 2: Incorporating Cognitive/Metacognitive Strategies within Inquiry-Based
Learning Models

While cognitive and metacognitive strategy instruction is often delivered using explicit or teacher-directed instructional methods, these strategies can also be successfully incorporated into inquiry or discovery-based learning models, particularly when teachers carefully consider their use of supplementary instruction time before and after the inquiry lesson. Thus, the value of these strategies can be yoked across pedagogical approaches.

Ms. Bell, a middle school science teacher, and Mr. Powell, a special education teacher, are co-teaching a physics unit about motion. The district follows an inquiry-based science curriculum in which students engage in hands-on labs and discovery learning to explore scientific concepts. Students are currently learning about the difference between speed and velocity and have examined the difference between the two by following structured inquiry labs with ultrasonic motion detectors. As a chapter assessment, Ms. Bell is planning a guided inquiry lesson where students will design and execute their own scenarios to demonstrate their understanding of the difference between speed and velocity:

- *Prompt 1: Design and execute a scenario where (a) the speed and velocity of a moving object are equal, and (b) where the speed and velocity of a moving object are **not** equal.*
- *Prompt 2: Describe a scenario when measuring the **velocity** of an object is a more meaningful/ useful measurement than measuring its **speed**. **Justify** your response.*

Based on the assessments from previous lessons, Mr. Powell believes some students have developed the skills and understandings to both design and execute their own examples to show the difference between speed and velocity. However, assessment results also suggest that some students may still need support to complete this activity. Mr. Powell decides to use a variety of cognitive and metacognitive strategies to help all students both during the lesson (i.e., Tier 1 instruction), and through supplementary Tier 2 and Tier 3 instruction for some students.

Supports for All (Tier 1): Cognitive/Metacognitive Scaffolding

When the cognitive demands of a task outweigh the ability of a learner to complete it successfully on their own, teachers have an opportunity to provide the essential support (i.e., scaffolding) enabling learners to bridge the gap (Wood et al., 1976). Like in other instructional contexts, cognitive scaffolds used within inquiry models can take many forms, such as graphic organizers to help support learners' planning and organization, verbal or written prompts to guide the learner in self-monitoring the steps in a procedure, or probing questions that can help build or activate a learner's conceptual knowledge. Teachers who attend to the cognitive strategies required for successful inquiry-based learning are well positioned to support all learners. When teachers collaborate to ensure these skills are taught and reinforced across the tiers, they can provide learners with pre-planned and timely supports that help them accomplish challenging tasks, such as those needed for scientific inquiry in the middle-grades (Flick, 2000).

Mr. Powell designed a scaffolded planning document for students to use as a cognitive and metacognitive support during the lesson (see Figure 14.2). At the top of this document, he included definitions with visual representations for both speed and velocity as well as self-monitoring prompts to serve as metacognitive cues when they are planning their scenarios (e.g., Does the direction of the motion matter in this scenario?). As the students work, both Mr. Powell and Ms. Bell also ask probing questions to groups to direct student thinking as needed (e.g., What path is the ball traveling when you throw it? Does it change direction?).

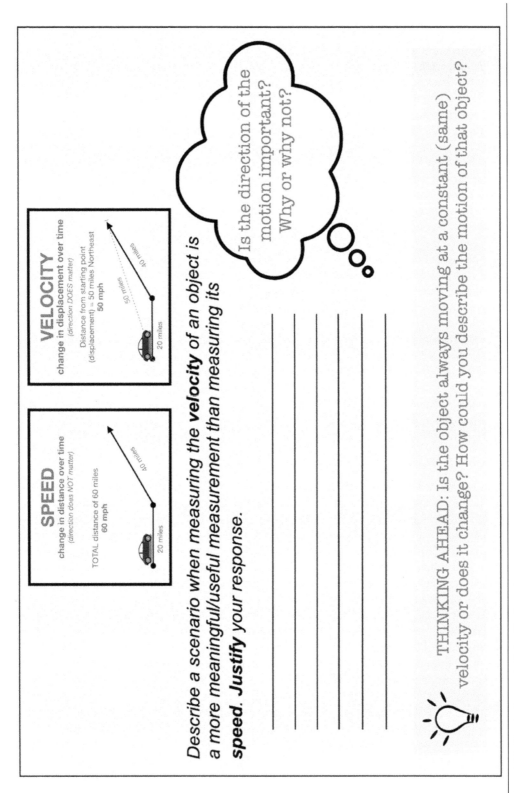

Figure 14.2 Planning Document with Cognitive Support

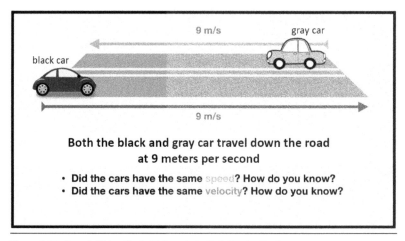

Figure 14.3 Example Picture Card with Prompts for Explicit Instruction Lesson

Tier 2 or 3 Instruction Before the Lesson: Explicit Teaching of Conditional Knowledge

Students with more complex learning needs who will be taught using constructive learning approaches can benefit from Tier 2 instruction *before* they engage in the whole-class lessons to reduce the cognitive load associated with more complex learning tasks (Sweller, 2012). Tier 2 pre-teaching can include explicit instruction in conditional knowledge needed for strategy usage and can incorporate scaffolds such as mnemonics to support, for example, declarative and procedural knowledge. Supplemental instruction such as this can equip learners with knowledge and skills that position them for successful future learning.

Built into his daily schedule, Mr. Powell also has a supplemental resource room block to support some of the students in the class in different content areas. Although Mr. Powell sometimes uses this time for reviewing lessons, he decides to use this block for pre-teaching content prior to the Tier 1 lesson. Two students in Ms. Bell's science class are also in Mr. Powell's resource room, so he designed a direct instruction lesson prior to the guided inquiry lesson to review the definitions of speed and velocity, and to support conditional knowledge of deciding when it is more useful to measure velocity vs. speed. First, students watched a music video (e.g., Jam Campus, 2019) that serves as a mnemonic support to review the definitions, formulas, and situational context for speed and velocity. Next, Mr. Powell introduced a series of images, GIFs, and video clips showing different objects in motion in a careful sequence to build understanding of speed and velocity. After each clip, he leads students through a series of questions about the object to calculate the different parts of a speed or velocity equation (see Figure 14.3).

Tier 2 or Tier 3 Instruction After the Lesson: Supports for Thinking and Generalization

Students receiving Tier 2 or 3 services can benefit from more individualized instruction after learning new skills to solidify their understanding and improve their ability to generalize new knowledge and skills to other contexts. Explicit review of key concepts can help reinforce lesson objectives and clarify misconceptions, while metacognitive think alouds can help hone students' thinking (e.g., self-monitoring) and help demonstrate what they learned.

At the end of every science block, Ms. Bell and Mr. Powell build in 20 minutes of flexible instruction time that can be used for extra practice, enrichment, or Tier 2 instructional support. Because the students were grouped heterogeneously for the main activity, Mr. Powell wants to make sure the students needing Tier 2 or Tier 3 support for science can explain what their group designed for the lesson. While Ms. Bell facilitated some practice and enrichment for some students, Mr. Powell facilitated an explicit lesson review for the others. First, Mr. Powell presented a scenario of his own. He used a metacognitive think aloud to model an explanation for the students for each prompt. Next, one group at a time, he asked students to explain and model what their group designed while prompting or adding information as needed. After each scenario was presented, Mr. Powell prompted them through a series of questions and tasks to reinforce the concepts and promote generalization. For one task, he asked two students to stand 5 feet apart and try to throw the ball back and forth at about the same **speed**. *Then he asked the students how they would have to arrange themselves to throw the ball at the same* **velocity**. *One student had an idea to stand next to the first student and both throw the ball at the same speed* in the same direction *so the ball would be moving at the same velocity.*

Wrap Up

An essential aspect of effective supplemental strategy instruction is the extent to which it aligns with the teaching and learning students experience in Tier 1. The approaches to providing such instruction, described in the vignettes, illustrate a flexible range of opportunities teachers can use to support learners' cognitive and metacognitive growth. In particular, the ability to use data to individualize and intensify cognitive and metacognitive strategy instruction at Tier 2 is what allows educators to help bridge the gap between students' current independent performance and the desired grade-level learning outcomes they are pursuing.

Tips

- *Aligned.* Ensure Tier 2 supports are in direct alignment with Tier 1 instruction and goals, and teach students how to use relevant cognitive and metacognitive strategies. This alignment, achieved through educators' commitment to collaboration and ongoing communication, makes certain that supplemental strategy instruction can be impactful and applicable within the core instruction they receive at Tier 1.
- *Individualized.* Tier 2 strategy instruction should be tailored to build on individual students' strengths while also addressing their specific areas of need. The following materials can be tailored and/or intensified to facilitate independent cognitive and metacognitive strategy-use at Tiers 2 and 3: mnemonic charts, graphic organizers, cue cards with familiar picture-based examples to support background knowledge and recall/memory, learning strategies contracts or goal-setting sheets, high-interest and culturally-relevant reading passages/writing prompts/planning materials, themed writing folder materials matched to student interests/strengths, self-monitoring chart, self-reinforcement supports, lessons repeated to mastery, teacher-created self-talk infused into model, and student-created self-talk for use during guided practice and beyond (self-instructions, self-evaluation, self-reinforcement, self-control, focusing on attention, etc.).
- *Flexible.* Use cognitive and metacognitive strategy instruction flexibly to support student learning within varied instructional orientations (e.g., inquiry learning, direct instruction); students must employ these strategies in all learning contexts. By maintaining a focus on the essential strategies expert learners use to perform cognitive tasks, teachers can apply this high leverage practice across the full range of instructional orientations and with varying degrees of individualization and intensification, as determined by student needs.

Key Resources

- https://highleveragepractices.org/hlp-14-use-cognitive-and-metacognitive-strategies   https://intensiveintervention.org
- https://ThinkSRSD.com

- https://iris.peabody.vanderbilt.edu/module/srs/#content
- Powerful Writing Strategies for All Students (Harris et al., 2008)

References

Braun, G., Kumm, S., Brown, C., Walte, S., Hughes, M. T., & Maggin, D. M. (2020). Living in Tier 2: Educators' perceptions of MTSS in urban schools. *International Journal of Inclusive Education*, *24*(10), 1114–28.

Chambers, B., Slavin, R. E., Madden, N. A., Abrami, P., Logan, M. K., & Gifford, R. (2011). Small-group, computer-assisted tutoring to improve reading outcomes for struggling first and second graders. *Elementary School Journal*, *111*, 625–40.

de Boer, H., Donker, A. S., Kostons, D. D., & van der Werf, G. P. (2018). Long-term effects of meta-cognitive strategy instruction on student academic performance: A meta-analysis. *Educational Research Review*, *24*, 98–115.

Fien, H., Smith, J. L. M., Smolkowski, K., Baker, S. K., Nelson, N. J., & Chaparro, E. (2015). An examination of the efficacy of a multi-tiered intervention on early reading outcomes for first grade students at risk for reading difficulties. *Journal of Learning Disabilities*, *48*, 602–21.

Flick, L. B. (2000). Cognitive scaffolding that fosters scientific inquiry in middle level science. *Journal of Science Teacher Education*, *11*(2), 109–29.

Harris, K. R., Graham, S., & Adkins, M. (2015). Practice-based professional development and self-regulated strategy development for Tier 2, at-risk writers in second grade. *Contemporary Educational Psychology*, *40*, 5--6.

Jam Campus (2019, April 9). *Speed and Velocity Song | Science Music Video* [video]. YouTube. https://youtu.be/s4sdXMbiu10

Korinek, L., & deFur, S. H. (2016). Supporting student self-regulation to access the general education curriculum. *Teaching Exceptional Children*, *48*(5), 232–42.

Luke, S. D. (2006). The power of strategy instruction. In *Evidence for Education*. Volume I, Issue I. *National Dissemination Center for Children with Disabilities*.

Manning, B. H. (1991). *Cognitive self-instruction (CSI) for classroom processes*. SUNY Press.

McLeskey, J., Maheady, L., Billingsley, B., Brownell, M. T., & Lewis, T. J. (Ed.) (2018). *High leverage practices for inclusive classrooms*. Routledge.

Muhammad, G. (2020). *Cultivating genius: An equity framework for culturally and historically responsive literacy*. Scholastic.

Peltier, C., & Vannest, K. J. (2017). A meta-analysis of schema instruction on the problem-solving performance of elementary school students. *Review of Educational Research*, *87*(5), 899–920.

Pressley, M., & Harris, K. R. (2009). Cognitive strategies instruction: From basic research to classroom instruction. *Journal of Education*, *189*(1–2), 77–94.

Stevens, E. A., Vaughn, S., Swanson, E., & Scammacca, N. (2020). Examining the effects of a tier 2 reading comprehension intervention aligned to tier 1 instruction for fourth-grade struggling readers. *Exceptional Children*, *86*(4), 430–48.

Sugai, G., & Horner, R. H. (2009). Responsiveness-to-intervention and school-wide positive behavior supports: Integration of multi-tiered system approaches. *Exceptionality*, *17*(4), 223–237.

Sweller, J. (2012). Human cognitive architecture: Why some instructional procedures work and others do not. In K. R. Harris, S. Graham, T. Urdan, C. B. McCormick, G. M. Sinatra, & J. Sweller (Eds.), *APA educational psychology handbook, Vol. 1. Theories, constructs, and critical issues* (pp. 295–325). American Psychological Association. https://doi.org/10.1037/13273-011

Van Someren, M., Barnard, Y. F., & Sandberg, J. (1994). *The think-aloud method: A practical approach to modeling cognitive processes*. Academic Press.

Wood, D., Bruner, J. S., & Ross, G. (1976). The role of tutoring in problem solving. *Child Psychology & Psychiatry & Allied Disciplines*, *17*(2), 89–100.

15
Provide Scaffolded Supports

Troy V. Mariage
Michigan State University
Elizabeth A. Hicks
Michigan State University

Introduction

There are few things more rewarding than seeing students with some of the most intense learning needs grow and develop. Students with intensive learning needs are defined in this chapter as students whose needs may be such that they typically receive some of their instruction in small groups, pairs, or even 1-to-1 instruction (Tier 2, 3) for a portion of the day. These students most often have an Individualized Education Plan (IEP) and are provided tailored instruction that is delivered with greater intensity to address students' unique learning needs. This process involves the individually planned and systematically monitored arrangement of teaching procedures, adapted equipment and materials, and accessible settings (Disabled World, 2019; Yell, 2019). This definition encompasses the goals of the high-leverage practice of providing intensive scaffolded supports, described as the provision of supports that allows an individual to accomplish a task that they could not achieve independently.

Providing scaffolded support for students with intense needs is often necessary to keep them in their zone of proximal development (Vygotsky, 2012). Instruction within a student's zone of proximal development is challenging enough that students are not yet independent and may be successful with targeted supports, or scaffolds. Scaffolds can be pre-planned and frequently include the creation of tools (e.g., cue-cards, language stems, anchor posters, calculator) that are called on to bridge what a student knows to new learning, but also are provided in the moment as the teacher dynamically assesses the student's current functioning in their zone of proximal development (Reiser, 2004). This attunement to the student's current state of understanding demands that teachers and interventionists expand their assessment practices to include dynamic assessments suited to gathering in the moment data to move students toward independent performance (Grant et al., 2012).

Finally, our understanding of (dis)ability has shifted and changed as new research, learning theories, and societal values in areas of diversity, equity, and inclusion have evolved (Baines, 2014; Trent et al., 1998; Valle & Connor, 2019). Rather than being viewed solely as a pathology or deficit within an individual, it is now understood that (dis)ability is partly or even predominantly a function of society's response to a physical or mental condition that limits a person's movements, senses, or activities (Gargiulo & Bouck, 2020). A high school student with a severe reading decoding disability (e.g., dyslexia) gains access to all educational materials as a digital file that can be read aloud with a

DOI: 10.4324/9781003276876-20

free text-reading application, allowing them to concentrate on the meaning of the content and complete their high school diploma. A third-grade student on the autism spectrum with limited expressive language uses an Alternative and Augmented Communication (AAC) device to interact with peers, paraeducators, teachers, and family. A high school student with intellectual disabilities and challenges in working memory has video models of the six job tasks at their worksite loaded on their smart phone, allowing them to replay the performance of a model, imitate the model, and complete each task to be independently employed (Sherman & De La Paz, 2012). Each example illustrates the potential power of scaffolded supports—either temporary or permanent—to support all learners.

Narrowing the Focus

Effective teachers are responsive to the developmental needs of their students and know how to intensify scaffolded support when students are unable to complete a task without additional support or reduce scaffolded support when a student is ready to assume more responsibility for learning. This chapter first outlines several principles of scaffolded support that guide decision-making for teachers using this high leverage instructional practice. For students with more intense learning needs, it is important to combine scaffolded support with other high leverage practices, including explicit instruction (Archer & Hughes, 2011; Rosenshine, 2012), cognitive strategy instruction (Boardman et al., 2013; Graham et al., 2005), and positive behavioral supports (Sugai & Horner, 2020) to name just a few. The chapter includes two examples of teachers who provide intensive scaffolded support in conjunction with other high leverage practices to guide learners with complex needs (see Fuchs et. al., 2018 for taxonomy of intensive interventions).

In the first example, we observe two early elementary students on the autism spectrum who are just learning that words on the paper can represent concrete actions or events (Mariage et al., 2021). The teacher is faced with a situation whereby students view reading as an activity, but not as a tool to construct meaning or an interaction with the text. This example highlights how a teacher may use pre-planned scaffolds in concert with assessment and data-based decision making, principles of explicit instruction, and strategy instruction.

In the second example, we examine how a secondary special education teacher uses discussion to scaffold learning in a first lesson for their IEP student's understanding of main ideas and key details in informational text. We then examine how the teacher employed a series of tools to scaffold learning toward independently researching and writing informational essays over the remainder of the year. This combination of teaching reading and writing of informational text foregrounds the necessity of an abiding knowledge of the scope and sequence of the curriculum to provide intensive scaffolds and supports to allow students to access grade level curriculum. The chapter concludes with a summary wrap-up, additional tips, and additional resources to extend learning.

Chapter Overview

1. Describe four principles that guide a teacher's decision-making when creating scaffolded supports (e.g., tools) and planning activities where students share their thinking in ways that allow the teacher to provide or fade scaffolds on a moment-to-moment basis.
2. Describe ways that a teacher provided intensive direct instruction and scaffolded instruction to help her two young students on the autism spectrum begin to understand that reading written directions can result in a behavioral performance that allows them to accomplish desirable goals, including accessing a preferred item.
3. Describe how a secondary self-contained teacher organized teaching tools across a year to provide multiple scaffolds to accomplish an IEP student's goal of independently writing a research paper.

Using the HLP: Principles of Scaffolded Supports

Decisions about whether to add or fade support on a moment-to-moment basis or over time are not arbitrary, but informed by knowledge of the learner, their goals, and an understanding of the tools available to scaffold learning (CEC, 2017; Mariage et al., 2019). Four principles that guide decision-making about whether, how, and when to adjust support follow:

1. **Responsive instruction**. The essence of providing scaffolded support is one's ability to dynamically assess where learners are functioning on a particular skill, strategy, concept, or process (Wood et al., 1976). Teachers who provide effective scaffolded support are excellent observers who have a deep understanding of where a student or group of students is functioning based upon formal, informal, and dynamic assessment of understanding (Bakker et al., 2015). Teachers have a sense of what a student can do independently, but then create conditions where students make their understanding visible through thinking aloud as they are solving a problem, writing down their understanding, or performing a task. With this information teachers can then respond to a student's current level of understanding by adding or fading support on a moment-to-moment basis. Providing scaffolded support is based on data—information that a student provides in the moment and knowledge of the student learned over time.

2. **Knowledge of curricular goals and short-term objectives**. Effective teachers have a deep understanding of the scope and sequence of the curriculum in different content areas and understand that short-term objectives contain the prerequisite skills necessary to achieve a curriculum goal. Content knowledge is essential to effectively anticipate what tools and scaffolds may be necessary to bridge to the next objective. A hallmark of teachers who work with students who have intense learning needs is their understanding of task analysis, breaking down complex skills into smaller more manageable parts, and the necessity of teaching successive approximations of those skills to build up to a complete performance. For example, an algebra course requires students to solve linear equations; however, a student who has not yet mastered basic mathematical operations (e.g., addition, subtraction, multiplication, and division) will likely struggle. Continued work on foundational math skills while also providing scaffolds such as a calculator, a video of a teacher solving a linear equation that can be viewed multiple times, or mnemonics that outline the steps are ways to support learners access their grade level curriculum.

3. **Understanding the learner**. Providing scaffolded support is bi-directional and relational, as teachers are always considering the whole child. Teachers should seek to develop an understanding of how a student's ability and skills as well as their race, ethnicity, gender, sexual orientation, language, religion, and socio-economic background impact their school experience and relationships (Lawrence-Brown & Sapon-Shevin, 2015). Furthermore, a student's positive and negative experiences with education that define their personal school history and circumstances outside of school also are critical factors to consider (Milner, 2021). A student's comfort, trust, and perceived self-efficacy are often preconditions that determine whether and how much they share (Milner et al., 2019). For example, it is common for students with intense emotional-behavioral needs to be guarded to protect their dignity and avoid embarrassment. Without relational trust, a student may prevent the teacher from assessing what they know and curtailing opportunities for the teacher to scaffold performance. A teacher's ability to understand and leverage a student's motivation and engagement creates conditions for participation. This type of deep understanding is gained through observation of and interaction with a student in multiple contexts, both structured and unstructured, over time. When teachers design learning activities that are culturally relevant and personally meaningful to students (Milner, 2021), they create learning zones that allow them access to what a student already knows and can do to support the development of new skills and abilities.

4. **Gradually release responsibility**. The metaphor of a scaffold is that it is a temporary support to allow someone to accomplish a task or a portion of a task that they cannot complete on their

own. In many cases, the terminal goal is internalized, self-regulated, and independent perform-ance. This means that teachers need to have an eye on the future independent performance they would like the student to achieve. We have found that sharing or co-creating goals with a student can go a long way in transferring ownership of learning and behavior from the teacher to the student. Much of teaching resembles an apprenticeship process, where the teacher provides more explicit and direct instruction in the initial stages of teaching, while gradually inviting increased student participation in the form of guided and independent practice (Mariage et al., 2020). In one classroom, the teacher was directly teaching students discussion strategies from the SCORE strategy: **S**hare ideas, **C**ompliment others, **O**ffer help and encouragement, **R**ecommend changes nicely, **E**xercise self-control (Vernon et al., 1993). The teacher created a large SCORE poster, defined each strategy, explained where someone might use the strategy (e.g., in cooperative groups or working with a peer) and modeled sentence stems for students to emulate (e.g., I think that…, I liked the way Jason…). The teacher then developed a self-monitoring checklist that allowed students to self-evaluate whether they used the strategies in a group or partner activity. Initially, the teacher also filled out a self-monitoring SCORE Card and compared their ratings with the child's. This initial teacher rating was then faded to the provision of peer support or self-ratings, but when the teacher sensed student behavior was slipping, she reintroduced the self-monitoring SCORE Card as a booster lesson to remind students of the discussion norms. Providing scaffolded support is rarely a linear process and should not be viewed rigidly as learning often requires a return to more explicit teaching or re-teaching of a skill or strategy.

Example #1: Following Written Directions for Young Students on the Autism Spectrum

Two students, Leah and Juan, are in the third and second grades, respectively. Leah is a Caucasian female with autism who has low expressive language and engages in minimal social reciprocity. Juan is a Hispanic male whose behaviors include aggression, swearing, and refusal. He also exhibits low expressive language but engages in some social reciprocity with his peers. Both students have adequate decoding skills but struggle to understand what they read.

Jackie, the teacher, determined that one way to expose Leah and Juan's understanding of the text is by asking them to read and follow written directions. This task made visible her students' understanding of the text and gave Jackie information she needed to make decisions about the pro-vision of scaffolded support. Jackie set her objective as having her students read and accurately follow six-step directions on three consecutive trials. An example of a six-step direction would be: (1) Go to the blue table; (2) write your name on the top of the paper; (3) draw a square on the paper; (4) cut out the square; (5) put the square on the paper plate; (6) give the plate to your teacher. Jackie began by confirming that her students could read the direction words and match those words with a sample picture. Both students were able to successfully match the written word to an image of that object.

Having established that her two students could match a word to an image, Jackie wanted to iden-tify the top reinforcers that each student could obtain as the final direction in a sequence. Jackie conducted a preference assessment and identified both Leah and Juan's top reinforcers. The preferred item placed in the final direction served as a motivational scaffold—it was a tangible outcome that could be accessed by performing the directions accurately.

Jackie's next step was to establish a baseline of performance for both students. Jackie began by giving Leah and Juan a six-step direction sequence without a reinforcer. Each direction had to be successfully performed in the correct order. Jackie prompted each trial lesson by verbalizing the same directions to the student: "Read these directions out loud. Follow all the directions. If you don't know a word, I can tell it to you." After the student read the directions, they were again told to "follow these directions." Neither Leah nor Juan could follow all the directions in sequence.

Before beginning the intervention lessons, Jackie established a correction procedure to provide additional scaffolded support if a student was unable to perform the task. The correction procedure following an incorrect response involved the teacher stopping the trial, returning the child to the original starting point, and then moving through three intensifying scaffolded prompts: (1) Student rereads the directions and tries to follow them again; (2) Teacher reads the directions aloud and models the task, before saying "your turn"; and (3) Physical prompting where teacher and student follow the direction together. By grounding her correction procedure in a system of least prompts, Jackie ensures students will perform at their greatest level of independence.

Jackie was committed to using data-based decisions to guide her instruction. To do this, she made a simple graph with the number of trials across the horizontal axis and the number of directions attempted on the vertical axis, including baseline, 1-step, 2-steps, 3-steps, and on through 6 steps. Each student began with a one-step direction that included one of their preferred items. When Leah or Juan completed three consecutive trials without an error, Jackie then added one additional direction to the trials (e.g., 2-steps to 3-steps).

Jackie's graph showed both Leah and Juan began to make many errors in following three-step and four-step directions. Jackie observed students reading the directions before beginning the first step, but when the students moved to step two, they set the paper to the side and did not refer to the sequence. They were relying only on their memory to remember the steps in order and began to make errors.

Even with the correction procedure, this series of scaffolded steps with added support was insufficient to help Leah and Juan remember the directions in the correct order. Jackie concluded that the reinforcer in the final direction did not help the students follow the steps in order because the difficulty resided in the fact that the students did not have a cognitive strategy for using the written text as a memory scaffold. This led Jackie to adjust her instruction by adding additional scaffolded support. To provide only the minimal support needed, Jackie first engaged in whisper reading—she read the directions aloud in a whisper, while the students observed her state the directions and perform each direction. For Juan, this whisper reading was sufficient modeling, and he was quickly able to follow four, five, and then six-step directions.

Leah was not able to progress with the whisper reading model, so Jackie decided to teach Leah an explicit re-reading strategy. To teach the re-reading strategy, Jackie modeled the strategy with three 3-step directions. For each direction, she followed the teaching script:

> Watch me. I am going to read the directions and follow these directions. This direction says (pointing to each word as she reads) "First, go to the teacher table." This sentence says that I must go to the teacher table, so I need to walk to the teacher table. Watch me. Okay, I just followed that direction. I just went to the teacher's table. I did it! Good job! Now I need to read the next direction. Watch me. I am going to read this direction and follow this direction. "Second, draw a square on the paper with a pencil." Watch me. Okay, I just followed that direction. I drew a square on the paper. I did it! Good job!

Jackie continued this pattern by modeling the third and final step in the direction. She then repeated this sequence with the two additional three-step directions.

After intensification of scaffolded supports through explicit modeling and repeated practice, Leah was able to progress to four, five, and six-step directions with success. Leah learned to refer to her written direction paper, point to the sentence, read the sentence aloud, and then perform the direction. The explicit modeling condition was sufficient scaffolding to learn the re-reading strategy and allowed her to be successful.

Reflection on the Example

This example of teaching written directions to two students with intensive needs illustrates both planned and unplanned scaffolded supports. Jackie drew upon her knowledge of reinforcement, direct instruction, and cognitive strategy instruction to construct a carefully thought-out plan of instruction for her students with intensive learning, social, behavioral, and communication needs.

Responsive instruction. At the heart of Jackie's instruction were multiple forms of informal and formal assessment. Jackie plotted the data on a simple graph to visually observe whether her students were meeting the objective and then used the graph to inform her instruction. This data plotting allowed Jackie to see that there were multiple errors for both Leah and Juan, leading her to make the decision to add scaffolded support beyond the correction procedure. The students were not using the written directions on the paper even though the correction procedure asked students to observe the teacher modeling the behavior. The students needed even more support than initially anticipated, so Jackie directly taught the students the strategy of re-reading.

Knowledge of direct instruction principles. Jackie incorporated several key principles of direct instruction, including (1) immediate error correction with feedback—immediately returning student to the beginning when an error was made, (2) mastery learning—requiring 3 correct trials before adding a direction, (3) using successive approximations by starting with a single written direction and then adding another direction after mastery, and (4) conspicuous reinforcement by placing a highly preferred item in the final direction that students could obtain with successful direction following (see Table 15.1).

Example #2: Developing Comprehension and Composition Skills for Secondary Learners

This second example focuses on one student, DeMarcus; however, it is important to note that the teacher is individualizing and scaffolding the learning of each student in the class simultaneously. DeMarcus attends a diverse urban high school in a Midwest city in the United States that is the home of two car assembly plants and several large parts manufacturing facilities. DeMarcus' school has over 70 percent of the students receiving free and reduced priced lunch. DeMarcus is an eighth grader identified with intense learning needs who struggles with comprehending text written at the third-grade level. He also struggles with using text structure (e.g., categories and key details) to read and compose extended text. Reading comprehension and written composition of informational text are closely related, as both involve understanding superordinate and subordinate ideas. In reading informational text, we often look for main ideas and key details within paragraphs to help us identify and remember information. Similarly, when we are generating informational text in writing, we identify a category of information that is often indicated by a topic sentence and then a series of key details that provide information about that category.

To better understand their skills related to text structure, DeMarcus's resource teacher, Jenny, asked her students to write about something they were an expert in. DeMarcus chose to write about soccer:

SOCCER
I like soccer. Because it's a good sport. Because I can win a trophy. Because I like trophies. I could put them in my room. So, my room would look nice. Soccer is my life.

DeMarcus's writing illustrates several common challenges exhibited by students with learning disabilities, including identifying categories of information that are supported by key details, using an associative writing approach where ideas that come to mind are written down without attention to a pre-writing plan, and the failure to recognize the needs of an external audience (egocentric writing). When given an informational paragraph about an animal (e.g., Rattlesnake), DeMarcus struggled to identify the main idea, even when the main idea was listed in a clear topic sentence. As Jenny reviewed DeMarcus' writing compositions and his informational reading, it became evident that he was having difficulty identifying superordinate (i.e., categories/main ideas) and subordinate (i.e., details) information.

Table 15.1 Instructional Features for Intensifying Instruction and Providing Scaffolded Support

Instruction supporting intense needs	Purpose	Examples
Conduct preference assessment	• Identify menu of positive reinforcers	• Play Skyfall Spelling®; Skittle®; Doo Doo Light®
Data-based instruction	• Baseline assessment • Behavior charting and visual inspection	• Follow six-step directions without support • Chart number of correct directions followed
Error correction and immediate feedback	• Clear signal that behavior is errant • Does not reinforce errant behavior	• Return student to starting location upon error • Move immediately to restart activity
Clear signal and pacing	• Obtain attention of student • High opportunity to respond	• "Watch me"; "Read these directions…" • "Read these directions. Follow all of the directions"
Mastery learning	• Firm responses to promote independence • Internalization of skill, strategy, or process	• Three correct trials before adding direction • Teacher models re-reading strategy three times
Successive approximations	• Identify learning goal and reinforce part	• Add only one additional direction at a time
Conspicuous reinforcement	• Increase likelihood a response will occur	• Place highly preferred item as final direction
Prompt hierarchy	• Correction procedure • Predetermined levels of increasing support • Increase procedural fidelity of teacher	• Reread. Teacher model. Physical prompting. • Teacher script for each prompt level
Modeling and thinking Aloud	• Make visible and explicit a cognitive strategy	• Teacher models and performs re-reading strategy
Provide scaffolded support	• Support that allows independent performance • Memory scaffold	• Teacher adds explicit support to teach re-reading strategy • Written text can support memory
Reading skills	• Word reading accuracy and comprehension • Executive skill: Managing memory • Improve reading stamina • Making text "mean"	• Accuracy required to access reinforcer • Re-reading strategy is a memory scaffold • Student must accurately read more directions • Comprehension is required to advance

Jenny used DeMarcus's writing sample and reading assessment as key data sources in developing what she called a focus correction area—a specific area in the larger writing process that she could develop through a reading/writing intervention. Jenny identified two parallel processes to focus instruction: (1) identifying main ideas and key details in informational text and mapping those unto a graphic organizer, and (2) using the categories and key details on the graphic organizer to write coherent paragraphs.

Jenny knew that to create some early momentum and success when a student is learning a new skill or strategy, it is best to start with examples and text that are easily understood. To begin instruction, Jenny listed three words on the lines next to an oval on a graphic organizer, including Ford, Chevrolet, and Toyota (see Figure 15.1). Jenny then read the words and began to think aloud:

Jenny: I have a list of three words next to this oval. These three words are key details that give us information about what the category might be. I am going to read these words out loud and ask myself what main idea or category they represent: Ford, Chevrolet, and Toyota. I have heard of all of these. Me and my family have even owned these. Friends, what do you think the category is?

Students: Cars!

Jenny: Yes, these three words, Ford, Chevrolet, and Toyota are all types of cars, so I am going to write "Types of Cars" in the oval next to these details.

Jenny: Let's try another. Jessica, can you read these three key ideas or details?

Jessica: Refrigerator. Microwave. Stove.

Jenny: Okay, so refrigerator, microwave, and stove. Friends, turn to your partner and share what category you think these three words represent. (Pause briefly for sharing) What did you and your partner decide, DeMarcus?

DeMarcus: Things in your house.

Jenny: Okay, yes, these are all things we find in our home. True, but I'm wondering if anyone has more specific ideas about a category these might belong to? Kiesha, what did you and your partner talk about?

Kiesha: They are all in the kitchen?

Jenny: Yes, they sure are—each of these items is found in the house, but specifically in the kitchen. Can anyone think of a name that we call these things in our kitchen? (Pause. No response) I am thinking of a name. When I go to Lowe's® or Home Depot® to look for new things like a microwave, refrigerator, or stove, I go to this section of the store. App…

Kiesha: Appliances?

Jenny: Yes! Appliances. But I have a question. Are there other appliances in our house, besides these three?

Students: Yes.

Jenny: What are some of these? Dalia?

Dalia: Washer and dryer.

Jenny: Exactly right. But do we usually have our washer and dryer in our kitchen, where we prepare food?

Students: No.

Jenny: So, what do you think I should label this category (pause, no response)? So, they are appliances, but what special type of appliances? (Pause, no response). What room are these appliances in? (Students: Kitchen). So, what kind of appliances?

DeMarcus: Kitchen appliances?

Jenny: There we go. Refrigerator, stove, and microwave are kitchen appliances. So, I am going to write "Kitchen Appliances" in our oval.

This short example illustrates several aspects of providing scaffolded support. Jenny provided explicit instruction by modeling and thinking aloud so her students could see a *completed example* and hear the thinking of a knowledgeable other. She then provided *repeated practice* with a new set of details, but instead of completing the task by herself (I Do), she immediately seeks to *transfer control* to her students by having a student read the details and asking them if they can think of a category that represents those details (We Do). When DeMarcus responds with a partially correct category, things in your house, Jenny acknowledges his attempt and then *steps in* and asks if there are additional categories that might more accurately describe these objects. Kiesha correctly mentions that the objects are all found in the kitchen, but the group still does not have a more precise categorical label, so Jenny *steps in* to *build additional background knowledge* by telling a short story about going to a hardware store recently to search for an item and asks the students what section of the store this might be. With no answer forthcoming, she provides a *partially completed response* by saying "App…" This is then enough support for Kiesha to say "appliances."

Jenny seizes on this moment to further challenge students to be even more precise in their category language, by asking whether there are other appliances in a home. Dalia mentions that a washer and dryer are appliances. Jenny provides a *non-example* by asking her students if a washer and dryer are typically found in the kitchen, and the students respond "no." Rather than giving the students the answer, she *steps back* and asks a question: "So, what do you think I should label this category?" The students do not answer, but, again, rather than stepping in and giving the correct answer, she provides a verbal scaffold in the form of a *question*: "So, they are appliances, but what special type of appliances?" This is still met with silence, so she reframes the question, "What room are these appliances in?" This is then enough support for DeMarcus to say, "kitchen appliances." Jenny then continues the lesson by allowing students to practice on additional examples with partners (We Do) and independently (You Do).

While this was a critical first lesson for Jenny and her students to begin to have extensive practice with many types of details and their corresponding categorical label, it was only the beginning of a several months long instructional sequence. DeMarcus's annual IEP goal was to independently research a topic and write an informational essay containing an introduction, three categories with at least 4–5 details per category, and a concluding paragraph. As DeMarcus and the other students developed their skills throughout the school year, Jenny continued to provide scaffolded support through adjusting the tools she used over time. A timeline of some of the instructional scaffolds are shown in Figure 15.1.

Jenny next introduced a formal reading strategy to help identify main ideas and details in informational texts, called BURNS: **B**ox the paragraph, **U**nderline the key details, **R**ead the details, **N**ote the main idea in the margin, and **S**ummarize across the passage (Englert & Mariage, 2020). After modeling and thinking aloud through several examples (I Do), Jenny quickly moved into guided practice to involve DeMarcus and his classmates into using the BURNS strategy. Two forms of scaffolded support Jenny used early in the guided practice (We Do) phase of the lessons were to (1) underline the key details in a paragraph of text in advance for the students, and (2) include the main idea for a paragraph among a short multiple-choice list right below the paragraph. Since reading key details and trying to produce a common main idea or category is a difficult skill, limiting the choices to just four answers helped students, initially, to improve their accuracy. Over time, these temporary scaffolds were faded and removed.

Jenny then extended instructions to having students map entire multi-paragraph passages into a graphic organizer (Dexter & Hughes, 2011). For example, in a paragraph about how the Great White shark hunts, Jenny created a graphic organizer on a large chart paper (see Figure 15.2). Jenny's students identified five categories after they BURNS the passage, including (1) looks like, (2) how they hunt, (3) where it lives, (4) enemies and threats.

Jenny then introduced two additional sources of information on sharks, including a YouTube® video clip on facts about the Great White shark and an interview with a shark expert. Jenny gave each of her students a worksheet with the five categories listed as squares on the page. She also gave

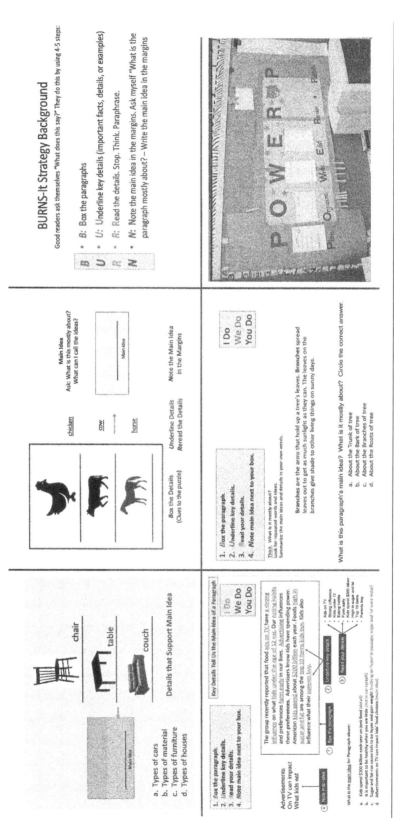

Figure 15.1 Building Understanding of Superordinate and Subordinate Ideas through Images, the BURN strategy, and POWER + P

Mentor Text for Body Paragraph

First, the great white shark is one of the most impressive looking creatures on earth. Its torpedo shaped body allows it to swim at high rates of speed through the water. Mother nature even helps the shark appear stealth-like in the water, because its white belly makes it difficult to see from below, while its gray-blue back is hard to see against the ocean depths from above. The adult great white shark weighs more than the average automobile at between 4000-6000 pounds—or 2 to 3 tons. Grown females can grow to 15-16 feet, or as far from the free throw line to the basket on a basketball court. Males are slightly shorter at 11-13 feet. It is no wonder that the great white shark is considered an apex predator with these kind of characteristics!

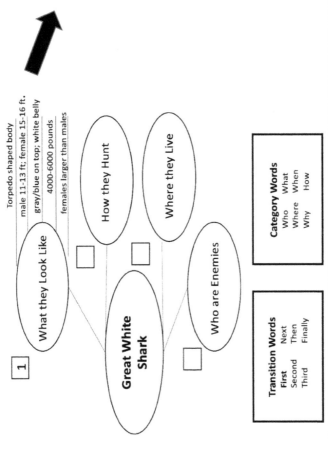

Figure 15.2 Providing Additional Scaffolded Supports for Sequencing, Transitions, Categories, and Paragraphs

the students five different colored sticky notes on a cardboard strip. Above each color was written the category label (e.g., Pink=looks like; Yellow=hunts; etc.). Jenny asked each student to have at least two new facts for each category. When a key detail came up in the videos, she paused the video and asked her students what they had just heard, what category the idea addressed, and gave them time to jot that idea on a sticky note and place it on the worksheet. When this additional research was completed, Jenny then had the students place their colored sticky notes on the large whole class web at the front of the room.

Finally, Jenny reconstructed the whole class web on the computer, so each of her students could have their own copy of the graphic organizer to scaffold their report writing. Jenny added several supports directly on the graphic organizer to elicit future conversations. She put a small box next to each category, so students could number the paragraphs in the order they wanted to write. Then, in the lower left corner, she placed a small box with the heading "Transition Words" and the words first, second, third, next, then, and last. This placement was meant to support a mini lesson on the use of transition words to signal the reader when they are reading a new paragraph or category of information. Finally, Jenny placed a completed paragraph of one of their categories that contained a clear topic sentence using a transition word (e.g., First), four detail sentences, and a concluding sentence. This model of the elements of a body paragraph served as mentor text for students to refer to as they wrote their remaining paragraphs. To provide a more permanent scaffold for students, Jackie developed a large poster in her room that included an exemplary model of a well-formed paragraph, writing the topic sentence in green, each detail sentence in yellow, and the concluding sentence in red to highlight the three main parts of her paragraph model.

Reflecting on the Example

This extended example of teaching superordinate and subordinate ideas gives insight into the many nuances of providing scaffolded support:

Knowledge of curriculum scope and sequence. DeMarcus' written expression goal on his IEP allowed Jenny to break down informational writing into its component parts. Jenny identified superordinate and subordinate ideas as an essential element in building coherent paragraphs. She crafted mini lessons on identifying the difference between categories and details through using a graphic organizer, and later provided direct instruction in writing an introductory paragraph, body paragraphs, complex sentences, topic sentences and concluding paragraphs.

Informal assessment. Jenny established a baseline of DeMarcus' writing ability by asking him to write a paper about something he was an expert in and to identify main ideas in informational passages. Jenny identified challenges in organization, paragraphs, transition words, topic sentences, depth of categories, breadth of categories, and audience sensitivity. Jenny used this data to begin to form her mini lessons on categories and details.

Step-in and step-back talk moves. Jenny listened carefully to her student's understanding of categories and key details as she moved through an "I Do, We Do, and You Do" sequence. When there was silence or the content was just outside a student or the group's learning zone, she stepped into model, think aloud, question, cue, or probe to provide only enough support for a student to successfully respond (Englert et al., 2007). If students were responding accurately or with partial accuracy, she would step back and continue to listen to students and allow them to construct knowledge together.

Cueing. In one instance, Jenny voiced the word "App..." to clue the students to a correct category. The students successfully identified that a refrigerator, microwave, and stove were all things found in the kitchen, but they could not produce the more exacting label of "appliances." Rather than give the answer, teachers can provide a cue or clue, so students maintain engagement and ownership in the construction of meaning.

Procedural facilitation, cognitive strategies, and mnemonics. Jenny used two procedural facilitators that both contained multiple cognitive strategies. Jenny taught her students a writing process called Cognitive Strategy Instruction in Writing across the entire year to remember the procedures that writers follow when composing a paper and that readers can use when identifying main ideas and key details in informational texts (Englert et al., 2006). To help her students remember the phases of the writing process and the strategies that good writers use, she used the mnemonic "POWER + P" to stand for **P**lanning, **O**rganizing, **W**riting, **E**diting, **R**evising, and **P**ublishing (see Figure 15.2 for classroom poster). The above lesson focused exclusively on the "organization" part of the writing process, but this was embedded within the larger writing process that made visible strategies for each phase.

The second procedural facilitation tool that taught cognitive strategies was the BURNS strategy (Englert & Mariage, 2020). Like POWER + P, BURNS is also a mnemonic to help students follow a procedure for identifying main ideas and details. Mnemonics are a memory scaffold to help students remember a sequence of procedures or steps that then prompt different strategies (e.g., **P**lan our writing: What is my topic? Who am I writing for? What do I know about my topic? Where can I get information? What text structure map can I use?).

Embedding scaffolded supports in tools. Jenny knew that her students would need additional mini lessons on writing effective informational reports. Several of these were supported directly on the graphic organizer. Jenny anticipated that some students might struggle in translating the graphic organizer to paragraph writing (from Organization to Writing, within the POWER + P procedure), so anticipated scaffolds she might use in the mini lessons, including (1) sequencing paragraphs, (2) common transition words, (3) a list of the 5 W + H words to help identify category labels (e.g., How they hunt; Where they live; Who their enemies are), and (4) a mentor text that include a topic sentence, detail sentences, and a concluding sentence. These extra supports on the graphic organizer provided clues and cues as students began to think about writing/drafting.

Completed or partially completed examples and non-examples. Students benefit from seeing complete examples of what they are striving to create. Completed examples such as mentor texts or a teacher created example provide a kind of gestalt, or whole, that then helps students have a clearer vision of what is expected. In our experience as special education teachers, having students compare examples and non-examples can be among the powerful teaching tools we are aware of for scaffolding understanding. In Jenny's class, she developed a model for all three parts of a research report, including an introductory paragraph, a body paragraph, and a concluding paragraph. Jenny also made examples and non-examples of each part of a research report and had students generate their own rubric by comparing examples and non-examples.

Wrap Up

For decades, researchers have tried to capture what the most effective teachers do in their classrooms. Terms like "withitness," responsive pedagogy, and attunement have all been used to describe the teacher who dynamically assesses and responds to their students' academic, social, motivational, communication, and behavioral needs on a moment-to-moment basis. We believe that these researchers were describing teachers who have mastered the high-leverage practice of providing scaffolded supports. These teachers can reengage the disengaged; give hope to those who do not have a deep supply; inspire those who struggle by breaking down complex tasks and scaffolding incremental gains; know when to step in and provide intense, explicit, and direct instruction on prerequisite skills that may be preventing a student from moving forward in their development. The most effective teachers also know how to step back to ensure that students have every opportunity to become self-regulated and self-determined learners. It is hard to imagine a more rewarding and challenging high-leverage practice than providing scaffolded support to learners with the most intense needs.

Tips

1. **Student Voice and Choice**. The most effective teachers not only transfer control of learning to students (We Do, You Do) as soon as they are able, but they create a classroom climate where students are *expected* to be valued and knowledgeable others for one another. While the teacher plays a critical role in providing explicit instruction, the most successful teachers often invite participation from the outset—they are co-learners with their students and seek their input as soon as possible. This creates ownership and buy-in from the beginning. These teachers also often provide students with choices. Nowhere is voice and choice more critical than when building multicultural, equitable, and culturally responsive learning communities in our classroom (Gay, 2018). When every child is represented in the curriculum and their voice and experiences are genuinely valued, we form a dialogical relationship with our students (Burbules, 1993). Scaffolding thrives most when students and teachers are comfortable in making public and explicit their thinking through talk, writing, art, and performance.

2. **Talk is Your Most Powerful Scaffold**. One of the most powerful cultural tools for scaffolding learning is talk (Chapin et al., 2013; van der Veen et al., 2017). When teachers elicit talk from their students, they gain insight into their level of thinking and can make an assessment on the spot about whether to follow up by asking questions (e.g., How do you think the shark uses vibration to hunt?), asking for a student to clarify their thinking (e.g., "Can you tell me more about that idea?"), to reinforce effort (e.g., "I like the way you and Samantha are thinking together"), and to build the dialogical relationship (e.g., "This was a difficult task, but you didn't give up and I am proud of you"). Listening to students as they think aloud gives the teacher and peers information about the student's understanding on a moment-to-moment basis. Student talk makes explicit conceptions and (mis)conceptions. When students engage in discussion, they hear their own thinking and can edit and revise their response as they interact with others.

3. **Scaffold Executive Skills**. We have found it helpful to consider executive skills, or skills necessary to execute or carry out a task, to provide direction on what areas might need scaffolded support. Executive skills include academic tasks, such as planning/prioritization, difficulty with task initiation, organization, sustaining attention, working memory, time management, flexibility, and metacognition (Dawson & Guare, 2018). They also include behavioral skills, including response inhibition, goal-directed persistence, and emotional regulation. Executive skills are crucial aspects of human development and can be assessed, taught directly and explicitly, and scaffolded just as an academic skill or cognitive strategy. Through attention to executive functioning difficulties, teachers can help students move toward becoming more self-regulated, self-determined, and more strategic learners.

4. **Providing Scaffolded Support is a Part of Planning Your Instruction**. While we have emphasized the moment-to-moment adjustment of support throughout this chapter, the most effective teachers learn to anticipate what types of scaffolds they may need (Ayala et al., 2012; Puntambekar & Hubscher, 2005). Over time, teachers become experienced at understanding common bottle necks in teaching different subject areas and develop a toolbox of potential scaffolds to employ whenever they are needed.

Key Resources

- Design a System of Scaffolded Supports: Strategic and Intensive Supports
  Pennsylvania Department of Education
  Retrieved from www.youtube.com/watch?v=OlnA1d8Xix8
- The IRIS Center. (2005). *Providing instructional supports: Facilitating mastery of new skills.*
  Retrieved from https://iris.peabody.vanderbilt.edu/module/sca/

- National Center on Intensive Intervention
  Retrieved from https://intensiveintervention.org/
- Scaffolding for Student Success
  Alberta Education
  Retrieved from www.youtube.com/watch?v=uKLDjmPk_RE
- Scaffolding Instruction for Students
  Teachings in Education
  Retrieved from www.youtube.com/watch?v=RUzMkLK4XbI

Baines, A. D. (2014). *(Un)Learning Disability: Recognizing and Changing Restrictive Views of Student Ability.* Teachers College Press.

In this book, AnnMarie Baines discusses how the term disability colors our perception of what students are capable of. Disability classification requires comprehensive assessment and reproduces views of capacity from a deficit and medical (pathological) perspective. This focus on the search for pathology can restrict how and what we see in our students. Recommendations for reimagining how we view (dis)ability are provided.

Lawrence-Brown, D., & and Sapon-Shevin, M. (2015). Condition Critical: Key Principles for Equitable and Inclusive Educa*tion.* Teachers College Press.

This edited book examines how discourses of power have historically served to position persons with disabilities from largely deficit-driven perspectives. However, through attention to critical perspectives, it is possible to create counter narratives that empower all people as society continues to focus on issues of equity and social justice.

Milner IV, R. (2021). Start Where You Are, But Don't Stay There: Understanding Diversity, Opportunity Gaps, and Teaching in Today's Classroom (2nd edition). Harvard Education Press.

To better address issues of inequity in education is to focus on what Milner refers to as "opportunity centered teaching" that positions all learners as capable and eager to learn, but who have differences in experiences and resources.

References

Archer, A. L., & Hughes, C. A. (2011). *Explicit instruction: Effective and efficient teaching.* Guilford Press.

Ayala, E., Brace, H. J., & Stahl, S. (2012). Preparing teachers to implement universal design for learning. In T. E. Hall, H. Meyer, & D. H. Rose (Eds). *Universal design for learning in the classroom: Practical applications* (pp. 135–52). Guilford Press.

Baines, A. D. (2014). *(Un)Learning disability: Recognizing and changing restrictive views of student ability.* Teachers College Press.

Bakker, A., Smit, J., & Wegerif, R. (2015). Scaffolding and dialogic teaching in mathematics education: Introduction and review. *ZDM Mathematics Education, 47*(7),1047–65. https://doi.org/10.1007/s11858-015-0738-8

Boardman, A. G., Swanson, E., Klingner, J. K., & Vaughn, S. (2013). Using collaborative strategic reading to improve reading comprehension. In B. B. Cook & M. Tankersley (Eds.), *Research-based practices in special education* (pp. 33–46). Pearson.

Burbules, N. (1993). *Dialogue in teaching: Theory and practice.* Teachers College Press.

Chapin, S., O'Connor, C., & Anderson, N. (2013). Classroom discussions in *Math: A teacher's guide for using talk moves to support the common core and more, grades K-6: A multimedia professional learning resource* (3rd ed.). Math Solutions Publications.

Council for Exceptional Children, & Collaboration for Effective Educator Development, Accountability and Reform. (2017). *High-leverage practices in special education*. Council for Exceptional Children.

Dawson, P., & Guare, R. (2018). *Executive skills in children and adolescents: A practical guide to assessment and intervention* (3rd. ed.). Guilford Press.

Dexter, D., & Hughes, C. A. (2011). Graphic organizers and students with learning disabilities: A meta-analysis. *Learning Disabilities Quarterly*, 34(1), 51–72. http://dx.doi.org/10.1177/0731948 71103400104

Disabled World (2019). *Special Education: Special Needs Students and Schools*. Disabled World. Retrieved March 23, 2022, from www.disabled-world.com//disability/education/special/

Englert, C. S., & Mariage, T. V. (2020). Strategy instruction to support struggling readers in comprehending expository main ideas. *Intervention in School and Clinic*, 56(2), 74–83. https://doi.org/10.1177/1053451220914892

Englert, C. S., Mariage, T. V., & Dunsmore, K. (2006). Sociocultural perspectives of writing instruction. In MacArthur, Graham, & Fitzgerald (Eds.), *Handbook of writing research* (pp. 208–21). Guilford Press.

Englert, C. S., Zhao, Y., Dunsmore, K., Collings, N. Y., & Wolbers, K. (2007). Scaffolding the writing of students with disabilities through procedural facilitation: Using an Internet-based technology to improve performance. *Learning Disability Quarterly*, 30(1), 9–29.

Fuchs, L. S., Fuchs, D., & Malone, A. S. (2018). The taxonomy of intervention intensity. *TEACHING Exceptional Children*, 50(4), 194–202. https://doi.org/10.1177/0040059918758166

Gargiulo, R. M., & Bouck, E. C. (2020). *Special education in contemporary society: An introduction to exceptionality* (7th ed.). SAGE.

Gay, G. (2018). *Culturally responsive teaching: Theory, research, and practice* (3rd. ed.). Teachers College Press.

Graham, S., Harris, K. R., & Mason, L. (2005). Improving the writing performance, knowledge, and self-efficacy of struggling young writers: The effects of self-regulated strategy development. *Contemporary Educational Psychology*, 30(2), 207–41. https://doi.org/10.1016/j.cedpsych.2004.08.001

Grant, M., Lapp, D., Fisher, D., Johnson, K., & Frey, N. (2012). Purposeful instruction: Mixing up the "I," "we," and "you." *Journal of Adolescent and Adult Literacy*, 56(1), 45–55. https://doi.org/10.1002/jaal.00101

Lawrence-Brown, D. & Sapon-Shevin, M. (2015). *Condition critical: Key principles for equitable and inclusive education*. Teachers College Press.

Mariage, T. V., Englert, C. S., & Mariage, M. F. (2020). Comprehension instruction for tier 2 early learners: A scaffolded apprenticeship for close reading of informational text. *Learning Disability Quarterly*, 43(1), 29–42. https://doi.org/10.1177/0731948719861106

Mariage, T. V., Englert, C. S., & Plavnick, J. B. (2021). *Teaching early learners with autism to follow written directions: Making text mediate action to promote independence*. Focus on Autism and Other Developmental Disabilities. https://doi.org/10.1177/1088357620943501

Mariage, T. V., Winn, J., & Dabo, A. (2019). Provide scaffolded supports. In J. McLeskey, L. Maheady, B. Billingsley, M. T. Brownell, & T. K. Lewis (Eds.), *High leverage practices for inclusive classrooms* (pp. 197–214). Routledge.

Milner, H. R. (2021). *Start where you are, but don't stay there: Understanding diversity, opportunity gaps, and teaching in today's classrooms* (2nd ed.). Harvard Education Press.

Milner, H. R., Cunningham, H. B., Delale-O'Connor, L., & Kestenberg, E. G. (2019). Chapter 4: Classroom management is about creating a caring environment. In *"These kids are out of control": Why we must reimagine "Classroom management" for equity* (pp. 97–132). Corwin, a SAGE Company.

Puntambekar, S., & Hubscher, R. (2005). Tools for scaffolding students in a complex learning environment: What have we gained and what have we missed? *Educational Psychologist*, *40*(1), 1–12. https://doi.org/10.1207/s15326985ep4001_1

Reiser, B. J. (2004). Scaffolding complex learning: The mechanisms of structuring and problematizing student work. *The Journal of the Learning Sciences*, *13*(3), 273–304. https://doi.org/10.1207/s15 327809jls1303_2

Rosenshine, B. (2012). Principles of instruction: Research-based strategies that all teachers should know. *American Educator*, *36*(1), 12.

Sherman, C. K., & De La Paz, S. (2012). Technology to facilitate the general education curriculum. In J. E. Aitken, J. P. Fairley, & J. K. Carlson (Eds.), *Communication technology for students in special education and gifted programs* (pp. 26–33). Information Science Reference (an imprint of IGI Global).

Sugai G, & Horner R. H. (2020). Sustaining and scaling positive behavioral interventions and supports: Implementation drivers, outcomes, and considerations. *Exceptional Children*. *86*(2), 120–36. https://doi.org/10.1177/0014402919855331

Trent S. C., Artiles, A. J., & Englert C. S. (1998). Chapter 8: From deficit thinking to social constructivism: A review of theory, research, and practice in special education. *Review of Research in Education*. *23*(1), 277–307. https://doi.org/10.3102/0091732X023001277

Valle, J. W., & Connor, D. J. (2019). *Rethinking disability: A disability studies approach to* inclusive practices (2nd ed.). Routledge. https://doi.org/10.4324/9781315111209

van der Veen, C., van der Wilt, F., van Kruistum, C., van Oers, B., & Michaels, S. (2017). MODEL2TALK: An intervention to promote productive classroom talk. *The Reading Teacher*, *70*(6), 689–700. https://doi.org/10.1002/trtr.1573

Vernon, S., Schumacher, J. B., & Deshler, D. D. (1993). The score skills: Social skills for cooperative groups. Edge Enterprises.

Vygotsky, L. S. (2012). *Thought and language, revised and expanded edition*. The MIT Press.

Wood, D., Bruner, J., & Ross, G. (1976). The role of tutoring in problem solving. *Journal of Child Psychology and Child Psychiatry*, *17*, 89–100. http://dx.doi.org/10.1111/j.1469-7610.1976.tb00381

Yell, M. L. (2019). *The law and special education* (5th ed.). Pearson.

16
Use Explicit Instruction

Kristen R. Rolf
Utah State University
Timothy A. Slocum
Utah State University

Introduction

Highly effective instruction for struggling learners requires *both* excellent instructional materials *and* excellent interactive teaching that delivers instruction clearly and responds to students' unique needs and strengths. Explicit Instruction is an evidence-based approach to both designing materials and delivering instruction that is effective for a wide range of learners. It has been shown to be effective for teaching many types of academic content (e.g., reading, writing, mathematics, science) and with students ranging from kindergarten to high school. It is comprised of 16 inter-related elements (see Table 16.1) that contribute to the effectiveness of the overall system (Archer et al., 2011). Explicit Instruction is designed to systematically prepare students to learn complex skills, present information clearly and unambiguously, support students to engage in new skills while receiving feedback, reduce support as students gain skills, and provide sufficient practice so that students are able to independently apply their new skills in a wide variety of situations.

In this chapter, we focus on how Explicit Instruction is used to deliver excellent interactive teaching based on carefully designed Explicit Instruction programs. Explicit Instruction programs focus on critical content, sequence skills logically so that earlier skills provide a foundation for later ones and break down complex skills into components that students can learn more easily. Explicit Instruction programs often include a user's manual, mastery tests, scripted lessons, and student materials. Lessons are organized and focus on critical skills. They provide step-by-step demonstrations of what students are to learn with clear, concise, and consistent language. They present examples and non-examples to show students exactly when and how skills are applied. Students are then actively engaged in practice with examples and non-examples. Initially, lessons provide scaffolding to support high levels of student success. These supports are gradually reduced and eliminated to increase students' independence. Later lessons include sufficient independent practice to enable students to reach mastery and fluency.

Effectively using an Explicit Instruction program is an intensification of the core instruction typically provided in Tier 1 and Tier 2 settings (Fuchs et al., 2014; Fuchs et al., 2017). For example, research-supported Explicit Instruction programs increase the *strength of instruction* through their systematic design, the *dosage of instruction* by providing numerous opportunities for students to make frequent relevant responses, *attention to transfer* by teaching for generalization and including

DOI: 10.4324/9781003276876-21

Table 16.1 Elements of Explicit Instruction

Content of instruction

1. Focus instruction on critical content

2. Sequence skills logically

3. Break down complex skills and strategies into smaller instructional units (Chunking)

Design of instruction

4. Design organized and focused lessons

5. Begin lessons with a clear statement of the lesson purpose and your expectations

6. Verify needed prior skills and knowledge before beginning instruction

7. Provide step-by-step demonstrations

8. Use clear, concise, and consistent language

9. Provide adequate ranges of examples and non-examples

10. Provide guided and supported practice

Delivery of instruction

11. Require frequent student responses

12. Monitor student performance closely

13. Provide immediate affirmative and corrective feedback

14. Deliver the lesson at a brisk pace

15. Help students organize knowledge

Independent practice and progress monitoring

16. Provide Purposeful Independent Practice (PIP).

opportunities for students to apply skills, and they provide an excellent basis for *behavioral support* by providing an instructional context in which students are engaged with relevant instructional tasks and can succeed by working hard and practicing self-regulation (Fuchs et al., 2017).

Explicit Instruction programs also provide a framework for further intensification of instruction while using the program(s). For example, when using an Explicit Instruction program, the teacher ensures that students are actively engaged by asking for frequent, relevant responses. They closely monitor student performance during the lesson and adjust their instruction accordingly; often through the use of specific error correction procedures, providing additional targeted practice, removing scaffolding, and providing specific praise. The ability to further intensify Explicit Instruction programs results in an efficient use of instructional time for the teacher and the students.

Narrowing the Focus

Selecting and implementing a high-quality research-validated Explicit Instruction program is the foundation of providing intensive instruction. This chapter will not focus on the design of programs, but rather will describe how to effectively use an Explicit Instruction program to intensify instruction.

We will also describe how to closely monitor student performance and further intensify instruction to meet individual students' needs when using an Explicit Instruction program.

Chapter Overview

1. Precisely placing students into instructional programs
2. Responding to student performance within interactive lessons:
   a. Immediate adjustments while teaching lessons
   b. Error analysis and adjustments to future lessons
3. Responding to student performance during independent practice, mastery tests, and external progress monitoring

Using the HLP

Precise Individualized Placement into Instructional Programs

Intensifying instruction using Explicit Instruction programs begins with identifying the most important areas for instruction, selecting a research-validated Explicit Instruction program, and determining an individualized starting point for instruction. Correct placement is the foundation of effective instruction and uses valuable instructional time efficiently. Placement into programs that are below the student's instructional level wastes instructional time on material already mastered. Placement into programs that are above the student's instructional level produces little learning and often frustrates both the student and the teacher. In this section, we describe the most important sources of data and how teachers can use them to determine an appropriate starting point.

Standardized achievement tests, including those used for special education eligibility assessment and state-mandated assessments, can help identify broad areas of strengths and weaknesses in students' academic skills. Although the results of such tests are not precise enough to suggest specific instructional goals, they can guide school personnel to areas that need more detailed assessment.

Each student's file (e.g. Individualized Education Plan, school records) may also provide valuable information. Ideally, the file will alert the teacher to recent instructional goals, progress monitoring data, accommodations, and strengths. Diagnostic tests can offer even more specific details about a student's strengths and weaknesses. Results from these tests can help the school team identify instructional goals and Explicit Instruction programs designed to meet the identified needs.

Results from curriculum-based measures can also be useful in selecting an Explicit Instruction program. Benchmarking assessments given at the student's grade level provide the school team with information about a student's performance relative to grade-level expectations. Progress monitoring assessments given at the student's instructional level provide important information about a student's progress and their responsiveness to past interventions. Ideally, the teacher is involved in administering the curriculum-based measures to observe student behavior during the assessment. Doing so may alert them to the student's specific strengths and challenges that may need to be addressed during instruction.

After reviewing all of the available information, the teacher is prepared to identify one or more Explicit Instruction programs that are likely to meet the student's needs. Next, they assess which program(s) might be a good match for the student. Well-designed Explicit Instruction programs include a placement test that identifies (a) whether the student has the prerequisite skills necessary to be successful in the program and (b) whether they should be instructed using a more advanced program. Placement tests vary in how precisely they prescribe exact starting places within programs. Teachers can use mastery tests within the program to further fine-tune the student's starting place in a program. To do so, the teacher administers the in-program mastery tests in order until the student does not meet the mastery criteria. For example, many Explicit

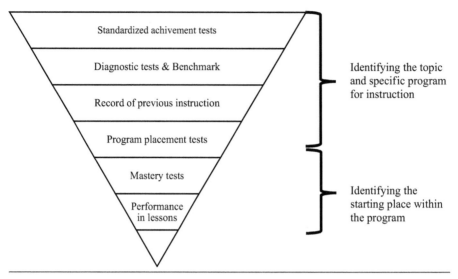

Figure 16.1 Intensifying Through Program Placement

Instruction programs include mastery tests every 10 lessons. If the placement test indicates that the program is appropriate for the student, the teacher can give the mastery test after Lesson 10 to see if the student already has the skills taught in the first 10 lessons. If the student passes the test for Lesson 10, the teacher can give the test for Lessons 20, 30, and so on. If the student does not pass the mastery test for lesson 40, instruction should begin with Lesson 31—just after the last mastery test that was passed. Even when carefully placing a student into a program on a particular lesson, initial placements should always be considered tentative and approximate. The final confirmation of an appropriate placement is student performance during lessons. Whenever a student is newly placed into a program, the teacher needs to pay particular attention to the student's success and struggles to verify appropriateness of the starting point and adjust the starting point, if necessary. Figure 16.1 summarizes the information that the teacher can use to appropriately place students in Explicit Instruction programs.

Vignette. Mr. Howard Ensures Focus on Critical Content

Mr. Howard has been a special education teacher at Desert Rock Elementary School in a small rural district in the southwest for 10 years. His main role is to support students who need intensive reading instruction, although he also provides intensive instruction in the areas of mathematics and writing. Some of his students were well-served by attending a high-quality reading group in the general education setting supplemented by small group instruction delivered by him and a paraprofessional (i.e., Tier 2 services). However, some of his other students were not progressing with this arrangement, so he implemented more intensive instruction (i.e., Tier 3 services). These students are quite diverse in their reading instruction; some receive small group instruction, some one-on-one, and some have a combination of the two.

Tori recently moved to Desert Rock from a neighboring district and is in fourth grade. She is an outgoing girl who makes friends easily. Although new to the school, she already has many friends and is well-liked by her classmates. Her mother and step-father are supportive and interested in her education. She was diagnosed with a specific learning disability in reading at the beginning of third grade. Tori is aware that she doesn't read as well as many of the kids in her fourth-grade class. As a result, she avoids reading out loud as much as possible.

Mr. Howard was able to obtain a copy of Tori's records from her last school. Standardized achievement test scores given during her evaluation for special education services indicate decoding skills at the first-grade level and listening comprehension at the fourth-grade level. Scores from the state-required standardized tests administered in the spring of third grade show that she was at grade-level in mathematics and was below grade level in reading. Her records show that she received core reading instruction in her third-grade classroom last year. After she was diagnosed with a learning disability, she spent an extra 30 minutes three times per week working on reading from the third-grade reading program in the resource room.

Based on the information he has, Mr. Howard can see that he will need to provide substantial support to Tori in reading. To further verify, he gives her three oral reading fluency benchmark assessments and finds that she reads fourth grade material at an average of 15 words per minute with only 70 percent accuracy. As he looks at all the data, Mr. Howard concludes that Tori needs intensive reading instruction with a focus on decoding. This will include a very powerful and focused reading program, responsiveness to her individual needs, and substantial instructional time devoted to reading. He knows that this is a big ask in terms of school resources and sacrifices of other valuable things that her school time could be devoted to, but it is clear to Mr. Howard that helping Tori develop strong and fluent decoding skills will open innumerable doors for her, so this investment is a must.

Mr. Howard decides to use an Explicit Instruction remedial decoding program that is well-supported by research. He gives the program's placement test to confirm that this program is the right level for Tori and to determine her starting point in the program. The placement test results indicate that she has the skills necessary for the program and that she should begin on Lesson 1. This confirms Mr. Howard's assumptions based on the standardized achievement test and oral reading fluency assessment results. He is curious if Tori has the skills to start later in the program. He gives Tori the mastery test that comes after Lesson 10. She answers 90 percent of the items correctly. This meets the criterion for passing the mastery test, so Mr. Howard administers the mastery test that comes after lesson 20. She answers 75 percent of the items correctly. This is below the criterion for passing the mastery test, so Mr. Howard decides he will start Tori at Lesson 11. Mr. Howard has two other students who have similar needs, so he will form a small instructional group with the three students.

Responding to Student Performance within Interactive Lessons: Immediate Adjustments during Lessons

In the following sections, we describe specific ways that teachers can intensify instruction when they are using these programs. Intensifying and individualizing instruction requires that the teacher closely monitor each student's performance and make appropriate adjustments throughout each lesson. This rapid, interactive responsiveness does not require additional testing or test interpretation. Instead, it requires that the teacher pay close attention to student responses during instruction and adjust instruction accordingly. This is sometimes called formative assessment.

Explicit Instruction programs include many opportunities for students to respond (both orally and in writing) during each lesson. Student responses are a rich source of information that teachers can use to determine if instruction needs to be adjusted. For example, during a lesson in which a group of four students read 10 letter sounds together in unison, the teacher is able to assess all four students on all 10 letter sounds in relatively little instructional time. The students' performance confirms that the instruction is effective or alerts the teacher to the need for making adjustments. It is important that the teacher have a systematic data collection routine to ensure data can be used for future lessons.

Praising and Correcting Student Responses. The teacher's most immediate response to students during a lesson is to affirm and praise accurate responses and correct inaccurate ones. Praising correct responses is important because it provides clear, positive feedback to students. Students with intensive instructional needs are often unsure if they are answering correctly, and their motivation to persevere during a challenging lesson may have been undermined by a history of struggling in school. Clear and frequent feedback raises students' awareness of their performance and may be very motivating when the lesson is difficult. The instructional and motivational effects of praising correct responses can be intensified by doing so frequently and immediately, especially during challenging parts of lessons. As students become more proficient, the amount of positive feedback may be reduced.

Explicit Instruction programs are designed to provide clear instruction that does not confuse students. When they are implemented effectively, students usually make few errors during a lesson. Even so, errors are an expected part of the learning process. Consistent and high-quality error corrections are extremely helpful for all learners, and they are *necessary* for those who have not benefitted from past instruction. Many students who need intensive instruction have developed misunderstandings and ineffective strategies during their time in school. Correcting errors is especially important for replacing misunderstandings and unreliable strategies with more accurate knowledge and effective skills.

An important principle for intensifying error corrections is to *immediately correct every error that is relevant to the lesson's objectives*. Students make errors because something is unclear or they have not mastered the content/skill. Effectively correcting errors provides immediate feedback to the student, teaches the correct response, allows the student to practice the correct response, and provides another opportunity for the teacher to assess the student's skill(s) after a short period of time. When teachers inconsistently correct errors, students may be confused about whether a response was correct or incorrect. This leads to additional errors and slows the pace of student learning.

High-quality error corrections include the following three steps: (1) model the correct response or guide the students in responding correctly; (2) test (Present the item again right away.); and (3) delayed test. (Present the same item or a similar one after a short delay.)

The first step in an error correction is to model or guide the student(s) to the correct answer. Deciding upon which of the two methods to use depends on the material being taught. If an error is based on a fact that the student is learning, or if guiding the student(s) to the correct answer would be too complicated or time-consuming, then the teacher gives the answer. When the student is learning a skill or procedure, the teacher guides the student to the correct answer. For example, when correcting a student who made an error while attempting to solve a subtraction problem that required renaming, the teacher guides the student by providing reminders of the steps for correctly solving the problem. In the second step of the correction, the teacher presents the item again to test whether the student now answers correctly. This step provides important information to the teacher about the student's learning and gives the teacher an opportunity to re-teach if the student still has misunderstandings. An additional benefit of this step is that the student can observe their own immediate progress by correctly responding to the item. The third step is to present the item again after a short delay. Typically, this takes place after the student has engaged with a few other items. The purpose of the delayed test is to provide the student with an opportunity to answer correctly without immediate support. If the student responds correctly, the teacher may be confident that the correction was effective. If the students do not respond correctly, the teacher can further intensify instruction by re-teaching, testing, and providing additional delayed tests before moving on in the lesson. At times, students may have persistent errors that require repeated corrections. The teacher must be prepared to do this while keeping a positive attitude and encouraging the student.

Vignette. Mr. Howard Supports Learning Through Corrections and Affirmations

In the first few weeks of instruction, it is clear to Mr. Howard that Tori has developed many misconceptions and unhelpful habits when decoding. She frequently makes errors when reading letters, has weak phonological skills, and inconsistently reads sight words. Mr. Howard keeps instruction positive by frequently reminding her and the other students that errors are part of learning and he will always help them correct errors so they can improve.

One day, Mr. Howard was teaching a lesson that included Explicit Instruction on letter sounds. Mr. Howard's interactions with the students are provided below, as well as notes highlighting how Mr. Howard intensified instruction through correcting errors:

1. Mr. Howard: (points to "a"). What sound does the letter make, Tori?
2. Tori: /e/   *{an error}*
3. Mr. Howard: That letter says /a/. Everybody, what sound?   *{model and test}*
4. All students: /a/   *{correct response on the test}*
5. Mr. Howard: Yes! We'll come back to that one again later.   *{affirmation}*
6. (Mr. Howard asks all of the students to read three other letters.)
7. Mr. Howard: (points to "a"). What sound, Tori?   *{delayed test}*
8. Tori: /a/   *{correct on delayed test}*
9. Mr. Howard: Excellent! You remembered!   *{praise}*

During the lesson, Mr. Howard notes that Tori and another student are making multiple errors on letter sounds. At the end of the lesson, he returns the letter sounds and asks the students to read them again. This is an additional delayed test and intensifies instruction by providing more targeted practice. Tori reads "a" correctly, and Mr. Howard gives her a big smile and a high-five. Tori beams and says "I'm getting really good at this!"

Mr. Howard employed all of the steps for correcting errors described above. When Tori incorrectly read "a," Mr. Howard immediately corrected the error by modeling the correct sound. Mr. Howard modeled the correct sound because it was the clearest approach to correcting the error. Notice that Mr. Howard provided a test of the missed sound right after correcting the error. He asked the entire group to read "a" to ensure that none of the students became confused as a result of her error. Mr. Howard affirmed the students' correct response to the test before asking them to read three other letters. He then provided a delayed test to Tori by asking her to read "a" again. She read the letter correctly, so he affirmed her correct response and continued with the lesson. (If she had incorrectly read the letter, he would have corrected the error using the same procedures again.) At the end of the lesson, Mr. Howard provided additional practice and a delayed test for Tori. He will remember to check on this in the next lesson.

Pacing. Throughout this section, we refer to pacing as the speed with which a teacher teaches a lesson rather than the idea that teachers need to teach certain lessons on specified days to "keep pace" with other groups or classes. Teachers intensify instruction by presenting lessons at a brisk pace. This makes good use of valuable instructional time and keeps students attentive and engaged. Teaching at a brisk pace can feel like a balancing act—the teacher moves as quickly as possible without compromising clarity and causing student errors. When material is more difficult for students, the pace slows somewhat; when it is easier, the pace increases. For example, when students are initially learning to sound out words, the pace of instruction may slow because the teacher must provide sufficient "think time" to allow students to figure out the words. But as the students become more proficient at sounding out, less "think time" is needed and the lesson can proceed at a quicker pace. Additionally, pacing varies within a lesson depending on the difficulty of each task. Determining an appropriately brisk pace requires closely monitoring student responses and behavior during a lesson and adjusting accordingly.

Vignette. Mr. Howard Varies Pace of Instruction

Each reading lesson in Mr. Howard's Explicit Instruction program introduces new content that may be challenging and includes review exercises that are easier. Mr. Howard knows that a brisk pace is different for different types of exercises. One day, a lesson included a review of CVC words (e.g., hop, cap, run). Knowing that this would be easier for the students, Mr. Howard moved quickly through this list. He provided minimal think time between words because the students had previously mastered reading this type of word. The lesson also introduced VCe words (e.g., hope, time, cape). Mr. Howard anticipated that this exercise would be more difficult for the students. He carefully taught the rule for reading this type of word and provided extra think time. This extra think time supported the students to read the words correctly by allowing them to figure out each word before saying it out loud. After the students read the words the first time, Mr. Howard had them read the words a second time with less think time between each word. Over the next few days, he gradually reduced the amount of think time he gave the students before reading VCe words to help them build fluency with this type of word.

Extra Guided Practice. Explicit Instruction programs provide guided practice in which students are supported with scaffolding as they actively respond to new tasks. The guided practice exercises include sufficient scaffolding to enable students to be successful, and may include the teacher assisting students or the students assisting each other. The scaffolding is gradually removed as students gain skills to build their independence. However, even the best programs cannot predict the amount of practice that each student will need as the scaffolding is removed. The teacher must make this decision based on student performance. The teacher intensifies instruction by adjusting the amount of practice to meet each student's individual needs throughout the process of removing the scaffolding.

There are several simple ways that teachers can adjust the amount of practice to fit the students' needs. One is the "repeat until firm" procedure. Using this procedure, the teacher repeats an exercise until the students can complete all items consecutively without errors. For example, an exercise in an Explicit Instruction mathematics program may present a set of eight shapes. For each shape, the students say if it is a polygon and if it is a quadrilateral. When the exercise is first presented, the students make three errors. The teacher praises the correct responses and corrects the errors. Then, the teacher begins again with the first item and challenges the students to get all eight items correct. This simple procedure uses student performance to determine the amount of practice the students' need—when their errors show that students need extra practice, the teacher provides it by going through the items again; when they need little practice, the teacher moves on to the next exercise.

A second simple procedure for expanding and targeting practice to meet students' precise needs is the "good-bye list." In this procedure, the teacher notes errors that the students make during a lesson. At the end of the lesson, the teacher presents the items to the students again. The teacher continues to present the items for a number of days. Each time the students correctly answer an item, the teacher puts a star by the item. After the students earn a previously specified number of stars for an item (usually five), the teacher removes the item and they all say "Good-bye!" to the item. This method for providing extra practice is especially useful when students are learning facts or skills that require relatively little time (e.g. math facts, letter sounds, reading words).

When providing additional practice on exercises that students find particularly difficult, students may become frustrated and/or discouraged. Teachers can encourage their students by explaining how the extra practice will help them and reinforcing their efforts. Reminding students that sports stars and musicians only perform their amazing feats after extensive practice, or temporarily switching to another task, may also be helpful.

Vignette. Mr. Howard Adjusts Amount of Guided Practice

Since joining Mr. Howard's reading group, Tori has mastered many letter sounds. Mr. Howard has also begun teaching Tori how to sound out words. One exercise looks like this:

1. Mr. Howard: I'll point under each sound. You say the sounds out loud without stopping between the sounds.
2. Mr. Howard points under each sound in "sam"
3. Students: ssssaaammm.
4. Mr. Howard: Now, read it the fast way. (Signals.)
5. Students: sam
6. Repeat steps 2–4 with mat, pet, and ram

One day, Tori and her classmates repeatedly make errors on this exercise. Mr. Howard's first response is to praise the students for their efforts and correct every error. He also begins providing additional practice on this skill. His primary strategy for providing additional practice is "repeat-until-firm." On the first day, Mr. Howard repeated the exercise four times before the students completed each item correctly. The students were engaged and motivated. The next day, Mr. Howard presented the same exercise to the students using different words. Initially, the students made several errors when sounding out and reading the words the fast way. Mr. Howard corrected every error. After presenting every item in the exercise, he said, "We're going to do that again because I think you can do even better!" The students responded with groans, appeared distracted during the exercise, and continued to make errors. Mr. Howard realized that forcing the students to repeat the exercise multiple times at this moment would not be effective. Instead, he taught the next exercise in the lesson, which happened to be easier for the students. He praised them for accurate and fluent reading, and they grew more motivated. Later in the lesson, he returned to the challenging exercise. This time, the students were more energized and engaged, and they only made one error. Mr. Howard praised them and presented the exercise again. The students accurately completed the exercise, and Mr. Howard pointed out their growth. On the third day, the students completed the same type of exercise without any errors on the first try. Mr. Howard did not provide any extra practice for this skill that day because the students' accuracy and fluency had improved.

Responding to Student Performance: Error Analysis and Adjustments to Future Lessons

The strategies of intensifying instruction by correcting all errors and providing extra practice on difficult items will be sufficient in many situations. Sometimes, it is important to examine the errors a student makes in order to provide even more targeted instruction. Error analysis is the process of examining students' errors to determine the likely cause(s) of the errors. The first step in analyzing errors is collecting data by recording student errors during a lesson. The second step is to examine the errors, noting what kinds of items are missed and how the student is responding incorrectly to identify the error pattern(s). After identifying the error patterns and their probable cause(s), teachers can develop targeted instruction and practice to address these error patterns.

Students often make repeated errors when learning a new procedure (e.g., sounding out words, multiplying fractions). When this occurs, the teacher examines each step in the procedure looking for steps that cause errors regularly. When the teacher finds the step(s) associated with the error(s), they re-teach the step and provide practice until it is mastered. Then the teacher returns to the full procedure. For example, a student may be making repeated errors when subtracting multi-digit numbers. The teacher watches the student work and carefully examines errors in the student's written work over several days. The teacher notices that the student does not rename when necessary. The teacher responds by reteaching the procedure for renaming when subtracting and provides practice. When this skill is strong, the student returns to full procedure for subtracting multi-digit numbers. The teacher watches carefully on the first few problems to check whether the student renames properly.

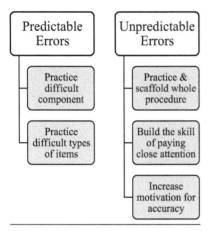

Figure 16.2 Common Results of Error Analysis

A second common situation requiring error analysis is when a student is learning a large number of items that are practiced together. For example, reading connected text involves decoding a large number of different words; spelling words correctly from dictation or in composition requires spelling a large number of words; arithmetic computation involves a large number of basic arithmetic facts; or identifying all the states in the United States on a map requires knowing locations and names for the 50 states. In these situations, a student may be accurate on some items or types of items, but inaccurate on others. If the student is identifying states on a map, the teacher can simply record which states the student misses and provide additional instruction and practice on those. When the student has mastered the difficult states, the teacher would provide practice on the full set of states. When practicing the full set, the teacher might give extra practice on items that had previously caused errors.

Sometimes, there is no clear pattern in student errors. There are three common causes of unpredictable errors. One cause is that the student is learning a new procedure that requires coordination of several components and they simply have not practiced enough to orchestrate all the components consistently. The teacher can provide support by asking questions that help the student attend to each component. For example, if a student is making unpredictable errors in multiplying multi-digit numbers, the teacher can ask, "What is the first thing you do?" After completing first step, the teacher asks, "What is the next thing you do?" and so on through the problem. A second cause of unpredictable errors is that a student has not learned to attend carefully to the items. This is often the case for readers who guess words rather than sounding them out. When the problem is learning to attend carefully, the teacher must be even more careful to correct every error because these are opportunities for the student to learn to pay more attention to the details of the items (e.g., words). Also, the teacher can add to their correction a component that requires the student to notice a critical aspect of the item. In the case of reading accurately, the teacher can add a step to the correction in which the student says each sound in the word. A third cause of unpredictable errors is low student motivation. Working carefully, paying close attention to details, and applying new skills that have not yet been thoroughly learned can be quite effortful. Confirmation of correct responses, recognition, and praise can be powerful motivators for many students. If this is not sufficient, the teacher can create simple systems and games that enhance motivation. Figure 16.2 summarizes some of the common results of error analysis.

Vignette. Mr. Howard Analyzes Errors and Addresses Component Skill

Tori and the other students in her reading group are learning to sound out words. To successfully sound out words, Tori will need to say the sound for each letter the slow way (e.g., "mmmaaannn") and then say the word the fast way (e.g., "man"). The Explicit Instruction reading program Mr. Howard is using has already provided extensive practice on these two sub-skills, and Mr. Howard has been careful to ensure that all of his students have mastered them both before combining them to sound out words. In this lesson, the group sounds some words out correctly but not others. Mr. Howard uses corrections and the "repeat-until-firm" strategy. These strategies for intensifying instruction are effective for two of the students, but Tori continues to make frequent errors.

Mr. Howard mentions this problem in a team meeting with Ms. Hamilton, the school psychologist, and Ms. Cho, the reading specialist. Ms. Cho asks whether Tori's errors are because (a) she doesn't say the right sounds for the letters, or (b) she says the words correctly the slow way but not the fast way. Mr. Howard sees that Ms. Cho is trying to figure out if one of the component skills is the cause. So, the next day, Mr. Howard keeps track of Toni's errors. He immediately notices that most of her errors involve saying the wrong sounds for letters. He then starts tracking which letters cause the errors, so he knows how to intensify instruction for Tori.

In a few days, it becomes clear that Tori's errors are the result of confusing "a" and "e." Tori says the right sounds for the letters in isolation, but she confuses the sounds when sounding out words. Ms. Cho suggests that Tori is accurate but not fluent—she can perform the skill in isolation but not in more complex situations. Ms. Cho suggests two possible strategies for intensifying instruction for Tori. One, Mr. Howard could use flashcards to build Tori's fluency with letter sounds. Two, he could provide more scaffolding for sounding out. Before sounding out a word, Mr. Howard could point under each letter and ask Tori to say the sound for the letters one at a time. That way, Tori could practice the easier task of saying each sound before sounding the entire word. Because Tori is already accurate on sounding out many words, Mr. Howard decides to add the scaffolding for words with the letters that are giving her trouble (a, e). Now he uses the following routine when asking Tori to sound out words that include "a" and "e":

- Mr. Howard: (Points to a new word: "man.") Tori, I want you to tell me the sound for each letter in this word. (Points to the "m.") What sound does this letter make?
- Tori: /m/
- Mr. Howard: Yes. (Points to the "a.") What sound?
- Tori: /a/
- Mr. Howard: Right. (Points to the "n.") What sound?
- Tori: /n/
- Mr. Howard: Super. You read all the letters perfectly! Now, sound out the word. Say each sound as I slide my finger under the letter. (Mr. Howard slides his finger under the letters of "man")
- Tori: mmmaaannn
- Mr. Howard: What's the word?
- Tomi: man
- Mr. Howard: Excellent! That was a tricky one, and you nailed it!

Mr. Howard carefully monitored Tori's performance and found that the extra scaffolding improved Tori's accuracy immediately. Mr. Howard realized he needed to gradually remove the extra scaffolding to make sure that Tori mastered sounding out words independently. Within a few days, Tori was able to sound out all words accurately and independently.

Responding to Independent Practice

Purposeful independent practice is critical for building knowledge and skills that students retain over time and use in complex situations. Active student responding is even more frequent during purposeful independent practice than other parts of the lesson. When students are engaged in high-quality independent practice, they are responding continuously. For example, students may be reading orally to build fluency, completing math problems, or writing responses to material they have read.

During purposeful independent practice, the teacher is focused on building at least three different kinds of skills. First, the teacher is supporting learning of the academic skills that are the explicit targets of the lesson. Second, the teacher is promoting skills related to understanding and following instructions. And third, the teacher is building the skills and motivation necessary for working productively for increasing lengths of time. As with all other parts of instruction, the teacher must monitor independent practice carefully and respond thoughtfully to enable students to master the material. Although this part of a lesson is called "purposeful *independent* practice," the teacher is highly involved. Teachers cannot assume that students (especially those with intensive instructional needs) already have the skills and motivation to work independently. Students with more intensive instructional needs may experience more difficulty applying skills during independent practice and may make more errors than other students. The teacher must closely monitor the students, continue to provide positive and corrective feedback, analyze errors to identify patterns, and reteach and provide additional practice, as necessary. This is intensification of instruction during independent practice. When the student is successful with this level of support, the teacher builds independence in the student by gradually reducing the frequency of check-ins and praising independence, accuracy, persistence, and productivity.

Vignette. Mr. Howard Analyzes Errors and Addresses Component Skills in Independent Practice

The Explicit Instruction reading program includes written work on simple reading comprehension. For example, students independently read words and circle the matching picture or read sentences and answer questions. The first time the reading group is assigned independent work that involves reading words and circling the matching pictures, two of the three students in the group pick up their pencils and begin working immediately. Tori does not pick up her pencil and quietly looks around the room. Mr. Howard is not sure if Tori is not completing the independent work because (a) she lacks the reading skills necessary for the task; (b) she doesn't understand the directions; or (c) she doesn't know how to work independently.

In order to clarify the instructions and test whether the problem is with the reading skill, Mr. Howard provides some scaffolding for the instructions (and temporarily eliminates the issue of knowing how to work independently).

- Mr. Howard: (points to first item) What is this word?
- Tori: mmmaaannn. Man.
- Mr. Howard: Right. Which picture should you circle?
- Tori: (points to the picture of the man) This one.
- Mr. Howard: Good. Go ahead and circle it.
- Tori: (circles the correct picture).
- Mr. Howard: Terrific. Now do the next one on your own and tell me when you are done. (He draws a line after the next item to emphasize that she only needs to do one item.)

Now Mr. Howard knows that Tori has the skills necessary to complete the task. He has also provided scaffolding for the directions, so Tori is very likely to know how to do the next item. By asking Tori to complete just one item independently, he is providing scaffolding for the skill of working independently.

- Tori: (after completing the item) I'm done.
- Mr. Howard: You got that one just right! Now, try these next two and then let me know. (He draws a line after the next two items, again emphasizing the small, manageable task.)

Mr. Howard is still not sure if Tori's lack of independence is because she has not developed the skill of working independently or because she gets attention and has to complete less work by quietly sitting without asking for help. Mr. Howard plans to address both these possibilities by gradually increasing the number of items that Tori does independently and praising her for independently and correctly completing items.

- Tori: (after completing the two items) Mr. Howard, I'm done.
- Mr. Howard: Perfect! And you didn't need my help. Now do you think you can do the remaining four of these on your own?
- Tori: Sure.
- Mr. Howard: Great! Let me know when you're done. (He draws a line after the items.)
- Tori: (after completing the four items) I'm done.
- Mr. Howard: Great, you got all four of these on your own!

The next day, Mr. Howard reduces scaffolding for understanding the directions by simply asking Tori what she has to do rather than telling her. He also continues to increase the amount of work she does between check-ins.

- Mr. Howard: What do you need to do in this section?
- Tori: (describes the task)
- Mr. Howard: Yes. Do this row and call me over when you are done. (Draws a star at the end of the row.)

Later in the program, a new kind of task required students to read a sentence and write several words in response to a question. Mr. Howard suspected that this was going to be challenging for Tori, so he watched her when she got to this point in the independent work. She read the sentence but sat without writing the answers. Mr. Howard could see that Tori would need more support to complete this difficult task, so he increased the scaffolding once again.

- Mr. Howard: What do you need to do here?
- Tori: Write the answer.
- Mr. Howard: Exactly. Do this one and call me over when you are done. (Draws a star after the first item)
- Tori: Done.
- Mr. Howard: Excellent. That's the right answer and nice handwriting! Now do these next two and let me know (draws a line after the next two items.)

He knows that all his students are in different places in the process of learning to work independently, so they will need different supports. Also, he knows that new and difficult tasks may require temporary extra supports. He watches his students carefully and continually adjusts his support to provide enough for the student to be successful.

Responding to Mastery Tests

Well-designed Explicit Instruction programs include regular mastery tests (approximately every 10 lessons) that assess the specific skills that have been taught in recent lessons. Earlier in this chapter, we described using mastery tests for placing students into appropriate lessons. The primary use of mastery tests is to determine whether a student needs additional instruction and practice on specific skills. Mastery tests are particularly important when the teacher has needed to correct many errors, add additional scaffolding, and/or provide extra practice. These supports are vital for promoting learning, but if they are not faded out, they may give the illusion that the students have reached mastery when they have not. Administering the mastery tests as directed by Explicit Instruction programs provides a check on whether the students have mastered all of the expected material with the expected level of independence. In general, it is important that extra supports and scaffolds *not* be used on mastery tests so the teacher can assess the students' skills at the level expected at that point in the program.

If teachers closely monitor student performance as we have suggested in this chapter, the results of the mastery tests usually will not be surprising. At times, however, students will not meet the criteria for passing a mastery test. Some well-developed Explicit Instruction programs include specific remediation procedures for students who do not pass mastery tests. These remediation procedures assist teachers with analyzing error patterns and determining how to re-teach specific content and/ or skills. The remediation usually involves repeating earlier lessons and/or exercises and ensuring that students reach mastery before moving on. After completing all of the remediation procedures, the teacher re-administers the mastery test. Typically, students meet passing criteria at this time and are prepared to move on to the next lesson. Students who do not meet the passing criteria need additional re-teaching and targeted practice.

If the Explicit Instruction program does not include remediation guidance along with mastery tests, then the teacher needs to use error analysis (as described above) to analyze student error patterns and develop re-teaching and targeted practice. If errors are widespread and performance is far below criterion, they should consider repeating the last five to 10 lessons. If errors are more isolated, they should identify the exercises that work on the weak skill in the last five to 10 lessons and repeat only those specific exercises.

Vignette: Mr. Howard uses mastery test to drive remediation

After about two months, the students in Mr. Howard's reading group have successfully passed multiple mastery tests from the Explicit Instruction reading program. During the last eight lessons, however, they've been introduced to VCe words (e.g., make, hope, mine). They are now reading lists of words that mix VC and VCe words (e.g., mad, hope, mine, pin, top). They have made frequent errors on long versus short vowel sounds. That is, when they see "made" they sometimes say "mad," and when they see "hop" they sometimes say "hope." Mr. Howard has corrected all errors, praised reading correctly, and intensified instruction by providing extra practice, but he is not sure if they will pass the upcoming mastery test. As expected, they do not meet the 90 percent correct criterion. The Explicit Instruction reading program Mr. Howard is using does not include remediation procedures, so Mr. Howard must problem solve by analyzing the students' errors. He checks all the errors on the mastery tests and confirms that almost all the mistakes involve confusing VC and VCe words. He was aware of errors on these types of words during lessons and this is additional support that the problem is specific to these words. He decides the remediation needs to be aimed specifically at reading VC and VCe words.

Because his students are having trouble with the medial vowel sounds, Mr. Howard notes the exercises in which this skill is first introduced and all the exercises that require its use (i.e., lists that mix both types of words). For the next three days, he spends half of his reading time on these exercises. On the fourth day he administers the mastery test again. This time, his students meet the criteria for passing. In addition to the overall criterion, Mr. Howard looks at their accuracy on the targeted type of words to make sure every student has mastered this skill. He is pleased to find that every student is accurate on at least 9 out of 10 of these words. The next day, he moves on to the next lesson.

External Progress Monitoring

Multiple sources of data are needed for making informed instructional decisions. Monitoring student responses during teacher-led instruction and independent work allows teachers to respond immediately and intensify instruction through error corrections and repeating items. Analyzing error patterns across lessons and on assessments supports teachers to intensify instruction through re-teaching and providing additional, targeted practice. Both of these types of progress monitoring are based on daily performance in lessons.

It is also important to monitor progress with assessments that are not part of the instructional program. This is because a student may be performing well in the program but fail to improve sufficiently outside the program. Instructional level curriculum-based measures are useful for monitoring student progress and may indicate if an instructional program is effective for a student. If a student's progress monitoring results do not show consistent growth, the instructional program (as it is being implemented) may not be effective for that student. This is a time for the team to engage in careful problem solving. As always, the first step is for the team to carefully examine the student's strengths and weaknesses—which specific skills appear to be the problem and which are strong? They should also review all other information regarding these skills, especially recent performance in the Explicit Instruction program. After reviewing the data, the team has several choices. They could (a) intensify the implementation of the current program using the techniques described in this book; (b) add a supplementary program that targets the weak skill areas; or (c) change programs.

If the program includes instruction on the weak skill, includes the components of Explicit Instruction, and the student is showing some progress, then we recommend further intensification within the current program. If the program does not include strong instruction and practice on the weak skill, the team should consider adding a supplemental program that targets this skill. However, the team must weigh potential advantages of adding a supplemental program against the costs of splitting instructional time between two programs and possible conflicts in the ways the two programs teach skills. It is possible for teachers to use so many different programs that students do not have sufficient time to make progress with mastery in any of the programs and to be confused by the mixed messages they get from the different programs. If the main program is research-validated and includes the components of Explicit Instruction, the team should consider changing programs to be a last resort. Although sometimes necessary, changing programs can disrupt progress, and the transition may take away from limited instructional time. However, if the program is not research-validated or does not include the components of Explicit Instruction, a change in program may be necessary to produce adequate learning in the long run.

Vignette on Intensification of EI Program due to Failing Mastery Test and ORF Plateau

Throughout the entire school year, Mr. Howard monitored his students' progress using Oral Reading Fluency curriculum-based measures. Around the time his students stopped passing mastery tests on the first attempt, Mr. Howard noticed their oral reading fluency progress monitoring scores plateauing. He brought both types of data (mastery tests and progress monitoring) to the school psychologist, Ms. Hamilton, the reading specialist, Ms. Cho, and the principal, Mr. Jones, and asked for their input. He was concerned that the Explicit Instruction reading program might not be working.

Ms. Hamilton, Ms. Cho, and Mr. Jones thanked Mr. Howard for bringing multiple sources of data for them to review as a team. They reminded Mr. Howard of all of the research supporting the Explicit Instruction program Mr. Howard chose. They also pointed out that the students have been making progress, although it had slowed in the recent weeks. Ms. Cho suggested that Mr. Howard intensify the Explicit Instruction program by providing additional, targeted practice outside of the usually scheduled lesson time. She noted that the group is at a level where they are reading short passages of connected text and that these passages will become longer in upcoming lessons. Reading these texts will provide excellent application of all their decoding skills. She suggested providing additional time for students to re-read the passages to build their fluency. Mr. Jones approved of this suggestion and offered to work with Mr. Howard to provide a paraprofessional who could conduct this extra practice.

After making arrangements with Mr. Jones, Mrs. Wise, the paraprofessional assigned to Mr. Howard's classroom, began supervising extra practice on passage reading for the students in Mr. Howard's group for 20 minutes every afternoon. The extra practice sessions appeared to help, as the students' accuracy and fluency improved during their usual lesson. In addition, all of the students passed the next mastery test on their first attempt. A couple of weeks later, the students' oral reading fluency progress monitoring scores also started to improve. After two more months of extra daily practice, the students' progress monitoring data were consistently improving so the team decided to discontinue the extra practice. Instead students would spend this time with their peers in the general education classroom. The team scheduled a time to reconvene in three weeks to review the data and re-institute the additional practice, should it be necessary.

Wrap Up

Explicit Instruction programs provide a strong foundation for intensification of instruction. The components of Explicit Instruction are themselves forms of intensification compared to programs that lack these components. But importantly, when using an Explicit Instruction program, the teacher is in a position to individualize and further intensify. Intensification follows the simple pattern of carefully watching student performance throughout the lesson, from mastery tests, and from curriculum-based assessments, then responding to it by making adjustments to teaching and practice. This chapter has described many ways this pattern of observation (data collection) and responding can be applied—from simple praise and corrections based on momentary observations through significant additions to the standard program based on mastery tests and curriculum-based assessments. It all comes down to closely monitoring student learning and responding to students so that every instructional minute can be as productive as possible.

Tips

1. Use research-validated Explicit Instruction programs to intensify instruction.
2. Place students appropriately within Explicit Instruction programs to make the most out of instructional time.
3. Monitor student performance closely during lessons and respond by giving clear positive and corrective feedback.
4. Analyze error patterns and provide extra practice to intensify Explicit Instruction programs.

Key Resources

1. Archer, A. L., & Hughes, C. A. (2010). *Explicit Instruction: Effective and Efficient Teaching.* Guilford Press.
2. This classic book thoroughly describes each component of Explicit Instruction and provides numerous real-world examples of how it can be implemented. This is the most complete resource for understanding Explicit Instruction.
3. Explicit Instruction website. https://explicitinstruction.org/ This website is the companion to the book *Explicit Instruction*. It provides free videos of Explicit Instruction lessons in various subject areas and at various grade levels. An excellent source for seeing Explicit Instruction in action.
4. NCII Course modules on Explicit Instruction: https://intensiveintervention.org/training/course-content/explicit-instruction

    This online course includes modules on intensifying instruction through (a) modeling and practice; (b) eliciting frequent responses; (c) providing feedback and maintaining a brisk pace; and (d) evaluating explicit instruction.

References

Archer, A. L., & Hughes, C. A. (2010). *Explicit Instruction: Effective and Efficient Teaching*. Guilford Press.

Baker, S., Lesaux, N., Jayanthi, M., Dimino, J., Proctor, C. P., Morris, J., ... & Newman-Gonchar, R. (2014). Teaching *academic content and literacy* to English learners in Elementary and Middle School. IES Practice Guide. NCEE 2014-4012. Washington, DC: National Center for Education Evaluation and Regional Assistance (NCEE), Institute of Education Sciences, U.S. Department of Education. Retrieved from https://whatworks.ed.gov/.

Christenson, S. L., Thurlow, M. L., Ysseldyke, J. E., & McVicar, R. (1989). Written language instruction for students with mild handicaps: Is there enough quantity to ensure quality?. *Learning Disability Quarterly, 12*(3), 219–29.

Cooper, J. O., Heron, T. E., & Heward, W. L. (2021). *Applied behavior analysis (3rd ed.)*. Pearson.

Frye, D., Baroody, A. J., Burchinal, M., Carver, S. M., Jordan, N. C., & McDowell, J. (2013). *Teaching math to young children: A practice guide* (NCEE 2014-4005). Washington, DC: National Center for Education Evaluation and Regional Assistance (NCEE), Institute of Education Sciences, U.S. Department of Education. Retrieved from the NCEE website: http://whatworks.ed.gov

Fuchs, L. S., Fuchs, D., & Malone, A. S. (2017). The taxonomy of intervention intensity. *Teaching Exceptional Children, 50*(1), 35–43.

Fuchs, D., Fuchs, L. S., & Vaughn, S. (2014). What is intensive instruction and why is it important? *Teaching Exceptional Children, 46*(4), 13–18.

Gersten, R., Beckmann, S., Clarke, B., Foegen, A., Marsh, L., Star, J. R., & Witzel, B. (2009). *Assisting Students Struggling with Mathematics: Response to Intervention (RtI) for Elementary and Middle Schools*. NCEE 2009-4060. Washington, DC: National Center for Education Evaluation and Regional Assistance (NCEE), Institute of Education Sciences, US Department of Education. Retrieved from https://whatworks.ed.gov/.

Graham, S., Bollinger, A., Olson, C. B., D'Aoust, C., MacArthur, C., McCutchen, D., & Olinghouse, N. (2012). *Teaching Elementary School Students to Be Effective Writers: A Practice Guide*. NCEE 2012-4058. What Works Clearinghouse.

Graham, S., McKeown, D., Kiuhara, S., & Harris, K. R. (2012). A meta-analysis of writing instruction for students in the elementary grades. *Journal of educational psychology, 104*(4), 879.

Hughes, C. A. Morris, J. R., Therrien, W. J., & Benson, S. K. (2017). Explicit instruction: Historical and contemporary contexts. *Learning Disabilities Research and Practice, 32*(3), 1–9.

Kamil, M. L., Borman, G. D., Dole, J., Kral, C. C., Salinger, T., & Torgesen, J. (2008). *Improving Adolescent Literacy: Effective Classroom and Intervention Practices. IES Practice Guide*. NCEE 2008-4027. National Center for Education Evaluation and Regional Assistance (NCEE), Institute of Education Sciences, US Department of Education. Retrieved from https://whatworks.ed.gov/.

Kostewicz, D. E., & Kubina Jr, R. M. (2011). Building science reading fluency for students with disabilities with repeated reading to a fluency criterion. *Learning Disabilities: A Multidisciplinary Journal, 17*(3), 89–104.

Kroesbergen, E. H., & Van Luit, J. E. (2003). Mathematics interventions for children with special educational needs: A meta-analysis. *Remedial and special education, 24*(2), 97–114.

Siegler, R., Carpenter, T., Fennell, F., Geary, D., Lewis, J., Okamoto, Y., Thompson, L., & Wray, J. (2010). *Developing effective fractions instruction for kindergarten through 8th grade: A practice guide* (NCEE #2010-4039). Washington, DC: National Center for Education Evaluation and Regional Assistance, Institute of Education Sciences, U.S. Department of Education. Retrieved from whatworks.ed.gov/ publications/practiceguides.

Solis, M., Ciullo, S., Vaughn, S., Pyle, N., Hassaram, B., & Leroux, A. (2012). Reading comprehension interventions for middle school students with learning disabilities: A synthesis of 30 years of research. *Journal of Learning Disabilities, 45*(4), 327–40.

Star, J. R., Caronongan, P., Foegen, A., Furgeson, J., Keating, B., Larson, M. R., Lyskawa, J., McCallum, W. G., Porath, J., & Zbiek, R. M. (2015). *Teaching strategies for improving algebra knowledge in middle and high school students* (NCEE 2014-4333). National Center for Education Evaluation and Regional Assistance (NCEE), Institute of Education Sciences, U.S. Department of Education. Retrieved from the NCEE website: http://whatworks.ed.gov.

Swanson, H. L. (2001). Searching for the best model for instructing students with learning disabilities. *Focus on Exceptional Children, 34*(2), 1.

Therrien, W. J., Taylor, J. C., Hosp, J. L., Kaldenberg, E. R., & Gorsh, J. (2011). Science instruction for students with learning disabilities: A meta-analysis. *Learning Disabilities Research & Practice, 26*(4), 188–203.

Vaughn, S., Gersten, R., & Chard, D. J. (2000). The underlying message in LD intervention research: Findings from research syntheses. *Exceptional children, 67*(1), 99–114.

Vaughn, S., Gersten, R., Dimino, J., Taylor, M. J., Newman-Gonchar, R., Krowka, S., Kieffer, M. J., McKeown, M., Reed, D., Sanchez, M., St. Martin, K., Wexler, J., Morgan, S., Yañez, A., & Jayanthi, M. (2022). *Providing Reading Interventions for Students in Grades 4–9* (WWC 2022007). Washington, DC: National Center for Education Evaluation and Regional Assistance (NCEE), Institute of Education Sciences, U.S. Department of Educations. Retrieved from https://whatworks.ed.gov/.

17
Use Flexible Grouping

Lawrence Maheady
SUNY Buffalo State
Kristen R. Rolf
Utah State University
Timothy A. Slocum
Utah State University

Introduction

Flexible grouping is a data-driven practice in which teachers create a variety of fluid groups (e.g., whole class, small groups, and partners) to meet specific student needs (McDonald, 2014). Teachers use formative assessment data, student preferences and interests, and learning objectives to group and regroup students often (e.g., daily; Brulles & Brown, 2018). Flood and colleagues (1992) noted that teachers who use flexible grouping assume that "every instructional episode demands careful attention to matching students' needs with the most appropriate group experience" (p. 615).

Special education teachers (SETs) use flexible grouping to accommodate learning differences, promote in-depth academic discussions, and facilitate collaborative student interactions. Students can work collaboratively or independently within flexible groups, and instruction may be teacher or student led (Colon et al., 2021). The general goal is to give students opportunities to interact with peers in meaningful ways while meeting important learning goals (Vaughn & Bos, 2012). Flexible grouping may also provide extra support for students during lessons, increase their motivation and/or interest, and promote personal and social responsibility (McKeen, 2019).

Narrowing the Focus

Chapter 17 includes multiple grouping arrangements (i.e., whole groups, small groups, partners, & one-to-one) that change often for differing amounts of time, and in response to ongoing measures of student performance. It is difficult, therefore, to conceptualize flexible grouping as a distinct and/or replicable practice. With this in mind, we identified two instructional strategies with considerable empirical support that include flexible grouping arrangements—Direct Instruction (DI) same-skill flexible groups (Engelmann & Carnine, 1991) and Juniper Gardens Children's Project Class Wide Peer Tutoring (CWPT; Greenwood et al., 1997)—provided a brief rationale for their use, and shared two vignettes to show how they were applied to intensify instruction for students with disabilities receiving Tier 3 services. Although we illustrate the use of flexible grouping within the context of specific teaching strategies, flexible grouping may be used effectively in a variety of instructional situations.

DOI: 10.4324/9781003276876-22

Chapter Overview

1. Describe the rationale for using two evidence-based practices to help novice SETs use flexible grouping.
2. Outline procedural steps for using CWPT and DI same-skill groups to improve student learning outcomes.
3. Provide two vignettes that describe how both EBPs were used to intensify instruction for students with disabilities.
4. Identify important instructional resources for using flexible grouping and intensifying instruction.

Using the HLP: Intensifying Instruction Using Two Evidence-Based Practices

According to the National Center for Intensive Intervention (NCII), teachers can intensify instruction by increasing (a) student opportunities to practice and receive positive and corrective feedback (e.g., more and/or longer sessions and smaller group sizes); (b) instructional alignment (e.g., allocating more time to specific target behaviors); (c) attention to learning transfer (e.g., pre-teaching content and embedding guided practice on target skills); and (d) student engagement and motivation (e.g., use peer support, group contingencies, and contingent rewards). Here, we examine how DI flexible same-skill groups and Juniper Gardens' CWPT can be used to intensify instruction for students receiving Tier 3 services.

Using small groups to intensify instruction. Special education teachers can use small *homogeneous* (i.e., same-skill) and/or *heterogeneous* (i.e., mixed-skill) groups to meet different student learning goals. Homogeneous groups are used to provide focused, intensive instruction for students with *similar* academic strengths, needs, and/or interests. Vellantino (2000) noted that they are configured often to meet short-term instructional goals and objectives. To maximize instructional intensity, teachers can reduce group sizes (i.e., one to three students was most effective for improving achievement; Iverson et al., 2005), provide more time to ensure student mastery (McLeskey & Waldron, 2011), and use practices that produce high rates of student responding (e.g., response cards and choral responding) (Heward & Wood, 2015). The first vignette describes how DI same-skill (i.e., homogeneous) groups were used to improve the performance of middle school students with emotional impairments.

Vignette 1: Flexible Grouping in Direct Instruction—Middle School, Remedial Reading Instruction

Ms. Baldwin is a fifth-year special education teacher in a large urban district. She works with a team of administrators, special education teachers, related service personnel, and paraprofessionals who are committed to ensuring that every special education student receives specialized instruction that meets their needs. Her primary role is teaching literacy to a caseload of 30 students who all require intensive instruction related to decoding. Mr. Tso is a paraprofessional assigned to her classroom.

Ms. Baldwin's students who need intensive instruction in reading have one class period (60 minutes) of teacher-led reading instruction followed by another class period (60 minutes) devoted to additional literacy activities (e.g., fluency, extra practice, and writing instruction). She refers to these two class periods as one instructional block. Her 30 students are scheduled in two instructional blocks—about 15 students in each.

Before the Beginning of the School Year

Ms. Baldwin plans to intensify and individualize literacy instruction by creating small instructional groups within each of her instructional blocks. To facilitate this, she works with the administrators to assign her students to the most appropriate classes. They work together to create a daily schedule for students that will enable them to receive all the intensive instruction they need. For students that Ms. Baldwin taught last year or are coming from the local elementary schools, she and the administrators review progress monitoring and program assessment data from the end of the previous year to inform their scheduling decisions. For new students coming from outside of the school district, Ms. Baldwin does her best to collect information from the most recent school and knows she will most likely need to collect additional data on her own. Although Ms. Baldwin and the administrators do their best to create supportive schedules for each student, the entire team is aware that they may need to make changes after students arrive and they are able to collect new data—they keep their plans flexible so they can meet students' needs.

Beginning of the School Year

Ms. Baldwin selected Direct Instruction (DI) in reading (Carnine et al., 2015) because it is well-supported by research for providing intensive instruction. The program has multiple levels designed to address the needs of students with various remedial reading needs. Each level includes small group teacher-led instruction, written work designed to build both comprehension and writing skills, and partner reading. She plans to create small groups out of the 15 students that are assigned to each instructional block to further individualize and intensify her instruction.

During each instructional block, she plans to use three types of grouping: small group for teacher-led instruction, pairs of students for fluency practice, and individual work for writing and supplemental practice. These three strategies for flexibly grouping her students are a starting point for organizing her instruction within each instructional block. The strategies intensify instruction by reducing group size, increasing instructional time on highly relevant tasks, and focusing the instruction on skills that are critical for each individual student.

During students' first days at school, Ms. Baldwin uses data to create the small groups within each instructional block. She knows that the standardized test scores from past years are not recent or specific enough to drive decisions about where to begin instruction within the program for each individual student. For students whom Ms. Baldwin taught last year using the same instructional program, she reviews her records from the end of last year. She notes what level of the program they were in, the last lesson they completed, and their reading fluency at the end of the year. She then gives the most recently passed mastery test to the students again. All students passed the test, giving her confidence that she can pick up where she left off with these students. (If any had not passed, she would have given them the next most recent mastery test. If they still had not passed, she would have continued giving them mastery tests in backwards order until they passed. She would have started instruction for these students at that point in the program.) For the students who are new to Ms. Baldwin, she reviews the available instructional data. None of the new students were taught using the instructional program she plans to use, so she gives fluency and placement tests to all students. Fluency tests provide initial benchmarks and give her a basis for pairing students for partner reading. The placement tests are brief, come from the instructional program, and are specifically designed to identify the precise skills necessary to succeed in a particular program level. Results will give her an indication of which program level(s) students need, but they will not specify exactly which lesson(s) within the level to begin instruction. To determine an exact starting point, she gives the first mastery test in the appropriate level to the students. If they pass, she gives them the next. She continues with this process until students do not pass a mastery check. These data give her a clear indication of which lesson the students need to begin instruction.

Ms. Baldwin uses the instructional data to organize her small reading groups. Because decoding involves learning a sequence of skills in which earlier skills provide the foundation for later skills, Ms. Baldwin is careful to ensure that each group is composed of students with very similar current instructional needs (i.e., homogeneous grouping). If students in each group already have similar instructional skills and needs, then she can teach lessons that will meet all their needs. This arrangement uses instructional time very efficiently. She knows that if she created groups of students with very different skill levels, some would have already mastered the skills in the lesson and others would not have the skills necessary to be successful. This would waste valuable instructional time and frustrate everyone.

Based on available information, Ms. Baldwin places all students in each instructional block into two smaller groups. One group has seven students, and the other has eight. Both groups are in the same instructional program, but one group is starting at the beginning of the program (Lesson 1) and the other group is starting a little over halfway through the program (Lesson 40). During the first, class period, Ms. Baldwin provides teacher-led instruction to one small group while Mr. Tso supervises students in the other small group as they work individually to complete written comprehension work. Halfway through the period, the small groups swap teachers and activities. In this way, the team will provide intensive small group instruction to all students and give students opportunities to work individually on tasks where that is more appropriate. This flexible grouping strategy uses instructional time efficiently and ensures that Ms. Baldwin engages with each student daily. During the second, class period of the instructional block, Ms. Baldwin and Mr. Tso provide fluency-building activities to pairs of students, additional writing instruction to individuals, and targeted supplemental reading practice for individual students. Aware of the need to use every instructional day to its fullest, Ms. Baldwin has her groups organized in the first week and begins instruction before the week ends.

Ms. Baldwin and Mr. Tso know that adjustments to instructional groups sometimes need to be made, and they look for indications that a group is not meeting any student's needs. Students may make errors on the first day of instruction because they are not familiar with routines, they have not been in school for some time and have forgotten material over the summer, they are no longer accustomed to paying close attention, and they may not have every skill necessary for the group. Ms. Baldwin and Mr. Tso expect to correct errors frequently and are prepared to do so in a supportive manner. They want their students to know that errors, and being corrected, are a healthy part of the learning process. At the same time, they monitor error patterns carefully for signs that a student would benefit from being in a different instructional group.

One Week Later...

Over the course of the first five days of instruction, Ms. Baldwin notices that one of the new students, Mateo, is doing better than expected. Mateo was very shy and extremely hesitant during placement testing, and she had placed him in the group beginning at Lesson 1. Over the last few days, his confidence has increased, and he has been accurate during teacher-led instruction and independent work. Ms. Baldwin asked Mr. Tso how he was doing during partner-reading and independent work. Mr. Tso said that Mateo writes extremely slowly but all his independent work was completed accurately (suggesting he is comprehending the content). Mateo had no problems in his partner reading, and he appeared to be very fluent and accurate during fluency-building activities.

Ms. Baldwin wonders if Mateo did not display his best reading skills on the placement tests. She decides to watch his performance during teacher-led instruction and asks Mr. Tso to do so as well. One week later they agree that Mateo may be able to work at a higher level. Ms. Baldwin gives the mastery test for Lesson 20, and Mateo passes easily. He also easily passes the test from Lesson 30. On the Lesson 40 test, he misses a few items and results suggest that he should start instruction around Lesson 40. This confirmed that Mateo's current group was not meeting his academic needs.

The other group was now on Lesson 50. To prepare him to join them, Ms. Baldwin asks Mr. Tso to teach Mateo individually starting with Lesson 40 until he is caught up with the other group and can join them. They decide the best time to provide this instruction is during the time for supplemental targeted reading practice (i.e., second class in instructional block). Mr. Tso teaches the lessons to

Mateo over the next few days, and he is soon able to join the other group. Ms. Baldwin suspects that there will be areas that initially are very challenging for Mateo in this group, so she tells Mr. Tso that she will note exercises that are difficult and will ask him to review and practice them individually with Mateo. When she tells Mateo about the change, she congratulates him on his excellent work in reading and emphasizes that she knows he can do this more challenging work. She makes a point to celebrate this advancement with Mateo and emails his parents with the good news.

On the first day in his new group, Mateo is simultaneously proud of his accomplishment, excited for the new challenge, and a little intimidated by the new work. Ms. Baldwin encourages him by reminding him that mistakes are the process of learning. She makes sure she stays positive with all her students and gives corrections with a positive and supportive attitude. She carefully notes topics on which Mateo makes only occasional errors and topics that are more difficult. Ms. Baldwin asks Mr. Tso to repeat the difficult exercises from each lesson until Mateo can read all the words without errors. In the next two weeks, the need for extra practice on difficult exercises gradually diminishes. Ms. Baldwin sends fewer exercises to be practiced and as a result, Mateo spends more time on written comprehension and fluency work with Mr. Tso. This flexible combination of support in the small group and highly targeted extra practice helps accelerate Mateo's learning, and soon he is participating in the group with high levels of accuracy and very few errors. He is proud of his accomplishments, and Ms. Baldwin reminds him that this is a result of his hard work, persistence, and his learning from previous mistakes.

Ms. Baldwin used flexible grouping strategies with Mateo by making an initial placement decision based on data, monitoring his performance during instruction, verifying his performance with additional assessment data, providing individualized instruction to support transitioning him to the more advanced group, and continuing to give additional support as he adjusts to his new instructional group. She will continue to monitor his performance in the new group using data from the lessons, assessment data, and progress monitoring data. If the data show a need, she will adjust again to make sure she provides instruction that meets Mateo's changing needs. Ms. Baldwin considers this process to be a critical part of *intensification* of instruction—doing what is necessary so each student receives the most appropriate lesson each day and builds their skills as quickly as possible.

Six Weeks After Instruction Began

For the first few weeks of school, students in the group that started at Lesson 1 progressed nicely. They made few errors during teacher-led instruction and completed their independent work accurately with little assistance. After about a month, they received instruction on reading words with single and double consonants (e.g., hoping and hopping). Despite Ms. Baldwin teaching the lessons as designed, students struggled with this skill—their accuracy decreased, they needed more assistance with independent work, and getting through lessons took much longer. Additionally, they did not pass the next mastery test. Ms. Baldwin knows that continuing to teach new lessons to students who have not mastered previous content is not in their best interest. Their progress will slow, and they will not master new skills.

She decides to re-teach the lessons beginning with the lesson that first introduced single and double consonants and use "Good-bye Lists." Good-bye lists are a simple and quick way to provide extra, highly targeted practice. She writes down every word the students do not read correctly the first time on the white board. At the end of the lesson, before saying "good-bye" to her students, she has them read through the list as a group. She puts a check mark next to every word read correctly. After a word has five checkmarks by it, she erases it from the list. The students respond well to this. Their accuracy increases during teacher-led instruction, the number of words on the "Good-bye List" decreases, and they complete independent work with less support from Mr. Tso. Ms. Baldwin continues to monitor student errors during teacher-led instruction. As student skills become more fluent, Ms. Baldwin can move more quickly through lessons and Mr. Tso can focus on providing more support for writing and oral reading fluency.

Ms. Baldwin and Mr. Tso use flexible groupings to adjust the content and intensity of instruction for this group. Initially, Ms. Baldwin re-taught lessons and they replaced some independent practice time with additional small group practice led by Mr. Tso. He increased the intensity of instruction by providing targeted practice on words students found challenging during lessons. After student accuracy improved during teacher-led instruction, Ms. Baldwin and Mr. Tso removed the extra targeted practice because it was no longer needed. They used the instructional time that had been devoted to extra practice to make more progress in the instructional program and toward other instructional objectives.

End of 1st Trimester

At the end of the first trimester, both of Ms. Baldwin's groups are doing well. Carefully teaching the lessons, collecting and reviewing data regularly, and responding to the needs of her students means that they are all becoming more proficient readers. They know and follow her classroom routines and make few errors during each lesson. The additional instructional time gained from student progress allows her to intensify instruction by teaching more than one lesson during a class-period. When they finish one lesson, Ms. Baldwin begins the next one during the same class-period and takes full advantage of all instructional minutes (rather than waiting until the next day to begin the next lesson). Often, she can complete one and a half lessons in a single session. As a result, her students will complete more than one program level in one year and narrow the achievement gap between them and their same-grade peers. Ms. Baldwin is using flexible grouping to increase progress through the curriculum in response to student performance. She is aware that both mastery and progress are critical for her students to succeed.

Throughout the Year

Ms. Baldwin continues to monitor her students closely and use flexible groupings throughout the school year. Classroom data, program assessment data, and progress monitoring data show that students are progressing at different rates within their groups. As with the examples above, Ms. Baldwin adjusts her instruction and grouping practices to provide extra support or to accelerate student learning, as needed. Table 17.1 summarizes the main strategies Ms. Baldwin uses to respond to each student's needs. She implements the flexible grouping strategies intentionally, collects and reviews student data to monitor progress, and adjusts, as necessary, to flexibly meet each students' needs. Throughout the year, her grouping choices are always driven by data and maintain a fluidity that allows her to respond quickly to each student's changing needs.

In contrast to the initial vignette, the second describes a middle-school special education teacher's use of a specific evidence-based, peer-tutoring strategy to intensify instruction and improve middle school students' science vocabulary skills during resource room instruction. Mr. Rodriguez learned about Juniper Gardens Children's Project CWPT during two required graduate research courses and worked collaboratively with the instructor and a research team partner to (a) develop relevant instructional materials (e.g., concept cards, pre- and post-test vocabulary assessments); (b) demonstrate accurate use of tutoring procedures (i.e., CWPT training materials, role-plays on campus and on site, and adapted CWPT fidelity checklists); and (c) conduct a single case study to examine tutoring effects on student science vocabulary performance. (It is important to note that this level of professional development and support is not common in most settings, therefore, other means of training and support will be needed to assist teachers in CWPT implementation).

Table 17.1 Flexible Grouping Strategies

For students who...	Adjust grouping by...
Make expected progress using core (Tier 1) instruction	Use core (Tier 1) instruction
Make expected progress using core (Tier 1) instruction but occasionally struggle with a particular skill	Provide additional, targeted practice (may be part of whole-class instruction, small group instruction, paired practice, or individual practice, depending on the needs of the students)
Regularly need additional support to make expected progress using core (Tier 1) instruction	Pre-teach and/or re-teach lessons Add daily, targeted, empirically supported supplemental (Tier 2) instruction in addition to core (Tier 1) instruction Provide instruction in small groups Provide targeted paired or individual practice
Do not make expected progress using core (Tier 1) instruction plus supplemental (Tier 2) instruction	Provide intensive (Tier 3) instruction using an empirically supported explicit and systematic instructional program. • Use the program's placement test and mastery tests to accurately determine the starting point for each student • Intensify data-based decision making by closely monitoring student performance during instruction and increasing the frequency of progress monitoring • Repeat lessons and/or provide additional, targeted practice (e.g., Good-bye Lists, repeating exercises) during the lesson Group students in small, homogeneous instructional groups during teacher-led instruction to use instructional time more efficiently Increase the amount of time devoted to instruction Provide additional, targeted paired or individual practice
Progress at a faster rate than their peers	In core (Tier 1) instruction: • Provide targeted enrichment activities in addition to core (Tier 1) instruction. In supplemental (Tier 2) instruction: • Review data and determine if current level of additional support is still needed. If not, reduce or stop supplemental instruction. • If additional support is still needed, increase pace and/or level of difficulty of instruction. • Continue to closely monitor student performance and make data-based decisions. In intensive (Tier 3) instruction: • Determine if placement within the instructional program is appropriate and advance student, if necessary. • Increase the pace of instruction by teaching more than one lesson per day. • Continue to closely monitor student performance and make data-based decisions.

Vignette 2: Using Juniper Gardens' CWPT to Improve Science
Vocabulary—Middle-School Resource Room

Tutoring is a supplemental instructional service that has been used to remediate, enrich, and accelerate student learning (Sanford, 2021). Tutoring practices have included adults and peers, and peer-tutoring programs have been delivered in same-age, cross-age, and class-wide formats. Hattie (2012) indicated that well-designed tutoring programs produce large effect sizes (i.e., .70 to .90) on elementary and secondary students' reading and math achievement.

Juniper Gardens CWPT is a within-class, reciprocal peer tutoring program with an extensive evidence base. It has been used to improve student achievement in literacy, math, and a variety of content areas in elementary and secondary general and special education classrooms (Kamps et al., 2008). CWPT was developed as an activity to *practice* previously taught content and skills to be used in place of independent work. There are four primary CWPT components (a) weekly competing teams; (b) highly structured, reciprocal tutoring procedures; (c) daily point earning, public posting, and contingent rewards; and (d) direct practice of targeted academic content and skills.

Mr. Rodriguez was a second year, special education teacher in a small urban school district. His instructional responsibilities included providing direct Tier III literacy instruction for two small groups of six, 5th and 6th grade students with high incidence disabilities in a resource room and "push in" services in math and science general education classes. Although students were making adequate academic progress overall, they needed more intensive instruction on critical science vocabulary to improve their performance. Mr. Rodriguez felt that CWPT would give students more opportunities to respond and receive feedback *within* lessons, increase instructional time on targeted skills (i.e., science vocabulary), and provide multiple engagement and motivation supports (e.g., group contingencies, public posting, and contingent rewards).

Mr. Rodriguez initially aligned his science vocabulary instruction with district-adopted curricula and existing general educator practice and used multiple Tier I and II interventions, but students continued to struggle in science. He decided to intensify his science vocabulary instruction by using the CWPT program. He adapted the standard CWPT protocol by (a) creating two instructional teams (i.e., one per classroom) that competed *across* rather than within classrooms; (b) using science concept cards to increase content alignment; and (c) including novel team rewards (e.g., mystery motivators) for improved individual and team performance.

Pre-teaching and Material Development

Mr. Rodriguez initially administered a comprehensive pretest of important science vocabulary (i.e., 100 words) over five, 15-minute sessions. Important science vocabulary terms were derived from two sources (a) district-adopted curricula materials for 5th & 6 grade science and (b) high frequency, grade level science vocabulary identified in *Visible Learning for Science, K-12 Text* (Almarode et al., 2018). Mr. Rodriguez conducted an error analysis, identified common missed vocabulary terms, and used this information to (a) create a series of *concept cards* for use during tutoring sessions, and (b) make weekly pre- and post-test assessments.

Concept cards (i.e., flashcards) were created based on student pre-test performance and allowed Mr. Rodriguez to cluster important and related content materials. Table 17.2 shows two sample concept cards that were used to teach content related to clouds and matter. Students used five or six concept cards each week and completed 10-item assessments based on this content on a pre- and post-test basis. (All tutoring-related materials including point totaling sheets and scoreboards were made *prior to* implementing CWPT and weekly pretests were given immediately after posttests each week.)

Table 17.2 Two Science Vocabulary Concept Cards with Definitions and Related Questions

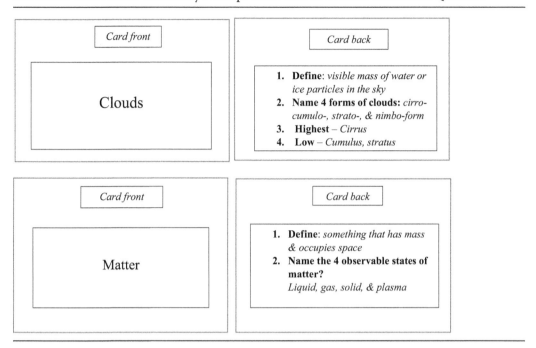

Table 17.3 provides a detailed lesson plan for how Mr. Rodriguez used CWPT to improve science vocabulary. His primary instructional goals were to increase student understanding of important science terms and help them make real-life connections between words and their uses (e.g., temperature can be used to determine the health of people). Science content was pre-taught each week using explicit instruction and concrete, student-friendly definitions. Instead of having students practice science content *independently* as he had been doing, Mr. Rodriguez used CWPT. The tutoring manual, however, did not specify the amount of time or number of CWPT sessions to schedule each week. Tutoring sessions in other content areas (e.g., math, reading, and spelling), however, were typically 20 to 30 minutes in length and occurred two to four times per week. Given Mr. Rodriguez instructional context, he scheduled three, 20-minute CWPT sessions each week. These sessions were adjusted in intensity (e.g., more and/or longer sessions) once based on student weekly posttest performance.

Weekly competing teams. Each week, Mr. Rodriguez assigned six students in each class to three sets of tutoring pairs based on the previous week's pretest performance. Student performance was ranked *privately* from highest to lowest (i.e., % correct) and then divided into two columns (i.e., split half ranking). The three highest-scoring students were placed in column 1 in descending order and the next three were ranked the same way in the second column. The highest-scoring student in the first column was paired with the highest scorer in column 2, the two second-highest scorers were paired, and so on. Tutor pairs remained the same for one week and were reconfigured based on subsequent pretest performance. The goal was to give students opportunities to work collaboratively with all classmates. Tutor pairs were encouraged to work quickly and collaboratively to earn as many individual and team points as possible during daily CWPT sessions and on weekly science assessments.

Structured tutoring roles. Students retrieved tutoring materials from their respective CWPT folders and sat near partners. Tutoring roles were reciprocal; students served as both tutors and tutees for equal amounts of time. Mr. Rodriguez set a large timer for 10 minutes and said, "ready begin." Tutors (a) held up each concept card (front facing tutees); (b) asked tutees to *say and write*

Table 17.3 Sample 5th–6th Grade Lesson Plan for CWPT Using Science Vocabulary Concept Cards

College and Career-Ready Standard
Determine or clarify the meaning of unknown and multiple meaning words and phrases based on grade-level
    reading and content. (MS–ESS$_{2-5}$)

Objective: To identify the meaning and uses of important science terms

Pre-teaching procedures: Comprehensive pre-assessment of science knowledge & identification and
    understanding of important vocabulary terms and real-life applications. Use of weekly pre- and post-test
    assessments. Science vocabulary was pre-taught using explicit instruction and concrete, student-friendly
    definitions.

Objective: To identify the meaning and uses of important science terms

Materials:
The instructional routine should be conducted at least twice per week after initial teacher-led instruction.

- Whiteboards or paper, and pen or pencil
- Five to six concept cards with vocabulary terms & questions related to real-life uses
  (e.g., precipitation, temperature, clouds, matter, molecule, and water vapor)
- Point totaling sheets, class scoreboards, procedural checklist, & mystery reward box

Suggested Schedule & Group Size

Schedule: Two to three, 20-minute practice sessions per week
Group size: Six students assigned to weekly tutoring pairs based on preassessment scores
Note: The script is intended as a model. It describes pre-teaching principles and activities as well as
             procedures for implementing CWPT in sample lessons.

Activity	Sample script and procedures
Intervention principles Use precise, simple language to teach key concepts and procedures.	**Today we will learn the meanings of some new science terms and how the words can be used in real-life situations. Learning new science terms will help you to understand more words and better understand the words we are using in our science lessons.** *Display and say the word ("temperature"). Ask students to say the word with you ("temperature") and make sure they pronounce them correctly.* **Temperature is a measure of hotness and coldness of an object or environment.**
Use explicit instruction and modeling with repetition to teach concepts and/or demonstrate steps in a process. Provide concrete practice opportunities and give positive and corrective feedback.	**In your science book, you will see how doctors use temperature to determine someone's wellness. Doctors take someone's temperature to determine if they are generally healthy or sick. When your body temperature is around 98.6 degrees, it is considered normal.** **What does temperature mean? (the hotness, or coldness of object or environment).**

Table 17.3 Cont.

	Provide several examples of the use of temperature in sentences. Ensure sentences help students to identify word meanings and uses. Be sure to explain examples by highlighting key characteristics shared about the meaning of the word.
Have students explain new concepts, in their own words, incorporating the important terms you have taught. Provide feedback	**Here is another example of the word temperature in a sentence. Let's see if we can explain the meaning of the sentences. "If I wanted to know if the bath water was ok, I could take the temperature." What does temperature mean?** *(the hotness or coldness of objects or the environment).* **That's right, to find out if the bath water is ok, I can measure the temperature. Can someone tell me how they would measure water temperature?** **(Accompany student responses with visual representations of thermometers)**
Provide repeated opportunities to practice using the word correctly and provide feedback.	**Here is another sentence. "The doctor's thermometer showed that the person's temperature was 103.4 degrees." What does temperature mean?** *(hot and above normal).* **What might the doctor tell the patient?** *(You may be sick because you have a high temperature).*
	Now I am going to ask you a few more questions about temperature. Would a temperature of 10 degrees be hot or cold? *(cold)* **Why?** *(A temperature of 32 degrees, is considered freezing; 10 degrees is lower.)* **That's right, 10 degrees is below a freezing temperature, so it would be very cold.** *Continue with additional practice opportunities. Be sure to have students explain their thinking.*
	Repeat above steps to introduce the word, "precipitation" and so on until all new vocabulary terms are introduced and reviewed
Provide repeated opportunities to practice using the word correctly and provide feedback.	**To practice the meanings and uses of our new science terms, we will be using Class Wide Peer Tutoring at least twice each week. CWPT is an academic game to help you learn science vocabulary terms and their uses.**
	Put students into tutoring pairs based on weekly pre-test performance, explain that they will take turns being tutors and tutees for 10 minutes each. Tutors (a) present concept cards to *tutees* (i.e., *vocabulary words facing partners*); (b) ask them to define terms & answer questions (orally & in writing); and (c) provide positive and corrective feedback (and points). Tutees (a) respond orally and in writing to vocabulary terms and questions; (b) correct errors noted by tutors; and (c) calculate daily point totals and writing numbers on top of practice sheets.

(continued)

Table 17.3 Cont.

	Teacher says, *"Ready to begin"* and sets timer for 10 minutes. While students work in pairs, teachers move around classroom providing feedback and "bonus points" to students providing acceptable academic responses and/or using appropriate tutoring procedures.

Structured tutoring procedures

Tutees say and write short definitions and responses to each science term and questions. Tutors assign 5 points for correct responses (i.e., accurate definitions & answers to questions). If responses are incorrect, tutors say "good try," provide correct responses, and ask tutees to say and write correct answers three times. If tutees correct errors, they earn 2 points. If errors are uncorrected, tutees get 0 points, and next concept cards are presented. Students are encouraged to complete as many items as they can in 10 minutes. *("The more items you complete, the more points you and your team earn toward a class wide reward").*

When timer goes off *(10 minutes)*, students are told to reverse roles and follow the same teaching procedures. Teacher circulates and awards bonus points.

After second 10-minute intervals, students are told to add up individual point totals and write the totals on top. They then exchange papers with partners who verify totals by signing their initials. Individual point totals are then entered on daily CWPT scoreboard *(posted prominently in class)*, daily and cumulative team totals are calculated and reviewed by the teacher.

Following at least two CWPT sessions, students are given weekly science quizzes individually. *(Quizzes contain recently reviewed vocabulary terms & questions).* Students are told that they can earn 10 points *(i.e., individual and team)* for each quiz item completely correctly. Individual quiz scores are added to weekly team totals. If pre-determined goals are met, the class earns "Team of the Week" certificates and opportunities to earn "mystery rewards." If weekly goals are not met, the class is encouraged to try harder next week.

Error Correction	Error correction is done in two ways in CWPT. First, within CWPT sessions, tutors identify and correct errors immediately and constructively. (i.e., "Nice try, a better response would be ___. Now say and write the answer three times and earn two more points"). Second, student performance on weekly science vocabulary quizzes allows teachers to assess maintenance of student understanding and to provide additional feedback as needed. Vocabulary terms (and concept cards) that were incorrect on weekly quizzes should be included in subsequent tutoring sessions and quizzes.

Table 17.3 Cont.

Instructional Considerations	<ul><li>Encourage students to use new vocabulary words during school day and at home. Provide positive feedback when students use words in instructional and non-instructional contexts.</li><li>Ask students to give synonyms for words and used them in sentences.</li><li>Review new words frequently, provide opportunities for students to interact with words by (a) using them in new sentences; (b) relating them to other known words; and (c) categorizing words.</li><li>Provide individual opportunities to write and illustrate situations where words may be used.</li></ul>

Note: This table was adapted from the vocabulary instructional routine: new vocabulary template provided by the National Center on Intensive Intervention. https://intensiveintervention.org/

the terms, definitions, and responses to related questions; and (c) provided immediate positive and constructive feedback (i.e., verbal and points) based on tutee responses.

In Table 17.1, for example, if tutees correctly pronounced *clouds* and provided an acceptable definition, tutors said, "that's right" and awarded 10 points (i.e., marked on point totaling sheets). If tutees correctly noted the four types of clouds and identified cirrus as the highest and cumulus or stratus as the lowest cloud formations, they earned 30 additional points (i.e., 10 for each question/ item). On the second concept card, students could earn 50 total points by correctly reading and defining "matter" and stating its four observable states (i.e., 10 points for each item).

When tutees made errors, they were corrected immediately. Tutors, (a) said "good try"; (b) provided acceptable responses (i.e., contained on concept cards); and (c) asked tutees to say and write correct responses two times. If tutees corrected their errors (step c), tutors awarded five points per item. If tutees did not correct responses (e.g., refused or made mistakes in corrections), no points were given, and the next concept card was presented. Students completed as many cards and questions as possible before time elapsed. They knew that the more items they completed correctly, the more points they earned individually and for the team. When the timer went off, students quickly reversed roles and followed the same tutoring procedures for the next 10 minutes.

Daily point earning, public posting, and rewards. In addition to earning points for accurate and corrected responses during daily CWPT sessions, students also earned "bonus points" for appropriate social and tutoring behavior. Mr. Rodriguez gave *bonus points*, for example, to tutors who maintained a brisk pace; provided clear, immediate, and concise feedback; awarded the appropriate number of points; used error correction procedures; and gave unsolicited supportive comments. Tutees earned bonus points by working quickly and accurately, correcting errors immediately and without comment, and producing high-quality academic responses. He typically awarded 15 to 20 bonus points per student by writing numbers on top of daily point totaling sheets. He used different colored pens each day to minimize the possibility of "point inflation."

After students served in both roles, they added individual and bonus points, recorded totals, and exchanged papers with partners to check for accuracy. If partners agreed with point totals, they wrote their initials, and earned 20 bonus points for accurate point totaling. Individual student points were written on a CWPT scoreboard and daily and cumulative team totals were entered and displayed *publicly* on a laminated scoreboard in the front of the classroom. Public posting when used appropriately (e.g., important target behaviors and improving performance trends) has a long history of positive academic and motivational effects.

Students also earned points based on their performance on weekly, 10-item science vocabulary posttests. They completed assessments *independently* and earned 20 points for each correct response (i.e., 200 points maximum). Individual quiz points were added to cumulative weekly totals for each class. The class with the most points earned "Team of the Week" certificates that were signed by members and posted prominently in the classroom. Winning team members also had a chance to earn mystery motivators. It is also possible for both teams to "win" each week by meeting pre-set criteria (e.g., class average of 80 percent and higher on weekly post-tests).

Mystery motivators (MM) are unknown rewards delivered based on successful completion of preset criteria (i.e., higher tutoring point total; Rhode et al., 2020). Mr. Rodriguez decorated 10 sealed envelopes that contained paper slips with the names of different high preference rewards (e.g., extra free time, drop work coupons, and snacks). Envelopes were sealed, dangled from the ceiling, and hyped by the teacher during the week (e.g., "*Your team is barely ahead of the other group, let's have a good practice session*"). The winning team of the week voted on which envelopes to pick, and rewards were *shared* at the most convenient time.

Direct practice of targeted academic skills. CWPT is flexible and can be used in multiple subjects, across varied ages (e.g., grades 1–10), and with different target behaviors. In reading, tutoring pairs alternate reading aloud and answering comprehension questions; in math, they take turns solving word and computation problems; and in spelling, they alternate spelling target words orally and in writing. Here, Mr. Rodriguez targeted science vocabulary and related questions and created sets of concept cards for students to practice the information. CWPT procedures increased student response opportunities within sessions, provided immediate positive and corrective feedback, and used contingent rewards for motivation. Mr. Rodriguez taught students to make simple line graphs showing weekly science quiz scores to monitor their ongoing performance.

As part of a master's project, Mr. Rodriguez also used a single case research design (i.e., A-B-A-B) to compare the effects of CWPT to his existing practice (i.e., baseline; explicit instruction + independent work) on student weekly post-test performance. Results showed a functional relationship in that all 12 target students had higher vocabulary post-test scores when CWPT was used. Performance changes were immediate and large (i.e., one to two letter grades) and there was less than 5 percent overlapping data points. All but one student also reportedly preferred using CWPT to working independently.

Wrap Up

Flexible grouping involves the use of multiple instructional arrangements (i.e., whole groups, small groups, partners, and one-to-one) that change often for differing amounts of time, and in response to formative measures of student performance. This chapter described the general parameters of this HLP and described two, evidence-based practices that special education teachers can use to intensify instruction and meet evolving student needs. The brief vignettes showed how teachers used DI same-skill flexible groups and class-wide peer tutoring procedures to improve academic outcomes (i.e., literacy and science vocabulary) for students receiving Tier III services.

Tips

1. Select teaching practices with the most empirical support and instructional relevance, implement them with integrity, and monitor the ongoing impact on important student outcomes.
2. Train students directly to use selected practices, monitor the fidelity (i.e., accuracy and consistency) with which they are used, and retrain students if accuracy falls below 90 percent.
3. Use short, formative assessments (e.g., exit tickets, "muddiest point," and one-minute quizzes) to monitor student performance and guide instructional decision-making.

Key Resources

National Center on Intensive Intervention

The National Center on Intensive Intervention (NCII) works with school districts to build capacity to support the implementation of data-based individualization in reading, math, and behavior. The Center (a) reviews commercially available academic and behavioral assessments and interventions and helps districts identify the most relevant programs; (b) provides ongoing technical assistance, training, and coaching to support implementation; (c) disseminates information via monthly webinars, videos, and presentations; and (d) conducts formative evaluations to inform the field and improve the Center's functioning. Key resources include, academic and behavior monitoring tools, academic intervention tools, and a data-based individualization framework for intensive intervention.
www.air.org/centers/national-center-intensive-intervention

Peer Tutoring Resource Center

Launched in November 2013, the Peer Tutoring Resource Center was created to help K-12 teachers develop and maintain peer tutoring programs in their classrooms and schools. The website provides links to resources for setting up different types of programs and research on best practices. A blog highlights successful peer tutoring practitioners and provides expert advice on pressing K12 education topics and a forum offers opportunities to learn from one another, ask and share experiences, challenges, and successes. www.peertutoringresource.org/

Comprehensive, Integrated, Three-Tiered (Ci3T) Model of Prevention

Ci3T is a data-driven model to prevent learning and behavioral challenges from developing and to respond effectively if they do arise. Ci3T provides a comprehensive and integrated framework to help schools utilize resources to support the academic, behavioral, and interpersonal needs of SWDs and others who struggle in schools. Ci3T provides information, training, and support for schools to promote collaboration and teaming and uses data-informed professional development to create positive and supportive learning environments.
www.youtube.com/watch?v=vyepd_175fg

HLP #17 Use Flexible Grouping

This video (17:08 minutes) provides an overview of the background and rationale for using flexible grouping and demonstrates three key components of this HLP through video exemplars from real classrooms. The first key component is that groups should be highly structured and include clear directives. The second is that some groups should be homogeneous, and others should be heterogeneous to provide an appropriate setting for the goals of the lesson. The third key component is that the use of flexible groups does not occur in a vacuum. https://highleveragepractices.org/hlp-17-use-flexible-grouping

Project IRIS

IRIS is a national center designed to improve educational outcomes for students, particularly those with disabilities from birth to age 21, by using evidence-based practices and interventions. Two particularly relevant modules include (a) video on the use of flexible grouping and (b) a case study on effective room arrangements. https://iris.peabody.vanderbilt.edu

References

Almarode, J., Fisher, D., Frey, N., & Hattie, J. (2018). *Visible learning for science, grades K-12: What works best to optimize student learning?* Corwin Press.

Brulles, D., & Brown, K. L. (2018). *A teacher's guide to flexible grouping and collaborative learning: Form, manage, assess, and differentiate in groups.* Free Spirit Publishing Co.

Carnine, D. W., Silbert, J., Kame'enui, E. J., Slocum, T. A., & Travers, P. (2015). *Direct instruction reading* (6th Ed.). Pearson.

Colon, G., Zgliczynski, T., & Maheady, L. (2021). Using flexible grouping. In J. McLeskey, L. Maheady, B. Billingsley, M., Brownell, & T. Lewis (Co-Eds.). *High leverage practices for inclusive educational settings* (2nd Ed., pp. 237–50). Routledge.

Engelmann, S., & Carnine, D. W. (1991). *Theory of instruction: Principles and applications* (Rev. ed.). ADI Press.

Flood, J., Lapp, D., Flood, S., & Nagel, G. (1992). Am I allowed to group? Using flexible grouping patterns for effective instruction. *Reading Teacher*, *45*(8), 608–16.

Greenwood, C. R., Delquadri, J. C., & Carta, J. J. (1997). *Together we can: Class Wide Peer Tutoring for basic academic skills*. Sopris West.

Harris, L. M., Archambault, L., & Shelton, C. C. (2021). Issues of quality on Teachers Pay Teachers: An exploration of best-selling US history resources. *Journal of Research on Technology in Education*, DOI: 10.1080/15391523.2021.2014373

Hattie, J. C. (2012). *Visible learning for teachers: Maximizing impact on learning*. Routledge.

Heward, W. L., & Wood, C. R. (2015, April). Improving educational outcomes in America: Can a low-tech, generic teaching practice make a difference? The Wing Institute. Available at: www.winginstitute.org/uploads/docs/2013WingSummitWH.pdf

Iverson, S., Tunmer, W., & Chapman, J. (2005). The effects of varying group size on the reading recovery approach to preventive early intervention. *Journal of Learning Disabilities*, *38*, 456–72.

Kamps, D., Greenwood, C., Arreaga-Mayer, C., Veerkamp, M., Utley, C., Tapia, Y., Bowman-Perrott, L., & Bannister, H. (2008). The efficacy of Class Wide Peer Tutoring in middle schools. *Education and Treatment of Children*, *31*, 1–34.

McDonald, L. (2014). Flexible grouping as a differentiation instruction strategy. Retrieved on February 22, 2021 from www.teachhub.com/classroom management/2014/09/flexible-grouping-as-a-differentiated-instruction-strategy/.

McKeen, H. (2019). The impact of grade level flexible grouping on math achievement scores. *Georgia Educational Researcher*, *16*(1), 48–62. Retrieved from https://files.eric.ed.gov/fulltext/EJ1206 047.pdf.

McLeskey, J., Maheady, L., Billingsley, B., Brownell, M., & Lewis, T. (Eds.) (2019). *High-leverage practices for inclusive settings*. Routledge & Council for Exceptional Children.

McLeskey, J., Maheady, L., Billingsley, B., Brownell, M., & Lewis, T. (Eds.) (2021). *High-leverage practices for inclusive settings (2nd Ed)*. Routledge & Council for Exceptional Children.

McLeskey, J., & Waldron, N. L. (2011). Educational programs for elementary students with learning disabilities: Can they be both effective and inclusive? *Learning Disabilities Research and Practice*, *26*(1), 48–57.

Rhode, G., Jenson, W. R., & Williams, N. A. (2020). *The tough kid book, (3rd ed.)*. Rowman & Littlefield.

Sanford, D. R. (2021). *The Rowman & Littlefield guide for peer tutors*. Pearson.

Vaughn, S. & Bos, C. S. (2012). *Strategies for teaching students with learning and behavior problems (8th Ed.)*. Houghton Mifflin.

Velantino, C. (2000). *Flexible grouping*. Houghton Mifflin Company. Retrieved from www.eduplace.com/science/profdev/articles/valentino.html

18
Use Strategies to Promote Active Student Engagement

Moira Konrad
The Ohio State University
William L. Heward
The Ohio State University

Introduction

Intensive instruction is a defining characteristic of special education (Heward et al., 2021), and much has been written about how to effectively provide intensive instruction. In most multi-tiered support models of special education, intensifying instruction entails reducing the number of students being taught and/or increasing the duration of instruction. Neither small groups nor longer periods of instruction ensure an effective lesson. Effective lessons require appropriate well-designed curricula, explicit instruction, systematic feedback, and—the focus of this chapter—actively engaged students.

Student Engagement and Effective Intensive Instruction

The positive correlation between increased student engagement during instruction and improved learning outcomes is one of the most robust findings of educational research (see reviews by Ellis et al., 1994; Hattie, 2009; Rosenshine & Berliner, 1978; Swanson & Hoskyn, 2001; Van Camp et al., 2020). Researchers have developed a variety of metrics for assessing student engagement: most notably, on-task behavior (Karweit & Slavin, 1982); academic learning time (Fisher et al., 1980); opportunities to respond (Greenwood et al., 1984), and, the focus of this chapter, active student responding (ASR; Heward, 1994). Active student response occurs when a student makes a detectable, lesson-specific response. The kinds of responses that qualify as ASR are as varied as the lessons teachers teach. Depending on the purpose of the lesson, any of the following may count as ASR: words segmented into phonemes, improper fractions converted to mixed numbers, chemical equations balanced, geometric figures drawn, state capitals named, topic sentences written, letters traced, coins counted, angles measured, words keyboarded, history facts stated.

Narrowing the Focus

Although active student responding is an important component of effective instruction in all teaching formats and settings, our focus is intensifying small-group instruction with ASR. We describe six ASR teaching tactics and suggest practical ways to implement and adapt them for a range of learners with disabilities

DOI: 10.4324/9781003276876-23

Chapter Overview

1. Tactics for increasing active student responding (ASR).
2. Applied example of a highly skilled teacher implementing the ASR tactics.
3. Getting the most out of ASR.

Using the HLP

Once appropriate learning goals have been identified and sequenced (see Chapters 11 and 12), teachers are tasked with designing, delivering, and evaluating lessons that help students attain those goals. Lessons with high rates of student engagement yield better learning outcomes than lessons with low rates of engagement (States et al., 2019).

Tactics for Increasing Active Student Responding

There are many ways to increase ASR—far too many to discuss in this brief chapter. We will describe six ASR tactics that are relatively easy and inexpensive to implement and have a solid evidence base. Additionally, even intensive instruction is usually administered in a group format, making it a challenge to ensure every student is actively engaged in learning, so the techniques described below focus on those that can be delivered in group arrangements.

Unison response tactics. The most common method for generating student participation during group instruction is posing a question or problem and calling upon a student who has raised their hand to answer. Although the student called upon makes an active response to the lesson, their classmates are often passive observers at best. Another problem with calling upon individual students to respond is that high achievers answer most questions while low achievers, for whom active participation is needed most, make few or no responses (Böheim et al., 2020).

Unison response techniques—specifically, choral responding and response cards—offer a solution. With each of these methods, the teacher poses a question or problem for the entire class or group, and all students respond in unison. Student responses may be vocal (choral response), selected (pre-printed response cards) or written (write-on response cards). Tables 18.1 and 18.2 provide detailed descriptions of how to use these tactics.

In addition to strong research evidence demonstrating positive effects of choral responding and response cards on students' learning and behavior (Common et al., 2020; Kamps et al., 1994; Marsh et al., 2021), the tactics are easy for teachers to implement, require few if any materials, and can be applied in any classroom.

Guided notes and structured worksheets. Often students need to write longer responses, either because they are learning new content and need to take notes or because they are learning a new skill and need to practice it. Two effective paper-pencil methods for increasing ASR are guided notes and structured worksheets.

Guided notes are teacher-prepared handouts that "guide" students through a lecture or demonstration with standard cues and specific spaces in which to write key facts, concepts, or relationships (Konrad et al., 2011). To complete their guided notes, students must respond throughout the lecture by listening, looking, thinking, and writing about the lesson's content. In addition to enabling students to actively respond to the lesson and improving retention of course content, guided notes help students easily identify important information and produce an accurate set of notes to study. Students at all achievement levels in elementary through postsecondary classrooms perform better on tests of content retention when they use guided notes (Jimenez et al., 2014; Konrad et al., 2009). Table 18.3 describes how to prepare and use guided notes.

Structured worksheets provide students with a series of problems/items or a sequence of steps to be completed during teacher-led group instruction. Unlike worksheets that students complete

Table 18.1 Steps and Tips for Using Choral Response

Preparing for Choral Response

1. Prepare students to engage in choral response activities:
   - Teach students the cues you will use to signal them when to respond in unison.
   - Model several trials and have students practice with choral response.
   - Provide feedback on how well they are following directions.
2. Prepare the trials in advance:
   - Make sure each question or item you present only has one correct answer.
   - Practice before the lesson so you can deliver instruction at a smooth and lively pace.
   - Make notes to remind you when in the lesson you will intersperse individual turns.
   - Plan how you will note items that need more practice (e.g., a plus or minus sign on your data sheet).

Teaching with Choral Response

1. Present the question or item (e.g., "What is the square root of 81?" "Which branch of government is responsible for passing laws?").
2. Provide students with wait time appropriate for the question—longer wait times for new content and questions requiring multiple steps or more complex thinking.
3. Signal students to respond (e.g., "everybody").
4. Listen to students' responses and provide feedback based on majority response. It is not so important who is making which response; it is easy to tell if students are "getting it" by hearing how firm, clear, and unison the response is. If you hear errors or tentative responses, provide the correct answer and repeat the question or item immediately *and* a little later in the lesson.
5. Intersperse individual turns: Now and then, instead of signaling a unison response, call on an individual student to answer the question. Present the question or item first (as if it will be another choral response item) and *then* call on a student by name. This means all students need to be prepared to respond. Individual turns should also be used to give low-achieving students opportunities to shine in front of their classmates. After a low-achieving student chorally voices a correct response, repeat the question several trials later and call on that student to answer individually.
6. Maintain a lively pace throughout the activity.

Tips for Maximizing Effectiveness of Choral Response

- Move around the room while leading choral response activities to monitor student engagement and accuracy of responses.
- Make sure students are placed such that you can readily hear them responding; this is particularly important for students who are struggling with the content or skills.
- Consider video recording your choral response exercises—watch the videos and self-evaluate for number of trials presented, consistency of feedback, engagement of students, and level of student and teacher enthusiasm. Set goals to improve!
- Have fun with choral responding.! Bring a high level of energy and excitement to the activity, and mix it up sometimes. For instance, have students give responses in a whisper voice or a robot voice, or call on one side of the room and then the other side.

independently, structured worksheets provide all students in the group with a series of teacher-directed learning trials. Properly designed structured worksheets can be very effective during the acquisition stage of learning. Students follow along as their teacher completes the worksheet on a smart board, document camera, or the oft-forgotten but still effective overhead projector. Because students receive feedback after each response, the likelihood they will repeat errors is greatly reduced. Choral responding and/or response cards can be used to provide students with ASR in addition to the written responses they make to complete their structured worksheets. Table 18.4 provides steps and guidelines for using structured worksheets.

Fluency-building tactics. Fluency is the combination of accuracy and speed that characterizes competent performance. A person who is fluent performs a skill automatically, without hesitation,

Table 18.2 Steps and Tips for Using Response Cards

Preparing for Response Cards

1. Prepare students to engage in response card activities:
   - Teach them what cues you will use when they are to hold up and put down their cards.
   - Model several trials and have students practice using response cards.
   - Provide feedback on how well they are following directions.
2. Prepare the trials in advance:
   - Practice the trials and signals before the lesson so you can deliver instruction at a smooth and lively pace.
   - Plan how you will note items that need more practice (e.g., a plus or minus sign on your data sheet).

Teaching with Response Cards

1. Present the question or item to the group of students (e.g., "What is the coefficient in this expression?" "Which branch of government interprets the laws?")
2. Provide students with wait time appropriate for the question—longer wait times for questions that require multiple steps or more complex thinking.
3. Give students a signal to respond (e.g., "cards up").
4. Scan students' responses and provide feedback based on majority response. If students make errors, provide the correct answer and repeat the question or item immediately and a little later in the lesson.
5. Randomly intersperse individual turns. In a small group where you can see each student's response (as well as how dependent they are on peer models or teacher prompts), this may not be necessary. However, if students know individual turns are coming, this may help motivate them to engage in the group practice.
6. Maintain a lively pace throughout the activity.
7. Remember that students can learn from watching others; do not let them think looking at classmates' response cards is cheating.

Tips for Preprinted Response Cards

- Design the cards to be easy for you and your students to see (e.g., consider size, print type, color codes).
- Make the cards easy for students to manipulate and display (e.g., put answers on both sides; attach a group of related cards to a ring).
- Begin instruction with a small set of cards (perhaps only two), and gradually add cards as students' skills improve.

Tips for Write-On Response Cards

- Limit length of responses to one to three words.
- Give each student a "sock pocket" (i.e., sock with dry erase markers inside). Have them put the sock on their non-dominant hand, so it is ready to erase answers quickly, while keeping their writing hand ready to write. Give each student at least two markers so they will be prepared with a backup if needed.
- Let students doodle on their response cards for a few minutes after the lesson as a reward for good behavior and participation.

as if by second nature. Students who achieve fluency with a new skill show better retention, demonstrate greater endurance, and are more likely to use the skills in novel situations (Binder, 1996; Codding et al., 2011; Stocker et al., 2019). Additionally, students fluent with component skills (e.g., multiplication facts and subtraction algorithms) may learn composite skills (e.g., long division) more quickly (Johnson & Street, 2012)

The two fluency-building tactics described here—timed practice trials and SAFMEDS—can be conducted as teacher-directed ASR activities in small-group or whole-class instruction, peer-managed arrangements, or self-directed practice activities. Table 18.5 provides guidelines for fluency-building tactics.

Table 18.3 Guidelines for Guided Notes

Preparing for Guided Notes
1. Prepare students to engage in notetaking with guided notes:
   - Provide example of guided notes and explain what different cues mean (e.g., a line means write what the teacher writes on the line; a pencil symbol means stop and respond to a reflection question).
   - Practice with a brief set of guided notes and provide feedback on how well students are following directions and filling in the notes.
2. Prepare materials in advance:
   - Prepare the lesson presentation, making sure to present information in a logical sequence and linear structure.
   - Intersperse slides as stopping points for a variety of other activities (e.g., written reflection, choral response, response cards).
   - Copy the information into a word processing document. If using presentation software (e.g., PowerPoint), use the outline function to make it easy to copy and paste into a word processing document.
   - Delete key words and phrases and replace with lines to serve as cues for students to write.
   - Print the guided notes and fill them out (as a student would) while practicing the lesson presentation. This will ensure there is sufficient space to write and will help assess the flow and timing of the lesson before delivering it to students.

Teaching with Guided Notes
1. Distribute guided notes and instruct students to follow along with your presentation.
2. Monitor to be sure students are following along.
3. Stop several times during the presentation to engage students in a variety of other lesson-related activities (e.g., discussion, written reflection, choral response, response cards).
4. Collect students' completed guided notes on an intermittent schedule and reward them for complete and accurate responses.

Tips for Maximizing Effectiveness of Guided Notes
- Consider including learning target for the day's lesson at the top of the guided notes. Then design the guided notes as a standalone "packet" of information and activities designed to help students reach that learning target. For instance, embed cues for students to stop and engage in fluency practice, response cards, choral response, reading assignments, online exercises, writing tasks, or homework can help students see how all these different activities support mastery of the learning target for that set of guided notes.
- Teach students how to use guided notes to study for upcoming tests or quizzes. For example, help them create flashcards or study guides and show them how to quiz themselves or classmates by turning guided notes items/bullets into questions.
- Vary the length of responses to keep students on their toes, but keep responses short (i.e., usually not more than 3–4 words). This will allow the lesson to move at a brisk pace.
- Use clip art and other images sparingly and only when they enhance and support the target skills. Otherwise, they may just become distracting, particularly for students with attention challenges.

Giving students the opportunity to perform a skill as many times as they can in a brief period is an excellent way to intensify instruction and build fluency. Practice in the form of 1-minute timings helps students with and without disabilities achieve fluency with a wide range of skills (Fishley et al., 2012; Greene et al., 2018; Ramey et al., 2016). It is best to use timed trials once students have already acquired the skills and have moved on to the practice stage of learning.

Say All Fast a Minute Each Day Shuffled (SAFMEDS) consists of a deck of cards with a question, vocabulary term, or problem on one side of each card and the answer on the other (Kubina et al., 2016). A student answers as many items in the deck as they can in one minute. The student looks at the question or problem, states the answer out loud, flips the card over to reveal the correct answer,

Table 18.4 Guidelines for Structured Worksheets

Preparing for Structured Worksheets

1. Prepare students to engage in structured worksheets:
   - Provide examples of structured worksheets and explain what different cues mean (e.g., a line means write what the teacher writes on the line; a star means try it on your own).
   - Practice with a brief structured worksheet and provide feedback on how well students are following along.
2. Prepare materials in advance:
   - Remember, structured worksheets focus on skills rather than content. Prepare the worksheet to follow a model-lead-test format. Make sure there are enough practice items for each of these stages: model, lead, test.
   - Because students will be following along as they learn the skills, a document camera, smart board, or overhead projector will work best. This allows the teacher to complete the skills in real time as students follow along.
   - If the skill involves multiple steps, build the worksheet in a chain-like fashion, wherein students will practice the first step before moving on to the next step.
   - Print the worksheet and complete it (as a student would) while practicing the lesson presentation. This will ensure there is sufficient space to write and will help assess the flow and timing of the lesson before delivering it.

Teaching with Structured Worksheets

1. Distribute worksheets to students and instruct them to follow along with your presentation.
2. Present the rule or skill students will be learning.
3. Monitor to be sure students are following along.
4. Stop several times throughout the presentation to engage students in a variety of other lesson-related activities (e.g., choral response, response cards).
5. Only move on to "test" items if students seem to be "getting it" based on your observations of the "lead" items and other ASR activities. If they are not getting it, determine if they just need more practice (in which case, use the "test" items as additional "lead" items with more teacher support) or if the skill needs to be broken down into smaller steps.
6. Collect students' completed worksheets and use the "test" items as assessment of the day's learning objective(s). Or provide the correct responses and have students self-correct.

Tips for Maximizing Effectiveness of Structured Worksheets

- Consider including the learning target(s) for the day's lesson at the top of the worksheet and then again at the end of the worksheet as a self-assessment.
- Include completed problems/models for students to refer to while responding. Remember, structured worksheets are used primarily when students are learning how to do something new. The models and prompts can be withdrawn in subsequent lessons after students begin to respond correctly.
- Have students respond to single items with feedback and self-correction before having them attempt a series of items or problems.
- Build multi-step skills in chain-like fashion. After students have learned to perform the first step with high accuracy, learning trials can be expanded to include the next step, and so on.

---

and then puts the card on either a "correct" or "incorrect" pile. Having the answer on the card allows for use during the acquisition stage of learning as feedback is built into the activity.

An Applied Example

Ms. Alma uses a variety of active student responding tactics to intensify instruction for fourth graders in both resource and inclusion settings. This highly-skilled special educator typically spends half of each school day co-teaching in a regular classroom and half of her day providing literacy and

Table 18.5 Guidelines for Fluency Building

Preparing for Fluency Building

1. Prepare materials:
   - Prepare flashcards, worksheets, and other materials needed for fluency trials. Keep in mind there are many premade materials available for little to no cost; a quick web search will yield many resources.
   - Create a "system" for the materials. For instance, each student might have a pouch or a file folder that contains their flashcards, a graph for tracking progress, and a self-monitoring sheet to remind them the steps in conducting fluency trials.
2. Prepare students to engage in fluency activities:
   - Teach students how to use the fluency system developed in Step 1 above.
   - Have them practice self-timings and timings with peers.
   - Model and have students practice engaging in the activities, and provide feedback on how well they are following the steps in the system.

Teaching with Fluency-Building Activities

1. Give students clear directions when it is time to begin a fluency activity. Making it a regular part of the class routine will help students become fluent at fluency activities.
2. Actively circulate while students are working on fluency activities to provide feedback and prompting when needed. Emphasize proficiency with feedback; in other words, tell them how many they got correct rather than giving them a percentage correct.

Tips for Maximizing Effectiveness of Fluency-Building Activities

- Emphasize fluency during the *practice* stage of learning. During the acquisition stage of learning students should focus on learning how to perform the skill correctly. Students who try to "go fast" before they can execute a skill correctly more often than incorrectly may end up "practicing errors" instead of building fluency.
- Keep the time for each fluency-building trial brief. Brief sprints of 10 seconds, then 15 seconds, 20 seconds, and so on, can help students gradually build their fluency (Kostewicz & Kubina, 2011). One minute is sufficient for most academic tool skills. For skills that require writing (e.g., timed writing exercises), trials may be up to 3 minutes.
- Do fluency building daily. For example, one or two oral reading time trials could be conducted at the end of each day's lesson.
- Make fluency building fun. Timed practice trials should not be presented as a test; they are a learning activity that can be approached like a game.
- Follow fluency-building activities with a more relaxed activity.
- Encourage students to set personal goals and try to beat their best scores.
- Have students keep track of their progress by graphing their best performance each day.

Adapted from W. L. Heward, S. R. Alber-Morgan, and M. Konrad, 2022, *Exceptional Children: An Introduction to Special Education* (pp. 25–26). Copyright Pearson.

---

math instruction in a resource room. This example focuses primarily on Ms. Alma's use of the ASR tactics for math instruction in her resource room.

Each Friday, Ms. Alma sets goals for the upcoming week. To assist in goal setting, she examines the student performance data she has collected during the week, consults with her general education colleagues to see what they are teaching, examines the grade level standards, and reviews each student's IEP. (See Chapters 11 and 12 to learn more about setting goals and aligning instruction with those goals.) This week, Ms. Alma's instruction will focus on divisibility rules to help her students achieve a fourth-grade math standard related to factors and multiples, while also addressing her students' individualized goals related to multiplication, division, and fractions.

A consistent routine helps promote a variety of ASR activities. When students enter Ms. Alma's resource room, they pick up individualized pouches of flashcards and check the smart board to see if today's fluency-building practice will be teacher-directed, with partners, or self-directed. The flashcards in each student's pouch match their current skill level—some students are working on addition and subtraction facts, some on multiplication and division facts, and some on identifying equivalent fractions. Ms. Alma sets a timer for 5 minutes and instructs everyone to begin. She has trained her students how to run timed trials with partners, practice by themselves, graph their performance, and problem-solve when they get stuck. While her students work with their flashcards, Ms. Alma takes attendance, collects fluency data for one or two students (individualized education program [IEP] probes), and monitors to be sure all students are engaged.

When the timer sounds, students put their flashcards back into their pouches, place them in their desks, and take out their write-on response cards and "sock pockets" (i.e., sock with dry erase markers inside). Students put the sock on their non-dominant hand, so it is ready to erase answers quickly. Then Ms. Alma leads a brisk response card review of problems and concepts from previous lessons. These reviews always include practice of what was learned yesterday (to prime students for today's lessons) and often include skills learned earlier in the year (to promote and check maintenance of mastered skills). Today's response card review includes practice applying the divisibility rules for 2, 5, and 10, a vocabulary review of the terms *factor* and *multiple*, and several multiplication and division fact problems. During these daily 5-minute response card reviews, each of Ms. Alma's students typically makes and receives feedback for a minimum of 20 responses.

While students put away their response cards, Ms. Alma distributes a structured worksheet for the day's new skill: the "3" divisibility rule (see Figure 18.1). Chantelle has a visual impairment and receives a large print version of the worksheet; Li has a writing disability and receives a version that allows circling or highlighting answers instead of writing them out. After sharing today's learning target and lesson agenda with the students, Ms. Alma uses a document camera to model the steps in the worksheet and students follow along and complete their worksheets. But before they even write anything on the worksheet, she leads the group through "skip counting" by 3s. This choral responding activity serves as a review for the students and is a fun way to build momentum for the rest of the lesson.

She then leads students through the top portion of the worksheet to review the multiples of 3. Then the students write the multiples of 3 on the worksheet, following along with Ms. Alma as she writes them. Ms. Alma knows that having students both *say* the multiples and *write* the multiples increases their ASR and promotes generalization.

Next, Ms. Alma presents the divisibility rule, which she has broken down into three steps. Rather than teaching all three steps at once, she goes through one step at a time. After modeling a few examples of Step 1, she provides several choral response opportunities. If students respond firmly (prompt and correct), she proceeds to Step 2 and repeats the process of modeling and then practicing with choral response with this step and then again with Step 3. If students respond hesitantly or inconsistently, she provides additional trials with write-on response cards to gain a better sense of which students are struggling and what is causing the errors.

When students are firm with all three steps of the rule, Ms. Alma gets them talking and writing about math with a brief partner activity that also promotes social interaction. Structured guidelines for this activity support participation of all of her students, including those with anxiety or behavioral challenges. This partner work includes a cumulative activity in which students apply the divisibility rules they have learned thus far to the same set of numbers. Ms. Alma circulates about the classroom, listening and watching to ensure students are learning. She praises correct responses and active participation, provides corrective feedback as needed, and takes note of any common challenges.

She ends class with an "exit ticket" to document students' mastery of the day's objective. Following the lesson, she examines each student's exit ticket and uses their data to help her plan for tomorrow.

Later in the week, Ms. Alma's students will apply the divisibility rules they have learned in a cumulative practice with a "Quiz, Quiz, Trade" collaborative activity (Kagan & Kagan, 2009). She

The 3 Rule

A number is divisible by 3 if the sum of the digits is divisible by _____. So, if you add up all the digits and 3 can evenly go into that number (in other words 3 is a *factor*), then the number is divisible by 3. Let's try some. First, make a list of the first 13 numbers that are divisible by 3 beginning with 0. In other words, what are the first 13 *multiples* of 3?

_____, _____, _____, _____, _____, _____, _____, _____, _____, _____, _____, _____, _____

Now, let's test out the rule. Use the divisibility rule to see if the number in the first column is divisible by 3.

Number	Step 1: Add up the digits in the number	Step 2: Is the sum divisibly by 3?	Is the original number divisibly by 3?
166	1 + 6 + 6 = 13	No	No
21			
2,118			
40			
23,022			
262,001			

Work with your partner to come up with your own numbers that are divisible by 3.

An example of a two-digit number that is divisible by 3: _____

An example of a three-digit number that is divisible by 3: _____

An example of a four-digit number that is divisible by 3: _____

🖉 In your own words, describe how you know your numbers were divisible by 3? _____

_____

_____

_____

Cumulative Practice with Your Partner

Number	Divisible by 3?	Divisible by 2?	Divisible by 5?	Divisible by 10?
333				
565				
4,000				
1,128				

Figure 18.1 Structured Worksheet from Ms. Alma's Lesson on Divisibility Rules

Note: What makes this worksheet effective is that students are following along with the teacher who is modeling the skill, embedding additional ASR (choral response, response cards, and cooperative learning), providing feedback, and using students' responses to guide her lesson.

gives each student a task card that has two questions on the front (e.g., "Is 327 divisible by 3?" and "Tell me how you know?") and the answers on the back. The students partner up and one partner asks the other partner the question on the card. The second partner answers, and the first partner provides feedback, which includes stating the divisibility rule that applies. The partners then switch roles. After they have each had a turn (Quiz, Quiz), the partners trade (Trade) cards and then move to another partner in the room to start the Quiz, Quiz, Trade routine again. Because this is a small-group class, every student will get a chance to Quiz, Quiz, Trade with every other student in the room, which is a great way for them to build their social and communication skills while practicing math. After they have gone through the first set of cards, each student will get a new card and the whole process begins again.

Throughout this activity, Ms. Alma documents students' successes and notes any academic, social, or communication challenges. This helps her prepare her end-of-week assessment and start planning for next week.

Getting the Most out of ASR

To get the most out of ASR for learners with disabilities, teachers must carefully consider instructional design and delivery and the individual needs of their students. Below are some considerations for using ASR in small-group, intensive instruction arrangements.

Keep the lesson's goal front and center. For maximum effectiveness, ASR tactics must be aligned with instructional goals and embedded within explicit systematically sequenced instruction (see Chapters 12 and 16). Each opportunity to respond should move students toward the intended learning goal. Sharing with the students the lesson goal, the success criteria, and an agenda showing how they will achieve the goal helps the students and teacher keep the lesson goal front and center. Ms. Alma posts her lesson goal (learning target) on the board each day and reads it aloud to the students (e.g., "I can use the 3 divisibility rule to quickly identify if a number is divisible by 3"). She then tells them how they will show they have learned the skills and points to the posted agenda to show them the activities they will do to get there: "At the end of class today, I'll give each you an exit ticket with five numbers on it. Next to each number, you will write 'yes' or 'no' to tell me if it is divisible by 3. To prepare you for success, here's our agenda for today's lesson…"

Teachers should be careful to match practice opportunities to their goals when designing lessons because students need ample ASR directly aligned to upcoming assessments to optimize learning outcomes. If students will be expected to *write* their responses at the end of the lesson or on a test next week, then ASR during the lesson must include *written* responses.

Prevent faulty stimulus control. (Halbur et al., 2021) When designing opportunities for students to respond to instruction teachers must be cognizant of faulty stimulus control. To ensure students are not responding to an irrelevant feature of the instructional materials, teachers can use the "blackout technique" (Vargas, 1984). Faulty stimulus control is evident if students can respond correctly when the relevant content is removed (blacked out). For example, in a phonics lesson, students' responses may appear to show letter-sound correspondences, but their responses are under the stimulus control of some non-phonics feature of the activity, such as pictures or color or size of font. As a result, students can be "right for the wrong reason."

Presenting items in a predictable format can also lead to faulty stimulus control. For instance, when presenting students with true/false questions during a choral responding or response card activity, be careful to arrange items in random order so students have to respond to the intended instructional stimulus and *not* to a predictable pattern. Similarly, during flashcard fluency practice, Ms. Alma makes sure students shuffle their cards, so they have to respond to the presented stimulus instead of a predictable order of the cards. Ms. Alma knows that faulty stimulus control might occur during error correction as well. When "her students make an error during" a choral response or response card activity, she corrects the error and then makes sure students try the missed item again. However, and this is critical, when the students engage in the corrected attempt, they must be responding to the appropriate stimulus. This means she needs to ask the question or present the item again (so the students are not just repeating back the correct answer), and if there is a visual stimulus (e.g., a math problem on the board), students need to be looking at that math problem while she is presenting the cue for them to respond.

Motivate and have fun. Many students with disabilities have long histories of negative school experiences. Skilled special educators recognize this and provide instruction that not only targets important skills but also motivates students and makes learning fun. There are many ways to do this, but we will focus on three ASR-specific areas teachers can focus on: pacing, variety, and surprise.

Keeping a brisk pace while leading students through ASR activities helps improve motivation because it helps keep students on task and keeps things moving (so students don't get bored or dwell on their mistakes). Teachers who plan their learning trials and prepare their materials prior to teaching have an easier time maintaining a brisk pace. The best way to increase pacing without rushing students is to shorten intertrial intervals. Practicing lessons in advance and have routines and classroom management systems in place helps teachers move along at a good pace.

Despite the benefit of routines and structure, variety when presenting lessons plays a significant role in maintaining student motivation. Creating lessons with a variety of ASR activities makes it easier to maintain student attention, helps students become well-rehearsed in each type of activity, and allows the teacher to easily switch back and forth among them. Similarly, although predictable routines are important, it is also fun to have some surprises in the form of *indiscriminable contingencies* such as random spot checks and group contingencies (Hunter et al., 2015; Kelshaw-Levering et al., 2000; Rhode et al., 2020), in which the learner cannot discriminate whether or not the next response will produce reinforcement (Cooper et al., 2020). Each day, Ms. Alma randomly chooses a student as the potential "response card hero" and watches that student a little more carefully than the others during the response card activities. The students do not know who has been selected. If the hero consistently responds on her signals and participates in all the learning trials, at the end of the day she announces who the hero was. That hero then earns a point toward a class pizza party and receives recognition in that student's preferred way (e.g., some stand up for applause, some get a note sent home to family, and some get a one-on-one acknowledgement from a friend or teacher). If the selected student does not meet her expectations, Ms. Alma tells the class they will have another chance tomorrow but does not "call out" the target student.

Ms. Alma evaluates students' written assignments using a technique called intermittent grading (Heward et al., 1991). At the end of each day, she collects her students' worksheets and selects a couple items to check. She decides which items to check in advance—some are strategically selected because they sample a critical skill from the lesson, and some are selected randomly. This saves considerable time on grading, and because they never know which items will be checked (the indiscriminable contingency), they are motivated to complete every item with their best efforts. If all students completed the "checked" items the class gets a point toward a pizza party. She looks for accuracy as well as completeness and students earn a second point if all items are correct. If there are accuracy errors, she makes note of patterns to help inform upcoming lessons.

Accommodate individual differences. Compared to large-group instruction, teachers are better able to identify individual students' needs and tailor their instruction accordingly during small-group instruction. For instance, when Ms. Alma's students write their responses on response cards, if she notices one student consistently making errors, she pairs that student with a peer who is mastering the content and continues providing feedback throughout the activity. Later, when students are working in groups or independently, she spends some one-on-one time with that student providing additional practice trials. She adjusts these practice trials to include modeling, prompting, less challenging items, and/or prerequisite skills. For more ideas about how to adapt instruction, see Chapter 14.

Promote maintenance and generalization. ASR activities can be carefully designed to promote generalization and maintenance. For instance, teachers can plan ASR that requires students to use various types of response modalities. In Ms. Alma's lesson, students respond in writing (on both response cards and worksheets) and vocally.

Building in reviews and "spaced practice" (i.e., distributing practice across time rather than having students engage in "massed practice") also promotes generalization and maintenance (Kang, 2016). Ms. Alma knows this and makes sure to include sufficient review and practice of previously learned skills in every lesson.

It is important to probe for maintenance and generalization throughout ASR activities and use these assessment data to plan upcoming lessons. For more suggestions on promoting maintenance and generalization, see Chapter 21.

Adjust instruction based on student performance. ASR not only gives students practice; it also gives teachers feedback on their instruction. These data allow teachers to make real-time instructional decisions. However, there are some considerations related to using ASR as data that are particularly important for learners with disabilities. First, and most important, is to remember there is no time to waste. If students are not acquiring skills, high rates of ASR let the teacher know this sooner rather than later. This information allows teachers to break down skills further when needed and to identify and teach missing prerequisite skills.

Although this chapter emphasizes the importance of ASR for student learning, teachers should know that more ASR is not always better. Although too much practice is not usually a problem (Scott et al., 2011; Stichter et al., 2009), sometimes additional practice is a waste of time (Cuvo et al., 1995). The number of practice trials needed is a moving target. Teachers should use student performance data and their best professional judgment as the number of responses may need to vary based on student composition in a class or topic. Frequent ASR "lets teachers know" when students have mastered a skill and are ready for new learning targets so erring on the side of too much ASR is likely better than erring on the side of too little.

Wrap Up

The most effective ASR techniques (a) capture and maintain students' attention; (b) provide students opportunities to practice and master skills; (c) give students feedback on their responses; and (d) provide teachers information on student performance that enable "on-the-fly" adjustments to the lesson. When deciding on what ASR tactic to use with students, teachers should implement them in ways that include all four of these criteria. Certainly, an activity that allows students to turn to partners and discuss a topic is better than no active responding, but it does not meet all these criteria so should not be considered adequate ASR and should be limited in terms of how much time it takes within a lesson. Of course, there are good reasons to have students pair up and discuss—practice of social and communication skills and building community in the classroom, for instance—but it is important for teachers to intentionally plan these types of activities and be clear about what they seek to accomplish with them. Increasing active student responding within well-designed lessons is one of the most impactful ways to intensify instruction and have fun along the way.

Tips

- *Keep the scripts and materials for ASR handy and durable to allow reuse in upcoming lessons.* For example, print out the list of questions used during a preprinted response card activity and keep it with the set of accompanying response cards. Label the materials with a key phrase related to the learning target so when planning a review of that curriculum content, they can be easily located. Plan these reviews strategically but also capitalize on serendipitous moments of extra time. Even with the myriad demands on teachers' time, teachers may be able to use ASR as "sponge activities" to soak up any little pocket of time available in their schedule.

- *Normalize error correction.* Part of what makes ASR strategies so effective is they allow teachers to reinforce student learning and provide corrective feedback when students make mistakes. Set the tone in your classroom—right from the beginning—that everyone makes mistakes (Lemov, 2010) and then correct them in a straightforward, supportive way.

- *Use the "foot-in-the-door" technique with general education colleagues.* For example, if you are in a co-teaching arrangement, offer to lead a review at the start of every lesson featuring choral responding and response cards. After your co-teacher witnesses their students engaged and having fun, they will be more likely to start using these tactics. You might then offer to assist in developing guided notes for the next lesson, to collaborate in planning a Kagan cooperative learning activity (Kagan & Kagan, 2009), or to plan and lead a cumulative review game before the next test.

- *Use ASR tactics to pre-teach.* Even if opportunities to co-teach are not available, you will still collaborate with general educators. For students who receive instruction in both special and regular classrooms, you can use ASR strategies in the resource room to *pre-teach* a lesson that will later be taught in the regular classroom. This gives the student more exposure to the content, thus intensifying instruction, and helps the student feel confident and prepared to engage with their peers in the regular classroom. Imagine, for example, getting a student ready for a cooperative learning activity in the regular math class where students will work in small groups to sort numbers as "prime" or "composite." You might conduct multiple trials identifying prime and composite numbers using choral response and/or response cards and then have students pair up to do an abbreviated version of the number sort they will be doing later in the regular classroom. The student is not only more likely to learn the material with the extra practice, but also gain the added social benefit of being well prepared to assist their peers without disabilities in their cooperative learning group.

- *Expand your repertoire of ASR tactics.* Consider using some of the many "high-tech" tools for increasing for active participation. Be very intentional in selecting these tools; don't just embed technology for the sake of technology. Tools that best support instruction (a) are aligned and designed to meet specific goals; (b) incorporate systematic feedback; and (c) encourage students to respond in a variety of ways. There are also a variety of cooperative learning and peer-mediated systems that can promote high levels of ASR. The Kagan cooperative learning activities (Kagan & Kagan, 2009), like the one used by Ms. Alma, and classwide peer-assisted tutoring systems (Gardner et al., 2007) are excellent ways to engage students in responding to instruction while encouraging prosocial peer interaction.

Key Resources

Response Card Exchange: Gaddis, T. (2022). *Response Card Exchange.* https://padlet.com/rcshare/response-card-exchange-kjdlxv69zcbo801t

States, J., Detrich, R. & Keyworth, R. (2019). *Active student responding (ASR) overview.* The Wing Institute at Morningside Academy. www.winginstitute.org/instructional-delivery-student-respond

Twyman, J. S., & Heward, W. L. (2018). How to improve student learning in every classroom now. *International Journal of Educational Research, 87,* 78–90. doi.org/10.1016/j.ijer.2016.05.007

References

Binder, C. (1996). Behavioral fluency: Evolution of a new paradigm. *The Behavior Analyst, 19*(2), 163–197.

Böheim, R., Urdan, T., Knogler, M., & Seidel, T. (2020). Student hand-raising as an indica- tor of behavioral engagement and its role in classroom learning. *Contemporary Educational Psychology*, 62. 101894. https://doi.org/10.1016/j.cedpsych.2020.101894

Chard, D. J., & Kame'enui, E. J. (2000). Struggling first-grade readers: The frequency and progress of their reading. *The Journal of Special Education, 34*, 28–38.

Codding, R. S., Burns, M. K., & Lukito, G. (2011). Meta-analysis of mathematic basic-fact fluency interventions: A component analysis. *Learning Disabilities Research & Practice, 26*(1), 36–47.

Common E. A., Lane, K. L., Cantwell, E. D., Brunsting, N. C., Peia Oakes, W., Germer, K. A., & Bross, L. A. (2020). Teacher-delivered strategies to increase students' opportunities to respond: A sys- tematic methodological review. *Behavioral Disorders, 45*(2), 67–84.

Cuvo, A. J., Ashley, K. M., Marso, K. J., Bingju, L. Z, & Fry, T. A. (1995). Effect of response prac- tice variables on learning spelling and sight vocabulary. *Journal of Applied Behavior Analysis, 28*, 155–173.

Ellis, E. S., Worthington, L. A., & Larkin, M. J. (1994). Executive summary of the research synthesis of effective teaching principles and the design of quality tools for educators (Technical Report No. 6). Eugene, OR: University of Oregon, National Center to Improve the Tools of Educators. Retrieved March 28, 2015, from http://eric.ed.gov/?id=ED386854

Fishley, K. M., Konrad, M., Hessler, T., & Keesey, S. (2012). Effects of GO FASTER on morpheme definition fluency for high school students with high-incidence disabilities. *Learning Disabilities Research & Practice, 27*, 104–15.

Gardner III, R., Nobel, M. M., Hessler, T., Yawn, C. D., & Heron, T. E. (2007). Tutoring system innovations: Past practice to future prototypes. *Intervention in School and Clinic, 43*(2), 71–81.

Greenwood C. R., Delquadri J., & Hall R. V. (1984). Opportunity to respond and student academic performance. In Heward W. L., Heron T. E., Trap-Porter J., & Hill D. S. (Eds.), Focus on behavior analysis in education (pp. 58–88). Charles Merrill.

Halbur, M. E., Caldwell, R. K., & Kodak, T. (2021). Stimulus control research and prac- tice: Considerations of stimulus disparity and salience for discrimination training. *Behavior Analysis in Practice, 14*(1), 272–82.

Hattie, J. (2009). *Visible learning: A synthesis of over 800 meta-analyses relating to achievement.* Routledge.

Heward, W. L. (1994). Three "low-tech" strategies for increasing the frequency of active student response during group instruction. In R. Gardner III, D. M. Sainato, J. O. Cooper, T. E. Heron, W. L. Heward, J. Eshleman, & T. A. Grossi (Eds.), *Behavior analysis in education: Focus on measurably superior instruction* (pp. 283–320). Brooks/Cole.

Heward, W. L., Heron, T. E., Gardner, R., III, & Prayzer, R. (1991). Two strategies for improving students' writing skills. In G. Stoner, M. R. Shinn, & H. M. Walker (Eds.), *A school psychologist's interventions for regular education* (pp. 379–398). National Association of School Psychologists.

Heward, W. L., & Wood, C. (2015). *Improving educational outcomes in America: Can a low-tech, gen- eric teaching practice make a difference?* Wing Institute. Online at: www.winginstitute.org/uplo ads/docs/2013WingSummitWH.pdf

Heward, W. L., Alber-Morgan, S. R., & Konrad, M. (2022). *Exceptional children: An introduction to special education* (12th ed.). Pearson.

Hunter, W. C., Maheady, L., Jasper, A. D., Williamson, R. L., Murley, R. C., & Stratton, E. (2015). Numbered heads together as a tier 1 instructional strategy in multitiered systems of support. *Education and Treatment of Children, 38*(3), 345–62.

Jimenez, B. A., Lo, Y., & Saunders, A. (2014). The additive effects of scripted lessons plus guided notes on science quiz scores of students with intellectual disabilities and autism. *Journal of Special Education, 47*, 231–44.

Johnson, K., & Street, E. M. (2012). From the laboratory to the field and back again: Morningside Academy's 32 years of improving students' academic performance. *Behavior Analysis in Practice*, *13*(1), 20–40.

Kagan, S., & Kagan, M. (2009). *Kagan cooperative learning*. Kagan Publishing.

Kamps, D. M., Dugan, E. P., Leonard, B. R., & Daoust, P. M. (1994). Enhanced small group instruction using choral responding and student interactions for children with autism and developmental disabilities. *American Journal on Mental Retardation*, *99*, 60–73.

Kang, S. H. (2016). Spaced repetition promotes efficient and effective learning: Policy implications for instruction. *Policy Insights from the Behavioral and Brain Sciences*, *3*(1), 12–19.

Karweit, N., & Slavin, R. E. (1982). Time-On-Task: Issues of timing, sampling, and definition. *Journal of Educational Psychology*, *74*(6), 844–51.

Kelshaw-Levering, K., Sterling-Turner, H. E., Henry, J. R., & Skinner, C. H. (2000). Randomized interdependent group contingencies: Group reinforcement with a twist. *Journal of School Psychology*, *37*, 523–34.

Konrad, M., Joseph, L. M., & Eveleigh, E. (2009). A meta-analytic review of guided notes. *Education and Treatment of Children*, *32*, 421–44.

Konrad, M. K., Joseph, L. M., & Itoi, M. (2011). Using guided notes to enhance instruction for all students. *Intervention in School and Clinic*, *46*, 131–40.

Kubina, R. M., Yurich, K. L., Durica, K. C., & Healy, N. M. (2016). Developing behavioral fluency with movement cycles using SAFMEDS. *Journal of Behavioral Education*, *25*, 120–41.

Lemov, D. (2010). *Teach like a champion: 49 techniques that put students on the path to college*. Jossey-Bass.

Maheady, L., Mallette, B., Harper, G. F., & Sacca, K. (1991). Heads together: A peer-mediated option for improving the academic achievement of heterogeneous learning groups. *Remedial and Special Education*, *12*(2), 25–33.

Marsh, D. J., Cumming, T. M., Randolph, J. J., & Michaels, S. (2021). Updated meta-analysis of the research on response cards. *Journal of Positive Behavioral Education*. https://doi.org/10.1007/s10864-021-09463-0

Ramey, D., Lydon, S., Healy, S., McCoy, A., Holloway, J., & Mulher, T. (2016). A systematic review of the effectiveness of precision teaching for individuals with developmental disabilities. *Review Journal of Autism and Developmental Disorders*, *3*, 179–195.

Rhode, G., Jenson, W. R., & Williams, N. A. (2020). *The tough kid book: Practical classroom management strategies* (3rd ed.). Sopris West.

Rosenshine, B., & Berliner, D. C. (1978). Academic engaged time. *British Journal of Teacher Education*, *4*, 3–16.

Scott, T. M., Alter, P. J., & Hirn, R. (2011). An examination of typical classroom context and instruction for students with and without behavioral disorders. *Education and Treatment of Children*, *34*(4), 619–642.

States, J., Detrich, R. & Keyworth, R. (2019). *Active student responding (ASR) overview*. The Wing Institute at Morningside Academy. www.winginstitute.org/instructional-delivery-student-respond

Stichter, J. P., Lewis, T. J., Whittaker, T. A., Richter, M., Johnson, N. W., & Trussell, R. P. (2009). Assessing teacher use of opportunities to respond and effective classroom management strategies: Comparisons among high- and low-risk elementary schools. *Journal of Positive Behavior Interventions*, *11*, 68–81.

Stocker, J. D., Schwartz, R., Kubina, R. M., Kostewicz, D., & Kozloff, M. (2019). Behavioral fluency and mathematics intervention research: A review of the last 20 years. *Behavioral Interventions*, *34*, 102–117.

Swanson, H. L., & Hoskyn, M. (2001). Instructing adolescents with learning disabilities: A component and composite analysis. *Learning Disabilities Research and Practice*, *16*(2), 109–119.

Van Camp, A. M., Wehby, J. H., Brittany, H., Martin, L. N., Wright, J. R., & Sutherland, K. S. (2020). Increasing opportunities to respond to intensify academic and behavioral interventions: A meta-analysis. *School Psychology Review*, *49*(1), 31–46.

Vargas, J. S. (1984). What are your exercises teaching? An analysis of stimulus control in instructional materials. In W. L. Heward, T. E. Heron, D. S. Hill, & J. Trap-Porter (Eds.), *Focus on behavior analysis in education* (pp. 126–141). Merrill.

19
Use Assistive and Instructional Technologies

Michael J. Kennedy
University of Virginia
Rachel L. Kunemund
University of Virginia
Lindsay M. Griendling
University of Virginia
Ryan O. Kellems
Brigham Young University

Introduction

The 19th High-Leverage Practice for Students with Disabilities is easy to wrap one's head around but can be difficult to implement in a way that results in positive outcomes for students (Howorth & Kennedy, 2021). The perceived ease in understanding stems from technology's impossibly outsized (and yet increasing) role in modern life. For example, it would be difficult to find a teacher who claimed they used zero technology as part of their instructional day. However, rapid changes and empirical evidence to support the use of specific technology-based products or approaches with various populations usually lags far behind the marketplace and implementation (Kennedy & Boyle, 2017). Therefore, with the omnipresent nature of technology comes difficulty in decision making and implementation for use with students with disabilities (Boyle & Kennedy, 2019). This is especially true for students with intensive academic needs. All students with disabilities have individualized education plans (IEPs) that prescribe specially designed instruction, accommodations and modifications, and technology tools and devices needed for communication or learning (or both). However, students with more intensive academic needs may require technology tools/devices that educators are less familiar with, making selection and implementation a bit more challenging.

Narrowing the Focus

Using assistive and instructional technology in special education is a broad topic, especially given the wide range of technology implemented currently in schools. However, it is important to specifically consider how students with disabilities who require intensive intervention can benefit from the selection, implementation, and assessment of educational technology. Educators may face challenges and be unsure how to navigate the process of identifying, selecting, implementing, and assessing instructional and assistive technology for students with intensive academic needs. The challenge stems from changing relationships between students' abilities and needs, the demands of

DOI: 10.4324/9781003276876-24

the curriculum/individual lessons, and how technology is used to deliver instruction or support student access (or both). Unfortunately, there is no precise roadmap or guaranteed effective strategies for using technology to support intensive needs of students—if there was, chapters like this would be short, and redundant with what readers already knew to do. Instead, researchers, teacher educators, special educators, our general education colleagues, families, and other stakeholders are left to do the best they can with what we do have. Fortunately, our cupboards are not barren.

In this chapter we review how to: (1) identify and evaluate technology for its appropriateness for specific student needs; (2) incorporate this technology into the classroom; (3) assess the effectiveness of the technology; and (4) put it all together with other HLPs. Our focus is on students with intensive academic needs; however, the frameworks and empirical evidence presented is appropriate for any student with an IEP.

Using the HLP: Identifying and Evaluating Effectiveness of Technology Devices

The IEP team should always be at the fore of making decisions regarding adoption of assistive and instructional technology devices for students with IEPs (Kennedy & Boyle, 2021). However, the team does not always have the necessary expertise or awareness of tools/products to make informed choices. Some districts have a dedicated technology specialist, but this is a luxury many teams cannot rely upon—especially in the post-COVID era of teacher shortages. Fortunately, there are multiple ways IEP team members can learn about effective assistive technology (AT) and instructional technology (IT) options.

First, membership and engagement with professional organizations such as the Innovations in Special Education Technology (ISET) division within the Council for Exceptional Children (www.isetcec.org) and Universal Design for Learning Implementation and Research Network (UDL-IRN; https://udl irn.org) can help members access new research and emerging ideas. Both organizations produce resources for members that support awareness and implementation of effective technology options. This includes *Journal of Special Education Technology* (JSET, https://journals.sage pub.com/home/jst) which, as the journal of record for ISET, publishes original research articles and practitioner-oriented pieces around technology use for students with disabilities. The UDL-IRN hosts an annual summit and operates numerous special interest groups for colleagues to share information and resources. Both organizations offer webinars, published products, affinity groups, and other networking opportunities.

The Office of Special Education Programs (OSEP) within the US Department of Education (https://osepideasthatwork.org) sponsors several centers and organizations that conduct research and disseminate findings (https://osepideasthatwork.org/find-center-or-grant). One is the Center for Innovation, Design, and Digital Learning (CIDDL, https://ciddl.org). CIDDL produces content for teacher educators, researchers, and school-based practitioners to learn about technology implementation options, and network with others interested in this field. This center offers numerous free resources including networking options for faculty and doctoral students, blogs, implementation guides for teacher education coursework, and research and practice briefs.

Another OSEP resource is the National Center on Accessible Educational Materials (AEM; https://aem.cast.org). The AEM Center is located within the Center for Applied Special Technology (CAST; www.cast.org), which is the foremost champion of universal design for learning (UDL). The leaders at the AEM Center produce content that helps practitioners and teacher educators consider and implement accessibility into their teaching when using technology. Their offerings include technical assistance, coaching, and resource libraries. The video for HLP #19 Use Assistive and Instructional Technology (https://highleveragepractices.org/hlp-19-use-assistive-and-instructional-technologies) was a collaboration between AEM, CAST, and the Collaboration for Effective Educator Development, Accountability, and Reform (CEEDAR) Center https://ceedar.education.ufl.edu.

CEEDAR produces top content that often includes technology resources (see https://ceedar. education.ufl.edu/wp-content/uploads/2014/10/IC-11_FINAL_05-26-15.pdf). CEEDAR works with states around the country to incorporate evidence-based practices into educator's pedagogical repertoires, which includes use of technology. This center provides a wide range of content that users can access including affinity groups, innovation configurations, videos, and other online resources.

A final OSEP-sponsored center that disseminates content related to technology use is the IDEA and Research for Inclusive Settings (IRIS) Center (www.iris.peabody.vanderbilt.edu). The IRIS Center produces content (e.g., online modules) for a range of topics that support teaching and learning (e.g., behavior management, IEP construction and implementation). They have a specific module related to assistive technology (https://iris.peabody.vanderbilt.edu/module/at/), amongst other content related to use of technology. All told, OSEP has made significant investments in the dissemination of evidence-based and other critical uses and implementations of technology.

OSEP also has a discretionary grant competition dedicated to technology: The Stepping Up Technology Implementation program. A searchable database of funded projects is available here: https://publicddb.osepideasthatwork.org. Each Stepping Up project focuses on supporting teachers' and other stakeholders' understanding and implementation of evidence-based technology to support some aspect of student learning, behavior, or social functioning. Readers are encouraged to learn about both current and prior funded projects, and contact the lead researcher of the project to learn more and gain access to relevant instructional or other materials. Products, including technology, created under these programs are considered Open Education Resources (OER) meaning that they are available to the public. The Institute for Education Sciences (IES; https://ies.ed.gov) also has a technology strand within their main funding mechanisms for the National Center for Education Research and National Center for Special Education Research. IES also maintains a searchable database of technology-focused grantees https://ies.ed.gov/funding/ grantsearch/index.asp with links to project abstracts and publications.

Mentioned earlier, CAST (www.cast.org) offers a range of high-quality resources related to assistive and instructional technology options that help make learning accessible and effective for students. While CAST is best known for its work related to UDL (www.cast.org/impact/universal-design-for-learning-udl), they offer a range of technology-driven tools and services to support accessibility and learning for students.

These resources are certainly not all available options for IEP team members to learn about effective technology options for students with intensive needs. What each of these resources has in common is their development and dissemination by qualified researchers and experts in our field. Many technology products used in education are peddled by companies seeking profit. While this is a necessary mechanism of business, the issue is that many of these products are promoted for classroom use prior to rigorous field testing evaluating its effectiveness. Without rigorous field testing, such products cannot be recommended for use with our students—especially students with significant support needs. Greater trust can be placed in assistive and instructional technologies that were developed and disseminated by field experts who received federal funding and sponsorship, as these products are research-based and rigorously tested to establish evidence for their use.

Technology is Not a Panacea

As noted, technology has become integrated into nearly every aspect of society, but not all tech is effective or appropriate for students with disabilities (Thomas et al., 2019). Educators in the 21st century have access to an unprecedented amount of educational content online, yet the credibility and usefulness of available information has never been more in doubt. As one example, Beahm et al. (2019) noted the widespread use of Pinterest and Teachers Pay Teachers (TPT) amongst practitioners seeking resources and potentially effective practices. While Pinterest and TPT may have some interesting materials and may occasionally facilitate teachers' use of evidence-based practices, the majority of content being disseminated on these sites is not evidence-based, is unlikely to incorporate culturally-informed practices, and could even be harmful. Yet, these sites undoubtedly receive more traffic in a day than high-quality OSEP and other agency-sponsored dissemination sites receive in a month or more. What is it about the content on Pinterest, TPT, and similar sites that earns practitioners' trust and business? In simple terms, content disseminated on those sites is easy to find and ready to deploy.

In any given situation, especially when stressed or rushed, we do what is expedient and available. This does not make teachers and other education stakeholders uninformed—it is a reality, given the demands associated with the daily work of teaching under the constraints of limited time, experience, and other resources. A teacher, juggling many competing responsibilities, is likely not going to click through a module that takes 30–60 minutes to consume, regardless of the quality of information therein, when they can find a handout on TPT in 60 seconds and use it with students a few minutes later. Therefore, it is our critical mission and challenge to to accept this reality of teacher behavior and innovate pathways to ensure evidence-based practices reach students. A good first step toward this goal is for teachers, families, and other stakeholders to learn about and visit the sites and organizations noted above. Then, through careful matching of high-quality products to student needs, improvements for student performance can be expected.

Incorporating Technology into the Classroom

As noted, access to high-quality sites and resources like those noted above is necessary, but not sufficient for changing teacher practice with respect to technology use. Especially in the case of students with more significant support needs, the selection and implementation of assistive and instructional technologies must be a joint effort among all IEP team members. Fortunately, there are specific frameworks that can aid IEP teams' decision making. One such framework is SETT (Student, Environment, Tasks, and Tools; Zabala, 2005). The SETT framework offers guiding questions that IEP teams can use as a guide as they collectively decide upon, adopt, and evaluate effectiveness of technologies that are being used to support students with disabilities across environments. These questions are provided in Table 19.1.

The SETT framework has guided many IEP teams to make knowledgeable decisions about technology use for students with disabilities. In many ways SETT mimics the IEP process in that the

Table 19.1 Guiding Questions for the SETT Framework

Student	• What is/are the area(s) of concern? • What are the student's current abilities related to the concern(s)? • What are the student's current needs related to the concern(s)? • What are the student's interests, preferences, and expectations?
Environment	• What attitudes and expectations are placed on the student? • What technological, physical, or instructional access issues exist? • What is the arrangement of instructional and physical environments? • What materials, equipment, or other supports are currently available?
Tasks	• What specific tasks enable progress toward IEP goals and objectives? • What specific tasks does the student need to do to actively participate?
Tools	• Will the student be unable to make progress without AT? • What AT devices and services will help the student succeed?

Source: Zabala (2005).

team carefully considers student needs from a variety of angles and creates a plan to provide needed supports. However, technology selection and adoption are often limited to the imagination and knowledge of the team. While SETT can be a helpful starting point for technology-focused discussions among IEP teams, it does not guarantee satisfactory answers will be produced or available. The final T in SETT—which stands for *Tools*—is where teachers, families, and other stakeholders often need the most support.

To determine if students will make progress without assistive technology, the IEP team members who are interacting with the student and the tool(s) across various environments need access to solid data collection mechanisms, measurable objectives, and consistent implementation. Too often, the IEP team may be tempted to answer this prompt within SETT with anecdotes and assumptions. While the experience and wisdom of the respective members of the team is valuable, additional precision with respect to student performance is needed when making decisions. Ongoing progress monitoring, use of standard treatment protocol interventions, and careful tracking of implementation as noted by the National Center on Intensive Intervention (www.intensiveintervention.org) is needed. In the final section of this chapter, we highlight how HLP 19 intersects with the other 21 HLPs, including practices 1–3 on collaboration, and 4–6 on assessment.

The 2nd question within the Tools prompt in SETT asks what AT devices and services will help the student succeed? This prompt in Zabala's (2005) framework is absolutely needed; however, the IEP teams' capacity for adequately addressing this prompt is greatly dependent upon their knowledge, experience, access to tools, and understanding of the student's needs relative to curricular demands. If responses to the first three prompts in SETT (Student, Environment, Tasks) are thorough, there may be sufficient data available to successfully identify the necessary technology tools. As previously discussed, however, technology options are always changing and may be costly, limiting the availability of such to certain users. Thus, although a student may legitimately need assistive or instructional technologies, the team may not know enough to recommend an appropriate tool, or may not have enough available resources to obtain an appropriate tool.

Therefore, use of the SETT framework pairs perfectly with resources created by and disseminated through OSEP, CEC, ISET, IES, UDL-IRN, and CAST resources noted in the previous section. Rather than relying on IEP team members' knowledge, which may be based solely on past experiences or learning, taking explicit time to review content and speak to experts who are readily available through these organizations can drastically improve the options available to teams. No one person knows everything there is to know about technology and implementation. Therefore, taking advantage of federal investments and other organizations created to serve the field is a terrific option.

Assessing Effectiveness

Once the IEP team has determined the students' strengths and needs, considered how the demands of the curriculum will impact learning potential, and identified AT or IT options, a plan is needed to evaluate success. Often, people assume the presence of technology automatically means good things are occurring. Unfortunately, this is a mistake. IEP teams need a mechanism to evaluate the extent to which the selected technology is a good match for students' needs. This means careful collection of performance data, given the use or lack of specific tools, and examining of additional options when the initial choice(s) are not supporting the student as intended (Kennedy & Boyle, 2021).

To support the IEP team as they move forward in collaborative and iterative processes to identify and implement effective assistive and instructional technology options, the Quality Indicators for Assistive Technology Services (QIAT) comprises a comprehensive set of guidelines for facilitating assistive technology identification and evaluation. While there are eight sets of quality indicators (see https://qiat.org/indicators/), Table 19.2 provides an overview (QIAT Leadership Team, 2015).

As the SETT framework questions posed in Table 19.1 mention, it is important to ensure the technology matches the skills and goals the student is working towards. Selecting appropriate skills,

Table 19.2 Quality Indicators for Assessment, Implementation, and Evaluation of Assistive Technology Needs

Assessment	Implementation	Evaluation
Assessment procedures are clearly defined and consistently applied.	AT is implemented according to a collaboratively developed plan.	Team members share data collection responsibilities.
Assessments are conducted by a team with the collective knowledge and skills of possible AT solutions.	AT is integrated into the student's daily activities across environments.	Data are collected on specific achievements identified by the team and related to one or more goals.
Functional assessments are conducted across applicable environments.	Persons supporting the student across all environments where AT is used share implementation responsibilities.	Evaluation includes quantitative and qualitative measurement of changes in the student's performance and achievement.
Assessments and trials are completed within a reasonable timeframe.	The student is provided opportunities to use a variety of strategies/AT to learn which are most effective.	Effectiveness is evaluated for a range of activities across environments.
Assessment data pertaining to the student, environments, and tasks inform AT recommendations.	Implementation involves learning opportunities for the student, family, and staff.	Data help teams identify supports and barriers to AT use to determine if changes are needed.
Recommendations are clearly documented.	Assessment data informs initial implementation and progress monitoring data informs needed adjustments.	Changes are made when evaluation data indicate that such changes are needed.
AT needs are reassessed when the student's needs are not being met with current devices and/or services.	Implementation includes management and maintenance of equipment and materials.	Evaluation of effectiveness is an iterative process that is continuously reviewed.

Source: QIAT Leadership Team (2015).

behaviors, and tasks is an important part of incorporating technology into instruction. Skills should be selected that are beneficial for the learner and at the learner's ability level, in addition to being well-defined and observable.

Part of assessing the effectiveness of assistive technology, or any intervention for that matter, is quality data collection. However, deciding how to collect data and what exactly to collect data on can be overwhelming for IEP team members. Further, determining what to do with the data collected and how to analyze it can be a barrier. Fortunately, there are resources available to aid in data collection and organization. The National Center on Intensive Intervention, for instance, has a ready-made data collection tool that can be used for progress monitoring purposes accessible on their website (https://intensiveintervention.org/resource/student-progress-monitoring-tool-data-collection-and-graphing-excel; Kearns, 2016). Further, to facilitate team decision making and organization related to the data, NCII also offers a set of Data Teaming Tools (https://intensiveintervention.org/implementation-intervention/data-teaming).

Putting it all Together

To conclude this chapter, we discuss strategies for making informed and effective decisions for students with disabilities and their access and use of assistive and instructional technologies in line with use of other HLPs. Once you have identified student areas of need, selected technology, and evaluated for effectiveness, the next step is to incorporate technology where appropriate in other areas of education (see Figure 19.1). HLP 19 is well situated within the other 21 practices to be used alongside and in combination. As the HLPs are intended to guide practice across multiple grade levels and content areas, many HLPs are used concurrently to support student needs (McLeskey et al., 2017).

Collaboration

The three collaboration HLPs are critical for ensuring the IEP team is working as closely together as possible in school and at home. Technology use spans home and school. Therefore, decisions related to technology acquisition and use are among the most important the team makes. The SETT framework, alongside other questions the IEP team undertakes when understanding a student's needs can be a very effective tool to guide thinking and decision making. In addition, the various members of the team bring knowledge about technology options and can visit OSEP and other agency sites and resources to learn about new tools.

HLP 1 is to collaborate with professionals to increase student success. With respect to technology selection and implementation, teachers, staff, administrators, and other stakeholders need to understand the needs of each individual child in light of their plan of study, and what technology options are available to them. This may mean liaising with district office specialists, or, if not available, county or state level resources to identify new practices or options. These specialists can also help determine how the technology can be paid for. In sum, ongoing conversations amongst team members to think about the role of assistive and/or instructional technologies in supporting students should be an ongoing and explicit action taken by professionals.

HLP 2 is to organize and facilitate effective meetings with professionals and families. All readers will be familiar with how teaching and communication went online during the COVID-19 pandemic. An unintended consequence was realizing that communication with families can occur at unusual times relative to school hours and past traditions and can give more chances for families to engage school personnel. In addition, these additional lines of communication can also extend to students, in giving them chances to access learning and their teachers when not able to be at school.

HLP 3 is to collaborate with families to support student learning and secure needed services. Throughout this chapter we have noted the role of the IEP team in using various sources of data and

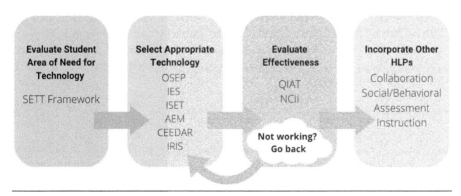

Figure 19.1 Putting It All Together

expertise to brainstorm and adopt appropriate technology options for students. Technology offers the opportunity to communicate with family members from various cultural and linguistic backgrounds in ways not used or possible in the past. Using family knowledge and expertise regarding the student is always essential and can support more valid recommendations for the selection and implementation of appropriate technology. In sum, knowledge of and mastery of the collaboration HLPs will lead to stronger implementation of HLP 19.

Assessment

The three assessment HLPs are also intertwined with using assistive and instructional technologies for students with disabilities. Establishing clear, data-driven approaches for understanding student technology needs in light of academic and functional needs, as well as the demands of the curriculum, is essential. In addition, communicating with families and using their input to make technology-related decisions is important.

HLP 4 is to use multiple sources of information to develop a comprehensive understanding of a student's strengths and needs. The SETT and QIAN frameworks are applied examples of how IEP teams can collaborate to gather needed information from a range of sources and make informed decisions. As noted, often technology adoption decisions are made for convenience of availability and stakeholder knowledge. The gathering of multiple waves of data across time and settings will help the team recognize a wider array of student strengths and needs, which then shines a light on places where a technology option can be successful. The various agencies and centers noted in the first section of this chapter can then be consulted to support team decision making. HLP 5 is to interpret and communicate assessment information with stakeholders, and HLP 6 is to use student assessment data, analyze instructional practices, and make necessary adjustments that improve student outcomes. Both HLPs connect to HLP 19 in ways similar to those noted above in terms of the IEP team making informed decisions for adoption and evaluating effectiveness.

Social/Behavioral

Technology can be a good option for helping students learn key social skills and expected behaviors in classrooms. HLP 7 is to establish a consistent, organized, and respectful learning environment. Technology has numerous applications to implement this HLP including use of video modeling of appropriate behaviors, use of behavior-tracking software, and students using self-monitoring software. HLPs 8 and 22 are to provide positive feedback to guide student behavior and learning. Teachers can push feedback in the form of emojis, points, or other reinforcements using various technologies when needed. Students also receive feedback from various software being used for learning to keep them engaged. HLP 9 is to teach social behaviors. Teachers can again look to technology as an option to create social stories, modeling videos, and offer performance options using tech. HLP 10 is to conduct functional behavioral assessments and behavior support plans. Technology is likely an option here for teachers collecting data, but also could be a reinforcement mechanism for students, or included in replacement behaviors. This could include using an alternative/augmentative communication device instead of a vocal utterance.

Instruction

To conclude, the 19th HLP, using assistive and instructional technology, intersects in numerous ways with the other 10 instruction HLPs. For example, HLPs 11–13 and 15 all implicitly involve the IEP team's process of selecting appropriate technology to support student outcomes. These HLPs also align with the collaboration and assessment domains. Therefore, when teachers and IEP teams identify long- and short-term goals, decide upon plans for systematically designing instruction, make adaptations to support outcomes, and use scaffolds, technology should be considered at all junctures. Many of the adaptations and scaffolds teachers use can be technology-driven and connected to specific IEP goals, and incorporated as an integral part of specially designed instruction provided to students.

When teaching using explicit instruction, use of technology should be considered. This could include specific videos, images, slides, simulations, or other flexible options. When the teacher models, gives guided and independent practice, the student should learn how the technology can help them access instruction and then succeed in demonstrating learning. The students might also use assistive or instructional technologies within groupings of various sizes (HLP 17), and as a mechanism to remain engaged throughout the lesson (HLP 18). Teachers may also use technology for the purposes of intensifying instruction (HLP 20). That is, they could use technology to deliver reading or mathematics instruction, monitor student progress, and aid in instructional decision making moving forward.

Finally, technology is a terrific option for students to learn to generalize and maintain their learning across various learning settings (HLP 21). As one of the main goals of special education, helping students to succeed across their various settings and tasks is critical, and the omnipresent use of technology is logical. For students with intensive needs, their use for technology to communicate, access the environment, and learn will not end with twelfth grade. Therefore, receiving explicit instruction on how to use their various technology devices to succeed and function acrosss a range of environments (i.e., in the school, home, and community) is crucial.

Wrap Up

Technology is everywhere in schools and society. Students with disabilities can use technology for a range of purposes and achieve wonders that were not possible in the recent past. Teachers, staff, families, and other stakeholders should use all available sources of data, and reputable sources of information to identify high quality and appropriate technology. By using frameworks such as SETT, and always considering the role of technology across implementation of all 22 HLPs, students have powerful tools that can support them in accessing and achieving across the range of environments in which they operate daily.

Tips

Instructional and assistive technology can be used to support students with IEPs across multiple domains (e.g., behavior, communication, academic). Here we offer a few "quick tips" that can be applied across each of these areas.

1. When selecting technology teachers should prioritize assessing technology to ensure that it is developmentally appropriate, addresses the desired outcome (e.g., mathematics instruction), type of technology, and of course the cost. There are various options and guidelines for assessing technology. Ok et al. (2016) provide a rubric teachers can use to aid in their decision-making process.
2. Teachers should continuously monitor progress as a new technology is implemented to ensure that it is effective or determine if changes need to be made. There are many progress monitoring templates available dependent on the domain being measured, the National Center on Intensive Intervention (https://intensiveintervention.org/) offers a number of progress monitoring tools.
3. As technology is used across many contexts and domains (e.g., communication and speech) it is important that teachers collaborate with other service providers and family members to ensure

that the technology is used consistently and with the highest quality. Family members and service provides may need training in implementing the technology in other contexts (e.g., home, community), but may also have expertise (e.g., speech language pathologist) that can be useful in using educational technology.

Key Resources

When selecting educational technology, a great place to start is ISET which is a professional organization that focuses on technology in special education (www.isetcec.org).

CIDDL (https://ciddl.org) and the National Center on Accessible Educational Materials (https://aem.cast.org) are both OSEP-funded centers that provide excellent resources related to research-based educational technology. When selecting technology from the above resources, or anywhere for that matter, it is important to assess that technology in terms of appropriateness for a specific student and outcomes.

The NCII site has a premade data collection tool for progress monitoring (https://intensiveintervention.org/resource/student-progress-monitoring-tool-data-collection-and-graphing-excel; Kearns, 2016) and they also offers a set of Data Teaming Tools (https://intensiveintervention.org/implementation-intervention/data-teaming).

References

Beahm, L. A., Cook, B. G., & Cook, L. (2019). Proceed with caution: Using web-based resources for instructing students with and at risk for EBD. *Beyond Behavior, 28*(1), 13–20

Boyle, J., & Kennedy, M. J. (2019). Innovations in classroom technology for students with disabilities. *Intervention in School and Clinic, 55,* 67–70. DOI: 10.1177/1053451219837716

Howorth, S. K, & Kennedy, M. J. (2021). High Leverage Practice 19: Use assistive and instructional technology. *Teaching Exceptional Children.* DOI: 10.1177/0040059921995661.

Kearns, D. M. (August, 2016). *Student progress monitoring tool for data collection and graphing [computer software].* US Department of Education, Office of Special Education Programs, National Center on Intensive Intervention.

Kennedy, M. J., & Boyle, J. (2017). The promise and problem with technology in special education. In J. M. Kauffman, D. P. Hallahan, & P. C. Pullen (Eds.) *Handbook of special education, 2nd edition* (pp. 606–14). Taylor & Francis.

Kennedy, M. J., & Boyle, J. (2021). That really escalated quickly—Online learning moves into the mainstream: Introduction to the special issue. *Journal of Special Education Technology, 36,* 63–6. DOI: 10.1177/01626434211006052.

McLeskey, J., Barringer, M-D., Billingsley, B., Brownell, M., Jackson, D., Kennedy, M., Lewis, T., Maheady, L., Rodriguez, J., Scheeler, M. C., Winn, J., & Ziegler, D. (2017, January). High-leverage practices in special education. Arlington, VA: Council for Exceptional Children & CEEDAR Center. © 2017 CEC & CEEDAR.

Ok, M. W., Kim, M. K., Kang, E. Y., & Bryant, B. R. (2016). How to find good apps: An evaluation rubric for instructional apps for teaching students with learning disabilities. *Intervention in School and Clinic, 51*(4), 244–252. https://doi.org/10.1177/1053451215589179

QIAT Leadership Team. (2015). *Quality indicators for assistive technology: A comprehensive guide to assistive technology services.* CAST Professional Publishing.

Thomas, C. N., Peeples, K. N., Kennedy, M. J., & Decker, M. (2019). Riding the special education technology wave: Policy, obstacles, recommendations, actionable ideas, and resources. *Intervention in School and Clinic, 54,* 295–303. DOI:s 10.1177/105345121881920.

Zabala, J. (2005). Ready, SETT, go! Getting started with the SETT framework. *Closing the Gap: Computer Technology in Special Education and Rehabilitation, 23*(6), 1–3.

20
Provide Intensive Instruction

Sarah A. Nagro
George Mason University

Sara D. Hooks
Towson University

Dawn W. Fraser
Johns Hopkins University

Kevin Monnin
George Mason University

Introduction

Under the umbrella of special education services, the Individuals with Disabilities Education Act (IDEA; 2006) defines *specially designed instruction* as "adapting, as appropriate to the needs of an eligible child under this part, the content, methodology, or delivery of instruction to address the unique needs of the child that result from the child's disability" (34 C.F.R. §300.39[b][3]). This regulation is a first step in defining the type of instruction students with disabilities should receive. Riccomini et al. (2017) explained that specifically designed instruction in special education includes a combination of high leverage practices (HLPs), considerations of learner characteristics, and intensive instruction. When the instruction provided has failed to adequately support students' academic learning, particularly after receiving supplemental, research-supported interventions, intensive instruction becomes especially important. As defined by the Council for Exceptional Children in partnership with the Collaboration for Effective Educator Development, Accountability, and Reform (CEEDAR) Center, providing intensive instruction is when:

> Teachers match the intensity of instruction to the intensity of the student's learning and behavioral challenges. Intensive instruction involves working with students with similar needs on a small number of high priority, clearly defined skills or concepts critical to academic success. Teachers group students based on common learning needs; clearly define learning goals; and use systematic, explicit, and well-paced instruction. They frequently monitor students' progress and adjust their instruction accordingly. Within intensive instruction, students have many opportunities to respond and receive immediate, corrective feedback with teachers and peers to practice what they are learning.
>
> *(McLeskey et al., 2017, p. 25)*

DOI: 10.4324/9781003276876-25

This chapter explains foundational information about providing intensive instruction and includes examples and resources for using essential components of intensive instruction. The next section will narrow the focus of this chapter by defining key terms related to intensive instruction and then lead into an overview of the major chapter topics. Educators looking to better understand and use intensive instruction will learn about essential functions and examples for use.

Narrowing the Focus

Providing intensive instruction is comprehensive in scope resulting in direct alignment with many other HLPs. In this section, we will explain the interconnectivity between other HLPs and intensive instruction as well as define key terms specific to providing intensive instruction to students with disabilities. *Intensifying instruction* means using research-based strategies and tools that have not yet been tried during less intensive instruction (during Tier 1 or even Tier 2). This approach to instruction requires frequent monitoring of student progress so teachers can adjust their intensive instruction according to ever-changing student needs (see HLP 11). Additionally, during intensive instruction, teachers strive to create many opportunities for students to practice high-priority skills and actively participate in learning (with peers) (see HLP 18). Finally, teachers provide immediate, corrective, specific, and individualized feedback to reinforce the learning objectives (see HLP 22). This process of modifying instruction, monitoring student progress, providing opportunities for students to respond, and giving feedback begins with careful consideration of where to begin instruction and what to prioritize.

The need for intensive intervention is first determined when teachers, using multiple sources (e.g., diagnostic data, formative and summative data, and progress monitoring data), determine that current levels of support and instruction are not adequately meeting a student's needs. This may be evidenced by a lack of adequate progress in their current education setting toward their individualized education program (IEP) goals or general curriculum learning standards despite receiving additional, research-based supports. Once the need for providing intensive instruction to a given student is identified, the process of data-based individualization (DBI) begins. Data-based individualization is a research-based, systematic, explicit, and personalized approach to deciding how to intensify instruction for students with significant needs. DBI is a systematic approach that includes starting from a valid intervention, monitoring student progress when using the intervention, exploring why the intervention alone is not enough, determining what changes are needed, implementing proposed changes, and monitoring the success of such changes in regard to student progress (National Center on Intensive Intervention [NCII], 2018). To summarize, DBI helps educators provide a starting point (i.e., start from a valid intervention), recognize when change is needed (i.e., well-documented insufficient progress), and clarify how to track the success of teacher choices regarding intensifying instruction (i.e., progress monitoring). Having said this, the actual use of intensive instruction takes many forms and draws on several other HLPs.

The essential components of intensive instruction are (a) clearly defining learning goals; (b) using systematic, explicit, engaging, and well-paced instruction; (c) frequently monitoring students' progress and adjusting their instruction accordingly; (d) creating many opportunities for students to practice and respond to what they are learning with teachers and peers; and (e) creating many opportunities for students to receive immediate, corrective feedback. In practice, providing intensive instruction can mean reducing the size of instructional groups, changing the pace of instructional delivery, adding instructional time to target high-priority academic student needs, strengthening the direct connection between student needs and intervention, increasing the frequency or duration of helpful interventions, and integrating academic and behavioral supports (Kennedy et al., 2019). Table 20.1 outlines the essential components of providing intensive interventions and highlights interconnectivity with other instruction HLPs. We do not detail

Table 20.1 Interconnectivity Between Providing Intensive Instruction and Instruction HLPs

Essentials of HLP 20	Aligning Instruction HLPs 11–22
1. Clearly defining learning goals.	HLP 11: Identify and Prioritize Long- and Short-Term Learning Goals: Teachers use grade-level standards, assessment data and learning progressions, students' prior knowledge, and IEP goals and benchmarks to make decisions about what to emphasize, and develop long- and short-term goals accordingly. HLP 17: Use Flexible Grouping: Teachers use homogeneous and heterogeneous small learning groups to accommodate learning differences, promote in-depth academic-related interactions, and teach students to work collaboratively. They embed strategies to maximize learning opportunities and participation.
2. Using systematic, explicit, and well-paced instruction, and frequently monitoring students' progress and adjusting their instruction accordingly.	HLP 12: Systematically Design Instruction Toward a Specific Learning Goal: Teachers provide the foundation for more complex learning by activating students' prior knowledge, sequencing lessons that build on each other, and making connections explicit, in both planning and delivery. HLP 13: Make Adaptations: Teachers select materials and tasks based on student needs; use relevant technology; and make modifications by highlighting relevant information, changing task directions, and decreasing amounts of material so that students can meet instructional goals. HLP 14: Teach Cognitive and Metacognitive Strategies to Support Learning and Independence: Teachers explicitly teach cognitive and metacognitive processing strategies to support memory, attention, and self-regulation of learning. Learning involves not only understanding content but also using cognitive processes to solve problems, regulate attention, organize thoughts and materials, and monitor one's own thinking. HLP 16: Use Explicit Instruction: Teachers make content, skills, and concepts explicit by showing and telling students what to do or think while solving problems, enacting strategies, completing tasks, and classifying concepts.
3. Creating many opportunities for students to practice and respond to what they are learning with teachers and peers	HLP 15: Provide Scaffolded Supports: Scaffolded supports provide temporary assistance to students so they can successfully complete tasks that they cannot yet do independently and with a high rate of success. HLP 18: Use Strategies to Promote Active Student Engagement: Teachers use a variety of instructional strategies that result in active student responding. Active student engagement is critical to academic success. HLP 19: Use Assistive and Instructional Technologies: Teachers select and implement assistive and instructional technologies to support the needs of students with disabilities. They select and use augmentative and alternative communication devices and assistive and instructional technology products to promote student learning and independence. HLP 21: Teach Students To Maintain And Generalize New Learning Across Time And Settings: Effective teachers use specific techniques to teach students to generalize newly acquired knowledge and skills in places and situations other than the original learning environment and maintain their use in the absence of ongoing instruction.
4. Creating many opportunities for students to receive immediate, corrective feedback.	HLP 22: Provide Positive and Constructive Feedback to Guide Students' Learning and Behavior The purpose of feedback is to guide learning and behavior and increase motivation, engagement, and independence, leading to improved student learning and behavior. Effective feedback must be strategically delivered, goal directed, and includes ways to improve performance.

Note: Definitions of HLPs from https://highleveragepractices.org/four-areas-practice-k-12/instruction

all the instruction HLPs in this chapter, but we do think it is important for educators to note that there is direct alignment between the instruction HLPs and all essential components of providing intensive instruction.

Chapter Overview

1. Clearly defining learning goals.
2. Using systematic, explicit, and well-paced instruction.
3. Frequently monitoring students' progress and adjusting their instruction accordingly.
4. Creating many opportunities for students to practice and respond to what they are learning with teachers and peers.
5. Creating many opportunities for students to receive immediate, corrective feedback.

Using the HLP

Clearly Defining Learning Goals

Students with disabilities requiring intensive instruction benefit from individualized modifications, adaptations, and supports to access grade-level content (HLP 13) (National Center on Educational Outcomes, 2013). Teachers are charged with prioritizing the most important academic skills to teach such as those that will allow students to benefit across all areas of their lives while balancing federal requirements to provide all students access to the general curriculum (HLP 11) (Apitz et al., 2017). Such a balance might be struck when teachers identify the highest priority learning goals for a given unit or segment of curriculum, and then plan to simplify the breadth and depth of knowledge covered in support of this high-priority skill rather than excluding portions of the general curriculum altogether.

For example, as outlined in Apitz and colleagues (2017), teachers can identify learning goals and then follow a step-by-step process for adapting text such as a story, passage, or potentially even word problems for one or more student(s) to directly support student learning given a specific goal or set of goals. First, a teacher can outline the story or passage to create a framework for adapting the text. Second, the teacher can identify key themes of the text and develop activities to specifically support these key themes. These activities are likely going to be narrow in scope when compared to the general curriculum, but they will help clarify key aspects of the lesson. Third, teachers can identify key vocabulary to target to build comprehension for students and help students make connections to everyday contexts or personal interests. The selected vocabulary should directly align with the high-priority learning goals so that the learning experience is cohesive and potentially results in improved student learning. Next, using the outline, key themes, and vocabulary, teachers can identify the main events in the story or passage and include those in the adapted version of the text as written by the teacher. Finally, the teacher can pair pictures or visual supports with the text to clarify meaning and emphasize the key themes and vocabulary. The teacher may use this modified text in combination with research-based literacy interventions to intensify the instruction for a given instructional group identified as needing this level of intensive support.

Making decisions about how to adapt and modify the curriculum stems from student needs and subsequent target goals. If the student's needs are in decoding, clearly defined learning goals should target skills explicitly linked to decoding rather than implicitly linked through broad literacy goals. For example, the teacher may explicitly target one or more of the elements of decoding such as phonological awareness, alphabetic knowledge, or orthographic knowledge. Within these components, teachers can set even more specific learning goals, such as the understanding of phonemes, syllables, and blends. Setting specific and clearly defined goals is essential because when the learning goals are too broad or vague, it becomes difficult for teachers to measure and then track student progress toward such nebulous goals.

Learning goals can and likely will include a range of content-specific goals such as accurately identifying grade-level vocabulary as well as targeting preferred learner characteristics such as sustained engagement, task completion, and skill generalization. Otherwise put, learning goals can address both declarative and procedural knowledge. For example, "Erin will understand the plant life cycle and be able to draw connections to other natural cycles." Learning goals can also be written at different levels of complexity across retrieval, comprehension, analysis, and knowledge utilization (Marzano, 2009). Further, learning goals can be used for a lesson, a unit, or an entire school year based on the purpose. This flexibility allows teachers to clarify exactly what is being targeted with clear directions for learning expectations, how goals will be observed and desired student performance will be demonstrated, and how long each goal will be prioritized.

Using Systematic, Explicit, and Well-Paced Instruction

Systematic, explicit instruction is carefully planned, structured, and logically sequenced (HLP 12 and 16). Careful and intentional planning allow the teacher to thoughtfully build the lesson structure, ensuring the essential components of systematic instruction are included. Lessons are structured in a predictable sequence from beginning to end. When lessons follow the same structure, students do not have to learn *how* the information will be presented (Nagro et al., 2019). This allows the students to focus their attention and energy on the skill or concept being taught. Content is taught in a logical sequence, allowing students to build on prior knowledge as they learn increasingly difficult skills and concepts. During systematic, explicit, and well-paced instruction teachers aim to (a) maximize time on task or learning engagement; (b) promote high levels of success; (c) cover more academic content; (d) increase time spent in instructional groups; (e) scaffold instruction (HLP 15); and (f) address different forms of knowledge (Archer & Hughes, 2010). Teachers activate the student's prior knowledge at the beginning of the lesson, directly linking what they already know to what they will be learning (HLP 12).

Systematic, explicit instruction can be used to teach a wide variety of concepts and skills across all content areas and grade levels. For example, skills ranging from mathematical operations (e.g., multiplying) and processes (e.g., finding the value of x) to phonics (e.g., letter-sound correspondence), the writing process (e.g., creating an outline), and the scientific method (e.g., constructing a hypothesis) can all be the focus during explicit instruction.

The pace of instruction can significantly impact student success, regardless of what skills are being taught. Students who require intensive instruction typically require additional time to process the information presented. Moving too quickly through the content or presenting too much information at once prevents the students from processing the information and, in turn, comprehending the content (Smith et al., 2016). However, if the pace of instruction is too slow, students become disengaged and no longer attend to the lesson. One way to think about finding the right pace is to visualize a rubber band around you and your students. If the rubber band is too slack (i.e., the pace is too slow), the rubber band will slip off and you will lose the group. If the rubber band is too tight (i.e., the pace is too quick), the rubber band will snap and you will lose the group. If the rubber band is at the right tension (i.e., an appropriate match between content and pace), you will successfully hold the group together.

Similarly, instruction should be engaging. Students should have frequent opportunities to respond and share previously mastered information. Appropriate instructional pace and methods for engagement can, and likely should, vary within and between lessons. Monitoring progress during instruction allows the teacher to adjust the lesson pace in the moment to meet the students' needs throughout the lesson.

Frequently Monitoring Students' Progress and Adjusting Their Instruction Accordingly

Teachers monitor student progress during practice and adjust instruction according to their performance. Some students may need additional examples or parts of examples, while others may need to see the skill being modeled again. It is essential to monitor student progress throughout the lesson so instruction can be adjusted accordingly. Students who require intensive instruction have likely struggled with the content in the past. This recurring struggle to grasp the content may result in failure, and repeated failure likely has negative emotional effects (Chohan, 2018). Therefore, failing to adjust instruction according to their present level of knowledge and skill only perpetuates the student's lack of success, and continued negative feelings of self-esteem.

Progress monitoring can, and should, also be systematic and explicit. In addition to monitoring progress during instruction to adjust in the moment, progress monitoring should also involve intentional planning prior to instruction, collecting data during instruction, then graphing and analyzing data after instruction to evaluate student progress. If the student is making sufficient progress, no adjustments are needed, and intensive instruction continues. If the data show the student is not making sufficient progress, additional adaptations that further intensify instruction are explored (HLP 13). This process is repeated throughout the intervention to ensure the student is consistently making sufficient progress. Teachers should not be discouraged by slow progress; instead, they need to be persistent and keep in mind aspects of the DBI process. Figure 20.1 includes an easy mnemonic for remembering how to increase access to the academic content for students with significant support needs using intensive instruction with an emphasis on progress monitoring (Hooks, 2015). Notice the cyclical nature of this process since progress monitoring is ongoing and allows educators to systematically track the success or need for additional changes to existing instructional approaches based on student performance.

Creating a progress monitoring plan includes specifying the monitoring tool to be used for data collection, identifying the student goal, and determining the frequency the data will be collected and reviewed (HLP 11). An effective monitoring tool is sensitive enough to capture student growth over a short period of time (Jung et al., 2018). An efficient monitoring tool is easy to administer and should be linked to instruction (Lindstrom, et al., 2019). Effective and efficient monitoring tools include standardized tools such as the Dynamic Indicators of Basic Early Literacy Skills (DIBELS) Oral Reading Fluency measure and informal curriculum-based measures (CBM) such as Dolch sight word lists, math computation probes, and writing prompts.

Academic and behavior monitoring tool charts are available on the NCII website, providing teachers with several options of progress monitoring tools and includes descriptions of the tool, associated grade levels, and skill areas. NCII provides several additional resources for DBI including tools for data teaming, goal setting, and graphing, allowing teachers new to DBI to effectively engage in the process. Graphing the data provides a visual representation of the student's progress making it easier to identify trends and determine if the student is making sufficient progress to meet their goal. Teachers can even share the graphed data with families and students to support school-family collaboration.

Case in Point: Ms. Martinez

Through thoughtful and intentional planning, Ms. Martinez designed a lesson using systematic, explicit instruction to teach four third-grade students to calculate the areas of an irregular shape or figure. Ms. Martinez uses the same lesson structure, regardless of content, so her students are familiar with the sequence of the lesson and how the information will be presented. After reviewing the lesson objective, which is written clearly on the board, Ms. Martinez activates her students' prior knowledge by asking them to share what they already know about area. This is done by a think-pair-share

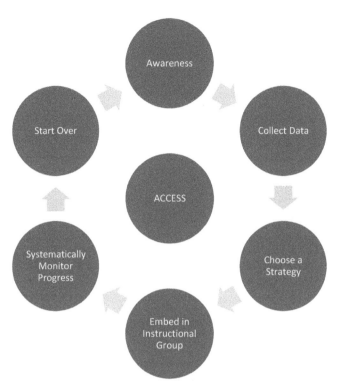

This mnemonic helps teachers remember the steps for increasing access to academic content using intensive instruction. The cyclical nature of this process reflects the ongoing process of progress monitoring.

Figure 20.1 Increasing ACCESS to Academic Content

activity. First, students are asked to write down what they know about area on a piece of paper or in a warm-up journal. While they are writing, she is actively walking around the room, paying careful attention to students who may look stuck. After one minute, students are encouraged to pair up with a partner and share what they have written.

As she walks around the room, Ms. Martinez closely monitors the discussions for identifiers of understanding and engagement and takes note of each student's present level of knowledge. Ms. Martinez now has a baseline measure of the students' prior knowledge which allows her to monitor progress throughout the lesson. This also provides her with an opportunity to adjust instruction according to the student's needs. She may need to provide a more in-depth review of calculating the area of a regular shape before proceeding with the lesson. When students have finished sharing in their pairs, a whole-class discussion of calculating areas begins.

Ms. Martinez summarizes what the students shared about their knowledge of area and provides a clear, concise definition of the term. She then uses the definition to explicitly link the students' existing knowledge to the process of calculating the area of an irregular shape. After students had a conceptual understanding of areas of irregular shapes, Ms. Martinez modeled one way to calculate the area. Ms. Martinez used teacher talk to talk through the procedural steps and the conceptual reasoning. She even models asking herself questions about what to do next and what to do if she gets stuck. She provides extra time for the students to process the information before moving to the next step. As she is modeling, she pays careful attention to the students, monitoring their understanding and engagement levels using her data collection chart. When she sees confused expressions or disengaged students, Ms. Martinez adjusts her pacing to match the needs of her students. Ms.

Martinez provides additional examples when she notices more frequent student errors on her data log (see Nagro et al., 2018 for downloadable data collection forms).

While modeling the process, Ms. Martinez provides multiple examples of shapes found in real-life settings ranging from oddly shaped swimming pools and hot tubs to complex gardens and playgrounds. Although Ms. Martinez is using real-life examples of irregular shapes, she is careful not to assume that all students have prior experience and knowledge of the items. After using several examples to model the process, Ms. Martinez provides the students with opportunities for practice. Some students have additional visuals on their desk, others are working with guided notes, and others still have access to a prerecorded example on their tablets. Each student is receiving intensified supports scaffolding their learning experience as appropriate given their individual needs (HLP 15). While the students practice, Ms. Martinez is monitoring student progress by circulating the room and logging student progress so she can provide additional instruction and/or supports as needed. Additionally, Ms. Martinez collects exit tickets from the class that are customized for each student to target individual student goals for the math lesson. Ms. Martinez has been graphing student accuracy throughout this unit using the individualized exit tickets to help her understand where each student is making progress or needs additional support. Ms. Martinez will continue this cycle of "ACCESS" (see Figure 20.1) throughout her teaching.

Creating Many Opportunities to Practice and Respond to What Students are Learning With Teachers and Peers

An evidence-based engagement approach, referred to as providing opportunities to respond (OTR) is a teacher-action such as questioning, prompting, or cuing that initiates a student response followed by immediate, corrective feedback (MacSuga-Gage & Simonsen, 2015). Student responses can include verbal, gestural, or written responses from students (Simonsen et al., 2010). Frequent OTR are associated with improved academic achievement and behavioral outcomes for students in general education, special education, and students who are at-risk for academic underachievement (Common et al., 2020). Benefits of high rates of OTR include increased engagement, more opportunities for students to practice skills, and immediate feedback for teachers to monitor student understanding (HLP 18). Despite the evidence of positive effects of increased OTR, students with language, learning, and behavioral needs are typically offered fewer OTR than their higher achieving peers (Green et al., 2021). Therefore, students who need the most practice to reinforce their skills and knowledge in fact often receive less practice, which increases the opportunity gap for students with disabilities and others who struggle to learn.

Not all students will respond in the same way to high-quality, research-based, differentiated instruction or more specifically to a carefully chosen intervention. All students can benefit from increased OTR, but it is particularly important for students considered "low- or non-responders" to supports provided in tiers one and two. These students may be hesitant to participate in traditional opportunities to respond (e.g., raising a hand to answer a question in a whole-group class discussion). Once an educator tracks how students are responding (e.g., accuracy and fluency of responses), they can choose a strategy to increase the rate and accuracy of student responses and apply the strategies in a more intensive and individualized setting. Strategies to increase OTR include increased presentation rate, choral responding, response cards, and peer-mediated methods, which are subsequently described.

First, increased presentation rate refers to fast instructional pacing that includes frequent opportunities for students to respond but allows for sufficient wait time. Faster pacing can reduce off-task behavior and increase accurate responding and participation for students with learning and behavioral needs in small groups and individuals with autism in one-to-one settings (Tincani

& Crozier, 2007; Lamella & Tincani, 2012). This fast pace does not mean spending less time providing direct instruction for concepts and skills. On the contrary, students receiving intensive intervention will likely need to spend more time and repetition to fully develop a skill or conceptual understanding. Students with disabilities may need 10–30 times more practice opportunities to retain and generalize their learning. In a small group or individual setting, teachers can provide a structured and supportive environment that offers more frequent and targeted questioning to elicit student responses with corrective feedback. Teachers should plan for a variety of scaffolded questions to elicit students' responses to ensure that the OTR are related to the students' individualized learning goals.

Next, choral responding occurs when the teacher issues a question or prompt with the expectation that all students will respond in unison. Choral responding is an effective way for teachers to engage students in a larger group. However, it can make it difficult to formatively assess understanding for students with intensive learning needs. During small group instruction, it is more manageable for teachers to record accuracy of responses during choral responding. One helpful recommendation is to create a data collection tool related to students' learning goals prior to small group instruction so that teachers can record accuracy of responses. Similarly, response cards are another strategy studied to increase OTR. Response cards involve a discrete set of student responses provided to the students using flash cards, a handheld dry erase board, or through adaptive technology (HLP 19) to allow students to respond to teacher prompts or questions by indicating (e.g., holding up or pressing a corresponding button on a tablet) their desired response. Benefits of response cards include increased academic responding, decreased behavior problems, and increased achievement (Common et al., 2020). Teachers can visually monitor the accuracy of responses and log concerns as necessary. Response cards may also engage learners who are reluctant to respond due to low self-efficacy or delayed language skills. Furthermore, pre-printed response cards can support students' language learning needs and could also include the child's first language on one side and the response in English on the other side of the card.

Finally, peer-mediated methods can increase student responding in large and small group settings by increasing academic engaged time and by providing more opportunities to practice skills. Peer-mediated OTR allow the teacher to monitor student responses, and students receive timely feedback from peers. For intensive instruction, peer-to-peer interactions must be highly structured with designated role expectations. During whole-group peer-to-peer OTR, teachers should be intentional to pair students with intensive learning needs with capable and accepting peer models (HLP 17). Commonly used peer-to-peer responding could be in the form of a "think-pair-share" or "turn and talk." When providing students with intensive instruction in a small group, teachers can scaffold peer interactions for optimal interaction, engagement, and learning (HLP 15). The strategies discussed in this section can be embedded into almost any research-based intervention to increase intensity and to offer more opportunities for practice and feedback.

Case in Point: Mrs. Stanley

Mrs. Stanley uses OTR to monitor her students' understanding during whole-group instruction. She uses a variety of methods to monitor her students' progress and understanding during instruction in her fifth-grade inclusive classroom. For example, when providing whole group instruction, she uses questioning to elicit verbal responses, white boards for written responses, and asks for gestures such as thumbs up or thumbs down to check for understanding. At a professional development meeting, the fifth-grade team discussed formative assessment strategies that promote data-based individualization. Mrs. Stanley shared the strategies that she uses to engage students, monitor understanding, and make real-time instructional decisions. One team member asked how Mrs.

Stanley knows that "all" students are understanding during whole group instruction and if she noticed any students that do not respond consistently or accurately. This prompted Mrs. Stanley to consider her students with Individualized Education Programs (IEPs) and two of her English Language Learners (ELL) who are not making as much progress toward curricular goals as she would like to see.

After the professional development meeting, Mrs. Stanley became more aware of the type and frequency of OTR she was providing to individual students in her class and collected data on how a few of her students were responding. She noticed that her students learning English did not always respond when the whole class was prompted and that some of her students with IEPs did not display accurate responses on their white boards. Although Mrs. Stanley provided a variety of whole-group response strategies to engage her students and to check for understanding, she realized that some students needed a more intensive and targeted approach.

What Mrs. Stanley was experiencing is consistent with the premise of a multi-tiered system of supports (MTSS) in that not all students will respond in the same way to even high quality, differentiated instruction or even to targeted intervention. Once Mrs. Stanley became aware of how her students were responding, she chose a strategy to increase the rate and accuracy of student responses and apply the strategies in a more intensive and individualized setting. Strategies to increase OTR include increased presentation rate, choral responding, response cards, and peer-mediated methods. Mrs. Stanley started by becoming aware of the students who needed more OTR, so she was able to select from a variety of strategies based on each student's individualized learning needs. She continued to collect data to individualize her approach based on each student's needs and goals and started the process over to ensure continued progress over time.

Creating Many Opportunities for Students to Receive Immediate, Corrective Feedback

Immediate corrective feedback is an essential component of any intensive intervention and has been shown to increase maintenance of skills over time (HLP 22). Frequent OTR described in an earlier section allows for increased opportunities for teachers to deliver real-time verbal feedback to reinforce or redirect learning toward the desired outcome for each child. Figure 20.2 summarizes key aspects of providing immediate, corrective feedback (i.e., behavior-specific praise, connects to prior learning, prompts toward error correction, and practice to apply feedback) as outlined in this section. Feedback can either be verbal or written; however, in some cases verbal feedback may be more effective to ensure that students not only access the feedback but that they also understand how to apply it for future practice. Verbal feedback during intensive instruction can also reduce barriers associated with students' literacy and/or language skills. Regardless of if feedback is verbal or written, it must go beyond praise and correction to maximize learning and motivation for students with intensive learning or behavioral needs (Hooks & Pett, in press). Some students need support to first understand and make sense of the feedback they receive by referring to prior learning and second to take action for the next steps. The corrective feedback process for students with intensive learning or behavioral needs involves behavior-specific praise, explicit connections to prior learning, prompts that lead toward error correction, and specific actions to apply feedback in practice and for future learning.

Praise statements are an important part of providing feedback and are even more effective for improving student outcomes when praise is specific to a desired response or behavior. High rates of behavior-specific praise are associated with both improved behavior and academic outcomes, but despite evidence of effectiveness general praise statements are more frequently observed in classrooms, and students with disabilities in inclusive classrooms receive relatively low levels of behavior-specific praise (Royer et al., 2019). Similar to increasing use of OTR mentioned

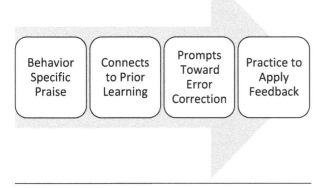

Figure 20.2 Key Aspects of Providing Immediate, Corrective Feedback

previously, teachers can self-monitor their use of behavior-specific praise to create awareness and increase implementation (Markelz et al., 2021). Effective teachers also carefully consider the type of behaviors that are acknowledged and praised related to the child's individualized learning goals.

Corrective feedback can and should be provided as part of teacher-student interactions in response to students' verbal and/or written responses. As part of intensive instruction, immediate and corrective feedback can either reinforce a desired response to increase the likelihood of repetition and retention or reshape an incorrect response to prevent future practice of undesired skills or behaviors. Praise and corrective feedback are important first steps, but students with intensive learning needs may require more explicit guidance regarding next steps and instruction for how to implement those steps by engaging with the feedback they received (Rabbani et al., 2022). Teachers can do this by making explicit connections to prior learning and future practice to build a bridge for students to apply prior skills and knowledge to new learning related to the learning or behavioral target. When teachers refer to prior learning, it makes learning relevant to what the child already knows so that students are empowered to take ownership of their own learning (Shing & Brod, 2016). Teachers can also promote agency and reduce learned helplessness by providing the child with a strategy to build upon their strengths. For example, "You can whisper read the text to yourself to see if there is anything missing from your story" (Hooks & Pett, in press, p. X).

The ultimate goal of providing feedback is for students to improve their performance and progress toward a specific learning or behavioral goal. Feedback must include direction for practice so that students have opportunities to apply the feedback from the previous steps and become aware of how their efforts result in progress over time. Otherwise put, it helps the child understand that the learning does not stop after the teacher's feedback concludes, and that specific actions lead to continuous improvement. When teachers communicate what and how the child can practice during intensive instruction, they promote growth-mindedness, since practice statements place emphasis on learning as a process rather than a product (Masters, 2014).

Case in Point: Mr. Paolini

Mr. Paolini knows that it is important to provide immediate and corrective feedback to all students, but especially for his students with diverse learning and behavioral needs. He takes pride in providing his students with feedback on their progress each day and regularly keeps students' families informed. Mr. Paolini uses the popular "compliment sandwich" approach (compliment-constructive criticism-compliment) to acknowledge something the child did well and to point out where they can improve. He likes to end with a positive, to leave students feeling good about their efforts and does the same when communicating with families about student progress.

At the end of a writer's workshop, Mr. Paolini confers with Isabelle, a student with a learning disability in his inclusive second grade classroom. He tells Isabelle "Good job producing three sentences!" and then points out what he wants Isabelle to work on by saying "Remember to begin your sentence with a capital letter." Mr. Paolini ends the interaction by giving a general praise statement of, "Keep up the good work!" Mr. Paolini recognizes the importance of providing immediate and corrective feedback to students with disabilities and consistently acknowledges his students' efforts. He praised Isabelle for producing three sentences and pointed out that she did not begin her sentence with a capital letter. If *written output* was one of Isabella's high-priority goals, Mr. Paolini successfully reinforced her production of three sentences. However, if the high-priority goal was *sequencing events*, the praise statement did not align with the desired outcome. Instead, Mr. Paolini might have said, "I like how your three sentences show the beginning, middle, and end of your story. Now try writing two sentences about what happened in the middle of your story. I can't wait to see what you write next!"

Wrap Up

In sum, the intensive instructional practices described in this chapter can be used within a MTSS to meet the needs of all learners, but can also be intensified to address the learning and behavioral needs for students considered low- or non-responders to intensify supports in Tiers 1 and 2. When teachers prioritize skills to teach (HLP 11), they can engage in more focused data collection, individualization (HLP 13), and provide more practice opportunities (HLP 18) related to a specific learning or behavioral target. Providing systematic instruction facilitates predictability for students to acquire the target skill more quickly since they do not have to first learn how the information will be presented. Furthermore, explicit instruction along with simple, concise language will help to provide clear expectations and methods for meeting learning goals without ambiguity. Providing frequent opportunities to respond with immediate, corrective feedback provides students with practice and provides immediate error corrections to prevent reinforcement of undesired outcomes (HLP 22). Taken together, the practices can be individualized based on frequent progress monitoring and data-based decision making.

Tips

- **Data-based individualizing**: When high-quality differentiated instruction in Tier 1 and targeted group interventions in Tier 2 are not effective for improving students learning or behavioral needs, teachers should use student progress data to individualize and intensify instruction. This may require increasing duration and intensity and reducing group size depending on the students' individualized needs.
- **Document and evaluate effectiveness often**: When modifications are made to interventions based on students' individualized needs, teachers should document and evaluate the effectiveness to guide future instruction. Sometimes strategies lose effectiveness over time for students with intensive needs.
- **Promote engagement in a culturally responsive way**: Engaging students is critical to learning. When engaging students, connect learning to students' lives. Understand the students' academic and cultural backgrounds and use this knowledge to inform your instruction.

- **Remember to involve families!** Teachers and practitioners should involve families to help make data-based decisions regarding intensive instruction. Each of these strategies can be further supported when families are engaged in their child's education (HLP 3).

Key Resources

- High Leverage Practice #20 Intensive Instruction: https://highleveragepractices.org/hlp-20-provide-intensive-instruction
- High Leverage Practice Guide #20: https://highleveragepractices.org/hlp-leadership-guides/hlp-20-guide
- CEEDAR Center, Culturally Responsive Teaching: https://ceedar.education.ufl.edu/wp-content/uploads/2014/08/culturally-responsive.pdf
- Council for Exceptional Children HLP #20: https://exceptionalchildren.org/sites/default/files/2021-01/HLP%2020%20Admin%20Guide.pdf
- National Center on Intensive Intervention: https://intensiveintervention.org/
- What Works Clearinghouse (database of intervention effectiveness): https://ies.ed.gov/ncee/wwc/

References

Apitz, M., Ruppar, A., Roessler, K., & Pickett, K. J. (2017). Planning lessons for students with significant disabilities in high school English classes. *Teaching Exceptional Children, 49*(3), 168–74. https://doi-org./10.1177/0040059916654900

Archer, A. L., & Hughes, C. A. (2010). *Explicit instruction: Effective and efficient teaching.* Guilford Press.

Chohan, B. I. (2018). The impact of academic failure on the self-concept of elementary grade students. *Bulletin of Education and Research, 40*(2), 13–25.

Common, E. A., Lane, K. L., Cantwell, E. D., Brunsting, N. C., Oakes, W. P., Germer, K. A., & Bross, L. A. (2020). Teacher-delivered strategies to increase students' opportunities to respond: A systematic methodological review. *Behavioral Disorders, 45*(2), 67–84.

Cooper, J. T., Whitney, T., & Lindo, A. S. (2018). Using immediate feedback to increase opportunities to respond in a general education classroom. *Rural Special Education Quarterly, 37*(1), 52–60. doi:10.1177/8756870517747121

Green, A. L., Olsen, A. A., & Nandakumar, V. (2021). Disparities across race and disability risk: Assessing teacher practices. *Psychology in the Schools, 58*(6), 1070–81.

Haydon, T., Marsicano, R., & Scott, T. M. (2013). A comparison of choral and individual responding: A review of the literature. *Preventing School Failure: Alternative Education for Children and Youth, 57*, 181–8. DOI: 10.1080/1045988X.2012.682184

Hooks, S. D. (2015). *The effects of training pre-kindergarten teachers to use self-management strategies to increase at-risk students' opportunities to respond to literacy prompts.* [Doctoral dissertation, Johns Hopkins University]. https://jscholarship.library.jhu.edu/handle/1774.2/39513.

Hooks, S. D., & Pett, J. (in press). Beyond the compliment sandwich; Try a WRAP! *Young Children.*

Jung, P.-G., McMaster, K.L., Kunkel, A.K., Shin, J. and Stecker, P.M. (2018). Effects of data-based individualization for students with intensive learning needs: A meta-analysis. *Learning Disabilities Research & Practice, 33*, 144–55. https://doi.org/10.1111/ldrp.12172

Kennedy, M. J., Cook, L., Morano, S., & Peeples, K. (2019). *High-leverage practice #20: Provide intensive instruction.* https://highleveragepractices.org/701-2-4-3-2/.

Lamella, L., & Tincani, M. (2012). Brief wait time to increase response opportunity and correct responding of children with autism spectrum disorder who display challenging behavior. *Journal of Developmental Disabilities, 24*, 559–73. doi: 10.1007/s10882-012-9289-x

Lindström, E. R., Gesel, S. A., & Lemons, C. J. (2019). Data-based individualization in reading: Tips for successful implementation. *Intervention in School and Clinic*, *55*(2), 113–19. https://doi.org/10.1177/1053451219837634

MacSuga-Gage, A. S., & Simonsen, B. (2015). Examining the effects of teacher-directed opportunities to respond on student outcomes: A systematic review of the literature. *Education and Treatment of Children*, *38*(2), 211–39.

Markelz, A. M., Riden, B. S., & Hooks, S. D. (2021). Increasing early childhood educators' behavior specific praise with wearable technology. *Journal of Early Intervention*, *43*(2), 99–116. https://doi.org/10.1177/1053815120927091

Martin, B., Sargent, K., Van Camp, A., & Wright, J. (2018). *Intensive Intervention Practice Guide: Increasing Opportunities to Respond as an Intensive Intervention*. Office of Special Education Programs. US Department of Education.

Marzano, R. J. (2009). *Designing & teaching learning goals & objectives*. Marzano Research Laboratory.

Masters, G. N. (2014). Towards a growth mindset in assessment. *Practically Primary*, *19*(2), 4–7.

McLeskey, J., Barringer, M-D., Billingsley, B., Brownell, M., Jackson, D., Kennedy, M., Lewis, T., Maheady, L., Rodriguez, J., Scheeler, M. C., Winn, J., & Ziegler, D. (2017, January). *High-leverage practices in special education*. Council for Exceptional Children & CEEDAR Center. https://highleveragepractices.org/sites/default/files/2020-10/Instructionfinal.pdf

Nagro, S. A., Hooks, S. D., & Fraser, D. W. (2019). Over a decade of practice: Are educators correctly using tertiary interventions? *Preventing School Failure: Alternative Education for Children and Youth*, *63*(1), 52–61. https://doi.org/10.1080/1045988X.2018.1491021

Nagro, S. A., Hooks, S., Fraser, D. W., & Cornelius, K. E. (2018). Whole-group response strategies to promote student engagement in inclusive classrooms [Reprinted in Special Issue: Putting high-leverage practices into practice]. *Teaching Exceptional Children*, *0*(4), 243–249. https://doi.org/10.1177/0040059918757947

National Center on Educational Outcomes (2013). Alternate assessments for students with disabilities. www.cehd.umn.edu/NCEO/TOPICAREAS/AlternateAssessments/ altAssessFAQ.htm

National Center on Intensive Intervention. (2018). *Breaking down the DBI process: Questions & considerations*. Author, Office of Special Education Programs, U.S. Department of Education. https://intensiveintervention.org/sites/default/files/NCII-placemat-508.pdf

National Center on Intensive Intervention. (n.d.). *Intensive intervention tools chart*. https://intensiveintervention.org/resource/tools-chart-user-guide

Rabbani, L. M., Alarabi, K. S., Alsalhi, N. R., & Al Qawasmi, A. A. (2022). Roles iinterplay between tteachers and sstudents in the pprovisions of ffeedback: Establishing a cgcommon ground. *International Journal of Early Childhood Special Education*, *14*(1).

Royer, D. J., Lane, K. L., Dunlap, K. D., & Ennis, R. P. (2019). A systematic review of teacher-delivered behavior-specific praise on K–12 student performance. *Remedial and Special Education*, *40*(2), 112–28.

Shing, Y. L., & Brod, G. (2016). Effects of prior knowledge on memory: Implications for education. *Mind, Brain, and Education*, *10*(3), 153–61.

Simonsen, B., Myers, D., & DeLuca, C. (2010). Teaching teachers to use prompts, opportunities to respond, and specific praise. *Teacher Education and Special Education*, *33*, 100–18. doi: 10.1177/0888406409359905

Smith, M., Saez, L., & Doabler, C. T. (2016). Using explicit and systematic instruction to support working memory. *eachingTeaching Exceptional Children*, *48*, 275–81. https://doi.org/10.1177/0040059916650633

Tincani, M., & Crozier, S. (2007). Comparing brief and extended wait-time during small group instruction for children with challenging behavior. *Journal of Behavioral Education, 16,* 355–67.

Wexler, J., Reed, D. K., Pyle, N., Mitchell, M., & Barton, E. E. (2015). A synthesis of peer-mediated academic interventions for secondary struggling learners. *Journal of Learning Disabilities, 48*(5), 451–70.

21
Teach Students to Maintain and Generalize New Learning Across Time and Settings

Sheila R. Alber-Morgan
The Ohio State University

Alyxandra Zavodney
The Ohio State University

Marcella M. Gallmeyer
The Ohio State University

Introduction

Teachers know their instruction is effective when their students achieve generalization and maintenance. That is, their students independently perform and apply skills they have learned in the classroom to other settings and situations, in novel or creative ways, and over time. Teachers cannot just "train and hope" (Stokes & Baer, 1977, p. 350) their students will go forth into the world and skillfully use what they acquired to mastery in the classroom. Most teachers, especially special education teachers, know firsthand that "train and hope" does *not* work, and "No one learns a generalized lesson unless a generalized lesson is taught" (Baer, 1999, p. 1). For these reasons, teachers must deliberately plan, teach, and assess for the three types of generalized outcomes—setting/situation generalization, response generalization, and response maintenance (Cooper et al., 2020).

Setting/situation generalization is transferring skills learned in the classroom to different places (e.g., home, other classrooms, community settings) or under different circumstances (e.g., same classroom but novel practice materials, another time of day, or a different teacher). With response generalization, students perform skills in new ways that were not directly taught (e.g., creativity, problem-solving). Response maintenance refers to how long a learner continues to perform a skill independently over time (e.g., weeks, months, years).

The ability to generalize and maintain newly learned skills is likely a challenge for most individuals, especially those with disabilities and/or intensive learning needs (e.g., Neely et al., 2018). Fortunately, students who need intensive instruction can benefit from a technology of generalization. Building on the seminal work of Stokes and Baer (1977), Cooper et al. (2020) delineated five strategies for programming for generalization and maintenance of newly learned skills as follows: (a) teach the full range of examples; (b) make the instructional setting similar to the generalization setting; (c) maximize contact with reinforcement in the generalization setting; (d) mediate generalization; and (e) train to generalize. This chapter presents various ways teachers can implement each of the five strategies so their students can achieve generalized outcomes.

DOI: 10.4324/9781003276876-26

Narrowing the Focus

All learners across age and ability levels can benefit a great deal from instruction that incorporates generalization programming. In a three-tiered response to intervention (RTI) model, generalization strategies can be used in whole class (Tier 1), small group (Tier 2), and one-on-one (Tier 3) instructional arrangements. This chapter focuses on using generalization strategies for students with mild disabilities who have intensive learning needs and require small group or one-on-one instruction. Specifically, we present special education teachers with recommendations for planning and implementing generalization strategies for students who need intensive interventions. These strategies will greatly increase their students' likelihood of independent functioning and success outside the classroom and over time.

Chapter Overview

1. Identify strategies teachers can use to program for generalization and maintenance of academic skills.
2. Explain how teachers can implement generalization strategies in their classrooms.

Using the HLP: Generalization Strategies

Teach the full range of examples. In general, the more examples the teacher presents when teaching a target skill, the more likely a student will generalize the skill to untrained examples (Cooper et al., 2020). To be most efficient, teachers should systematically select examples that represent the range of situations students are likely to encounter in the generalization setting (e.g., Barczak, 2019). For example, when teaching students to make a purchase with a credit card, have the student practice the skill at different places of business (e.g., restaurant, convenience store, grocery store) with different purchasing procedures (e.g., swipe card, insert card, tap card, or hand card to clerk). Teachers will know they have taught enough examples when the student can perform the skill with untrained examples (e.g., credit card purchase at fast food restaurant). See Table 21.1 for additional examples across content areas. Selecting the most relevant examples to customize instruction for individual learners is an excellent opportunity to be culturally responsive. For example, when teaching students to navigate, use maps that correspond to places in the student's current community and places where they or their parents lived in the past. Directly teach examples the student will more frequently encounter and assess for generalization with other likely, but less frequently occurring examples.

Make the instructional setting similar to the generalization setting. Students are likely to transfer skills to other settings or situations when features of the instructional setting are similar to those in the generalization setting. Two ways teachers can make the instructional setting similar to the generalization setting are by *programming common stimuli* and *teaching loosely*. When programming common stimuli, teachers identify critical features of generalization settings (e.g., visual or auditory prompts, materials, people) and include them during instruction. For example, setting up an area of the classroom to resemble a store (e.g., with signs, shelves, items with price tags, real money, cash register) so students can practice making purchases before going to real stores.

When programming common stimuli, teachers identify and incorporate critical stimuli necessary to perform the target skill. For example, when teaching students to complete a job application, teachers should collect job applications from a range of different businesses in the community to use as practice examples. Alert the student to the *critical* elements of the job application (e.g., space to write name, contact information, work history, references) and show how those elements appear in different places, fonts, colors, and formats on different job applications. Students should practice locating the critical stimuli when completing items on different authentic job applications.

Table 21.1 Examples of Multiple Exemplar Training Across Content Areas

Content Area	Target Skill	Direct Teaching Examples	Generalization to Untaught Examples
Social Studies	finding locations	school map neighborhood map city map state map	local zoo or park map map of different neighborhood map of different city country map
Science	identifying states of matter: solids, liquids, and gases	solids (rocks, wood, metal) liquid (water, oil, juice) gases (oxygen, carbon dioxide, helium)	solids (ice, sand, glass) liquids (mercury, gasoline) gases (vapor, ozone, freon)
Reading	following directions with recipes	microwave recipes (popcorn) blender recipes (smoothie) sandwich recipes (tuna salad) skillet recipes (scrambled eggs)	other microwave recipes (pizza) other blender recipes (soup) sandwich + skillet (grilled cheese)
Math	adding decimals	vertical problems horizontal problems with and without regrouping with manipulatives small group/one-on-one	vertical/horizontal problems using different numerals with/without regrouping using different numerals. without manipulatives general education class

In contrast to programming common stimuli, teachers can also promote generalization by varying the non-critical stimuli—this is called teaching loosely. Frequently varying unimportant stimuli will prepare students to perform the target skill under a range of conditions so they will not be impeded by unfamiliarity of the environment. With job applications, the varied non-critical stimuli include features such as the number and size of blank spaces to complete; size, color, and font type of print; and number of pages. Additionally, students can practice completing job applications at different times of the day, in different areas of the classroom, on different computers, and in the presence of different people.

When programming common stimuli, teachers can make the common stimuli transportable to other settings and situations when students need to use the target skill. Figure 21.1 shows an example of a functional transportable common stimuli prompt for decoding unknown words. After explicitly teaching each strategy, teachers can build them into the decoding prompt a few at a time. Then students can take the prompt to each of the settings where they will need to decode and understand vocabulary independently (e.g., other classes, in the library, doing homework, reading for pleasure). Pictures can be added to the prompt if the student needs them to understand the directions (e.g., Draw a pair of eyes under the directions, "Look"). Transportable stimuli can include the addition of cultural scaffolding (see Schema in Figure 21.1) by having students relate unknown words to their personal background knowledge and experiences.

Maximize contact with reinforcement in the generalization setting. For a variety of reasons, students may not be contacting reinforcement for doing the target skill outside of the classroom. Specifically, students may not perform the skill proficiently enough in the generalization setting to access reinforcement, students may be unmotivated to perform the skill, and/or target behaviors that are emitted may go unnoticed and unreinforced by significant others. The following approaches will increase the likelihood students will contact reinforcement outside of the instructional situation.

Decoding Strategies

Get Your Mouth Ready Look at the beginning sound, make that sound and slide all the way through the word.	**Cut** Look for parts you know.	**Blend** Say the sounds of part of the word and blend them together.
Look See the word from start to end.	**Skip, Read, Return** Skip the word you don't know, keep reading to the end of the sentence and return to the word.	**Reread** Go back to the beginning of the sentence and reread.
Try Does it look right? Does it make sense? Does it sound right?	**Picture Clues** Look at the pictures to see what they share.	**Schema** Think of your background knowledge and experiences

Figure 21.1 Functional Transportable Common Stimuli for Decoding Words

Teach the target behavior to criteria needed in generalization setting. Targeting fluency of responding will increase the likelihood students will perform the skill proficiently enough to contact reinforcement in the generalization setting. For example, while a student might meet the criteria of accurate word decoding in the resource room, he or she may not read fluently enough to contact reinforcement in the regular classroom. Teachers can build their students' fluency and mastery by using brief daily timed trials (e.g., 1-minute repeated readings). Identify criteria for mastery by collaborating with general education teachers and then clearly outline and plan materials for instruction so that students reach that criterion. Goal setting with self-graphing is an excellent motivational tool for increasing fluency of academic skills (e.g., Gilley et al., 2021; Ritter et al., 2021). Fishley et al. (2017) combined goal setting, fluency drills, and self-graphing using the GO FASTER strategy to build vocabulary knowledge. An example of how to combine these skills is teaching five morphemes, then conducting 30-second timed fluency drills followed by students self-graphing their data on a chart.

Figure 21.2 shows an example of a student self-recording sheet for oral reading fluency goals. Prior to completing a 1-minute oral reading timed trial, students can mark on the graph their words per minute goal for that day and fill in the title of the reading passage. After completing the timed trial, the student self-records by coloring in the column up to the number of words read. Teachers should direct students to examine their progress monitoring data and provide feedback on how much they are improving (e.g., "Wow, that's seven more words than yesterday!"). Being culturally responsive when selecting reading passages for individual students will likely increase their motivation and success. Identify topics and reading passages that relate to the student's background experiences. Better yet, allow students to choose their own reading passages and/or topics. If progress monitoring data show the student is not improving, the reading level of the passages may need to be adjusted or additional reinforcers may be needed to increase motivation.

Program unpredictable contingencies. Behaviors that are reinforced under intermittent and unpredictable schedules of reinforcement are more robust and enduring than behaviors on fixed and predictable schedules (Cooper et al., 2020). Teachers can program unpredictable contingencies in fun and motivating ways using activities such as classroom lotteries, group contingencies (e.g., Helton & Alber-Morgan, 2020), and mystery motivators (e.g., Coffee & Whitlock, 2020).

Figure 21.3 shows an example of an unpredictable group contingency using a BINGO chart for students to sign for various accomplishments such as turning in homework on time, sharing materials, and making quick transitions to the next activity. Throughout the day, the teacher "catches

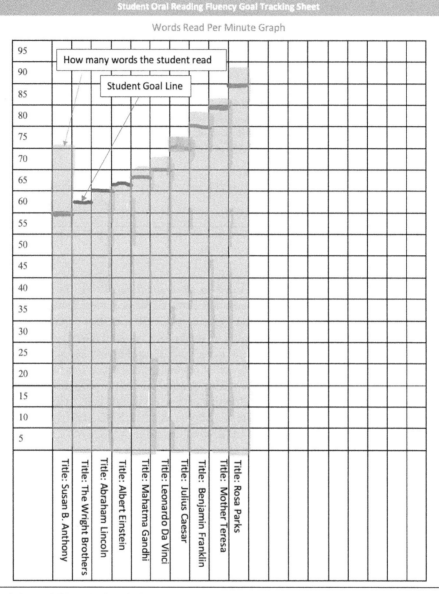

Student Oral Reading Fluency Goal Tracking Sheet

Words Read Per Minute Graph

How many words the student read

Student Goal Line

95
90
85
80
75
70
65
60
55
50
45
40
35
30
25
20
15
10
5

Title: Susan B. Anthony
Title: The Wright Brothers
Title: Abraham Lincoln
Title: Albert Einstein
Title: Mahatma Gandhi
Title: Leonardo Da Vinci
Title: Julius Caesar
Title: Benjamin Franklin
Title: Mother Teresa
Title: Rosa Parks

Figure 21.2 Student Self-Recording Sheet for Oral Reading Fluency

students being good" and provides a verbal prompt with specific positive feedback, such as, "Julie, thank you for quickly getting ready for group time, please go to the BINGO chart and write your name in any box." Give students many opportunities to sign the BINGO chart. At the end of the day (or instructional period), have a prize drawing and deliver the reward to each student whose name is signed in that box (e.g., For O-1, Demetrius, Oscar, and Julie will each receive a reward). The rewards can be selected from a predetermined list of suggestions made by students such as lunch with the teacher or extra screen time. These predetermined rewards can align with each column on the BINGO chart (e.g., B-lunch with the teacher, I-extra screen time, N-show and tell, G-pick from prize box, O-happy note to parents).

B	I	N	G	O
Lunch with teacher	Extra screen time	Show and tell	Pick from prize box	Happy note to parents
1 Mike	Bailey Julie Oscar	Oscar Brittany	Mike Demetrious	Demetrious Oscar Julie
2 Mike Demetrious Bailey	Mike Bailey	Bailey	Brittany	Mike Julie
3 Bailey	Oscar Julie Demetrious	Mike Brittany	Brittany Julie	Oscar
4 Oscar Julie	Bailey Demetrious		Bailey	Mike
5	Julie Brittany	Mike Demetrious		Demetrious Julie

Figure 21.3 Unpredictable Contingency Chart for Earning Rewards

Set behavior traps. Another approach that addresses student motivation is setting behavior traps (Alber & Heward, 1996; Cooper et al., 2020). Behavior traps are natural reinforcement contingencies that maintain and extend academic and social skills. When teachers use a student's fervent interests to design reinforcing individualized instruction across the curriculum, they are setting behavior traps. For example, a student who loves martial arts might be motivated to write stories, biographies, or instructions (language arts), research the history and geography of different kinds of martial arts (social studies), research the statistics of martial arts winners to compare or to make predictions (math), and learn about the physics of martial arts such as momentum equals mass times velocity (science).

Because behavior traps are based entirely on the individual interests of a student (e.g., comic books, athletes, musicians, sports, dolls, horses, race cars, cooking, swimming, origami), using this strategy is an ideal way to nurture a student's cultural identity and provide deeper meaning while targeting academic goals. Figure 21.4 shows a way to incorporate a behavior trap into a language arts activity for a student who is a big fan of the Denver Broncos. This type of writing activity provides flexibility for a wide range of student interests.

Ask significant others to reinforce the target behavior. When target behaviors are not reinforced in the generalization setting, they are unlikely to be maintained. For this reason, it is a good idea to

Must Do: _____Write a 5-Sentence Paragraph_____

All Done!

1.   _____Topic Sentence_____   ☑

My favorite football team is the Denver Broncos.

2.   _____Write Fact Sentence _____   ☑

The Denver Broncos played their first game in 1959 when they beat the Boston Patriots 13 to 10.

3.   ____Write Fact Sentence_____   ☑

The first Black man to play professional football, Gene Mingo, played for the Broncos from 1960 up until 1964.

4.   ____Write Fact Sentence____   ☑

Amazingly, the Broncos played their coldest game recorded of all time in 1983 when it was zero degrees in Kansas City.

5.   ____Write Concluding Sentence____   ☑

In conclusion, my favorite football team has an interesting history.

Figure 21.4 Example of a Behavior Trap for a Writing Activity

collaborate with significant others including the student's family members and school staff by asking them to notice and reinforce the occurrence of target behaviors with positive feedback and rewards. ClassDojo (www.classdojo.com) provides an easy and efficient way to communicate with students and their families. It uses a digital platform in which significant others can reinforce students for specific skills that are noted in the Dojo classroom. For example, Bella is a student who is working on self-advocating in situations where she may need teacher assistance. Each time Bella self-advocates, she receives positive feedback and is awarded Dojo points. Once her points are awarded, Bella's significant others can view her feedback and the points she was awarded for self-advocating. Knowing this information, Bella's guardians could then provide additional reinforcement after school.

Teach students to recruit reinforcement. Students can also learn to recruit their own reinforcement when teachers or significant others do not notice them engaging in desirable behaviors. Specifically, teachers should teach students to complete a portion of their work, signal adult attention (e.g., using a hand raise), and politely ask for feedback (e.g., "Please look at my work and tell me how I'm doing."). To prevent too much student recruiting, students can be taught to limit the number of times they recruit their teacher's attention during an independent work period (e.g., Owens & Lo, 2021; Rouse et al., 2014). For example, teachers can provide their students with a self-monitoring card with a limited number of boxes to check (e.g., three) each time the student recruits. Figure 21.5 shows an example of a recruiting prompt card that can be taped to a student's desk or notebook. The prompt lists the steps for recruiting, provides a box to check each time a recruiting response is made, and provides a place to self-evaluate performance.

Mediate Generalization. Mediating generalization is arranging for the transfer of the target skill by using additional prompts such as *contriving a mediating stimulus* or *teaching self-management*. Contriving a mediating stimulus is giving the student a transportable prompt to take to the different generalization settings as a reminder for how to perform a skill. Figure 21.1 is an example of a transportable prompt. Other examples include having the student set timers to remind them to complete certain tasks throughout the day. Peer buddies who help students stay on task or remember to complete a homework assignment can also be mediating stimuli.

Teaching self-management is instrumental for programming for generalized outcomes and maximizing independence. Self-management includes a range of behaviors such as self-setting goals, self-monitoring, self-assessment, self-recording, self-graphing, and self-reinforcement. Teachers should look for ways to incorporate self-management skills into any of the generalization strategies as part of an instructional package (e.g., self-graphing number of math facts answered per minute, checking off when a step in a series is complete, self-selecting a performance goal). By teaching self-management skills to their students, teachers can promote perseverance and resilience in overcoming obstacles, planning and organization, and the ability to set personal goals and take initiative.

Figure 21.6 shows an example of a self-monitoring task sheet for completing a science fair project. Teachers can use the "Get Ready, Do, Done" model (Ward & Jacobson, 2014) to divide the

Name: Bella	Date: March 5, 2022	
Directions	Check box	Self-evaluate
1. Complete part of my work. 2. Raise my hand. 3. Wait quietly for the teacher. 4. Ask teacher for feedback in a polite voice. 5. Say "Thank you." 6. Check a box	✓ ✓ ☐	☺ ☺ ☹ ☺ ☺ ☹ ☺ ☺ ☹

Figure 21.5 Example Prompt Card for Recruiting Reinforcement

Get Ready	Do	Done
What materials do I need? Where can I find the materials? _____ Construction Paper _____ Colored Pencils _____ Poster Board _____ Scissors _____ Glue _____ Computer	What steps do I need to do? How much time do I need for each step? _____ Write Hypothesis (5–10 min) _____ Write Method (10–15 min) _____ Write Procedure(s) (15–20 min) _____ Write Conclusion (10–15 min) _____ Write References (10–15 min) _____ Print Paragraphs (5–10 min) _____ Glue papers to poster (10–15 min) _____ Add Figures, Illustrations (10–15 min) _____ Place Title (2–5 min)	What will my assignment look like when it is done? Is there an example that I can look at? (Place picture of exemplar finished project here)
Gather the materials I need and find a spot to work.	Get started. Can I see the clock or timer?	Complete the task. Does it look the way I expected? What worked? What would I change next time?

Figure 21.6 Example of a "Get Ready, Do, Done" Form

task into manageable parts. Students should first look at the "Done" section as a reference for what the assignment should look like when it is complete. In the "Get Ready" section, students list the materials they need to complete the task. In the "Do" section, students list each step that must be completed and an estimated time allotment for each step. To increase self-efficiency, some students may find it beneficial to set a timer when completing each step. Once all items have been completed in each section, the checked items can be used by both students and teachers to assess work for completion.

Train to Generalize. Two approaches for training to generalize are *reinforce response variability* and *instruct the learner to generalize*. Reinforcing response variability is simply praising or rewarding creative or novel responses. For example, during a written expression activity, the teacher reinforces the student's use of a variety of novel adjectives and action verbs. When reinforcing response variability, teachers should be careful to only reinforce creative responses that are *correct*. When there is only one correct answer (such as with math facts and spelling orthography), teachers should not reinforce creative responses. In addition to reinforcing novel or creative responses, teachers must also continue to reinforce other correct responses that are not novel so students will continue to maintain those skills in their repertoire as well.

Another approach included in this strategy is *instructing the learner to generalize* which is simply reminding students to use the skill outside of the instructional setting. For example, "When you're doing this assignment at home, don't forget to use the algorithm card to guide you through the steps." After each lesson, teachers can prompt students to identify situations when they will use the strategy. The teacher might say, "When are you going to use the self-questioning strategy that we just practiced?" and help the student generate examples (e.g., when doing science homework, during silent reading time, in social studies class). Then check back with the student, "Did you remember to use the self-questioning strategy when you did your science homework?" and "How did you do?" A simple reminder and follow-up can result in generalized outcomes for a wide range of skills.

Wrap Up

Programming for generalization requires deliberate planning—teachers cannot just "train and hope" their students will achieve generalized outcomes. Deliberate planning for generalization requires identifying critical features of generalization settings (i.e., antecedent stimuli and reinforcers) and building those features into their classroom instruction. After identifying generalization goals for students, teachers can examine the strategies presented in this chapter and customize them to best fit individual learning needs for optimal student independence. Decades of empirical research have produced strategies that teachers can easily build into instruction to improve generalized outcomes for students with mild disabilities who need intensive interventions.

Tips

1. **Examine the generalization settings for features to incorporate into classroom instruction**. When ensuring the transfer of skills from one setting to the next it is important for practitioners to mimic the generalization setting as closely as possible during instruction. Incorporating different aspects of the generalization setting such as visual prompts, auditory stimuli, and physical features of the environment will assist students in making connections across settings and will decrease the likelihood of students requiring teacher assistance.

2. **Obtain knowledge about individual students' interests**. Arguably the most critical information practitioners can possess is knowledge of each of their students' unique interests. Obtaining this knowledge can come from formalized methods such as student interviews or informal methods such as observing the activities the student selects during free time, engaging in conversations with the student, or observing what the student likes to read. Overall, obtaining knowledge of students' interests and cultural backgrounds affords teachers and students opportunities to partner in creating deeper connections with academic content which can ultimately result in higher levels of motivation, conceptual understanding, and retention of material.

3. **Monitor progress of generalized outcomes**. When teaching new skills, teachers should frequently probe for generalization to untaught examples. This is necessary to monitor student progress, make instructional decisions, and determine mastery. Teachers should also probe for generalization prior to instruction to pre-assess what the student can already do in the generalization settings, and probe for generalization after instruction has ended to assess and promote maintenance.

4. **Collaborate with significant others to program for generalization**. The importance of creating a home-to-school connection cannot be overemphasized. Students' significant others'

partnership with school stakeholders is imperative for student academic engagement and achievement. To bolster this partnership, it is essential for significant others and school staff to regularly collaborate about what is happening in the classroom so that students can generalize skills between school, home, and community settings.

Key Resources

1. *Get ready do done*. CognitiveConnections. (n.d.). Retrieved May 4, 2022, from www.efpractice.com/projects-3-1
2. Kearns, D. M. (August, 2016). *Student progress monitoring tool for data collection and graphing [computer software]*. US Department of Education, Office of Special Education Programs, National Center on Intensive Intervention. https://intensiveintervention.org/resource/student-progress-monitoring-tool-data-collection-and-graphing-excel
3. Sayeski, K. L., Earle, G. A., Davis, R., & Calamari, J. (2019). Orton Gillingham: Who, what, and how. *Teaching Exceptional Children, 51*(3), 240–9.
4. Wright, J. (2015). How to: Manage Group behaviors with the element of surprise: The mystery motivator. Response to Intervention. Retrieved May 4, 2022, from www.interventioncentral.org/node/992118

References

Alber, S. R., & Heward, W. L. (1996). Gotcha! Twenty-five behavior traps guaranteed to extend your students' academic and social skills. *Intervention in School and Clinic, 31*, 285–9.

Baer, D. M. (1999). *How to plan for generalization*. PRO-ED.

Barczak, M. A. (2019). Simulated and community-based instruction: Teaching students with intellectual and developmental disabilities to make financial transactions. *Teaching Exceptional Children, 51*(4), 313–21.

Coffee, G., & Whitelock, S. (2020). Response cost raffle and mystery motivator. In M. I. Axlerod, M. Coolong-Chaffin, & R. O. Hawkins (Eds.), *School-Based Behavioral Intervention Case Studies: Effective problem solving for school psychologists* (pp. 142–60). Routledge.

Cooper, J. O., Heron, T. E., & Heward, W. L. (2020). *Applied behavior analysis* (3rd ed.). Pearson.

Fishley, K. M., Konrad, M., & Hessler, T. (2017). GO FASTER: Building morpheme fluency. *Intervention in School and Clinic, 53*(2), 94–8.

Gilley, D. P., Root, J. R., & Cox, S. K. (2021). Development of mathematics and self-determination skills for young adults with extensive support needs. *The Journal of Special Education, 54*(4), 195–204.

Helton, M. R., & Alber-Morgan, S. R. (2020). Improving young children's behavior with GAMES: Group-contingency approaches for managing elementary-classroom settings. *Young Exceptional Children, 23*(1), 24–35.

Neely, L., Garcia, E., Bankston, B., & Green, A. (2018). Generalization and maintenance of functional communication training for individuals with developmental disabilities: A systematic and quality review. *Research in Developmental Disabilities, 79*, 116–29.

Owens, T. L., & Lo, Y. (2021). Function-based self-advocacy training for students with or at risk for emotional and behavioral disorders in general education settings. *Journal of Emotional and Behavioral Disorders*, 10634266211039760.

Ritter, C., Morrison, J. Q., & Sherman, K. (2021). Differential effects of self-graphing on self-monitoring of early literacy outcomes in kindergarten students. *Journal of Behavioral Education, 30*(4), 559–77.

Rouse, C. A., Everhart-Sherwood, J. M., & Alber-Morgan, S. R. (2014). Effects of self- monitoring and recruiting teacher attention on pre-vocational skills. *Education and Training in Autism and Developmental Disabilities, 49,* 313–27.

Stokes, T. F., & Baer, D. M. (1977). An implicit technology of generalization. *Journal of Applied Behavior Analysis, 10,* 349–67.

Ward, S., & Jacobsen, K. (2014). A clinical model for developing executive function skills. *Perspectives on Language Learning and Education, 21*(2), 72–84.

22
Provide Positive and Constructive Feedback to Guide Students' Learning and Instruction

Kristen Merrill O'Brien
George Mason University

Michelle M. Cumming
Florida International University

Patricia Gann
Florida International University

Gino D. Binkert
George Mason University

Introduction

To guide the learning of students with disabilities, effective feedback is one of the most powerful instructional tools available to teachers (Hattie, 2012; Hattie & Timperley, 2007). Feedback is defined as the information provided to an individual about their performance or understanding (Hattie & Timperley, 2007). Providing feedback is critical to the learning process, as students need to know what they are doing accurately, how to correct any errors, and how to progress towards their learning goals. Given the importance of feedback to support students in learning new content and skills, providing positive and constructive feedback is a valuable high leverage practice (HLP) special education teachers can use in their instructional practice. Instructional feedback is particularly important for students with disabilities who require intensive intervention. Students with disabilities receiving intensive intervention often have difficulty with grade-level content and have significant instructional support needs, making it important that special education teachers are able to provide effective instruction through HLPs that increase students' understanding, including feedback.

Research has shown that students' learning and achievement improve when special education teachers provide effective feedback (Hattie et al., 2017; Hattie & Timperley, 2007). What is key to providing feedback, however, is that it is done effectively, as not all feedback has been shown to improve student outcomes (Shute, 2008). In fact, some types of feedback can be detrimental to student learning (Hattie & Clarke, 2019). Thus, in order to harness the power of instructional feedback for students with disabilities receiving intensive intervention, special educators need to know how to correctly use this HLP.

DOI: 10.4324/9781003276876-27

Narrowing the Focus

As there is a large body of research on feedback as an instructional practice, a thorough review of the literature on feedback is beyond the scope of this chapter. Although feedback can be delivered by various people (e.g., teachers, peers, oneself) and in many different ways (e.g., verbally, written, immediate, delayed, using technology), in this chapter we focus on the instructional feedback provided by a teacher to a student to guide students' academic learning (see HLP 8 on feedback to guide students' behavior). Throughout this chapter, we provide best practices for using positive and constructive feedback to guide learning for students with disabilities receiving intensive intervention.

Chapter Overview

1. Describe how to use three types of feedback (i.e., confirm, refine, clarify) to target students' learning needs at appropriate levels.
2. Describe essential features of feedback used to guide student learning.
3. Provide examples and non-examples of instructional feedback.
4. Explain how to teach students to receive and use feedback.
5. Describe how to monitor and intensify feedback to meet student needs.

Using the HLP

Having an understanding of how to effectively provide feedback to guide students' learning is an important HLP for all special educators. In this section, we present a case study of Miguel, followed by descriptions of how to use feedback to target students' needs at appropriate levels, the essential feedback features, how to teach students to receive and use feedback, and how to intensify feedback. Throughout this section, we provide examples of how Miguel's teacher uses feedback to support his learning.

Case Study: Meet Miguel

Miguel is a 5th grade student in self-contained class for students with varying exceptionalities who has an emotional and behavioral disorder (EBD) and, recently, has also been identified as having a specific learning disability (SLD) in reading. Although learning and processing difficulties were noted in his initial evaluation in third grade, a classification of SLD in reading was not considered due to two rule-out factors. First, Miguel's problematic classroom behaviors prevented him from fully engaging in academic instruction, particularly reading. Second, the IEP team determined, as a beginning English Language learner, Miguel's limited English proficiency at the time impacted his reading vocabulary and comprehension ability. Despite making progress with his English proficiency in third and fourth grade, Miguel's reading skills continued to be below grade level despite receiving instruction. A subsequent reevaluation in fifth grade revealed that Miguel had a SLD in reading. As a result, Miguel receives intensive reading instruction in a small group setting with Ms. Faust, his special education teacher.

Ms. Faust has set up her 90-minute intensive reading group to not only target students' word-reading difficulty through explicit instruction in phonics and grapheme-phoneme correspondence, but also develop students' reading fluency and comprehension with grade-level content. She uses screening and progress monitoring data to guide her lessons so that instruction corresponds to student need. Ms. Faust also ensures that lessons afford students plenty of opportunities to respond, engage in guided practice, and receive individualized feedback.

Types of Feedback: Confirm, Refine, or Clarify

Feedback is crucial to shaping student learning by simultaneously building academic achievement and minimizing problematic behaviors (e.g., off-task, disruptive behaviors) often associated with students' perception of tasks deemed too difficult (Collins & Cook, 2016; Oakes et al., 2018). Typically, feedback is part of a three-part contingency in which the teacher provides a cue (e.g., teacher tells student to solve the long division problem), followed by a student action (e.g., student solves the first problem), followed by teacher feedback (e.g., teacher notes the answer is correct or incorrect; Hattie & Clarke, 2019; Oakes et al., 2018). This process is repeated as needed to improve student learning outcomes. Feedback typically can either confirm understanding (e.g., "You followed each of the long-division steps in order. Your answer is correct!"), refine understanding (e.g., "I see you followed the first two steps correctly, but skipped the third step. Let's list the long-division steps again."), or clarify misunderstanding (e.g., "I think we got different answers on this problem. Let's look at the long-division steps together."). Overall, with a focus on learning, feedback can be a powerful means to decrease discrepancies between student understanding and performance (Hattie, 2012; Shute, 2008).

Focusing Feedback at the Appropriate Level

Whether confirming, refining, or clarifying, feedback is most powerful in enhancing students' academic success when it is (a) intricately intertwined with instruction; (b) based on learning needs; and (c) targeted at the appropriate level (Hattie & Timperley, 2007; Oakes et al., 2018). Specifically, teachers can engage in feedback that focuses on the accuracy of the task (i.e., task-level feedback), the processes students used to understand and/or complete the task (i.e., process-level feedback), the self-regulation students used to move forward with confidence and self-efficacy on the task (i.e., self-regulation-level feedback), or the student's personal attributes, such as intelligence (i.e., self-level feedback). Task-level feedback tends to relate to students' surface-level learning, such as when students learn, remember, reproduce, and apply learned knowledge. As students progress in deepening their learning, which involves more complex processes (e.g., knowledge construction, transferal to more challenging tasks), feedback should shift to the process and self-regulation levels. Although task-level feedback is powerfully effective, when it is relied on solely, it can actually limit students' ability to progress in enacting effective strategies or using self-regulation skills. As such, feedback should move students from task to process and then from process to self-regulation (Hattie, 2012), with teachers avoiding use of ineffective self-level feedback (e.g., "You are so smart!") that is typically *not* focused on the task and student learning goals. In the following sections, we provide more in-depth guidance on providing effective feedback at each level.

Task-Level Feedback

Feedback at the task level focuses on providing students guidance on whether they are doing the task correctly and/or how they can accurately complete the task by (a) adding more information; (b) correcting erroneous information; or (c) including different information (Hattie & Timperley, 2007). For example, if students do the task correctly, the teacher can confirm they did it correctly and encourage them to continue working on the next task (e.g., "You correctly calculated the slope! You are ready to move onto the next problem"). If teachers find that there is missing, erroneous, or incorrect information, feedback could focus on what students can do to improve the task. For instance, a teacher may provide the correct answer or indicate additional or different information is needed (e.g., "Please add a bit more information about your extended family members in your family tree assignment; it looks like you're missing the adjectives to describe your three favorite relatives"). Although this type of feedback is highly effective at improving academic outcomes (Thurlings et al.,

2013), teachers should determine whether task errors are due to errors related to interpretation rather than lack of knowledge. If students lack knowledge on how to do the task properly, then further instruction is far more effective than providing task-level feedback. For example, Ms. Faust notices that Miguel does not know how to read words ending in "gh" (e.g., trough). Instead of providing feedback on additional oral reading attempts, Ms. Faust provides further instruction. Once Miguel has been taught this skill, she can now use task-level feedback during instruction. Ms. Faust says to Miguel, "Wow, you read that entire list of words correctly, remembering that 'gh' is pronounced /f/ in cough, rough, and laugh! Now let's try reading these words in our passage."

Process-Level Feedback

Process-level feedback is focused on the process or strategies students use to comprehend and per-form a task (Hattie & Timperely, 2007). This type of feedback is most effective at enhancing deeper learning when students have a clear understanding of the task. Process- and task-level feedback are closely linked, as feedback at the process level can help students develop and use effective strategies to complete a task or, if they completed the task well, continue to use effective strategies (e.g., "I see you have found the correct number of atoms in the first element. Be sure to use the same strategy for the next element!"). Additionally, process-level feedback can help students search for additional information if needed or develop strategies to detect errors in their work. For example, if a student is missing important information from an assignment, the teacher can provide process-level feedback to guide the student in effectively searching for additional information and determining if found information is relevant to the task (e.g., "I see more information is needed about different types of fish in your science presentation. Please be sure to use the information searching strategy you learned to find and add important information about fish."). If the task has errors, the teacher can provide feedback on using strategies to detect and correct those errors. For example, to help Miguel address his difficulty with verb tense use in writing, Ms. Faust says, "Miguel, I would like you to use the strategy we learned previously by underlining all the verbs in your draft and then determine if the correct tense was used in the sentence."

Self-Regulation Level Feedback

Feedback at the self-regulation level refers to feedback that enhances students' ability to monitor and regulate their own thoughts, emotions, and actions towards a learning goal, so that they can become self-regulated learners (Nicol & Macfarlane-Dick, 2006). This type of feedback is particularly important for helping students deepen their learning and confidence by building internal feedback and metacognitive skills (i.e., thinking about their thinking) to effectively engage in self-regulation strategies. For instance, teachers can provide feedback aimed at actively building their students' self-assessing and self-monitoring strategies so that they can (a) review and evaluate the accuracy of their own work (e.g., "How can you effectively check your work?"); (b) assess the effectiveness of used strategies (e.g., "Which strategy was most beneficial?"); and (c) determine next steps needed to reach their learning goals, such as planning (e.g., "How can you reach your goal?"), modifying strat-egies (e.g., "What other strategy can you use?"), or increasing/reducing goal complexity ("You have met this goal, so how can we make it a little more challenging?"). Teachers can also foster students' use of help-seeking strategies (Hattie & Timperley, 2007; Nicol & Macfarlane-Dick, 2006). A critical piece of help-seeking behavior is related to emotions, such that students may avoid help-seeking if they perceive they may be embarrassed or ostracized; thus, teachers will need to be mindful of cre-ating a safe space for students. For instance, Ms. Faust determines Miguel has attained reading skill proficiency on a text and wants to move him up to the next reading level. She also wants to build his self-assessment and help-seeking skills as she notices he rarely asks for help. During class, she tells

Miguel, "If you encounter a word you do not recognize, I want you to use the learned strategies to sound it out and determine which strategy is most effective. If you encounter a word you can't sound out, please remember to come directly to me to ask for a cue on how to best sound out the word." Because less proficient learners tend to have minimal self-regulation skills, it will be important for teachers to focus on the task- and process-level before moving to the self-regulation level.

Self-Level Feedback

Feedback at the self-level refers to providing feedback (often positive) about the student as a person (e.g., intelligence, personality, appearance) and not on the task, the process, or self-regulation (Hattie & Timperley, 2007; Shute, 2008). Although often used in classrooms and combined with task-level feedback, self-level feedback (e.g., "You are so smart! Good girl!") is highly ineffective, as it contains no information about the task to help increase students' understanding or engagement. Additionally, self-level feedback may actually impede student learning, as it deflects attention from the task and places value judgements on the student, which can influence how they feel about themselves (Hattie, 2012; Nicol & Macfarlane-Dick, 2006). For instance, a student may be praised for being intelligent and, as a result, avoid tackling challenging assignments for fear of failing to meet this expectation. For example, Miguel read a paragraph aloud with no mistakes. Ms. Faust in her excitement wanted to say, "You are a rockstar reader and awesome student!" But she remembered the importance of avoiding self-level feedback. Instead, she said, "Miguel, I noticed how you sounded out each word using the strategy we learned. Well done!" Overall, when feedback is directed at the correct level, it can maximize students' learning and performance.

Effective Feedback Features

To effectively enact HLP 22, it is critical for teachers to have an understanding of what features of feedback are most important. Special educators should not only provide feedback that confirms, refines, or clarifies understanding and is aimed at the appropriate level of learning (i.e., task, process, or self-regulation), but they should also provide feedback that is (a) goal-directed and actionable; (b) specific; (c) immediate; (d) developmentally appropriate; and (e) culturally responsive. We describe each of these features below and give examples and non-examples of each in Tables 22.1 and 22.2.

Goal-directed and Actionable Feedback

To help students move their learning forward, students need to have a clear idea of their academic goals and their progress towards those academic goals. Feedback is the instructional tool teachers can use to help guide students from their current level of understanding or performance to their academic goal. It is, therefore, critical that teachers provide students with feedback that is goal-directed and actionable. To do so, teachers should provide feedback that helps students answer three questions (Hattie, 2012; Hattie & Timperley, 2007):

1. **Where am I going?** In this first feedback question, the focus is on clarifying the learning goal for the student. When answering this question, teachers provide feedback that clearly describes the expected outcome and what successful goal attainment looks like. For example, Ms. Faust says to Miguel, "Remember that today our goal is to figure out if a statement in our passage is fact or opinion. Let's go through each of the underlined statements to determine if they are a fact or an opinion."

Table 22.1 Feedback Examples during Intensive Instruction—Elementary Level

Feedback Feature	Lesson Scenario	Feedback Examples	Feedback Non-Examples
Goal-directed and Actionable	Malik is a 4th grader receiving intensive small group math instruction about place value.	• Malik, good work identifying the place and value of each underlined digit. You're off to a great start! • Let's look back at this number, Malik. The 8 is not in the hundreds place. Take a look again, and remember to use your place value chart to help you identify what place it is in.	• Good job, Malik. Keep working towards that math goal! • Uh oh, Malik, I don't think these are all correct. Let's try again.
Specific	Nadia is a 1st grader in 1-on-1 reading intervention lesson about retelling story events in sequential order.	• Yes, Nadia, that is the first event that happened. You put the picture in the first box because it is the start of the story. Great work! • Nadia, let's look at the picture you just put in the second box. It's a picture of when the wolf leaves the three pigs. Is that what happens right after the first picture? Remember, we want to find what happens next.	• Good girl, Nadia! • Way to go! • No, try again. • That's wrong. Any other ideas?
Immediate	Rosslyn is a 3rd grader receiving small math group instruction on multiplication.	• Rosslyn, that is correct; the answer to 4x2 is 8. Great job using the math manipulatives to create your 2 groups of 4! Do the next one and let me see how you set up the problem. • Ok, let's see how did you on setting up the next problem. Yes, that's perfect; you have 3 groups of 3! Now it's time to solve!	• Rosslyn, that answer you wrote on the last worksheet is incorrect. Go back and try again please. • Rosslyn, I circled the problems from last week's homework that you need to do again.
Developmentally Appropriate	Penelope is a 4th grade student in a small group science lesson on the correct order of the planets in the solar system.	• Penelope, you put your picture of Mars in the 2nd spot and picture of Venus in the 4th spot. Remember Mars, the red planet, comes after us in the 4th spot. Also, Venus is the hottest planet and next to the sun because it is so hot! • Remember our acronym: My Very (Venus) Easy Method (Mars) Just Speeds Up Nothing.	• Whoopsie, Penelope, we made an uh-oh! • Oh, rats! Someone needs to remember the differences between gas giants and planets that are not gas giants.
Culturally Responsive	Toshio is a 2nd grade student receiving small group intensive instruction in social studies.	• Toshio, I see that you are adding the cities you visited on your trip to see your grandmother in Japan. Do you know what else you need to include in your map? Remember to look at the first item on the directions list and check it off when done. Then look at the next item on the list.	• Toshio, you are so smart, just like your parents! • Toshio, this isn't done right. Fix it. • You need to add more detail to your map.

Table 22.2 Feedback Examples during Intensive Instruction—Secondary Level

Feedback Feature	Lesson Scenario	Feedback Examples	Feedback Non-Examples
Goal-directed and Actionable	Genevieve is a 10th grader receiving 1-on-1 instruction during the earth science block focused on igneous rocks.	• Great job, Genevieve! You finished matching the types of igneous rock, extrusive and intrusive! • Let's look at the graphic organizer asking for types of extrusive and intrusive rocks. You labeled granite as an extrusive rock. Reread your passage about intrusive rocks and what makes a rock intrusive.	• Almost, Genevieve! • You did great work! • Check your graphic organizer.
Specific	Amilios is a 9th grader receiving small group support during an algebra math block.	• Amilios, you're doing a great job of getting x by itself for rearranging equations. This is fantastic work! • Can you walk through this equation with a negative x and a negative on the other side of the equation? Whenever you multiple a negative by a negative, what should the result be? Take a look at your checklist support in your math notebook.	• You got this one wrong. Fix it, please. • We have done these multiple times; you should remember the process. • You only got one wrong, so it should be fine and won't hurt your grade.
Immediate	Malia is an 11th grader receiving small group English instruction on common idioms used in fiction passages.	• Malia let's stop and review the question you just answered on the idiom worksheet. • You wrote the definition of "cold shoulder" as someone turning their back on someone. That is the incorrect definition, so let's think this through and use previous context to help. Yes, you are correct Malia, it does mean to ignore someone!	• Malia, the last two homework assignments you have completed have some errors. Please fix them. • Malia I will be back around in 15 minutes. Reread your answers, as some of them might need to be redone.
Developmentally Appropriate	Evander is a 12th grader receiving 1-on-1 support in a social studies block focusing on the topic of geography.	• Evander, you are able to use the map to locate the state we live in and the capital of our state! • This question asks you to name the water between Asia and North America. You circled the Indian Ocean, but that is south of Asia and does not touch North America. Use this globe; put your finger on Asia and another finger on North America. What ocean is between your fingers?	• Evander, use the map legend and look west of North America and east of Asia. What is the body of water that is located there? • No, no, Evander. Be a good boy and reread the passage.

Table 22.2 Cont.

Feedback Feature	Lesson Scenario	Feedback Examples	Feedback Non-Examples
Culturally Responsive	Jerome is a 6th grader receiving small group instruction in his U.S. history class.	• I see that you are working really hard to complete your essay on the Civil War. The expectation is to include the history of a person who lived through the Civil War. Yesterday your small group brainstormed possible historical figures to include. Which historical figure did you connect with and why? Great! Please include details about them in your essay. Can you tell me what your next steps are going to be?	• You just learned about the Civil War. Add more stuff. • There is so much information missing from this assignment. You're not trying hard enough.

2. **How am I going?** This second feedback question gives the student information about their progress towards the learning goal and how to continue working towards the learning goal. Often, this type of feedback specifies targeted criteria for success, past performance, or how well the student did on a given part of the task. For instance, Ms. Faust says during their small group writing lesson, "Miguel, let's see how you're doing on proofreading your paragraph. You have found exactly where the quotation marks go to show that someone is speaking. Nice work! It looks like you may have forgotten to check for commas, so please go back through the paragraph and look for where you might need commas."

3. **Where to next?** To provide information on the third feedback question, teachers tell students how to enhance their learning. By providing students with feedback that illuminates how to advance their learning, teachers can support students' self-regulation, deepen their understanding, and provide them with additional strategies to support their learning. When answering the third feedback question, Ms. Faust tells Miguel during their reading lesson, "Wow, you have worked so hard the past few weeks on learning the new reading strategies that help us to understand what we are reading. Tomorrow you will get to pick which strategy to use and we'll see how it helps you when reading a new story!"

The three feedback questions work together to help close the gap between students' current understanding and their desired end-state. Specifically, the feedback questions contribute to a coordinated understanding for students about their learning goals and the standards for reaching them, how they are doing in achieving those goals, and how to accelerate their progress toward goal attainment. By using these three questions, teachers can effectively provide feedback that is goal-directed and provides actionable steps towards goals, thereby maximizing the instructional potential of feedback.

Specific Feedback

Another hallmark of effective feedback is providing feedback that is specific rather than generic (Conroy et al., 2009; Thurlings et al., 2013). Specific feedback goes beyond just telling students whether a response was correct or incorrect by elaborating details about their response or action (i.e., what was correct or how to improve it; Collins & Cook, 2016). Using specific feedback clearly and explicitly teaches students what to do and prevents ambiguity. Research has shown that feedback is much more effective when it is specific; when feedback lacks specificity, students may become frustrated or perceive the feedback as useless (Shute, 2008). Thus, when giving instructional feedback, teachers should first verify whether their answer is correct or incorrect, and then provide specific information about the answer. Providing clear and specific feedback gives students explicit, content-focused information about their responses, which is especially important for students with disabilities receiving intensive intervention who have difficulties with academic content and need direct and explicit instruction.

In today's small group reading lesson, students are working on identifying the main idea of a nonfiction text. Miguel is using a graphic organizer to practice finding the main idea and two supporting details. Miguel has a supporting detail listed as the main idea, so Ms. Faust says, "Miguel, let's look at this one carefully, as this is not the main idea. Remember, when we look for the main idea in our text, we're looking for the idea that it is mostly about. Does this tell us what the story is mostly about, or does it give us detail? Yes, you are right—this is a detail because it provides specific information. Take a look back to see what the story is mostly about." Later when Miguel correctly identifies the main idea, Ms. Faust says to Miguel, "Yes, Miguel, you are right! You have found the main idea because 'animals have features that help them live in certain places' is what our text is mostly about. Great work finding the main idea!"

Immediate Feedback

To maximize students' learning gains, feedback should be provided immediately (Chan et al., 2014; Collins & Cook, 2016). When teachers provide immediate feedback, students can adjust their performance on-the-spot during the learning task. Using immediate feedback thereby allows students to efficiently use that information during academic performance when the task is still relevant (Brookhart, 2008). Further, using immediate feedback instead of delayed feedback can prevent students from continuing to practice with errors. Providing immediate feedback is particularly important during academic tasks that are difficult or when learning new skills (Shute, 2008). Thus, for students with disabilities who have more intensive academic support needs, immediate feedback is critical for their learning, as it allows for real-time error correction or reinforcement of correct responses.

Given the benefits of immediate learning, especially for students with disabilities who have more significant academic needs, it is also important that teachers give students opportunities to modify their performance following immediate feedback. When students accurately correct their learning errors following feedback, teachers can then follow-up with immediate affirmative feedback to reinforce their response. Thus, a key part of immediate feedback is also allowing for ongoing opportunities to practice with additional immediate feedback.

As Miguel is working on his graphic organizer to identify supporting details in a nonfiction text, Ms. Faust knows how important it is to give him feedback immediately. For example, last week when Ms. Faust was working with another student and took longer than usual to give Miguel feedback, she realized he had done multiple practice opportunities incorrectly. Thus, in today's lesson, for each response that Miguel provides, Ms. Faust makes sure that she immediately follows his response with feedback. For instance, during the small group lesson, Miguel and his peers gave a thumbs up or down unison response to questions about the main idea. After each response, Ms. Faust immediately told students the answer and elaborated on why it was correct or incorrect. During independent practice, Ms. Faust gave Miguel feedback right after each of his responses on his graphic organizer.

Developmentally Appropriate Feedback

Another important feature of instructional feedback is using developmentally appropriate feedback. Teachers must consider students' ability levels and prior knowledge when determining what type of feedback to provide. Feedback should be explicit, clear, and understood by the learner. Thus, teachers should use appropriate word choice and complexity of feedback to align with student needs. If teachers provide too little information, the feedback may not benefit the student, but if they provide too much detail or feedback that is too complex for a student's developmental level, then the feedback will not be understood. Thus, teachers should aim for the "just right" amount of feedback that is developmentally appropriate for that particular student. To ensure that feedback is developmentally appropriate, teachers can check for student understanding following feedback (Brookhart, 2008). If students are not demonstrating that they understand the feedback, teachers should adjust their feedback to be more developmentally appropriate.

In today's small group reading lesson, Ms. Faust is teaching how to compare and contrast the ideas in two nonfiction texts about foreign countries. During independent practice, Ms. Faust notices that Miguel found two similarities between the countries, but he is struggling to identify two differences within the nonfiction texts. Ms. Faust says to Miguel, "Yipee, you've got it! But uh oh—where are the differences?" Miguel appears confused about what exactly to do, so Ms. Faust adjusts her feedback and says, "You've done well with identifying similarities, but now it's time to contrast your two foreign countries. Return to the nonfiction texts and look for disparities." Ms. Faust now sees that Miguel is looking confused and still does not quite understand. She adjusts her feedback once more to be developmentally appropriate by saying, "Miguel, excellent work finding two similarities between France and Spain. Remember that we also need to find two differences. Can you look back at what we read and find something that is different between the two countries?"

Culturally Responsive Feedback

When instructing students with disabilities who come from culturally and linguistically diverse (CLD) backgrounds (e.g., students of color, indigenous, non-English dominant, immigrant, religious minority; Wang et al., 2022), teachers will need to ensure their feedback is culturally responsive. Cultural responsiveness incorporates non-dominant cultural characteristics of students (e.g., values, perspectives, experiences) into instruction to enhance content meaning and relatability (Gay, 2002), resulting in greater student motivation, engagement, and academic achievement (Aronson & Laughter, 2016). With the aim of confirming, refining, or clarifying understanding, teachers will need to ensure their feedback focuses on (a) setting high expectations (e.g., complete assignment requirements); (b) promoting social justice by validating students' cultural and linguistic lived experience, and (c) considering students' instructional preferences (e.g., role plays, group instruction) and needs (Aceves & Orosco, 2014). For instance, some students may demonstrate linguistic diversity in use of nondominant language (e.g., creole), while other students may exhibit diversity in communication style (The IRIS Center, 2012). In some cultures, dramatic presentation (e.g., pronounced gestures, emphasis on certain words) is a valued communication style and may differ from the school culture. Thus, instead of viewing this communication style as negative, teachers should ensure feedback validates the student's communication style and guides them to meet assignment expectations (e.g., "Remember that in this essay you are to write about a character who is experiencing an emotion. Think about ways your family members' body gestures and words convey if they are happy, angry, sad, and excited. How can you show that your character is experiencing one of these emotions in your essay?"). Furthermore, some students, whose families may have been in the United States for many generations may be from collective cultures (e.g., Asian, Latinx, Native American, Hawaiian) and value communal learning and achievement. Those students may prefer to work in cooperative learning groups, where they collaboratively problem-solve and practice new skills (Gay, 2002), and may benefit from feedback given at the small group level as well as at the individual level ("Your group has a good beginning and ending to your play about going to the market, but the middle would benefit from more details. Please discuss with your group what details are important to add.").

When providing culturally responsive feedback, it will be important for teachers to ensure not only that they encourage students to connect to cultural identities and experiences (e.g., assignments on relevant historical figures, current events), but also make connections between students' background knowledge and instructional content (Linan-Thompson, et al., 2018). For instance, teachers can activate students' prior knowledge to enhance the accuracy of their task ("I see that you have completed most parts about your essay on the Navajo barter system, but you are missing the examples. Can you think about how your community uses the barter system and include those as examples?"). In essence, not only is it important for teachers to affirm a student's culture and lived experiences for effective feedback, but it also helps to create an environment of acceptance and mutual respect within the classroom. To this end, it is essential that special education teachers become familiar with the cultures of their CLD students (Gay, 2002).

Miguel is reading aloud and mispronounces a word, placing emphasis on a syllable as if he were speaking in Spanish. Ms. Faust gives him immediate feedback by saying, "You read that word very well, Miguel. But when we are reading in English, the word is pronounced…" Ms. Faust is using culturally responsive feedback by acknowledging and valuing the cultural and linguistical origins of Miguel's way of pronouncing the word, while giving him feedback on the expected way of reading it in English. Overall, when teachers engage in culturally responsive feedback, they play an important role in addressing issues of inequity and social justice.

Teaching Students to Receive and Use Feedback

Not only do special education teachers need to attend to the types of feedback to ensure they are aimed at the appropriate level and the various features of effective feedback, but teachers should also consider explicitly teaching their students how to receive and use feedback if these are skills the student has not yet acquired. The quality of a teacher's feedback statements will not matter if a student is not able to appropriately use the feedback provided (Hattie & Clarke, 2019). Just as students with disabilities receiving intensive intervention may need explicit strategy instruction in other academic areas, these students may need to be directly taught how to receive and use feedback.

First, as with any use of explicit instruction, special educators may need to directly teach students the purpose and forms of feedback, model how to receive and use feedback, and provide guided and independent practice opportunities in how to appropriately receive and use feedback. Throughout this instruction, teachers should provide ongoing feedback on students' performance. In addition to explicit instruction on how to receive and use feedback, teachers can also ensure that they are providing sufficient opportunities for students to use provided feedback. For example, as Archer and Hughes (2011) discuss, after teachers provide a corrective statement (i.e., refining or clarifying feedback), it is important to then have students give the correct response. By building in these opportunities and reinforcing students for using feedback, students will have scaffolded practice opportunities in how to use feedback (e.g., "Remember that a verb shows action in the sentence. You identified Hector as the verb, but Hector is a person and not an action word. Can you look again to see what word might show action in our sentence?... Yes! 'Danced' is the verb. Great work using my feedback to find the right answer!"). Finally, teachers can provide instruction on self-regulation skills so that students are able to regulate their emotions to effectively receive feedback, set learning goals and self-monitor their use of feedback towards those goals, and solve problems in their use of feedback (Smith et al., 2015).

As Ms. Faust is reflecting on this week's small group reading instruction, she sees that in her data notebook she documented several instances where she provided feedback to Miguel but he did not appear to receive and/or use it. She is also noticing signs of frustration from Miguel during reading since it is a difficult subject for him. Ms. Faust decides to begin by teaching Miguel a breathing technique to control his anger, as emotion regulation will be key to being able to first receive instructional feedback. She also decides to use explicit instruction to teach Miguel a step-by-step strategy for receiving and using academic feedback (1. Stay calm. 2. Listen to the feedback. 3. Ask yourself if the feedback is clear. 4. Ask questions if needed. 5. Take action.). Ms. Faust knows that Miguel will need individualized instruction to learn this strategy, so she plans to explicitly teach Miguel the steps in the strategy by first modeling with a think aloud to show Miguel how she would use the strategy in a given scenario, followed by guided and independent practice opportunities in using the strategy to effectively receive and use instructional feedback.

Intensifying Feedback

As we have discussed throughout this chapter, feedback is the information the teacher explicitly provides students to confirm, refine, or clarify their understanding and work towards their learning goals. Thus, for students with disabilities who are receiving intensive intervention, using effective feedback is particularly critical for their learning. Importantly, feedback can be altered to increase instructional intensity and its effectiveness (Stevenson et al., 2017). Special education teachers can use data on student performance along with self-assessment data on their use of feedback to adjust the intensity of feedback to meet student needs.

As described in HLP 20, ongoing progress monitoring and data-based decision making are key to providing intensive instruction, as special education teachers engage in a continuous cycle of making data-based instructional adjustments and monitoring student performance. If assessment data shows that a student is not responding to instruction, feedback is one instructional component that can be modified to intensify the intervention. First, feedback can be intensified by increasing its frequency. For example, if a student is receiving feedback after every five responses or at the end of the lesson, this may not be enough for the student, so the feedback can be intensified to occur after every response. Another method for increasing the frequency of feedback is to examine the opportunities that students have to respond during the lesson (see Chapter 18). By increasing student engagement and responses during a lesson, special educators can create additional opportunities for feedback. Feedback can also be intensified by increasing the specificity of the feedback, which can increase the clarity and explicitness of error correction or further reinforce appropriate actions. Finally, the content of feedback can be modified to increase the use of effective features of feedback. For instance, special education teachers can examine the information provided to students through feedback to verify that the feedback is aimed at the correct learning level (i.e., task, process, self-regulation), goal-directed and actionable, developmentally appropriate, and culturally responsive. As with all intensive instruction, once feedback is intensified through adjustments, it will be critical to continue to collect progress monitoring data on student performance and data on teachers' use of feedback.

Assessing Feedback to Intensify Instruction

To determine which adjustments should be made to intensify feedback, special educators should examine the feedback that is currently being provided to the student. One way to assess their feedback is by using the CEEDAR Center's (2021) High Leverage Practices Self-Assessment Tool, with which special educators can self-assess and reflect on their current use of HLP 22. The data special educators collect with the HLP 22 section of this assessment tool can illuminate any aspects of providing instructional feedback that may not be fully or accurately applied. Lower ratings on any items in the HLP 22 section indicate areas where special education teachers could implement instructional adjustments as a way to intensify instruction.

Table 22.3 HLP 22 Checklist—Special Education Teacher Self-Assessment of Instructional Feedback

Observation Information

Observer:
Date:
Lesson length and setting (e.g., subject, instructional grouping):
Target student:

Directions

During the observation, for each response the student provides, put a tally in the *Number of Student Responses*. If the teacher provides a feedback statement following that response, put a tally in the *Number of Feedback Statements*. For each feedback statement observed, put a tally for (a) each statement that is or is not aimed at the *appropriate instructional level* and (b) each *Feedback Feature* that is reflected by the statement. Refer back to the HLP 22 chapter for definitions and examples of feedback statement features, as needed, to ensure accurate counts.

Total Feedback Statements Observed

Number of Student Responses	*Number of Feedback Statements*
Total:	Total:

Feedback Statement Features

Aimed at the Appropriate Instructional Level (task, process, self-regulation)?		*Feedback Features*				
Yes	No	Goal-directed / actionable	Specific	Immediate	Developmentally appropriate	Culturally responsive
Total:	Total:	Total:	Total:	Total:	Total:	Total:

Another way to assess their use of feedback is to monitor the feedback they provide during instruction. In Table 22.3, we have created an HLP 22 checklist that teachers can use to self-monitor the feedback that they provide to students during a lesson. We recommend that when using this checklist, special education teachers should either (a) record a lesson and use the video evidence to complete the checklist or (b) have a colleague observe their instruction and use the checklist as they observe. After using the checklist, teachers can examine which effective feedback features could be potential areas for adjusting feedback to intensify instruction.

Finally, teachers may choose to gather additional data on their use of feedback by gathering student perceptions about the teacher's use of feedback. Special educators can ask students if the feedback they are given provides enough clarification and specificity, occurs at the right timing (i.e.,

Table 22.4 Example of a Completed HLP 22 Checklist—Special Education Teacher Self-Assessment of Instructional Feedback

Observation Information

Observer: *MS. FAUST*
Date: *OCTOBER 15*
Lesson length and setting (e.g., subject, instructional grouping): *15 MINUTES, READING SMALL GROUP*
Target student: *MIGUEL*

Directions

During the observation, for each response the student provides, put a tally in the *Number of Student Responses*. If the teacher provides a feedback statement following that response, put a tally in the *Number of Feedback Statements*. For each feedback statement observed, put a tally for (a) each statement that is or is not aimed at the *appropriate instructional level* and (b) each *Feedback Feature* that is reflected by the statement. Refer back to the HLP 22 chapter for definitions and examples of feedback statement features, as needed, to ensure accurate counts.

Total Feedback Statements Observed

Number of Student Responses	*Number of Feedback Statements*
11111 11111	*11111 11*
Total: *10*	Total: *7*

Feedback Statement Features

Aimed at the Appropriate Instructional Level (task, process, self-regulation)?		*Feedback Features*				
Yes	No	Goal-directed / actionable	Specific	Immediate	Developmentally appropriate	Culturally responsive
11111 1	*1*	*111*	*111*	*11111*	*11111 11*	*11111*
Total: *6*	Total: *1*	Total: *3*	Total: *3*	Total: *5*	Total: *7*	Total: *5*

immediacy) and frequency (i.e., amount), is clear and understandable, and provides helpful information about what to continue doing or change to work towards their learning goals. Oakes et al. (2018) suggest that teachers can share student data directly with the student when asking for their perspectives on provided feedback so that students can link the use of feedback to learning goals, processes, and outcomes.

Ms. Faust wants to assess her use of feedback with Miguel during small group reading instruction. Ms. Faust records her lesson after securing appropriate permissions, and as she watches the recording, she completes the HLP 22 Checklist. As shown in Table 22.4, Ms. Faust notices after analyzing the data that Miguel had 10 opportunities to respond during the 15-minute lesson, and she provided feedback after 7 of the 10 responses from Miguel (70% of statements received feedback).

Of Ms. Faust's 7 feedback statements, most (n=6; 86%) were aimed at the appropriate instructional level. When analyzing the feedback features, all 7 statements were developmentally appropriate, and most (n=5; 71%) were immediate and culturally responsive. Only 3 of the 7 statements (43%) were goal-directed and actionable and specific. Thus, Ms. Faust decides to intensify her use of feedback by (a) increasing the number of feedback statements overall (i.e., give Miguel feedback after each response); (b) use goal-directed feedback that provides Miguel with actionable steps towards his learning goals; and (c) provide specific feedback to clearly confirm, refine, or clarify Miguel's responses. Ms. Faust decides she will continue to monitor her use of feedback during instruction to ensure Miguel continues to make progress towards his reading goals.

Wrap Up

Using instructional feedback to guide students' academic learning is one of the most powerful tools available to special educators, especially for students with disabilities receiving intensive instruction. In this chapter, we explained how feedback can be used to confirm, refine, or clarify student responses and can be delivered at three levels (i.e., task, process, self-regulation) to be most effective. We described the critical features of feedback: (a) goal-directed and actionable; (b) specific; (c) immediate; (d) developmentally appropriate; and (e) culturally responsive. We also outlined how teachers can intensify their use of feedback to meet students' needs. Providing positive and constructive feedback is a critical practice for all special educators, and one that can greatly influence student success.

Tips

1. **Provide students with ongoing and frequent opportunities to respond during instruction to inform feedback.** Without providing students ample practice and ways to actively engage during a lesson, teachers will lack opportunities to provide feedback on student performance. Thus, feedback is linked to HLP 16, *Use Explicit Instruction* and HLP 18, *Use Strategies to Promote Active Student Engagement*.
2. **Create a positive classroom environment to support students' use of feedback.** For students to effectively receive and use teacher-provided feedback, special education teachers must create and maintain a safe, respectful, and culturally responsive learning environment (HLP 7, *Establish a Consistent, Organized, and Respectful Learning Environment*). By creating a positive classroom climate where teacher-student relationships are mutually respectful and diversity is valued by all, students will be in a learning environment that supports and facilitates the use of instructional feedback.
3. **Match the intensity of your feedback to the intensity of the student's instructional needs.** As with all intensive instruction (see HLP 20, *Provide Intensive Instruction*), special education teachers should adjust the intensity of instruction to meet students' needs. Similarly, teachers should adjust their feedback to support individual students' learning goals. Just as teachers should intensify their use of feedback for students with greater support needs, they can provide less intense (e.g., less frequent, less specific) feedback as students gain proficiency.

Key Resources

Archer, A. L., & Hughes, C. A. (2011). *Explicit instruction: Effective and efficient teaching*. Guilford Press.

CEEDAR Center (2021, August 5). *High-Leverage Practices Self-Assessment Tool*. https://highleveragepractices.org/assessment-tools-high-leverage-practices-students-disabilities

Hammond, Z. (2015). *Culturally responsive teaching and the brain: Promoting authentic engagement and rigor among culturally and linguistically diverse students.* Corwin; Sage.

Hattie, J., & Timperley, H. (2007). The power of feedback. *Review of Educational Research, 77*, 81–112. https://doi.org/10.3102/003465430298487

The IRIS Center (2012). *Classroom diversity: An introduction to student differences.* https://iris.peabody.vanderbilt.edu/module/div/

National Center on Intensive Intervention (n.d.). *Explicit Instruction Course, Module 7 Part 1: How Should Feedback Be Provided?* https://intensiveintervention.org/explicit-instruction-supporting-practices-feedback-pace

Kennedy, M. J., Peeples, K. N., Romig, J. E., Mathews, H. M., & Rodgers, W. J. (2018). High-leverage practices #8 & #22: Provide positive and constructive feedback to guide students' learning and behavior. https://highleveragepractices.org/hlps-8-and-22-provide-positive-and-constructive-feedback-guide-students-learning-and-behavior

Oakes, W. P., Lane, K. L., Menzies, H. M., & Buckman, M. M. (2018). Instructional feedback: An effective, low-intensity strategy to support student success. *Beyond Behavior, 27*(3), 168–74. https://doi.org/10.1177/1074295618799354

References

Aceves, T.C., & Orosco, M.J. (2014). *Culturally responsive teaching* (Document No. IC-2). University of Florida, Collaboration for Effective Educator, Development, Accountability, and Reform Center. https://ceedar.education.ufl.edu/wp-content/uploads/2014/08/culturally-responsive.pdf

Archer, A. L., & Hughes, C. A. (2011). *Explicit instruction: Effective and efficient teaching.* Guilford Press.

Aronson B., & Laughter J. (2016). The theory and practice of culturally relevant education: A synthesis of research across content areas. *Review of Educational Research, 86*(1), 163–206. https://doi.org/10.3102/0034654315582066

Brookhart, S. M. (2008). *How to give effective feedback to your students.* Association for Supervision and Curriculum Development.

CEEDAR Center (2021, August 5). *High-Leverage Practices Self-Assessment Tool.* https://highleveragepractices.org/assessment-tools-high-leverage-practices-students-disabilities

Chan, P. E., Konrad, M., Gonzalez, V., Peter, M. T., & Ressa, V. A. (2014). The critical role of feedback in formative instructional practices. *Intervention in School and Clinic, 50*, 96–104. https://doi.org/10.1177/1053451214536044

Collins, L. W., & Cook, L. (2016). Never say never: The appropriate and inappropriate use of praise and feedback for students with learning and behavioral disabilities. In B.G. Cook, M. Tankersley, & T. J. Landrum (Eds.), *Advances in learning and behavioral disabilities: Vol. 29. Instructional practices with and without empirical validity* (pp. 153–73). Emerald Publishing Limited.

Conroy, M. A., Sutherland, K. S., Snyder, A., AlHendawi, M., & Vo, A. (2009). Creating a positive classroom atmosphere: Teachers' use of effective praise and feedback. *Beyond Behavior, 18*(2), 18–26.

Gay, G. (2002). Preparing for culturally responsive teaching. *Journal of Teacher Education, 53*(2), 106–16. https://doi.org/10.1177/0022487102053002003

Hattie, J. (2012). *Visible learning for teachers: Maximizing impact on learning.* Routledge.

Hattie, J. & Clarke, S. (2019). *Visible learning: Feedback.* Routledge.

Hattie, J., Gan, M., & Brooks, C. (2017). Instruction based on feedback. In R. E. Mayer & P. A. Alexander (Eds.), *Handbook of research on learning and instruction* (2nd ed., pp. 376–417). Routledge. https://doi.org/10.4324/9781315736419

Hattie, J., & Timperley, H. (2007). The power of feedback. *Review of Educational Research, 77*(1), 81–112. https://doi.org/10.3102/003465430298487

The IRIS Center (2012). *Classroom diversity: An introduction to student differences.* https://iris.peabody.vanderbilt.edu/module/div/

Linan-Thompson, S., Lara-Martinez, J. A., & Cavazos, L. O. (2018). Exploring the intersection of evidence-based practices and culturally and linguistically responsive practices. *Intervention in School and Clinic, 54*(1), 6–13. https://doi.org/10.1177/1053451218762574

Nicol, D. J., & Macfarlane-Dick, D. (2006). Formative assessment and self-regulated learning: A model and seven principles of good feedback practice. *Studies in Higher Education, 31*(2), 199–218. https://doi.org/10.1080/03075070600572090

Oakes, W. P., Lane, K. L., Menzies, H. M., & Buckman, M. M. (2018). Instructional feedback: An effective, low-intensity strategy to support student success. *Beyond Behavior, 27*(3), 168–174. https://doi.org/10.1177/1074295618799354

Shute, V. J. (2008). Focus on formative feedback. *Review of Educational Research, 78*(1), 153–89. https://doi.org/10.3102/0034654307313795

Smith, S. W., Cumming, M. M., Merrill, K. L., Daunic, A. P., & Pitts, D. (2015). Teaching self-regulation skills to students with behavior problems: Essential instructional components. *Beyond Behavior, 24*(3), 4–11.

Stevenson, N. A., & Reed, D. K. (2017). To change the things I can: Making instruction more intensive. *Intervention in School and Clinic, 53*(2), 74–80. https://doi.org/10.1177/1053451217693365

Thurlings, M., Vermeulen, M., Bastiaens, T., & Stijnen, S. (2013). Understanding feedback: A learning theory perspective. *Educational Research Review, 9,* 1–15. https://doi.org/10.1016/j.edurev.2012.11.004

Wang, P., Jackson, D., Freeman-Green, S., Kamuru, J., & Driver, M. (2022). Integrating culturally sustaining pedagogy and evidence-based practices to support students with learning disabilities in a social justice mathematics lesson. *TEACHING Exceptional Children.* https://doi.org/10.1177/00400599221079640

23
Learning to Use HLPs for Intensive Interventions Reflections for Teachers, School Leaders, and Teacher Educators

James McLeskey
University of Florida
Bonnie Billingsley
Virginia Tech
Stephen D. Kroeger
University of Cincinnati

For many years, researchers have sought to identify practices that could be used by teachers to improve academic and behavioral outcomes for students with disabilities. While many effective practices have been identified by researchers, these practices have not been widely used by teachers (Cook & Odom, 2013; Grima-Farrell et al., 2011; McLeskey et al., 2018). Several scholars have speculated about why effective practices are often not used. For example, Carnine (1997) suggested that much of the research conducted on effective instruction is not designed to make a difference in classroom practice. Predictably, teachers then lack confidence in these practices, and perceive them to have limited utility in the classroom.

Cook and Odom (2013) extended this idea by contending that researchers have placed insufficient emphasis on studying how effective practices may be implemented in classrooms. Some scholars have suggested that the recent emergence of implementation science (Fixsen et al., 2019; Ward et al., 2022) provides a framework for studying how effective practices might be used in classrooms. Still other frameworks have been proposed that, to some extent, address this implementation of practice concern, including Multi-tiered Systems of Support (MTSS) and Data-Based Individualization (Edmunds et al., 2019; Peterson et al., 2019). This emphasis on examining the impact of context when investigating evidence-based or other effective practices, and using frameworks such as Implementation Science, Multi-tiered System of Support (MTSS) and Data-based Individualization (DBI) have shown some limited promise for increasing the use of effective practices in classrooms (Edmunds et al., 2019; Fixsen et al., 2019; Ward et al. 2022).

A number of teacher educators have contended that how teachers are prepared also contributes to the lack of use of effective or evidence-based practices in classrooms. In short, these scholars have contended that teacher preparation is not designed to prepare teacher candidates to use practices

DOI: 10.4324/9781003276876-28

in classrooms (McLeskey et al., 2018). Shortcomings of teacher preparation programs include the following:

- For the most part, the preparation of teachers occurs in settings removed from PK-12 classrooms, and emphasis is placed on knowing *about* effective practices rather than focusing on preparing candidates to *use* practices in classrooms (Ball et al., 2009).
- There are few direct connections between courses offered in teacher preparation programs and field experiences, resulting in fragmentation between theory and practice and a major focus on the "conceptual underpinnings of teaching" rather than the practices teachers will need to know how to use when they enter the classroom (Grossman et al., 2009, p. 275).
- The particular practices that teacher candidates learn to use are most often left to chance, as these practices are learned during field experiences, the component of preparation that teacher educators have the least control over (Grossman & McDonald, 2008). Furthermore, the practices that teacher candidates happen to learn in field settings may or may not be effective practices (McLeskey et al., 2018).
- Teacher candidates are thus seldom systematically taught to use effective or evidence-based practices that are the foundation of effective teaching practice during their preparation programs (Forzani, 2014; McLeskey et al., 2018).

To begin to address these shortcomings, scholars across disciplines in teacher education (e.g., Grossman et al., 2009; McDonald et al., 2013; McLeskey & Brownell, 2015; Windschitl et al., 2019) have recommended the identification of a limited set of practices that are highly effective in improving student outcomes (i.e., high-leverage practices). Of course, identifying these practices is only a necessary first step, followed by the need to design effective approaches that will support teacher candidates in learning to use these practices with students in classrooms.

Extensive research has been conducted regarding what is needed to design effective approaches to support the development of expertise in teaching and across other professions (Benedict et al., 2016; Brownell et al., 2019; Ericsson & Pool, 2016). This research has consistently demonstrated that learning to use complex skills requires carefully planned, structured opportunities to practice the skill (or instructional practice) in settings that are authentic, supported by feedback from an effective coach (Benedict et al., 2016; Brownell et al., 2019). When used in teacher education, these practice-based opportunities "provide candidates time to apply content pedagogy, to gain real experience, to understand school relationships—and, most importantly—to work with students within a supervised context" (Benedict et al., 2016).

A similar approach has also been shown to be effective when supporting practicing teachers to learn to use complex practices in their classrooms (Billingsley et al., 2019). In the next section, we provide some reflections for teachers regarding the information discussed in this book, and address the qualities of effective professional development that are needed to provide the necessary support for teachers to learn to use these HLPs effectively in their classrooms (Leko et al., 2022). This section is then followed by reflections for school leaders and teacher educators regarding the HLPs and supporting teacher candidates and current teachers as they learn to use these practices.

Reflections for Teachers

Many of the HLPs that are described in this book should be familiar to special education teachers, as these practices are addressed in textbooks, conference presentations, professional development activities, and so forth and are fundamental to delivering intensive interventions. However, you will also recognize that naming these practices is relatively simple, the difficult part comes in learning to use the practices in classrooms to provide intensive interventions for students with disabilities. As we noted previously, high quality professional development that will be most helpful in supporting teachers as they learn to use these practices in classrooms shares several components. For example, Desimone and Garet (2015) have identified five qualities of effective professional development (PD) that include:

1. *Active learning* that includes opportunities such as observing the use of the practice and trying the practice and receiving feedback, rather than passively listening to someone talk about the practice.
2. *Coherence* to ensure that the content, goals, and activities included in professional learning fit into the school curriculum and goals and align with the teachers knowledge and beliefs and the identified needs of their students.
3. *Collective participation* of a group of teachers who are motivated to learn the practice and willing to work collaboratively to support everyone in learning to use the practice.
4. *Sustained duration* through the school year to ensure that sufficient time is available to (a) gain knowledge regarding the teaching practice; (b) learn about the components of the practice; and (c) have sufficient opportunities to try out the practice with coaching and feedback. Research on professional learning of teachers has shown that it takes at least 20 hours of contact time, and often more, to have a good beginning in learning to use a complex practice.
5. *Content focus* of the professional learning provides a clear context for applying the practice and allow opportunities to focus on how students learn the content in a particular area (e.g., reading, mathematics).

We would encourage you to seek out professional development that is designed with most or all of these qualities in mind. We have found that principals often provide leadership for developing and supporting this type of professional development in highly effective, inclusive schools (e.g., DeMatthews, 2020; Hoppey et al., 2019; Hoppey & McLeskey, 2013; Waldron et al., 2011). At other times, small groups of teachers work collaboratively to support one another and share expertise in learning to use effective practices. If these types of professional learning opportunities are available in your school or school district, we would encourage you to take advantage of them.

Even if these types of collective professional learning are not available, our experience indicates that a valuable resource for learning to use complex practices that is available to all teachers is other teachers in your school or school district with expertise related to particular effective practices. We would encourage you to seek out these teachers, as they are often willing to have you observe in their classrooms, respond to questions and discuss issues related to using the practice. Furthermore, your principal or special education supervisor may be willing to work out the logistics so you can arrange a time when this teacher can come to your classroom to provide coaching regarding the use of the practice.

The HLPs for special educators obviously include a wide range of complex practices. Gaining expertise related to these practices should be done strategically (e.g., consider which will make the most difference as you provide intensive interventions for your students) and coherently by not taking on too many practices at once, and by planning your learning around a coherent group of HLPs. This could be done, for example, by addressing several HLPs that are needed to provide intensive instruction to a small group of early elementary students in reading (or some other content area and grade level that is relevant and important for you and your students). The HLPs that are addressed could then include HLP20 (provide intensive instruction), coupled with some combination of HLP15 (provide scaffolding), HLP16 (explicit instruction), HLP18 (promote engagement), HLP22 (provide feedback), HLP6 (formative assessment), and several others. Of course, you will already have expertise related to some of these practices, which with give you a head start on improving your expertise. Furthermore, practices we already know how to use could also be shared with others if you participate with one or more colleagues.

Finally, both the wisdom of practice and research have demonstrated that nothing is more important to improving academic and behavioral outcomes for students with disabilities than improving the practice of their teachers. This is especially the case for students who have more complex needs that require intensive interventions. We recognize that delivering this instruction in schools can be challenging, and very much appreciate the many teachers we know and have worked with who have taken on this demanding task. We hope you have found that the information we have provided regarding HLPs and intensive interventions in this book will make this task somewhat more manageable as your career proceeds. All the best in the years to come!

Reflections for School Leaders

The HLPs described in this book are relevant to principals' work as instructional leaders, as they support special and general education teachers' use of effective instructional practices. Although principals may have some preparation related to the legal requirements of special education, relatively few have preparation that addresses effective instructional practices that support students with disabilities (DeMatthews et al., 2020). Thus, leaders can use these chapters as a succinct guide for learning about practices that have a strong evidence base for student learning (Nelson et al., 2021) and share them with teachers in their schools.

Principals who are knowledgeable about these HLPs are also in a stronger position to communicate with professionals and families about the needs of students with disabilities. We identify four ways principals can use HLP to support teacher effectiveness through systemic school improvement (McLeskey et al., 2022), including using them as an instructional framework; providing content for induction and mentoring; identifying priorities for professional learning; and creating conditions to support quality instruction.

Using HLPs as an Instructional Framework

The HLPs provide an instructional framework to support communication and a shared language about effective instruction (Windschitl et al., 2012), providing guidance to all in the school about teaching students with disabilities. Principals should involve teacher leaders as they consider how to introduce and support these core practices throughout the school. One strategy is to begin with HLP 1 (collaborate with professionals to increase student success) as each student with a disability needs a program that is developed and coordinated among all educators in the school. For example, HLP 1 may be introduced to emphasize the importance of a collective responsibility for students with disabilities throughout the school and to consider the specific roles of special and general education teachers as they work in inclusive schools. HLP 1 also provides a foundation for teachers' work together as they use the assessment, social/behavioral, and instructional HLPs to address specific student needs.

Providing Content for Induction and Mentoring

HLPs may also serve as content for induction and mentoring, reducing the uncertainty about which instructional practices new special educators should use. Special educators who were taught HLPs in their preservice program should recognize some of these practices, creating coherence between their preservice development and expectations in their first year in the classroom (Billingsley et al., 2019). For new teachers who have not yet completed a teacher preparation program, these chapters provide a clear set of instructional guidelines.

Mentors across the district should work together to consider how HLPs will be incorporated in an induction program. They might consider priorities for HLPs during orientation to help new teachers set priorities for the first weeks of school (e.g., HLP 7, establish a consistent, organized, and respectful learning environment). Mentors and leaders should also consider how they will support special education teachers (SETs) in learning to use specific HLPs over time. For example, they may introduce a practice in a faculty meeting, schedule PD that reviews and demonstrates the practice, provide coaching as each teacher begins to use the practice, and assess progress through informal observations and feedback.

Identifying Priorities for Professional Learning

HLPs need to be systematically introduced and taught, using the same qualities of effective PD introduced earlier in this chapter (see Desimone & Garet, 2015). Supporting teacher learning through lesson study facilitates special and general education co-teaching as they apply an HLP to teaching in a specific content area (e.g., apply HLP 16 explicit instruction in reading instruction). Leaders may also consider encouraging teachers to become experts in a particular HLP, supporting a team of teacher leaders throughout the district who can support HLP development. Mentors and leaders should also consider observing the use of specific HLPs during instruction and discuss their use in informal, follow-up conferences. Finally, principals and district leaders may also consider sharing a list of the online HLP videos (see https://highleveragepractices.org/) and IRIS modules (see https://iris.peabody.vanderbilt.edu/resources/high-leverage-practices/) relevant to each HLP, providing resources teachers can use as they consider their specific learning goals.

Creating Conditions to Support High-Quality Instruction

Leaders and teachers need to consider the instructional conditions that support the use of specific HLPs. For example, to support flexible grouping (HLP 17) teachers need access to students with similar learning needs, and the time and materials necessary for instruction. Teachers may also need access to technology resources to incorporate assistive and instructional technologies (HLP 19) necessary to support student learning. Thus, the HLPs provide teachers and leaders with opportunities to consider the time, schedules, and resources needed to support instruction.

In summary, the HLPs provide leaders with a set of core practices they can use to support teachers' effectiveness in schools. These HLPs can be adopted as a framework for teaching students with disabilities in a school or district. At the same time. these HLPs should be supported flexibly, engaging teachers in discussions about their use. SETs also need opportunities to use practices beyond the 22 HLPs, which will be determined by their specific instructional roles (e.g., reading instruction, transition planning). Leaders who are knowledgeable about HLPs should be better able to support these practices, increasing both their effectiveness and credibility as instructional leaders.

Reflections for Teacher Educators

The following reflections are based on the work of colleagues and myself (Steve Kroeger) at the University of Cincinnati. As teacher educators, we know (Kourieos, 2019; Lampert & Graziani, 2009; Rawlins et al., 2019) that our preservice teachers must be able to skillfully combine teaching content with knowledge about their students. A toolbox of effective teaching skills is essential. Knowing how to support candidate growth in using effective strategies, moving from novice to an advanced beginner (Dreyfus, 2002), will influence how we prepare students in our programs. Yet, we also know that such movement in expertise requires extensive practice and support. Without such intensive practice our candidates will be able to implement few effective practices, and when they do implement them, it will be with inconsistent fidelity (Brock, 2016; Cox et al., 2013). We need reliable strategies for preparing candidates to use critical practices by the time they complete our programs.

Several years back, while co-teaching with a pair of middle childhood science educators, I observed them and their students using a rehearsal procedure that allowed the course participants to enact science lessons that they planned and then co-taught to each other. Digging deeper, I learned that they called the process *microteaching*. I quickly discovered that this decades-old practice had a substantial evidence base, suggesting its efficacy as a teacher preparation tool and strategy (Hattie, 2009). Over the past several years, to observe and participate in the goal of supporting our candidates in becoming advanced beginners, the faculty of our special education preparation program at the University of Cincinnati began to systematically develop the use of microteaching (Kroeger et al., 2022).

Microteaching is a practice learning opportunity (PLO) showing strong impact on the quality of teacher instructional behavior and student learning outcomes (Hattie, 2009). Microteaching uses a structured approach of bounded practice that makes it possible to focus on specific teaching behaviors (Allen & Eve, 1968). The practice learning opportunity asks teachers to assess the impact of their teaching practices on learning, collaborate with colleagues on professional development, and extend the expertise of coaches by engaging in active learning activities in the classroom (Cordingley et al., 2015; Opfer & Pedder, 2011; Postholm, 2012; Timperley et al., 2007; Wei et al., 2010). Microteaching has four sequential phases (see Figure 23.1). The process begins with a planning phase, followed by a recorded teaching session, then a written individual reflective commentary, and ending with a collaborative assessment phase (Kroeger et al., 2022).

The four phases of microteaching are broken down into components which are included in Table 23.1. During planning, learning goals and objectives are determined, as well as a data collection plan, peer recruitment and lesson planning. The microteaching phase consists of a 10–20-minute recorded lesson that demonstrates the use of an evidence-based practice used with a high leverage practice in a content area. The third phase is the reflective commentary where the candidate watches their recorded lesson and takes minute-by-minute notes of what they were doing and how students responded. The fourth phase is a collaborative assessment where the candidate leads a discussion about the lesson with peers and an instructional coach. They follow a protocol of ten questions for this discussion.

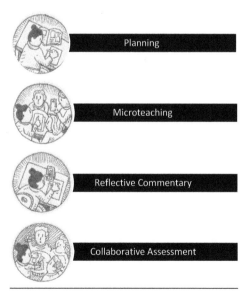

Figure 23.1 Four Phases of Microteaching

Table 23.1 Parts of the Four Phases of Microteaching

Microteaching is a system of bounded practice that makes it possible to focus on specific teaching behaviors		Purpose: Training, Diagnostic Evaluation, Innovation	
Phase 1	**Phase 2**	**Phase 3**	**Phase 4**
PLANNING	MICRO-TEACHING	REFLECTIVE COMMENTARY	COLLABORATIVE ASSESSMENT
• Identify and prioritize long & short-term learning goals • Develop the lesson plan • Communication skills, self-directed learning • Data collection, Recourses, EBP and HLPs • Plan the technology • Recruit peer support	• 10–20 minutes of instruction • Selected content area • Evidence-Based practice • High-Leverage Practice	• Individually, teacher completes analysis of the recorded teaching, asking: • *What was I doing and how were students responding?* • In a separate column, *what connections can I make to principles of learning-research?*	• Who reached the goal, and who struggled? • What part was problematic? • Misconceptions? • What practical experiences will help? • How to use what you learn about your students? • Collaboration: Celebrate or concerns? • Next Steps

Microteaching aligns well with several other practice-based approaches. Brownell and colleagues (2019, p. 341) identified eight approaches from the teacher preparation literature that incorporate the features of effective practice (see Table 23.2). Their review of the literature described the practice-based approaches, brief descriptions of each, impact on candidate outcomes and some general recommendations for use. The list they provided did not include microteaching. I have placed it with rehearsal (CEEDAR Center, n.d.) based on our experience and its parallel approach to rehearsal as it is described in Table 23.2.

Consistent with the knowledge base associated with practice-based learning, McDonald and colleagues (2013) highlighted a call for teachers to learn a set of core practices that require the use of in-the-moment professional judgment in a larger context of a community of practice. Citing what Mary Kennedy (1999) called the gap between what new teachers have learned and what they are able to do, the authors reimagined a learning cycle for preparing teachers. The learning cycle they proposed is conceptualized in four stages (see Figure 23.2). In one stage a core practice is introduced, modeled, and examined. In a second stage a core practice is planned and taught using microteaching or rehearsal (in our use of this cycle). In a third stage, a core practice is enacted with students. A fourth stage then includes a process of analysis and reflection that moves the practitioner forward.

The microteaching process, as we adapted it in our program, encapsulated each of the stages outlined by McDonald and colleagues (2013). To illustrate, we taught reciprocal teaching in one of our reading courses. Reciprocal teaching (Palinscar & Brown, 1984) is a set of cognitive and meta-cognitive strategies that support learning and independence (HLP14). Following Hovland's (2019) explanation of the reciprocal teaching process, we asked candidates to explicitly teach (HLP 16) each of the four reciprocal teaching skills of question asking, clarification, prediction, and summarization. The candidates microtaught five times across the semester, incrementally adding a new reading skill to the repertoire. In the fifth microteaching episode candidates were to seamlessly implement all four of the reciprocal teaching reading skills.

Table 23.2 Practice-based Approaches

Approach	Description
Case learning	Rich descriptions that provide information regarding the learner, context, and an instructional scenario to improve candidates' knowledge of instruction.
Rehearsal	Candidates teach peers who assume roles of K-12 learners using a particular practice in a tightly controlled setting (e.g., micro-teaching).
Virtual reality simulation	Similar to rehearsal, but candidates teach avatars in a tightly controlled setting.
Video analysis	Candidates view, analyze, and reflect upon a video of a lesson to better understand how instruction is enacted and the impact of instruction on student engagement and learning.
Peer/bug in ear coaching	Candidates are observed teaching and provided feedback from a peer or from a faculty supervisor.
Lesson study	Candidates are grouped into teams that plan, teach, observe, provide feedback, and revise lessons.
Aligned field experiences	Tightly coordinated, structured opportunities are provided for candidates to apply what they are learning from coursework in field experiences.

Source: Adapted from Brownell et al. (2019).

Figure 23.2 The Four Stages of the McDonald Learning Cycle
Source: Adapted from McDonald et al., 2013.

The microteaching process utilized the steps of the McDonald (2013) learning cycle in the following ways. Consider the reciprocal teaching skill of question asking. Step one, faculty introduced, explained, and modeled a lesson using question asking. Step two, in the plan and practice step, candidates planned a question asking lesson and then practiced their lesson with a small group of peers using microteaching. Step three, in the analysis and reflection step, two sub-steps were employed. Sub-step one, immediately after the lesson was delivered to peers, the microteacher completed a minute-by-minute reflective commentary of their video recording, usually captured on the microteacher's smart phone. Sub-step two, the microteacher gathered with a team of peers and an instructional coach to collaboratively analyze the lesson and make plans for future implementation. It was not until the spring semester that step four, enact with K12 students, that the candidates' additional microteaching lessons were implemented in a clinical setting.

To support duration of practice and cohesiveness of this learning approach, faculty members implement microteaching in several courses during the final two years of candidates preservice training (see Table 23.3). Third-year candidates are introduced to microteaching in a fall literacy methods course. They microteach five times in the semester implementing reciprocal teaching

Table 23.3 Cohesive Use of Microteaching Across the Program

When	Where	What
Junior Year Fall Semester	Reading Methods Course for students identified with Mild to Moderate learning needs	Microteach five times across semester implementing reciprocal teaching and explicit instruction. Does not involve K12 students
Junior Year Spring Semester	Reading Assessment course for students identified with Moderate to Intense learning needs	Microteach ten times and then deliver each of the lessons with K12 students
Senior Year Fall Semester	Student Teaching Seminar that accompanies student teachers in clinical placements	Microteach one lesson that is planned for student teaching
Senior Year Fall and Spring Semester	Student Teaching in a transition to work program focused on self-determination	Microteach three times with a focus on student goal setting and self-determination

and explicit instruction. In the spring semester of that same year all candidates implement ten microteachings in a clinical setting with students who are identified with intellectual disabilities. In the senior year candidates microteach once during the seminar that accompanies their student teaching. Finally, approximately eight preservice teachers complete three microteaching lessons while working in a transition-to-work program at the University. These lessons are focused on a self-determination goal that the K12 students developed at the beginning of the semester. What ties these microteaching experiences together is the commitment of the faculties to use microteaching to learn and then implement evidence-based and high leverage practices to effectively deliver ambitious, high-quality instruction.

Research and the wisdom of practice in teacher education have clearly established that preservice teachers need intensive ongoing training in the use of effective practices (such as evidence-based and high leverage practices) if they are to learn to use these practices in the classroom. One of the ways to provide that preparation is the systematic inclusion of microteaching and other practice-based strategies (see Table 23.2) into courses across a preparation program. Because of its flexible design, microteaching, as well as other practice-based strategies, can be used across several years of a program, including use in online and distance learning formats, to ensure that candidates are well prepared to deliver effective instruction when they enter the classroom.

The first time I implemented microteaching, I did so on my own, with little guidance from colleagues. This initial experience whetted my appetite for deeper learning about why the practice was so effective in engaging my students and supporting their learning of the course material. This powerful first experience led to an invitation to others to build an informal community of practice. Once I engaged at this collegial level, I experienced greater growth and insight about the process and learned from my colleagues new ways and approaches to implement microteaching with greater effectiveness. The ongoing use of the microteaching process multiplied our insights over time and supported the learning of our students with consistent forms of practice across our preparation program.

Then a few summers back, colleagues and I spent several weeks in online meetings with our CEEDAR colleagues and faculty from around the country examining how we were implementing this new practice in our program. Implementing a robust practice-based opportunity is not done lightly. The CEEDAR team and participants from several CEEDAR states helped us examine each step of the implementation process. We all learned as participants in this community of practice. We posed questions that we could not yet answer, and participants expertly pointed to areas that still needed to be improved. Over time, with a team of critical friends who were willing to ask questions and make suggestions, we established a practice-based process that is working relatively well, but still improving each semester.

This past year we initiated a microteaching study with an incentive grant from our state. We implemented microteaching across three different settings—one setting with our inservice teachers, a second setting with three early career inservice teachers, and a third setting with a faculty member from another university who was incorporating microteaching for the first time in one of her methods courses. Initial data and feedback from participants in these three settings were very positive. Throughout this work, we have learned that practice-based opportunities like microteaching have the potential for broad application across the life span of a teacher. The reflective process that is built into the practice creates space for increasingly vulnerable conversations about our practice and how to improve it. In our preparation program, there are multiple opportunities to explicitly name what we are doing and why we are doing it. Our candidates engage in open and critical discussion about their teaching in ways that are unrivalled, in our experience, in other teaching formats. Practice-based processes like microteaching are inherently collaborative, and because of that they help to build strong instructionally focused teams of learners.

Probably the single most important thing I have learned over the past few years concerning the microteaching process is that it has positioned me, as a faculty member, as a co-learner with the candidates. What I mean by this is that microteaching put enacted teaching and student response to that teaching at the center of a reflective and analytical conversation. Candidates and faculty, together, looked at how students were responding to instruction. We were sitting on the same side of the table, as colleagues, some younger less experienced, and others a little older with a bit more, observing and then discussing how we might improve our practice. This phenomenon felt different to me, new, more engaging from several perspectives. This process thrilled my teaching in ways I did not think possible.

Finally, an emerging body of scholarship and practical guidance has begun to emerge as teacher educators from across disciplines (e.g., mathematics, science, special education) have begun to share information regarding their experiences in defining HLPs and developing practice-based learning opportunities that can be used to support the development of expertise. We have included a few of these resources in Table 23.4 that we hope you will find useful.

Table 23.4 Recommended Resources for Teacher Educators Related to HLPs

1. Benedict et al. (2016). *Learning to Teach: Practice-Based Teacher Education.*	• This brief document describes essential features for providing high-quality, structured, and sequenced opportunities to practice within teacher preparation programs. • Describes teacher preparation programs that have enacted innovative strategies to embed practice-based opportunities into existing coursework and field experiences. • Describes several practice-based approaches that have been found to increase beginning teacher candidates' capacity for teaching. • Identified potential action steps that EPPs and districts
2. Brownell et al. (2019). *A continuum of pedagogies for preparing teachers to use high-leverage practices.*	• Provides a framework for preparing teacher candidates to learn to use high-leverage practices. • Describes practice-based approaches that are supported by research on teacher learning or student achievement. • Describes a practice-based approach to implementing HLPs

Table 23.4 Cont.

3. Grossman et al. (2009). *Redefining teaching, re-imagining teacher education.*	• This article provides an argument for re-conceptualizing teaching and teacher preparation to improve teacher practice. • Describes new directions in teacher education including organizing around core practices, reimagining the curriculum, and addressing pedagogical issues for teacher education programs. • Addresses the organizational challenges that teacher education programs must address as they support candidate learning of core practices in practice-based settings.
4. Kroeger et al. (2022). *Microteaching. An opportunity for meaningful professional development.*	• This article provides a step-by-step description of how to implement microteaching as a professional development tool. • The article follows a vignette of a teacher seeking to improve her practice with a small group of colleagues. • Forms that can be used and suggestions for implementation are included.
5. Maheady et al. (2019). *School-university partnerships: One institution's efforts to integrate and support teachers use of high-leverage practices.*	• Describes a teacher preparation program's work to integrate HLPs into coursework and clinically rich experiences in a dual certification program. • Describes the development of a set of 17 HLPs from both general and special education that provided a core curriculum for the dual certification program. • Emphasizes the importance of strong school-university partnerships to support the development and refinement of candidate use of HLPs.
6. McDonald et al. (2013). *Core practices and pedagogies of teacher education: A call for a common language and collective activity.*	• This article provides a review of changes in teacher education that have led to an emphasis on better supporting teachers in learning to use knowledge in action. • Provides a review of why core practices are a critical foundation for practice-based teacher preparation. • Describes a learning cycle that addressing practice-based experiences that address introducing and learning about the practice, preparing for a researching the practice, enacting the activity with students, and analyzing the enactment and moving forward.
7. McLeskey et al. (2017). *HLPs in Special Education: The final report of the HLP Writing Team..*	• This short book was written by CEC's High Leverage Practices Writing Team that developed HLPs for K-12 special education teachers. • Includes an introduction to the HLPs and a description of how they were developed. • Provides background information, description, and a brief research synthesis for each of the HLPs.
8. Windschitl et al. (2012). *Proposing a core set of instructional practices and tools for teachers of science.*	• An article that discusses why the identification of core practices is critical to improving the practice of teachers. • Reviews research informing the development of core practices. • Describes the development of core practices in science education. • Describes supporting tools and how they were used to support candidates in the learning to use core practices in a science education teacher preparation program. • Reflects on unexpected insights that arose from beginning to engage in this work.

Wrap Up

Over the last several years, teacher preparation programs in special education from across the United States have begun to focus on using HLPs as a central component of the curriculum of teacher preparation (e.g., Kroeger et al., 2022; Maheady et al., 2019). In short, they are aspiring to prepare teacher candidates to use a set of foundational, effective practices in classrooms before they enter the teaching profession. While this approach to preparation is common across many other professions (see Ericsson & Pool, 2016), it is obviously new for teacher education and professional development. Proceeding in this direction involves obvious risks—for example, in the past with many initiatives to improve teacher preparation, there has been a "proliferation of approaches driven more by the trend than by a deep understanding of how people learn to enact ambitious professional practice" (McDonald et al., 2013, p. 379). Given this history, we recommend proceeding with caution. We also recommend proceeding by collaborating with colleagues to "share the load" in developing research-based approaches to improving expertise (Brownell et al., 2019). All the best as you proceed with this work!

References

Allen, D. W., & Eve, A. W. (1968). Microteaching: *Theory into Practice, 7*(5), 181–5.

Ball, D., Sleep, L., Boerst, T., & Bass, H. (2009). Combining the development of practice and the practice of development in teacher education. *The Elementary School Journal, 109*(5), 458–74.

Benedict, A., Holdheide, L., Brownell, M., & Foley, A. (2016). *Learning to Teach: Practice-Based Preparation in Teacher Education*. Special Issues Brief, Center on Great Teachers & Leaders at American Institutes for Research, CEEDAR Center, University of Florida (pp. 1–44). Retrieved from http://ceedar.education.ufl.edu/wp-content/uploads/2016/07/Learning_To_Teach.pdf

Billingsley, B., Bettini, E., & Jones, N. D. (2019). Supporting special education teacher induction through high-leverage practices. *Remedial and Special Education, 40*(6), 365–79. https://doi.org/10.1177/0741932518816826

Brock, M. E. & Carter, E. W. (2016). Efficacy of teachers training paraprofessionals to implement peer support arrangements. *Exceptional Children, 82*(3), 354–71.

Brownell, M., Benedict, A., Leko, M., Peyton, D., Pua, D., & Richards-Tutor, C. (2019). A continuum of pedagogies for preparing teachers to use high-leverage practices. *Remedial and Special Education, 40*(6), 338–55. DOI: 10.1177/0741932518824990.

Carnine, D. (1997). Bridging the research-to-practice gap. *Exceptional Children, 63*, 513–21.

CEEDAR Center (n.d.). Microteaching-explicit instruction. https://ceedar.education.ufl.edu/portfolio/plo-microteaching/

Cook, B. G., & Odom, S. L. (2013). Evidence-based practices and implementation science in special education. *Exceptional Children, 79*, 135–44.

Cordingley, P., Higgins, S., Greany, T., Buckler, N., Coles-Jordan, D., Crisp, B., Saunders, L., & Coe, R. (2015). *Developing great teaching: Lessons from the international reviews into effective professional development*. Project Report. Teacher Development Trust. https://dro.dur.ac.uk/15834/1/15834.pdf

Council of Chief State School Officers and Collaboration for Effective Educator Development, Accountability, and Reform Center (2017). *PSEL 2015 and promoting principal Leadership for the success of students with disabilities*. Retrieved from www.ccsso.org/sites/default/files/2017-10/PSELforSWDs01252017_0.pdf

Cox, A. W., Brock, M. E., Odom, S. L., Rogers, S. J., Sullivan, L. H., Tuchman-Ginsberg, L., & Collet-Klingenberg, L. (2013). National Professional Development Center on ASD: An emerging national educational strategy. *Autism services across America*, 249–266.

DeMatthews, D. (2020). Undoing systems of exclusion: Exploring inclusive leadership and systems thinking in two inclusive elementary schools. *Journal of Educational Administration*, in press.

DeMatthews, D. E., Kotok, S., & Serafini, A. (2020). Leadership preparation for special education and inclusive schools: Beliefs and recommendations from successful principals. *Journal of Research on Leadership Education*, *15*(4), 303–29. https://doi.org/10.1177%2F1942775119838308

Desimone, L., & Garet, M. (2015). Best practices in teachers' professional development in the United States. *Psychology, Society, & Education*, *7(3)*, 252–63.

Dreyfus, H. L. (2002). *A phenomenology of skill acquisition as the basis for a Merleau-Pontian non-representationalist cognitive science*, Unpublished paper. Retrieved from https://philpapers.org/archive/DREAPO

Edmunds, R., Ghandi, A., & Danielson, L. (Eds.) (2019). *Essentials of Intensive Intervention.* Guilford Press.

Ericsson, A. & Pool, R. (2016). *Peak: Secrets from the new science of expertise.* Houghton Mifflin.

Fixsen, D. L., Van Dyke, M. K., & Blase, K. A. (2019). *Science and implementation.* Active Implementation Research Network. www.activeimplementation.org/wp-content/uploads/2019/05/Science-and-Implementation.pdf

Forzani, F. M. (2014). Understanding "core practices" and "practice-based" teacher education: Learning from the past. *Journal of Teacher Education*, *65*, 357–68.

Grima-Farrell, C. R., Bain, A., & McDonagh, S. H. (2011). Bridging the research-to-practice gap: A review of the literature focusing on inclusive education. *Australasian Journal of Special Education*, *35*, 117–36.

Grossman, P., Hammerness, K., & McDonald, M. (2009). Redefining teaching: Re-imagining teacher education. *Teachers and teaching: Theory and Practice. 15*(2), 273–89.

Hattie, J. (2009). *Visible learning: A synthesis of over 800 meta-analyses relating to achievement.* Routledge.

Hoppey, D., Black, W., & Mickelson, A. (2019). The evolution of inclusive practice in two elementary schools: Reforming teacher purpose, instructional capacity, and data-informed practice. *International Journal of Educational Reform*, *27*(1), 22–45.

Hoppey, D. & McLeskey, J. (2013), A case study of principal leadership in an effective inclusive school. *The Journal of Special Education*, *46*(4), 245–56.

Hovland, J. B. (2020). Inclusive comprehension strategy instruction. *Teaching Exceptional Children*, *52*(6), 404–13. DOI: 10.1177/0040059920914334

Kennedy, M. M. (1999). The role of preservice teacher education. In L. Darling-Hammond & G. Sykes (Eds.), *Teaching as the learning profession: Handbook of teaching and policy* (pp. 54–86). Jossey Bass.

Kourieos, S. (2019). Problematizing school-based mentoring for pre-service primary English language teachers, mentoring and tutoring: Partnership in learning, *27*(3), 272–94. DOI: 10.1080/13611267.2019.1630992

Kroeger, S. D., Doyle, K., Carnahan, C., & Benson, A. (2022). Microteaching: An opportunity for meaningful professional development. *Teaching Exceptional Children*, 1–10, DOI: 10.1177/00400599211068372#

Kroeger, S. D., & Doyle, K. (2021, April). *Microteaching—explicit instruction.* CEEDAR Center. https://ceedar.education.ufl.edu/portfolio/plo-microteaching/

Lampert, M., & Graziani, F. (2009). Instructional activities as a tool for teachers' and teacher educators' learning. *The Elementary School Journal*, *109*(5), 491–509.

Leko, M., Roberts, C., Zepp, S., Chandrashekhar, S., & Forsberg, M. (2022). The role of professional development in effective inclusive elementary schools. In J. McLeskey, F. Spooner, R. Algozzine,

& N. L. Waldron (Eds.), *Handbook of Effective Inclusive Elementary Schools: Research and Practice* (pp. 98–114). Routledge/Taylor & Francis.

Maheady, L., Patti, A., Rafferty, L., & del Prado Hill, P. (2019). School-university partnerships: One institution's efforts to integrate and support teacher use of high-leverage practices. *Remedial and Special Education, 40*(6), 356–64.

McDonald, M., Kazemi, E., & Kavanaugh, S. (2013). Core practices of teacher education: A call for a common language and collective activity. *Journal of Teacher Education, 64*(5), 378–86.

McLeskey, J., Barringer, M., Billingsley, B., Brownell, M., Jackson, D., Kennedy, M., Lewis, T., Maheady, L., Rodriguez, J., Scheeler, M., Winn, J., & Ziegler, D. (2017). *High leverage practices in special education: The final report of the HLP Writing Team.* CEC & CEEDAR Center.

McLeskey, J., Billingsley, B., & Ziegler, D. (2018). Using high-leverage practices in teacher education to reduce the research-to-practice gap. *Australasian Journal of Special Education, 42*(1), 3–16.

McLeskey, J., & Brownell, M. (2015). High-leverage practices and teacher preparation in special education (Document No. PR-1). Retrieved from University of Florida, Collaboration for Effective Educator, Development, Accountability, and Reform Center website: https://ceedar.education.ufl.edu/wp-content/uploads/2016/05/High-Leverage-Practices-and-Teacher-Preparation-in-Special-Education.pdf

McLeskey, J., Spooner, F., Algozzine, B., & Waldron, N.L. (2022). Time to support inclusion and inclusive schools (pp. 3–15). In McLeskey, J., Waldron, N.L., Spooner, F. & Algonzzine, B. *Handbook of Effective Inclusive Elementary Schools (2nd edition).* Routledge, Taylor-Francis.

Nelson, G., Cook, S. C., Zarate, K., Powell, S. R., Maggin, D. M., Drake, K. R., Kiss, A. J., Ford, J. W., Sun, L., & Espinas, D. R. (2021). A systematic review of meta-analyses in special education: Exploring the evidence base for high-leverage practices. *Remedial and Special Education.* https://doi.org/10.1177/07419325211063491

Opfer, D., & Pedder, D. (2011). Conceptualizing teacher professional learning. *Review of Educational Research, 81*, 376–407. DOI:10.3102/0034654311413609

Palinscar, A. S., & Brown, A. L. (1984). Reciprocal teaching of comprehension-fostering and comprehension monitoring activities. *Cognition and Instruction, 1*(2), 117–75.

Peterson, A., Danielson, L., & Fuchs, D. (2019). Introduction to intensive intervention: A step-by-step guide to data-based individualization. In R. Edmunds, A. Ghandi, & L. Danielson (Eds.) (2019). *Essentials of Intensive Intervention* (pp. 9–29). Guilford Press.

Postholm, M. B. (2012). Teachers' professional development: A theoretical review. *Educational Research, 54*(4), 405–429. DOI:10.1080/00131881.2012.734725

Rawlins, P., Anthony, G., Averill, R., & Drake, M. (2019). Novice perceptions of the use of rehearsals to support their learning of ambitious mathematics teaching. *Asian-Pacific Journal of Teacher Education.* DOI: 10.1080/1359866X.2019.1644612.

Timperley, H., Wilson, A., Barrar, H., & Fung, I. (2007). *Teacher professional learning and development: Best evidence synthesis iteration* (BES). Iterative Best Evidence Synthesis Programme, New Zealand Ministry of Education. http://educationcounts.edcentre.govt.nz/goto/BES

Waldron, N., McLeskey, J., & Redd, L. (2011). Setting the direction: the role of the principal in developing an effective, inclusive school, *Journal of Special Education Leadership, 24*(2), 51–60.

Ward, C., Farmer, S., Jackson, K., & Ihlo, T. (2022). Support for school change and improvement. In J. McLeskey, F. Spooner, R. Algozzine, & N. L. Waldron (Eds.). *Handbook of Effective Inclusive Elementary Schools: Research and Practice* (pp. 483–506). Routledge/Taylor & Francis.

Wei, R. C., Darling-Hammond, L., & Adamson, F. (2010). *Professional development in the United States: Trends and challenges.* National Staff Development Council. Retrieved from http://learning forward.org/docs/pdf/nsdcstudytechnicalreport2010.pdf?sfvrsn=0

Windschitl, M., Thompson, J., Braaten, M., & Stroupe, D. (2012). Proposing a core set of instructional practices and tools for teachers of science. *Science Education, 96*(5), 878–903.

Windschitl, M., Thompson, J., Braaten, M., & Stroupe, D. (2019). Sharing a vision, sharing practices: How communities of educators improve teaching. *Remedial and Special Education, 40*(6), 380–90.

Index

For Product Safety Concerns and Information please contact our EU
representative GPSR@taylorandfrancis.com
Taylor & Francis Verlag GmbH, Kaufingerstraße 24, 80331 München, Germany

www.ingramcontent.com/pod-product-compliance
Ingram Content Group UK Ltd.
Pitfield, Milton Keynes, MK11 3LW, UK
UKHW031042080625
459435UK00013B/560